Organizational
BEHAVIOR

A PRACTICAL APPROACH

Edited by Beth G. Chung
San Diego State University

University Readers™
San Diego, CA

Bassim Hamadeh, CEO and Publisher
Michael Simpson, Vice President of Acquisitions
Jamie Giganti, Managing Editor
Jess Busch, Graphic Design Supervisor
Seidy Cruz, Acquisitions Editor
Sarah Wheeler, Senior Project Editor
Natalie Lakosil, Licensing Associate

First published in the United States of America in 2014 by University Readers, an imprint of Cognella, Inc.

Trademark Notice: Product or corporate names may be trademarks or registered trademarks, and are used only for identification and explanation without intent to infringe.

Cover: Copyright © 2011 by iStockphoto.com/ShutterWorx. Copyright © 2011 by iStockphoto.com/Jamie Farrant.

Printed in the United States of America

ISBN: 978-1-60927-219-7 (pbk)

University Readers™
800.200.3908 | www.universityreaders.com

CONTENTS

INTRODUCTION TO ORGANIZATIONAL BEHAVIOR

John A. Wagner III & John R. Hollenbeck

Defining Organizational Behavior

Organizational behavior is a field of study that endeavors to understand, explain, predict, and change human behavior as it occurs in the organizational context. Underlying this definition are three important considerations:

1. Organizational behavior focuses on observable behaviors, such as talking in a meeting, running production equipment, or writing a report. It also deals with the internal states, such as thinking, perceiving, and deciding, that accompany visible actions.
2. Organizational behavior involves the analysis of how people behave both as individuals and as members of groups and organizations.
3. Organizational behavior also assesses the "behavior" of groups and organizations per se. Neither groups nor organizations "behave" in the same sense that people do. Nevertheless, some events occur in organizations that cannot be explained in terms of individual behavior. These events must be examined in terms of group or organizational processes.

Research in organizational behavior traces its roots to the late 1940s, when researchers in psychology, sociology, political science, economics, and other social sciences joined together in an effort to develop a comprehensive body of organizational knowledge. As it has developed, the field of organizational behavior has grown into three distinct subfields, delineated in Table 1.1: micro organizational behavior, meso organizational behavior, and macro organizational behavior.

Micro Organizational Behavior

Micro organizational behavior is concerned mainly with the behaviors of individuals working alone. Three subfields of psychology were the principal contributors to the beginnings of micro organizational behavior. *Experimental psychology* provided theories of learning, motivation, perception, and stress. *Clinical psychology* furnished models of personality and human development. *Industrial psychology* offered theories of employee selection, workplace attitudes, and performance assessment. Owing to this heritage, micro organizational behavior has a distinctly psychological

Table 1.1 Subfields of Organizational Behavior

Subfield	Focus	Origins
Micro organizational behavior	Individuals	Experimental, clinical, and organizational psychology
Meso organizational behavior	Groups	Communication, social psychology, and interactionist sociology, plus the origins of the other two subfields
Macro organizational behavior	Organizations	Sociology, political science, anthropology, and economics

orientation. Among the questions it examines are the following: How do differences in ability affect employee productivity? What motivates employees to perform their jobs? How do employees develop perceptions of their workplace, and how do these perceptions in turn influence their behavior?

Meso Organizational Behavior

Meso organizational behavior is a middle ground, bridging the other two subfields of organizational behavior. It focuses primarily on understanding the behaviors of people working together in teams and groups. In addition to sharing the origins of the other two subfields, meso organizational behavior grew out of research in the fields of *communication, social psychology*, and *interactionist sociology*, which provided theories on such topics as socialization, leadership, and group dynamics. Meso organizational behavior seeks answers to questions such as the following: What forms of socialization encourage co-workers to cooperate? What mix of skills among team members increases team performance? How can managers determine which prospective leader will be the most effective?

Macro Organizational Behavior

Macro organizational behavior focuses on understanding the "behaviors" of entire organizations. The origins of macro organizational behavior can be traced to four disciplines. *Sociology* provided theories of structure, social status, and institutional relations. *Political science* offered theories of power, conflict, bargaining, and control. *Anthropology* contributed theories of symbolism, cultural influence, and comparative analysis. *Economics* furnished theories of competition and efficiency. Research on macro organizational behavior considers questions such as the following: How is power acquired and retained? How can conflicts be resolved? What mechanisms can be used to coordinate work activities? How should an organization be structured to best cope with its surrounding environment?

Contemporary Issues

Considered both individually and collectively, the three subfields of organizational behavior offer valuable information, insights, and advice to managers facing the challenge of understanding and reacting to a broad range of contemporary management issues. According to a variety of sources, today's managers find five of these issues especially important: workforce diversity, team productivity, organizational adaptability, international growth and development, and ethical concerns.

Workforce Diversity

Within the societal cultures of the United States and Canada, subcultural differences once ignored by many managers now command significant attention and sensitivity. Historically, the North American workforce has consisted primarily of white males. Today, however, white males make up far less than 50 percent of business new hires in the United States, whereas women and African American, Hispanic, and Asian men account for increasingly large segments of the U.S. workforce. Moreover, in the last ten years the number of women and minorities assuming managerial positions in the U.S. workforce has grown by over 25 percent. It is becoming—and will continue to become—even more important for managers to know about and be ready to respond to the challenges deriving from individual differences in abilities, personalities, and motives. Knowledge about the workplace consequences of these differences, drawn from the subfield of micro organizational behavior, can provide managers with help in this regard.

Team Productivity

Management is becoming less of a process relying on top-down command and control, where managers have all the power and nonmanagerial employees have little say in what they do. For various reasons organizations now use greater amounts of *empowerment*—the delegation to nonmanagers of the authority to make significant

decisions on their jobs. Often, empowerment is accomplished by grouping employees into teams and then giving those teams responsibility for self-management activities such as hiring, firing, and training members, setting production targets, and assessing output quality. Guidance from meso organizational behavior precepts can help managers establish realistic expectations about the implementation difficulties and probable effects of team-based empowerment.

Organizational Adaptability

In today's business world, emphasis is shifting from the mass production of low-cost, interchangeable commodities to the production of high-quality goods and services, made individually or in small batches and geared to meet the specific demands of small groups of consumers. This shift requires greater flexibility than ever before and necessitates that quality receive greater emphasis than it has in the past. Companies are reacting by implementing programs that require new ways of dividing an organization's work into jobs and coordinating the efforts of many employees. Implementations of this sort benefit from insights derived from macro organizational behavior.

International Growth and Development

Fewer firms today limit their operations to a single national or cultural region than was once the case. Instead, multinationalism or even statelessness has become the norm. The resulting globalization is changing the way business is conducted, and it promises to continue to do so at an increasing pace. Managers facing this massive change must develop increased sensitivity to international cultural differences. All three subfields of organizational behavior have valuable advice to offer managers confronted with this challenge.

Ethical Concerns

Managing organizational behavior inevitably involves the acquisition and use of power. Thus, managers continually face the issue of determining whether the use of power in a given instance is effective and appropriate. One approach in dealing with this issue is to adopt the *utilitarianist* perspective and judge the appropriateness of the use of power in terms of the consequences of this use. Does using power provide the greatest good for the greatest number of people? If the answer to this question is "yes," then the utilitarian perspective would suggest that power is being used appropriately.

A second perspective, derived from the theory of *moral rights*, suggests that power is used appropriately only when no one's personal rights or freedoms are sacrificed. It is certainly possible for many people to derive great satisfaction from the use of power to accomplish some purpose, thus satisfying utilitarian criteria, while simultaneously causing the rights of a few individuals to be abridged. According to the theory of moral rights, the latter effect is an indication of inappropriateness. Power holders seeking to use their power appropriately must therefore respect the rights and interests of the minority as well as look after the well-being of the majority.

MANAGEMENT AND MANAGERS

John A. Wagner III & John R. Hollenbeck

Although managers and managerial jobs are ubiquitous in contemporary life, few people really understand what managers do as they perform their jobs. Could you tell someone what management is? What skills and abilities managers need to succeed in their work? How today's management practices have developed? Modern societies depend on the well-being of organizations ranging from industrial giants like General Electric and IBM to local businesses like the corner grocery store. In turn, all of these businesses depend on the expertise of managers. It is therefore important that members of modern societies, including you, know what management is, what managers do, and how contemporary practices have developed.

This chapter introduces management theory and practice. It begins by defining the concept of management in terms of the various functions that managers perform in organizations. Next, it describes the job of a manager in greater detail, focusing on the skills managers use and the roles they fill as they perform their jobs every day. The chapter then examines how modern management theory has evolved, discussing several key schools of thought about management and managers that have developed between the late 1800s and the present.

Defining Management

Management, defined most simply, is the process of influencing behavior in organizations such that common purposes are identified, worked toward, and achieved. To define management in greater detail, we must consider a closely related question: What is an organization?

Three Attributes of Organizations

An **organization** is a collection of people and materials brought together to accomplish purposes not achievable through the efforts of individuals working alone. Three attributes enable an organization to achieve this feat: a mission, division of labor, and a hierarchy of authority.

Table 2.1 Sample Mission Statements

Company	Mission
Hershey Foods	Hershey Foods' basic business mission is to become a major, diversified food company. … A basic principle that Hershey will continue to embrace is to attract and hold customers with products and services of consistently superior quality and value.
Polaroid	Polaroid designs, manufactures, and markets worldwide a variety of products based on its inventions, primarily in the photographic field. These products include instant photographic cameras and films, light-polarizing filters and lenses, and diversified chemical, optical, and commercial products. The principal products of the company are used in amateur and professional photography, industry, science, medicine, and education.

Source: Excerpted from annual stockholder reports.

Mission

Each organization works toward a specific **mission**, which is its purpose or reason for being. As illustrated in Table 2.1, a mission statement identifies the primary goods or services that the organization is intended to produce and the markets that it hopes to serve. An organization's mission helps hold it together by giving members a shared sense of direction.

Division of Labor

In every organization, difficult work is broken into smaller tasks. This **division of labor** can enhance *efficiency* by simplifying tasks and making them easier to perform. A classic example of this effect can be seen in the following analysis of the pin-making process by the eighteenth-century Scottish economist Adam Smith:

> One man draws out the wire, another straightens it, a third cuts it, a fourth points it, a fifth grinds it at the top for receiving a head. To make the head requires two or three more operations. [Using a division of labor such as this,] ten persons could make among them upward of forty-eight thousand pins a day. But if they had all wrought separately and independently they certainly could not each of them have made twenty; perhaps not one pin in a day.

The division of labor enables organized groups of people to accomplish tasks that would be beyond their physical or mental capacities as individuals. Few people can build a car by themselves, yet companies like Nissan turn out thousands of cars each year by dividing the complex job of building a car into a series of simple assembly-line tasks.

Hierarchy of Authority

The **hierarchy of authority** is another common organizational attribute. In very small organizations, all members of the organization may share equally the authority to make decisions and initiate actions. In contrast, in larger organizations authority is more often distributed in a pyramidal hierarchical pattern like that shown in Figure 2.1. At the top of this hierarchy, the chief executive officer (CEO) has the authority to issue orders to every other member of the organization and to expect these orders to be obeyed. At successively lower levels, managers direct the activities of

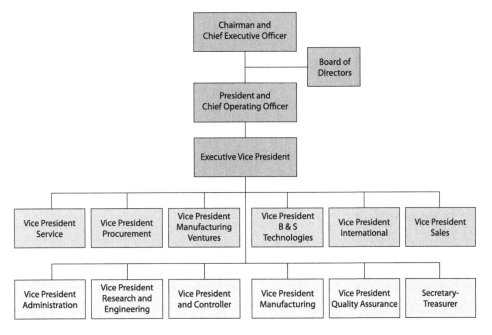

Figure 2.1 Briggs & Stratton Organization Chart. An organization chart is a graphic representation of a firm's hierarchy of authority. The organization chart in this figure shows the top and middle management of Briggs & Stratton, a manufacturer of small gasoline engines used in lawn mowers, snow blowers, and similar equipment. Note that the company is divided horizontally into various functional departments—such as manufacturing and sales—whose efforts are unified through authority relations that extend vertically between vice presidents and the CEO. Source: Based on information contained in annual stockholder reports.

people beneath them and are constrained by the authority of managers above them.

Formal Definition

The three attributes of organizations just described help clarify the role of management in organizational life. In a sense, the first two attributes are discordant, as the mission assumes the integration of effort whereas the division of labor produces a differentiation of effort. As a result, an organization's members are simultaneously pushed together and pulled apart. Managerial influence, derived partly from the third attribute of hierarchical authority, reconciles this conflict

and balances the two opposing attributes. This balancing act is what managers do and what management is all about.

Management is thus a process of planning, organizing, directing, and controlling organizational behaviors to accomplish a mission through the division of labor. This definition incorporates several important ideas. First, management is a process—an ongoing flow of activities—rather than something that can be accomplished once and for all. Second, managerial activities affect the behaviors of an organization's members *and* the organization itself. Third, to accomplish a firm's mission requires organization. If the mission could be accomplished by individuals working alone, neither the firm nor its management would be necessary. Fourth, the process of

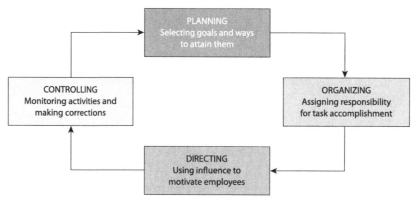

Figure 2.2 The Four Management Functions

management can be further divided into the four functions shown in Figure 2.2: planning, organizing, directing, and controlling.

Planning is a forward-looking process of deciding what to do. Managers who plan try to anticipate the future, setting goals and objectives for a firm's performance and identifying the actions required to attain these goals and objectives. For example, when Robert Iger meets with other Walt Disney Company executives to develop specifications for the attractions and concessions at theme parks under construction, he is engaged in planning. In planning, managers set three types of goals and objectives:

1. *Strategic goals* are the outcomes that the organization as a whole expects to achieve by pursuing its mission.
2. *Functional or divisional objectives* are the outcomes that units within the firm are expected to achieve.
3. *Operational objectives* are the specific, measurable results that the members of an organizational unit are expected to accomplish.

As shown in Figure 2.3, these three types of goals and objectives are linked together. The focus of lower-order objectives is shaped by the content of higher-level goals, and achieving higher-level goals depends on the fulfillment of lower-level objectives.

Goals and objectives are performance targets that the members of an organization seek to fulfill by working together—for instance, gaining control over 15 percent of the firm's market, or manufacturing less than one defective product for every thousand produced. Setting such goals and objectives helps managers plan and implement a sequence of actions that will lead to their attainment. For example, financial objectives growing out of Iger's planning meetings at Disney become targets that newly opened theme parks are expected to meet or exceed during their first few years in operation. Goals and objectives also serve as benchmarks of the success or failure of organizational behavior. When they review past performance, managers can judge the company's effectiveness by assessing its goal attainment. For example, Disney theme park managers can assess the success of their operations by comparing actual revenue and cost data with corporate profitability goals.

As part of the **organizing** function, managers develop a structure of interrelated tasks and allocate people and resources within this structure. Organizing begins when managers divide an

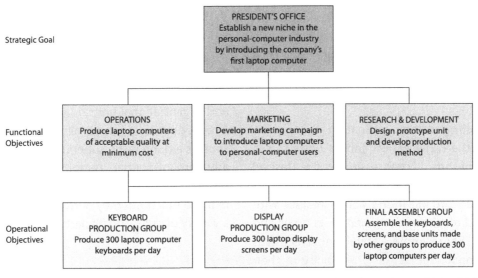

Figure 2.3 The Hierarchy of Goals and Objectives. An organization's strategic goals set boundaries within which functional objectives are established. In turn, functional objectives shape the objectives of operational units. Accomplishing operational objectives therefore contributes to the attainment of functional objectives and strategic goals.

organization's labor and design tasks that will lead to the achievement of organizational goals and objectives. In companies such as Whirlpool, Boeing, and IBM, assembly operations are devised and built during this phase. Next, managers decide who will perform these tasks. To make this determination, they analyze the tasks to identify the knowledge, skills, and abilities needed to perform them successfully. They can then select qualified employees or train other employees who lack the necessary qualifications to carry out these tasks.

Grouping tasks and the people who perform them into *organizational units* is another step in the organizing process. One type of organizational unit, a *department*, includes people who perform the same type of work. For instance, all employees who market an organization's goods or services can be brought together in a marketing department. Another type of unit, a *division*, includes people who do the company's work in the same geographic territory, who work with similar kinds of clients, or who make or provide the same type of goods or services. For example, Coca-Cola has a European division that does business in Europe. General Electric's financial services division markets only financial services.

The **directing** function encourages member effort and guides it toward the attainment of organizational goals and objectives. Directing is partly a process of communicating goals and objectives to members wherein managers announce, clarify, and promote targets toward which effort should be directed. For example, Jeff Bezos is directing when he meets with other top managers at Amazon.com to announce yearly sales objectives. Directing is also a process of learning employees' desires and interests and of ensuring that these desires and interests are satisfied in return for successful goal-oriented performance. In addition, directing may require managers to use personal expertise or charisma to inspire employees to overcome obstacles that might appear insurmountable. Apple Computer's Steve Jobs relies heavily on charisma to keep employees in his company excited about new products and market opportunities. In sum, directing is a process in which managers *lead* their subordinates, influencing them to work together to achieve organizational goals and related objectives.

Controlling means evaluating the performance of the organization and its units to see whether the firm is progressing in the desired direction. In a typical evaluation, managers compare an organization's actual results with the desired results as described in its goals and objectives. For example, Capital One executives might compare the actual profitability of their Visa card operations with the profitability objectives set during previous planning sessions. To perform this kind of evaluation, members of the organization must collect and assess performance information. A firm's accounting personnel might gather data about the costs and revenues of organizational activities. Marketing representatives might provide additional data about sales volume or the organization's position in the marketplace. Finance specialists might then appraise the firm's organizational performance by determining whether the ratio of costs to revenues meets or surpasses the company's target level.

If the evaluation reveals a significant difference between goals and actual performance, the control process enters a phase of *correction*. In this phase, managers return to the planning stage and redevelop their goals and objectives, indicating how differences between goals and outcomes can be reduced. The process of management then continues anew, as managers engage in additional organizing, directing, and controlling.

What Managers Do

Managers are the people who plan, organize, direct, and control so as to manage organizations and organizational units. Managers establish the directions to be pursued, allocate people and resources among tasks, supervise individual, group, and organizational performance, and assess progress toward goals and objectives. To succeed in these functions, they perform specific jobs, use a variety of skills, and fill particular roles.

Managerial Jobs

Although all managers are responsible for fulfilling the same four functions, not all of them perform exactly the same jobs. Instead, most organizations have three general types of managers: top managers, middle managers, and supervisory managers. Figure 2.4 illustrates the distinctive combination of planning, organizing, directing, and controlling performed by each type of manager.

Top Managers

Top managers, who are responsible for managing the entire organization, include individuals with the title of *chairperson*, *president*, *chief executive officer*, *executive vice president*, *vice president*, or *chief operating officer*. Managerial work at this level consists mainly of performing the planning activities needed to develop the organization's mission and strategic goals. Top managers also carry out organizing and controlling activities as determined by strategic planning. As part of the controlling function, they assess the firm's progress toward attainment of its strategic goals by monitoring information about activities both

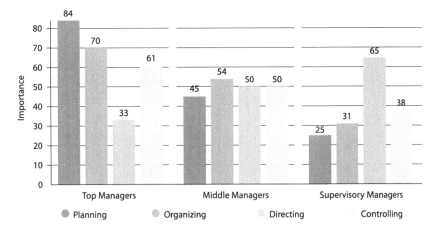

Figure 2.4 Managerial Functions and Types of Managers. Planning is the most important function of top managers. Middle managers fulfill all four management functions about equally. Directing is the most important function of supervisory managers.

within the firm and in its surrounding environment. Top management's responsibilities include adjusting the organization's overall direction on the basis of information reviewed in the controlling procedures. Because strategic planning, organizing, and controlling require a great deal of time, top managers have little time to spend in directing subordinates' activities. Typically, they delegate responsibility for such direction to middle managers lower in the hierarchy of authority.

Middle Managers

Middle managers are usually responsible for managing the performance of a particular organizational unit and for implementing top managers' strategic plans. As they work to transform these strategies into programs that can be implemented at lower levels of the company, middle managers help establish functional or divisional objectives that will guide unit performance toward attainment of the firm's strategic goals. For instance, middle managers in a company's marketing department might transform the strategic goal of attaining control of 35 percent of the company's market into objectives specifying the level of sales to be achieved in each of the company's 12 sales districts. Middle managers are also responsible for ensuring that the managers beneath them implement the unit goals and appropriately direct employees toward their attainment. Terms such as *director* or *manager* are usually a part of a middle manager's title—for example, *director of human resources* or *western regional manager*.

Supervisory Managers

Supervisory managers, often called *superintendents*, *supervisors*, or *foremen*, are charged with overseeing the nonsupervisory employees who perform the organization's basic work. Of the three types of managers, supervisory managers spend the greatest amount of time actually directing employees. Except for making small, on-the-job adjustments, they seldom perform planning and organizing activities. Instead, supervisory managers initiate the upward flow of information that middle and top managers use to control organizational behavior. They may also distribute many of the rewards or punishments used to influence nonsupervisory employees' behaviors. Their ability to control subordinates' activities is limited, however, to the authority delegated to them by middle management.

Managerial Skills

Not surprisingly, the skills that managers use to succeed in their jobs are largely determined by the combination of planning, organizing, directing, and controlling functions that they must perform. As shown in Figure 2.5, each level of management has its own skill requirements.

Conceptual skills include the ability to perceive an organization or organizational unit as a whole, to understand how its labor is divided into tasks and reintegrated by the pursuit of common goals or objectives, and to recognize important relationships between the organization or unit and the environment that surrounds it. Conceptual skills involve a manager's ability to *think* and are most closely associated with planning and organizing. These skills are used most frequently by top managers, who take responsibility for organization-wide strategic endeavors.

Included in **human skills** is the ability to work effectively as a group member and build cooperation among the members of an organization or unit. Managers with well-developed human skills can create an atmosphere of trust and security in which people can express themselves without fear of punishment or humiliation. Such managers, who are adept at sensing the aspirations, interests, and viewpoints of others, can often foresee others' likely reactions to prospective courses of action. Because all management functions require that managers interact with other employees to acquire information, make decisions, implement changes, and assess results, it is not surprising that top, middle, and supervisory managers all put human skills to use.

Technical skills involve understanding the specific knowledge, procedures, and tools required to make the goods or services produced by an organization or unit. For example, members of a company's sales force must have skills in selling. Accountants have bookkeeping or auditing skills. Maintenance mechanics may need to have welding skills. For managers at the top or middle of an organization's hierarchy of authority, who are far removed from day-to-day production activities, technical skills are the least important of the three types of skills to have. Such skills are more critical to the success of supervisory managers

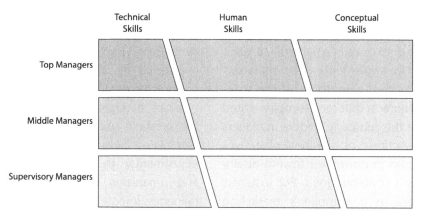

Figure 2.5 Managerial Skills

overseeing employees who use technical skills in performing their jobs.

Managerial Roles

Like skill requirements, **managerial roles** vary from one kind of manager to another. Indeed, the same manager may play more than one role at the same time. As shown in Table 2.2, these roles cluster together in three general categories: interpersonal, informational, and decisional roles.

Interpersonal Roles

In fulfilling interpersonal roles, managers create and maintain interpersonal relationships to ensure the well-being of their organizations or units. They represent their organizations or units to other people in the *figurehead role*, which can include such ceremonial and symbolic activities as greeting visitors, attending awards banquets, and cutting ribbons to open new facilities. Managers also function as figureheads when they perform public service duties, including such activities as chairing the yearly fund drive for the United Way or serving on the board of the local Urban League. In the *leader role*, they motivate and guide employees by performing such activities as issuing orders, setting performance goals, and training subordinates. Managers create and maintain links between their organizations or units and others in the *liaison role*. For example, a company president may meet with the presidents of other companies at an industry conference.

Informational Roles

Because they serve as the primary authority figures for the organizations or units they supervise, managers have unique access to internal and external information networks. In informational roles they receive and transmit information within these networks. In the *monitor role*, managers scan the environment surrounding their organizations or units, seeking information to enhance performance. Such activities can range from reading periodicals and reports to trading

Table 2.2 Ten Roles of Managers

Role	Description
Interpersonal roles:	
Figurehead	Representing the organization or unit in ceremonial and symbolic activities
Leader	Guiding and motivating employee performance
Liaison	Linking the organization or unit with others
Informational roles:	
Monitor	Scanning the environment for information that can enhance organizational or unit performance
Disseminator	Providing information to subordinates
Spokesperson	Distributing information to people outside the organization or unit
Decisional roles:	
Entrepreneur	Initiating changes that improve the organization or unit
Disturbance handler	Adapting the organization or unit to changing conditions
Resource allocator	Distributing resources within the organization or unit
Negotiator	Bargaining or negotiating to sustain organizational or unit survival

rumors with managers in other firms or units. In the *disseminator role*, managers pass information to subordinates who would otherwise have no access to it. To share information with subordinates, they may hold meetings, write memoranda, make telephone calls, and so forth. In the *spokesperson role*, managers distribute information to people outside their organizations or units through annual stockholder reports, speeches, memos, and various other means.

Decisional Roles

In decisional roles, managers determine the direction to be taken by their organizations or units. In the *entrepreneur role*, they make decisions about improvements in the organizations or units for which they are responsible. Such decisions often entail initiating change. For example, a manager who hears about a new product opportunity may commit the firm to producing it. She may also delegate the responsibility for managing the resulting project to others. The *disturbance handler role* also requires making change-oriented decisions. Managers acting in this role must often try to adapt to change beyond their personal control. For example, they may have to handle such problems as conflicts among subordinates, the loss of an important customer, or damage to the firm's building or plant.

In the *resource allocator role*, managers decide which resources will be acquired and who will receive them. Such decisions often demand difficult trade-offs. For instance, if a manager decides to acquire personal computers for sales clerks, he may have to deny manufacturing department employees a piece of production equipment. As part of the resource allocation process, priorities may be set, budgets established, and schedules devised. In the *negotiator role*, managers engage in formal bargaining or negotiations to acquire the resources needed for the survival of their organizations or units. For example, they may negotiate with suppliers about delivery dates or bargain with union representatives about employee wages and hours.

Differences among Managers

Just as the functions managers perform and the skills they use differ from one managerial job to another, so do the roles managers fill. In Figure 2.6, the roles of liaison, spokesperson, and resource allocator are shown as being most important in the jobs of top managers, reflecting top management's responsibilities for planning, organizing, and controlling the strategic direction of the firm. In addition, monitoring activities are more important for top managers than for other types of managers because they must scan the environment for pertinent information.

For middle managers, the leader, liaison, disturbance handler, and resource allocator roles are the most important. These roles reflect the importance of middle management's job of organizing, directing, and controlling the functional or divisional units of the firm. The role of disseminator is also important in middle managers' jobs, as these managers must explain and implement the strategic plans formulated by top management.

For supervisory managers, the leader role is the most important, as they spend most of their time directing nonsupervisory personnel. They also act as spokespeople who disseminate information within their groups and serve as liaisons who connect their groups with the rest of the organization. In addition, they acquire and distribute the resources that their subordinates need to carry out their jobs.

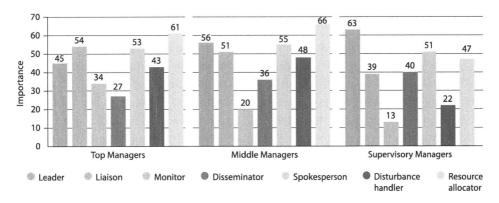

Figure 2.6 Managers' Jobs and the Roles They Fill. When researchers asked top, middle, and supervisory managers about the importance of the roles they perform, their answers provided the data illustrated graphically here. Note that the roles of figurehead, entrepreneur, and negotiator were not included in this survey. Source: Based on information from A. I. Kraut, P. R. Pedigo, D. D. McKenna, and M. D. Dunnette, "The Role of the Manager: What's Really Important in Different Management Jobs," *Academy of Management Executive* 3 (1989), 286–293.

The Nature of Managerial Work

To further analyze the classification of managerial roles just discussed, Henry Mintzberg observed a group of top managers at work for several weeks. After listing these managers' major activities and monitoring the time it took to perform them, Mintzberg found that the managers spent by far the most time in scheduled meetings. When combined with unscheduled meetings, this activity accounted for almost 70 percent of the managers' time. As Table 2.3 shows, the managers were left with barely a fifth of the day for desk work, and about a tenth for telephone calls and tours—walking around the company to see what was going on.

Mintzberg also recorded the amount of time consumed by each instance of each activity. As indicated in Table 2.3, scheduled meetings averaged a little more than an hour in length and ranged from less than 10 minutes to more than 2 hours. Unscheduled meetings were generally shorter, lasting from a few minutes to about an hour and averaging approximately 12 minutes each. Periods of desk work and tours to inspect the company averaged from 11 to 15 minutes each and were fitted in between scheduled meetings and unscheduled interruptions. Telephone calls were almost always quite short, averaging about 6 minutes each.

Based on his observations, Mintzberg concluded that managers' roles often require them to work in short bursts rather than in

Table 2.3 Distribution of Managerial Activities

Managerial Activity	Percentage of Workday Consumed	Average Duration
Scheduled meetings	59%	61 minutes
Desk work	22%	11 minutes
Unscheduled meetings	10%	12 minutes
Telephone calls	6%	6 minutes
Tours	3%	15 minutes

long, uninterrupted sessions. Such individuals frequently lack the time to complete rigorous planning, organizing, directing, and controlling. Rather than taking the form of a routine, well-planned course of action, managing can involve making nonroutine *incremental adjustments*. Clearly, managing is a fast-paced, active profession.

A Framework of Management Perspectives

Our discussions thus far are based on management thoughts and practices developed all over the world, many of which are thousands of years old. Consider the following:

1. As early as 3000 B.C., the Sumerians formulated missions and goals for government and commercial enterprises.
2. Between 3000 and 1000 B.C., the Egyptians successfully organized the efforts of thousands of workers to build the pyramids.
3. Between 800 B.C. and about A.D. 300, the Romans perfected the use of hierarchical authority.
4. Between A.D. 450 and the late 1400s, Venetian merchants developed commercial laws and invented double-entry bookkeeping.
5. In the early 1500s, Niccolo Machiavelli prepared an analysis of power that is still widely read.
6. At about the same time, the Catholic Church perfected a governance structure built upon the use of standardized procedures.

However, truly modern management practices did not begin to develop until the Industrial Revolution of the 1700s and 1800s. Inventions such as James Watt's steam engine and Eli Whitney's cotton gin created new forms of mass production that made existing modes of organization obsolete. Mass-assembly operations accelerated the pace of production dramatically and required the employment of large numbers of workers, overwhelming the small administrative staffs then employed by most companies. In addition, expertise became important to maintain production equipment, even though managers had little time to develop this expertise themselves. The field of industrial engineering, which first emerged because of the need to invent and improve workplace machinery, began to address the selection, instruction, and coordination of industrial employees. Toward the end of the Industrial Revolution, managers and engineers throughout North America and Europe focused on developing general theories of management.

1890–1940: The Scientific Management Perspective

Management theories initially took the form of *management principles* intended to provide managers with practical advice about managing their firms. Most of these principles were written by practicing managers or others closely associated with the management profession. Among the first principles to be widely read were those of the **scientific management perspective**.

All principles of scientific management reflected the idea that through proper management an organization could achieve profitability and survive over the long term in the competitive world of business. Theorists sharing the scientific management perspective devoted their attention to describing proper management and determining the best way to achieve it.

Frederick W. Taylor

The founder of scientific management, Frederick W. Taylor (1856–1915), developed his principles of scientific management as he rose from the position of laborer to chief engineer at the Midvale Steel Works in Philadelphia, Pennsylvania. These principles, which appear in Table 2.4, focused on increasing the efficiency of the workplace by differentiating managers from nonsupervisory workers and systematizing the jobs of both types of employees.

According to Taylor, an organization's profitability could be ensured only by finding the "one best way" to perform each job. Managers were charged with teaching workers this technique and implementing a system of rewards and punishments to encourage its use. Taylor reported that he used this approach to improve the productivity of coal shovelers at the Bethlehem Steel Company. As he observed these workers, he discovered that a shovel load of coal could range

from 4 to 30 pounds, depending on the density of the coal. By experimenting with a group of workers, Taylor discovered that shovelers could move the most coal in one day without suffering undue fatigue if each load of coal weighed 21 pounds. He then developed a variety of shovels, each of which would hold approximately 21 pounds of coal of a particular density. After Taylor taught workers how to use these shovels, each shoveler's daily yield rose from 16 tons to 59 tons. At the same time, the average wage per worker increased from $1.15 to $1.88 per day. Bethlehem Steel was able to reduce the number of shovelers in its yard from about 500 to 150, saving the firm about $80,000 per year.

Taylor's ideas influenced management around the world. In a 1918 article for the newspaper *Pravda*, the founder of the Russian Communist Party, Vladimir Lenin, recommended that Taylor's scientific management be used throughout the Soviet Union. In the United States, Taylor's

Table 2.4 Frederick W. Taylor's Principles of Scientific Management

1. Assign all responsibility to managers rather than workers.	Managers should do all the thinking related to the planning and design of work, leaving workers the task of carrying it out.
2. Use scientific methods to determine the one best way of performing each task.	Managers should design each worker's job accordingly, specifying a set of standard methods for completing the task in the right way.
3. Select the person most suited to each job to perform that job.	Managers should match the abilities of each worker to the demands of each job.
4. Train the worker to perform the job correctly.	Managers should train workers to use the standard methods devised for their jobs.
5. Monitor work performance to ensure that specified work procedures are followed correctly and that appropriate results are achieved.	Managers should exercise the control necessary to guarantee that workers under their supervision always perform their jobs in the one best way.
6. Provide further support by planning work assignments and eliminating interruptions.	Managers can help their workers continue to produce at a high level by shielding them from distractions that interfere with job performance.

Source: Based on information presented in F. W. Taylor, *The Principles of Scientific Management* (New York: Norton, 1911), pp. 34–40.

principles had such a dramatic effect on management that in 1912 he was called to testify before a special committee of the House of Representatives. Unions and employers both objected to Taylor's idea that employers and employees should share the economic gains of scientific management and wanted Congress to do something about it. Nevertheless, with the newspaper publicity he gained from his appearance, Taylor found even wider support for his ideas and was soon joined in his work by other specialists.

Other Contributors

The husband-and-wife team of Frank (1868–1924) and Lillian (1878–1972) Gilbreth followed in Taylor's footsteps in pursuing the "one best way" to perform any job. The Gilbreths are probably best known for their invention of *motion study*, a procedure in which jobs are reduced to their most basic movements. Table 2.5 lists some of these basic movements, each of which is called a *therblig* (*Gilbreth* spelled backward without inverting the *th*). The Gilbreths also invented the microchronometer, a clock with a hand capable of measuring time to 1/2000 of a second. Using this instrument, analysts could perform time-and-motion studies to determine the time required by each movement needed to perform a job.

Another contributor to scientific management, Henry Gantt (1861–1919), developed a task-and-bonus wage plan that paid workers a bonus besides their regular wages if they completed their work in an assigned amount of time. Gantt's plan also provided bonuses for supervisors, determined by the number of subordinates who met deadlines. In addition, Gantt invented the Gantt chart, a bar chart used by managers to compare actual with planned performance. Present-day scheduling methods such as the program evaluation and review technique (PERT) are based on this invention.

Harrington Emerson (1853–1931), a third contributor to scientific management, applied his own list of 12 principles to the railroad industry in the early 1900s. Among Emerson's principles were recommendations to establish clear objectives, seek advice from competent individuals, manage with justice and fairness, standardize procedures, reduce waste, and reward workers for efficiency. Late in his life, Emerson became interested in the selection and training of employees, stressing the importance of explaining scientific management to employees during their initial training. He reasoned that sound management practices could succeed only if every member of the firm understood them.

1900–1950: The Administrative Principles Perspective

At about the same time that Taylor and his colleagues were formulating their principles of scientific management, another group of theorists was developing the **administrative principles perspective**. In contrast to scientific management's

Table 2.5 Therblig Motions

Search	Transport empty	Transport loaded	Inspect
Find	Position	Disassemble	Assemble
Select	Rest	Preposition	Plan
Grasp	Use	Release load	Avoidable delay

emphasis on reducing the costs of production activities, this perspective focused on increasing the efficiency of administrative procedures.

Henri Fayol

Considered the father of modern management thought, Henri Fayol (1841–1925) developed his principles of administration in the early 1900s while serving as chief executive of a French mining and metallurgy firm, Commentry-Fourchambault-Decazeville, known as "Comambault." Fayol was the first to identify the four functions of management we have already discussed: planning, organizing, directing, and controlling. He also formulated the 14 principles shown in Table 2.6 to help administrators perform their jobs.

Fayol believed that the number of management principles that might help improve an organization's operation is potentially limitless. He considered his principles to be flexible and adaptable, labeling them principles rather than laws or rules

> to avoid any idea of rigidity, as there is nothing rigid or absolute in [management] matters; everything is a question of degree. The same principle is hardly ever applied twice in exactly the same way, because we have to allow for different and changing circumstances, for human beings who are equally different and changeable, and for many other variable elements. The principles, too, are flexible, and can be adapted to meet every need; it is just a question of knowing how to use them.

For Fayol, management involved more than mechanically following rules. It required that managers exercise intuition and engage in skillful behavior in deciding how, when, and why to put management principles into action.

Max Weber

Max Weber (1864–1920) was a German sociologist who, although neither a manager nor a management consultant, had a major effect on management thought. Like Fayol, he was interested in the efficiency of different kinds of administrative arrangements. To figure out what makes organizations efficient, Weber analyzed the Egyptian Empire, the Prussian army, the Roman Catholic Church, and other large organizations that had functioned efficiently over long periods of time. Based on the results of these analyses, he developed his model of **bureaucracy**, an idealized description of an efficient organization that is summarized in Table 2.7.

Weber's bureaucratic model provides for both the differentiation (through the division of labor and task specialization) and the integration (by the hierarchy of authority and written rules and regulations) necessary to get a specific job done. Weber believed that any organization with bureaucratic characteristics would be efficient. He noted, however, that work in a bureaucracy could become so simple and undemanding that employees might grow dissatisfied and, as a result, less productive.

Other Contributors

A number of other management experts have contributed to the administrative principles perspective. James Mooney (1884–1957) was vice president and director of General Motors and president of General Motors Overseas Corporation during the late 1920s, when he espoused his principles of organization. Mooney's *coordinative principle* highlighted the importance of organizing the tasks and functions in a firm into

Table 2.6 Fayol's 14 Principles of Management

Principle	Description
Division of work	A firm's work should be divided into specialized, simplified tasks. Matching task demands with workforce skills and abilities will improve productivity. The management of work should be separated from its performance.
Authority and responsibility	Authority is the right to give orders, and responsibility is the obligation to accept the consequences of using authority. No one should possess one without having the other as well.
Discipline	Discipline is performing a task with obedience and dedication. It can be expected only when a firm's managers and subordinates agree on the specific behaviors that subordinates will perform.
Unity of command	Each subordinate should receive orders from only one hierarchical superior. The confusion created by having two or more superiors will undermine authority, discipline, order, and stability.
Unity of direction	Each group of activities directed toward the same objective should have only one manager and only one plan.
Individual versus general interests	The interests of individuals and the whole organization must be treated with equal respect. Neither can be allowed to supersede the other.
Remuneration of personnel	The pay received by employees must be fair and satisfactory to both them and the firm. Pay should be distributed in proportion to personal performance, but employees' general welfare must not be threatened by unfair incentive-payment schemes.
Centralization	Centralization is the retention of authority by managers, to be used when managers desire greater control. Decentralization should be used if subordinates' opinions, counsel, and experience are needed.
Scalar chain	The scalar chain is a hierarchical string extending from the uppermost manager to the lowest subordinate. The line of authority follows this chain and is the proper route for organizational communications.
Order	Order, or "everything in its place," should be instilled whenever possible because it reduces wasted materials and efforts. Jobs should be designed and staffed with order in mind.
Equity	Equity means enforcing established rules with a sense of fair play, kindliness, and justice. It should be guaranteed by management, as it increases members' loyalty, devotion, and satisfaction.
Stability of tenure	Properly selected employees should be given the time needed to learn and adjust to their jobs. The absence of such stability undermines organizational performance.
Initiative	Staff members should be given the opportunity to think for themselves. This approach improves the distribution of information and adds to the organization's pool of talent.
Esprit de corps	Managers should harmonize the interests of members by resisting the urge to split up successful teams. They should rely on face-to-face communication to detect and correct misunderstandings immediately.

Table 2.7 Features of Bureaucratic Organizations

Feature	Description
Selection and promotion	Expertise is the primary criterion. Friendship criteria or other favoritism is explicity rejected.
Hierarchy of authority	Superiors have the authority to direct subordinates' actions. They must ensure that these actions serve the bureaucracy's best interests.
Rules and regulations	Unchanging regulations provide the bureaucracy's members with consistent, impartial guidance.
Division of labor	Work is divided into tasks that can be performed by the bureaucracy's members in an efficient, productive manner.
Written documentation	Records provide consistency and a basis for evaluating bureaucratic procedures.
Separate ownership	Members cannot gain unfair or undeserved advantage through ownership.

Source: Based on information presented in H. H. Gerth and C. W. Mills, trans., *From Max Weber: Essays in Sociology* (New York: Oxford University Press, 1946).

a coordinated whole. He defined coordination as the orderly arrangement of group effort to provide unity of action in the pursuit of a common mission. His *scalar principle* identified the importance of scalar—hierarchical—chains of superiors and subordinates as a means of integrating the work of different employees. Finally, Mooney's *functional principle* stressed the importance of functional differences, such as marketing, manufacturing, and accounting. He noted how work in each functional area both differs from and interlocks with the work of other areas as well as how the success of the larger firm requires coordination and scalar linkages among its different functional parts.

Lyndall Urwick (1891–1983), another contributor to the administrative principles perspective, was a British military officer and director of the International Management Institute in Geneva, Switzerland. Urwick made his mark by consolidating the ideas of Fayol and Mooney with those of Taylor. From Taylor, Urwick adopted the idea that systematic, rigorous investigation should inform and support the management of employees. He also used Fayol's 14 principles to guide managerial planning and control, and

Mooney's three principles of organization to structure his discussion of organizing. In this way, Urwick's synthesis bridged Taylor's scientific management and the administrative principles approach, and it integrated the work of others within the framework of the four functions of management identified by Fayol.

Mary Parker Follett (1868–1933), who became interested in industrial management in the 1920s, was among the first proponents of what later became known as *industrial democracy*. In her writings on administrative principles, Follett proposed that every employee should have an ownership interest in his or her company, which would encourage attention to a company's overall mission and goals. In promoting cooperation in the workplace, her work foreshadowed the human relations perspective, which is described next. Follett also suggested that organizational problems tend to resist simple solutions, because they typically stem from a variety of interdependent factors. Here again she anticipated later theorists, contributing to the contingency approach discussed later in this chapter.

1930–1970: The Human Relations Perspective

Although members of the scientific management and administrative principles perspectives advocated the scientific study of management, they rarely evaluated their ideas in any formal way. This omission was corrected in the mid-1920s, when university researchers began to use scientific methods to test existing management thought.

The Hawthorne Studies

The *Hawthorne studies*, which began in 1924 at Western Electric's Hawthorne plant near Chicago, Illinois, were among the earliest attempts to use scientific techniques to examine human behavior at work. As summarized in Table 2.8, a three-stage series of experiments assessed the effects of varying physical conditions and management practices on workplace efficiency. The first experiment examined the effects of workplace lighting on productivity; it produced the unexpected findings that changes in lighting had little effect but that changes in social conditions seemed to explain significant increases in group productivity. Additional experiments led the researchers to conclude that social factors—in particular,

workers' desires to satisfy needs for companionship and support at work—explained the results observed across all of the Hawthorne studies.

Later reanalyses of the Hawthorne experiments not only found weaknesses in the studies' methods and techniques, but also suggested that changes in incentive pay, tasks being performed, rest periods, and working hours led to the productivity improvements attributed by researchers to the effects of social factors. Nonetheless, the Hawthorne studies raised serious questions about the efficiency-oriented focus of the scientific management and administrative principles perspectives. In so doing, they stimulated debate about the importance of human satisfaction and personal development at work. The human relations perspective of management thought that grew out of this debate redirected attention away from improving efficiency and toward increasing employee growth, development, and satisfaction.

Douglas McGregor

Douglas McGregor (1906–1964) played a key role in promoting this redirection, through his efforts at sharpening the philosophical contrast between the human relations approach and the scientific management and administrative principles

Table 2.8 The Hawthorne Studies

Experiment	Major changes	Results
Stage I: Illumination study	Lighting conditions	Improved productivity at nearly all levels of illumination
Stage II: First relay-assembly test	Job simplification, shorter work hours, rest breaks, friendly supervision, incentive pay	30 percent productivity improvement
Second relay-assembly test	Incentive pay	12 percent productivity improvement
Mica-splitting test	Shorter work hours, rest breaks, friendly supervision	15 percent productivity improvement
Stage III: Interview program	—	Discovery of presence of informal productivity norms
Bank-wiring-room test	Incentive pay	Emergence of productivity norms

perspectives. McGregor used the term **Theory X** to describe his key assumptions about human nature, which appear in Table 2.9. He suggested that theorists and managers holding these assumptions would describe management as follows:

1. Managers are responsible for organizing the elements of productive enterprise—money, materials, equipment, people—solely in the interest of economic efficiency.
2. The manager's function is to motivate workers, direct their efforts, control their actions, and modify their behavior to fit the organization's needs.
3. Without such active intervention by managers, people would be passive or even resistant to organizational needs. They must therefore be persuaded, rewarded, and punished for the good of the organization.[21]

According to McGregor, the scientific management and administrative principles perspectives promoted a "hard" version of Theory X. Both perspectives favored overcoming employees'

resistance to organizational needs through strict discipline and economic rewards or punishments. McGregor added that a "soft" version of Theory X seemed to underlie the Hawthorne studies, as the Hawthorne researchers appeared to regard satisfaction and social relations mainly as being rewards for employees who followed orders.

Theory Y, a contrasting philosophy of management that McGregor attributed to theorists, researchers, and managers holding the human relations perspective, is based on the second set of assumptions shown in Table 2.9. According to McGregor, individuals holding Theory Y assumptions would view the task of management as follows:

1. Managers are responsible for organizing the elements of productive enterprise—money, materials, equipment, people—in the interest of economic ends.
2. Because people are motivated to perform, have potential for development, can assume responsibility, and are willing to work toward organizational goals, managers are

Table 2.9 Theory X and Theory Y Assumptions

Theory X assumptions:
1. The average person has an inherent dislike of work and will avoid it if possible.
2. Because they dislike work, most people must be coerced, controlled, directed, or threatened with punishment before they will put forth effort toward the achievement of organizational objectives.
3. The average person prefers to be directed, wishes to avoid responsibility, has relatively little ambition, and desires security above all.

Theory Y assumptions:
1. Expanding physical and mental effort at work is as natural as play and rest. The average person does not inherently dislike work.
2. External control and the threat of punishment are not the only way to direct effort toward organizational objectives. People will exercise self-direction and self-control in the service of objectives to which they feel committed.
3. Commitment to objectives is a function of the rewards associated with their achievement. The most significant rewards—the satisfaction of ego and self-actualization needs—can be direct products of effort directed toward organizational objectives.
4. Avoidance of responsibility, lack of ambition, and emphasis on security are not inherent human characteristics. Under proper conditions, the average person learns not only to accept but also to seek responsibility.
5. Imagination, ingenuity, creativity, and the ability to use these qualities to solve organizational problems are widely distributed among people.

Source: Based on information presented in D. McGregor, *The Human Side of Enterprise* (New York: McGraw-Hill, 1960), pp. 33–34, 47–48.

responsible for enabling people to recognize and develop these basic capacities.

3. The essential task of management is to arrange organizational conditions and methods of operation so that working toward organizational objectives is also the best way for people to achieve their own personal goals.

Unlike Theory X managers, who try to control their employees, Theory Y managers try to help employees learn how to manage themselves.

Other Contributors

Many management theorists, including Abraham Maslow and Frederick Herzberg, embraced the point of view embodied in McGregor's Theory Y and speculated about ways in which personal autonomy and group participation might encourage employee growth, development, and satisfaction. The works of these contributors also served as benchmark theories during the early development of research on micro and meso organizational behavior, as described later in this book.

1960–Present: The Open Systems Perspective

With the emergence in the 1960s of the **open systems perspective**, human relations concerns related to employee satisfaction and development broadened to include a focus on organizational growth and survival. According to the open systems perspective, every organization is a *system*—a unified structure of interrelated subsystems—and it is *open*—subject to the influence of the surrounding environment. Together, these two ideas form the central tenet of the open systems approach, which states that organizations whose subsystems can cope with the

surrounding environment can continue to do business, whereas organizations whose subsystems cannot cope will not survive.

Daniel Katz and Robert L. Kahn

In one of the seminal works on the open systems perspective, Daniel Katz and Robert Kahn identified the process shown in Figure 2.7 as essential to organizational growth and survival. This process consists of the following sequence of events:

1. Every organization imports *inputs*, such as raw materials, production equipment, human resources, and technical know-how, from the surrounding environment. For instance, Shell Oil Company hires employees and, from sources around the world, acquires unrefined oil, refinery equipment, and knowledge about how to refine petroleum products.

2. Some of the inputs are used to transform other inputs during a process of *throughput*. At Shell, employees use refinery equipment and their own know-how to transform unrefined oil into petroleum products such as gasoline, kerosene, and diesel fuel.

3. The transformed resources are exported as *outputs*—saleable goods or services—to the environment. Petroleum products from Shell's refineries are loaded into tankers and transported to service stations throughout North America.

4. Outputs are exchanged for new inputs, and the cycle repeats. Shell sells its products and uses the resulting revenues to pay its employees and purchase additional oil, equipment, and know-how.

According to Katz and Kahn, organizations will continue to grow and survive only as long as they import more material and energy from the environment than they expend in producing

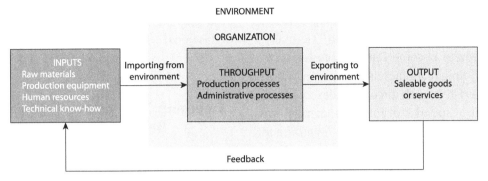

Figure 2.7 The Open Systems Perspective

the outputs exported back to the environment. *Information inputs* that signal how the environment and organization are functioning can help determine whether the organization will continue to survive. *Negative feedback* indicates a potential for failure and the need to change the way things are being done.

Fred Emery and Eric Trist

In Katz and Kahn's model, the environment surrounding an organization is both the source of needed resources and the recipient of transformed products. Accordingly, organizational survival depends on sensing that environment and adjusting to its demands. Describing environments and their associated demands so as to improve this sensing and adjustment process was the goal of Fred Emery and Eric Trist, two early theorists of the open systems perspective.

After noting that every organization's environment is itself composed of a collection of more or less interconnected organizations—supplier companies, competitors, and customer firms—Emery and Trist proposed the existence of four basic kinds of environments. The first kind, which they labeled the *placid random environment*, is loosely interconnected and relatively unchanging. Organizations in such environments operate independently of one another, and one firm's

decision to change the way it does business has little effect on its rivals. These organizations are usually small—for example, landscape maintenance companies, construction firms, and industrial job shops—and can usually ignore each other and still stay in business by catering to local customers.

Placid clustered environments are more tightly interconnected. Under these conditions, firms are grouped together into stable industries. Environments of this sort require organizations to cope with the actions of a *market*—a fairly constant group of suppliers, competitors, and customers. As a result, companies in placid clustered environments develop strategic moves and countermoves that correspond to competitors' actions. Grocery stores in the same geographic region often do business in this type of environment, using coupon discounts, in-store specials, and similar promotions to lure customers away from other stores.

Disturbed reactive environments are as tightly interconnected as placid clustered environments, but are considerably less stable. Changes that occur in the environment itself have forceful effects on every organization. For instance, new competitors from overseas, by increasing automation and changing consumer tastes in the U.S. automobile market, revolutionized the domestic auto industry in the 1970s and 1980s. In response, GM and

Ford had to change their way of doing business, Chrysler ultimately merged with Germany's Daimler-Benz to become DaimlerChrysler, and a fourth long-time manufacturer, American Motors, ceased to exist. In such circumstances, organizations must respond not only to competitors' actions but also to changes in the environment itself. Owing to their unpredictability, it is difficult to plan how to respond to these changes.

Turbulent fields are extremely complex and dynamic environments. Companies operate in multiple markets. Public and governmental actions can alter the nature of an industry virtually overnight. Technologies advance at lightning speed. The amount of information needed to stay abreast of industrial trends is overwhelming. As a result, it is virtually impossible for organizations to do business in any consistent way. Instead, they must remain flexible in the face of such uncertainty, staying poised to adapt themselves to whatever circumstances unfold. Today's computer and communications industries exemplify this sort of environment. Technological change and corporate mergers are creating and destroying entire categories of companies at ever-increasing rates.

Other Contributors

Emery and Trist suggested that organizations must respond in different ways to different environmental conditions. Tighter environmental interconnections require greater awareness about environmental conditions, and more sweeping environmental change necessitates greater flexibility and adaptability. Other open systems theorists, including Paul Lawrence, Robert Duncan, and Jay Galbraith, have similarly stressed the need for organizations to adjust to their environments. Their ideas, and those of other open systems theorists, form the basis of several current models of macro

organizational behavior, described in later chapters of this book.

Emerging: The Positive Organizational Behavior Perspective

As we have noted, the field of organizational behavior is rooted in part in the discipline of psychology. For this reason, changes in psychology have influenced thinking in organizational behavior as the two fields have continued to develop. One such area of cross-fertilization involves the area of "positive psychology." Noting that much of the research conducted in psychology during the last half of the 20th century examined cognitive and behavioral pathologies, that is, negative thoughts and activities, psychologists have recently begun suggesting that more attention be focused on human strengths and potential, thus, on positive psychological processes and outcomes. In introducing a special issue of the *American Psychologist* on the topic of positive psychology, Martin Seligman and Mihaly Csikszentmihalyi described positive psychological results at three levels of operation:

1. The intrapsychic level: well-being, contentment, and satisfaction; hope and optimism; and flow and happiness.
2. The individual level: the capacity for love and vocation, courage, interpersonal skill, aesthetic sensibility, perseverance, forgiveness, originality, future-mindedness, spirituality, high talent, and wisdom.
3. The interpersonal (group) level: the civic virtues and the institutions that move individuals toward better citizenship—responsibility, nurturance, altruism, civility, moderation, tolerance, and work ethic.

THE CHANGING ENVIRONMENT OF ORGANIZATIONS

Ricky W. Griffin & Gregory Moorhead

The environment of all organizations is changing at an unprecedented rate. The rise of social entrepreneurship by organizations such as Mercy Corps represents only one perspective on environmental change. Indeed, in some industries, such as consumer electronics, popular entertainment, and information technology, the speed and magnitude of change are truly breathtaking. YouTube, for instance, uploads over 60 hours of new video footage every hour. And it's only been during the last decade or so that smartphone technologies, Facebook, and social networking have become commonplace.

Even industries characterized by what have been staid and predictable environments, such as traditional retail and heavy manufacturing, also face sweeping environmental changes today. Understanding and addressing the environment of a business has traditionally been the purview of top managers. But the effects of today's changing environment permeate the entire organization. Hence, to truly understand the behavior of people in organizational settings, it is also necessary to understand the changing environment of business. This chapter is intended to provide the framework for such understanding. Specifically, as illustrated in Figure 3.1, we introduce and examine five of the central environmental forces for change faced by today's organizations: globalization, diversity, technology, ethics and corporate governance, and new employment relationships.

Globalization and Business

Perhaps the most significant source of change affecting many organizations today is the increasing **globalization** of organizations and management. Of course, in many ways, international management is nothing new. Centuries ago, the Roman army was forced to develop a management system to deal with its widespread empire. Moreover, many notable early explorers such as Christopher Columbus and Magellan were not actually seeking new territory but instead were looking for new trade routes to boost international trade. Likewise, the Olympic Games, the Red Cross, and other organizations have international roots. From a business standpoint, however, the widespread effects of globalization are relatively new, at least in the United States.

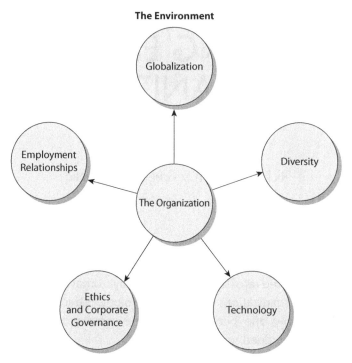

Figure 3.1   The changing environment of business presents both opportunities and challenges for managers today. Five important environmental forces are globalization, diversity, technology, ethics and corporate governance, and new employment relationships.

The Growth of International Business

In 2012, the volume of international trade in current dollars was about 50 times greater than the amount in 1960. Indeed, while international trade actually declined by 11 percent in 2009 due to the global recession, it increased by that same amount in 2010 as the economy began a slow rebound. Four major factors account for much of the growth in international trade.

First, communication and transportation have improved dramatically over the past several decades. Telephone service has improved, communication networks span the globe and can interact via satellite, and once-remote areas have become routinely accessible. Telephone service in some developing countries is now almost entirely by cellular phone technology rather than land-based wired telephone service. Fax and electronic mail technologies allow managers to send documents around the world in seconds as opposed to the days it took just a few years ago. And newer applications such as text messaging and Skype have made global communication even easier. In short, it is simply easier to conduct international business today than was the case just a few years ago.

Second, businesses have expanded internationally to increase their markets. Companies in smaller countries, such as Nestlé in Switzerland and Heineken in the Netherlands, recognized long ago that their domestic markets were too small to sustain much growth and therefore moved into the international arena. Many U.S. firms, on the other hand, have only found it advantageous to enter foreign markets in the last half-century. Now, though, most midsize and even many small firms routinely buy and/or sell products and services in other countries.

Third, more and more firms are moving into international markets to control costs, especially

Serving a Global Market

Tourism is projected by many to be the largest employer in the world within the next decade. While most think of the travel and tourism industry as consisting entirely of young people who are greeters at airports, restaurant servers, or front desk agents at hotels, the impact of the growing number of visitors ripples out across national economies to unexpected areas such as jobs in retail, construction, and manufacturing. The challenge for any international destination is to teach employees about the key differences that a non-native traveler will have that should be accommodated when that traveler arrives at a service experience. Whether the issue is one of language, customs, or service expectations, the employee serving the international customer must be alert to the many variations that different travelers will bring.

The post–9/11 period in the United States is a good example. This tragic act of terrorism created a surge of patriotism that spanned nearly all Americans in all jobs. This became an especially important issue for the American travel and tourism industry as American employees needed to display special sensitivity to international travelers, especially those from countries that had been publically hostile to the United States. Some of those travelers, when encountering this patriotism, found it at least mildly uncomfortable and sometimes frighteningly hostile. This problem was more likely once the travelers left portal cities and visited more remote locations less accustomed to dealing with international guests. Even at portal destinations, however, travelers reported checking into hotels after a long flight and being confronted with a desk agent wearing an American flag and a lapel button displaying an aggressively patriotic slogan. On the streets, people were flying flags on private residences and commercial buildings, and patriotic auto bumper stickers were everywhere. To some foreign travelers coming to the United States to conduct business or vacation, this display was intimidating.

An astute manager of a business-class hotel in New York, Los Angeles, or Washington, DC, might anticipate the problem and provide extra training to sensitize employees to the impact these strong visual might have on guests. Unfortunately, not every manager is astute, and outside the major ports of entry to the United States there were reports of situations where the hospitality to ensure a welcoming atmosphere for all visitors was not so well done. If an organization is supposed to be providing a service to all customers, then it is incumbent on managers to ensure that employees are prepared for the variations in customers. Theme parks know that visitors from some cultures avoid standing in any lines; these parks assist their employees in maintaining queue discipline by clearly defining their waiting lines with ropes and stanchions. In other words, organizations that serve international customers ensure that their employees are provided training and every assistance in managing those customers' experiences so that they and those around them are satisfied.

Discussion Question: If you have traveled to another country or are a traveler from another county, what reactions did you have to the things you saw and the people you first met upon entry into the foreign country? How did these affect your feelings about and perceptions of the country you entered?

to reduce labor costs. Plans to cut costs in this way do not always work out as planned, but many firms are successfully using inexpensive labor in Asia and Mexico. In searching for lower labor costs, some companies have discovered well-trained workers and built more efficient plants that are closer to international markets. India, for instance, has emerged as a major force in the high-tech sector. Turkey and Indonesia are also growing in importance. And many foreign automakers have built plants in the United States.

Finally, many organizations have become international in response to competition. If an organization starts gaining strength in international markets, its competitors often must follow suit to avoid falling too far behind in sales and profitability. Exxon Mobil Corporation and Chevron realized they had to increase their international market share to keep pace with foreign competitors such as BP and Royal Dutch Shell.

Cross-Cultural Differences and Similarities

The primary concern of this book is human behavior in organizational settings, so we now turn our attention to differences and similarities in behavior across cultures. While there is relatively little research in this area, interesting findings have begun to emerge.

General Observations At one level, it is possible to make several general observations about similarities and differences across cultures. For one thing, cultural and national boundaries do not necessarily coincide. Some areas of Switzerland are very much like Italy, other parts like France, and still other parts like Germany. Similarly, within the United States there are large cultural differences across, say, Southern California, Texas, and the East Coast.

Given this basic assumption, one major review of the literature on international management reached five basic conclusions. First, behavior in organizational settings does indeed vary across cultures. Thus, employees in companies based in Japan, the United States, and Germany are likely to have different attitudes and patterns of behavior. The behavior patterns are also likely to be widespread and pervasive within an organization.

Second, culture itself is one major cause of this variation. **Culture** is the set of shared values, often taken for granted, that help people in a group, organization, or society understand which actions are considered acceptable and which are deemed unacceptable. Thus, although the behavioral differences just noted may be caused in part by different standards of living, different geographical conditions, and so forth, culture itself is a major factor apart from other considerations.

Third, although the causes and consequences of behavior within organizational settings remain quite diverse across cultures, organizations and the ways they are structured appear to be growing increasingly similar. Hence, managerial practices at a general level may be becoming more and more alike, but the people who work within organizations still differ markedly.

Fourth, the same individual behaves differently in different cultural settings. A manager may adopt one set of behaviors when working in one culture but change those behaviors when moved to a different culture. For example, Japanese executives who come to work in the United States may slowly begin to act more like U.S. managers and less like Japanese managers. This, in turn, may be source of concern for them when they are transferred back to Japan.

Finally, cultural diversity can be an important source of synergy in enhancing organizational effectiveness. More and more organizations are coming to appreciate the virtues of diversity, but they still know surprisingly little about how to manage it. Organizations that adopt a multinational strategy can—with effort—become more than a sum of their parts. Operations in each culture can benefit from operations in other cultures through an enhanced understanding of how the world works.

Specific Cultural Issues Geert Hofstede, a Dutch researcher, studied workers and managers in 60 countries and found that specific attitudes and behaviors differed significantly because of the values and beliefs that characterized those countries. Table 3.1 shows how Hofstede's categories help us summarize differences for several countries.

The two primary dimensions that Hofstede found are the individualism/collectivism continuum and power distance. **Individualism** exists to the extent that people in a culture define themselves primarily as individuals rather than as part of one or more groups or organizations. At work, people from more individualistic cultures tend to be more concerned about themselves as

individuals than about their work group, individual tasks are more important than relationships, and hiring and promotion are usually based on skills and rules. **Collectivism**, on the other hand, is characterized by tight social frameworks in which people tend to base their identities on the group or organization to which they belong. At work, this means that employee–employer links are more like family relationships, relationships are more important than individuals or tasks, and hiring and promotion are based on group membership. In the United States, a very individualistic culture, it is important to perform better than others and to stand out from the crowd. In Japan, a more collectivist culture, an individual tries to fit in with the group, strives for harmony, and prefers stability.

Power distance, which can also be called **orientation to authority**, is the extent to which people accept as normal an unequal distribution of power. In countries such as Mexico and Venezuela, for example, people prefer to be in a situation in which authority is clearly understood

Table 3.1 Work-Related Differences in 10 Countries

Country	Individualism/ Collectivism	Power Distance	Uncertainty Avoidance	Masculinity	Long-Term Orientation
CANADA	H	M	M	M	L
GERMANY	M	M	M	M	M
ISRAEL	M	L	M	M	(no data)
ITALY	H	M	M	H	(no data)
JAPAN	M	M	H	H	H
MEXICO	H	H	H	M	(no data)
PAKISTAN	L	M	M	M	L
SWEDEN	H	M	L	L	M
UNITED STATES	H	M	M	M	L
VENEZUELA	L	H	M	H	(no data)

Note: H = high; M = moderate; L = low for INDIVIDUALISM/COLLECTIVISM H means High Individualism, L means High Collectivism and M means a balance of individualism and collectivism. These are only 10 of the more than 60 countries that Hofstede and others have studied.
References: Adapted from Geert Hofstede and Michael Harris Bond, "The Confucius Connection: From Cultural Roots to Economic Growth," *Organizational Dynamics,* Spring 1988, pp. 5–21; Geert Hofstede, "Motivation, Leadership, and Organization: Do American Theories Apply Abroad?" *Organizational Dynamics,* Summer 1980, pp. 42–63.

and lines of authority are never bypassed. On the other hand, in countries such as Israel and Denmark, authority is not as highly respected and employees are quite comfortable circumventing lines of authority to accomplish something. People in the United States tend to be mixed, accepting authority in some situations but not in others.

Hofstede also identified other dimensions of culture. **Uncertainty avoidance**, which can also be called **preference for stability**, is the extent to which people feel threatened by unknown situations and prefer to be in clear and unambiguous situations. People in Japan and Mexico prefer stability to uncertainty, whereas uncertainty is normal and accepted in Sweden, Hong Kong, and the United Kingdom. **Masculinity**, which might be more accurately called **assertiveness** or **materialism**, is the extent to which the dominant values in a society emphasize aggressiveness and the acquisition of money and other possessions as opposed to concern for people, relationships among people, and overall quality of life. People in the United States tend to be moderate on both the uncertainty avoidance and masculinity scales. Japan and Italy score high on the masculinity scale while Sweden scores low.

Hofstede's framework has recently been expanded to include **long-term** versus **short-term orientation**. Long-term values include focusing on the future, working on projects that have a distant payoff, persistence, and thrift. Short-term values are more oriented toward the past and the present and include respect for traditions and social obligations. Japan, Hong Kong, and China are highly long-term oriented. The Netherlands, the United States, and Germany are moderately long-term oriented. Pakistan and West Africa tend to be more short-term oriented.

Hofstede's research presents only one of several ways of categorizing differences across many different countries and cultures. His findings, however, are now widely accepted and have been used by many companies. They have also prompted ongoing research by others. The important issue to remember is that people from diverse cultures value things differently from each other and that people need to take these differences into account as they work.

Managerial Behavior Across Cultures

Some individual variations in people from different cultures shape the behavior of both managers and employees. Other differences are much more likely to influence managerial behavior per se. In general, these differences relate to managerial beliefs about the role of authority and power in the organization. For example, managers in Indonesia, Italy, and Japan tend to believe that the purpose of an organization's structure is to let everyone know who his or her boss is (medium to high power distance). Managers in the United States, Germany, and the Great Britain, in contrast, believe that organizational structure is intended to coordinate group behavior and effort (low power distance). On another dimension, Italian and German managers believe it is acceptable to bypass one's boss to get things done, but among Swedish and British managers, bypassing one's superior is strongly prohibited.

Figure 3.2 illustrates findings on another interesting point. Managers in Japan strongly believe that a manager should be able to answer any question he or she is asked. Thus, they place a premium on expertise and experience. At the other extreme are Swedish managers, who have the least concern about knowing all the answers. They view themselves as problem solvers and facilitators who make no claim to omniscience.

Some evidence also suggests that managerial behavior is rapidly changing, at least among

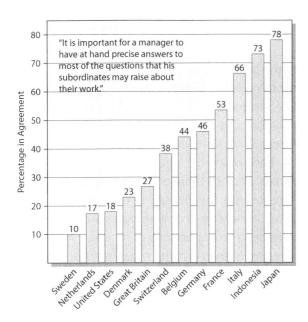

Figure 3.2 Differences Across Cultures in Managers' Beliefs about Answering Questions from Subordinates. Subordinates in various cultures have different beliefs regarding managers' ability to provide definite, precise answers to questions. Japan has the strongest expectations; Sweden has the weakest. Reference: from *International Studies of Management and Organizations,* vol. XIII, no. 1–2, Spring–Summer 1983.

European managers. In general, these managers are becoming more career oriented, better educated, more willing to work cooperatively with labor, more willing to delegate, and more cosmopolitan. Finally, a recent major global research project has investigated differences in leadership in different countries and produced some interesting results.

Diversity and Business

A second major environmental shift in recent years has been the increased attention devoted to the concept of diversity. **Workforce diversity** refers to the important similarities and differences among the employees of organizations. 3M defines its goals regarding workforce diversity as "valuing uniqueness, while respecting differences, maximizing individual potentials, and synergizing collective talent and experience for the growth and success of 3M." In a diverse workforce, managers are compelled to recognize and handle the similarities and differences that exist among the people in the organization.

Employees' conceptions of work, expectations of rewards from the organization, and practices in relating to others are all influenced by diversity. Managers of diverse work groups need to understand how the social environment affects employees' beliefs about work, and they must have the communication skills required to develop confidence and self-esteem in members of diverse work groups.

Unfortunately, many people tend to stereotype others in organizations. A **stereotype** is a generalization about a person or a group of persons based on certain characteristics or traits. Many managers fall into the trap of stereotyping workers as being like themselves and sharing a manager's orientation toward work, rewards, and relating to coworkers. However, if workers do not share those views, values, and beliefs, problems can arise. A second situation involving stereotyping occurs when managers classify workers into some particular group based on traits such as age or gender. It is often easier for managers to group people based on easily identifiable characteristics and to treat these groups as "different." Managers who stereotype workers based on assumptions about the characteristics of their group tend to ignore individual differences and therefore to make rigid judgments about others that do not take into account the specific person and the current situation.

Stereotypes can lead to the even more dangerous process of prejudice toward others. **Prejudices** are judgments about others that reinforce beliefs about superiority and inferiority. They can lead to an exaggerated assessment of the worth of one group and a diminished assessment of the worth of others. When people prejudge others, they make assumptions about the nature of the others that may or may not be true, and they manage accordingly. In other words, people build job descriptions, reward systems, performance appraisal systems, and management systems and policies that fit their stereotypes.

Management systems built on stereotypes and prejudices do not meet the needs of a diverse workforce. An incentive system may offer rewards that people do not value, job descriptions might not fit the jobs and the people who do them, and performance evaluation systems might measure the wrong things. In addition, those who engage in prejudice and stereotyping fail to recognize employees' distinctive individual talents, a situation that often leads these employees to lose self-esteem and possibly have lower levels of job satisfaction and performance. Stereotypes can also become self-fulfilling prophecies. If we assume someone is incompetent and treat the person as though he or she is incompetent, then over time the employee may begin to share the same belief. This can lead to reduced productivity, lower creativity, and lower morale.

Of course, managers caught in this counterproductive cycle can change. As a first step, they must recognize that diversity exists in organizations. Only then can they begin to manage it appropriately. Managers who do not recognize diversity may face an unhappy, disillusioned, and underutilized workforce.

Dimensions of Diversity

In the United States, race and gender have been considered the primary dimensions of diversity. The earliest civil rights laws, for instance, were aimed at correcting racial segregation. Other more recent laws have dealt with discrimination on the basis of gender, age, and disability. However, diversity entails broader issues than these. In the largest sense, the diversity of the workforce refers to all of the ways that employees are similar and different. The importance of renewed interest in diversity is that it helps organizations reap the benefits of all the similarities and differences among workers.

The **primary dimensions of diversity** are those factors that are either inborn or exert extraordinary influence on early socialization. These include age, race and ethnicity, gender, physical and mental abilities, and sexual orientation. These factors make up the essence of who we are as human beings. They define us to others, and because of how others react to them, these factors also define us to ourselves. These characteristics are enduring aspects of our human personality, and they sometimes present extremely complex problems to managers.

Secondary dimensions of diversity include factors that matter to us as individuals and that to some extent define us to others; however, they may be less permanent than primary dimensions and can be adapted or changed. These include educational background, geographical location, income, marital status, military experience, parental status, religious beliefs, and work experience. These factors may influence any given individual as much as the primary dimensions. Many veterans of the wars in Afghanistan and Iraq, for example, have been profoundly affected by their experience of serving in the military.

Who Will Be the Workforce of the Future?

Employment statistics can help us understand just how different the workforce of the future will be. Figure 3.3 compares the workforce composition of 1984, 1994, 2004, and projections for 2014. All workforce segments have increased as a percentage of the total workforce except the white male segment, which has declined steadily. This may not seem too dramatic, but it follows decades in which the white males have dominated the workforce, making up well over 50 percent of it. When one considers that the total U.S. workforce is over 150 million people, a small percentage decline is still large in absolute numbers.

We can also examine the nature of the growth in the workforce over the 10-year period from 2004 to 2014 (projected). Figure 3.4 shows the percentage of the growth attributable to each segment. For instance, over this 10-year period the total male portion of the workforce is expected to grow by 1.1 percent. Within this category, though, white males are expected to increase only by .8 percent while black males are projected to increase by 1.9 percent, Hispanic males by 2.8 percent, and Asian males by 2.7 percent. As can be seen, both white males and white females are expected to decline slightly as a percentage of the overall workforce while all other groups are projected to increase.

Examining the age ranges of the workforce gives us another view of the changes. In contrast to its standing in earlier decades, the 16–24 age group is growing more rapidly than the overall population—an increase of 3.4 million (14.8 percent) between 2000 and 2010. The number of workers in the 25–54 age group has increased by

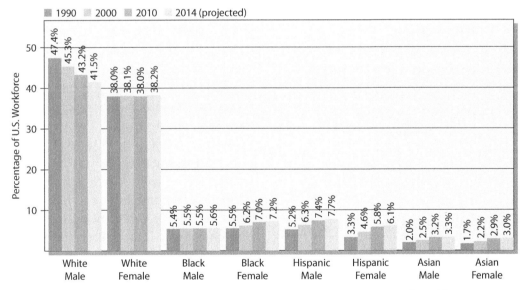

Figure 3.3 Workforce Composition 1990–2014. In the period between 1990 and 2014, all workforce segments are expected to increase as a percentage of the total workforce except the white male segment, which is has declined from 47.4% in 1990 to 43.2% in 2010 and is expected to decline further to 41.5 % by 2014. *Note*: The percentages for each year exceed 100 because of the number of individuals who report dual or multiple ethnicities. Source: Bureau of Labor Statistics, Labor Force Projections to 2014: Retiring Boomers, http://www.bls.gov/opub/ mlr/2010/11/art3full.pdf.

5 million (5.0 percent), and the number of workers in the 55 and older group has increased by 8.5 million (46.6 percent).

Global Workforce Diversity

Similar statistics on workforce diversity are found in other countries. In Canada, for instance, minorities are the fastest-growing segment of the population and the workforce. In addition, women make up two-thirds of the growth in the Canadian workforce, increasing from 35 percent in the 1970s to over 50 percent in 2010. These changes have initiated a workforce revolution in offices and factories throughout Canada. Managers and employees are learning to adapt to changing demographics. One study found that 81 percent of the organizations surveyed by the Conference Board of Canada include diversity management programs for their employees.

Increasing diversity in the workplace is even more dramatic in Europe, where employees have been crossing borders for many years. In fact, in

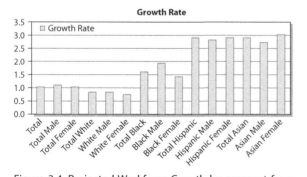

Figure 3.4 Projected Workforce Growth by segment from 2004 to 2014. As this figure illustrates, while the overall workforce is expected to grow by 1% between 2004 and 2014, the smallest growth will occur in the white male and white female categories, while the largest growth will occur in the Asian female category. Source: Bureau of Labor Statistics, Labor Force Projections to 2014; http://www.bls.gov/opub/mlr/2005/11/art3full.pdf.

1991 more than 2 million Europeans were living in one country and working in another. When the European Union further eased border crossings for its citizens in 1992, this number increased significantly. It was expected that opening borders among the European community members primarily would mean relaxing trade restrictions so that goods and services could move more freely among the member countries. In addition, however, workers were also freer to move, and they have taken advantage of the opportunity. It is clear that diversity in the workforce is more than a U.S. phenomenon. Many German factories now have a very diverse workforce that includes many workers from Turkey. Several of the emerging economies in Central Europe are encountering increasing diversity in their workforce. Poland, Hungary, and the Czech Republic, for instance, have experienced a steady influx of workers from the Ukraine, Afghanistan, Sri Lanka, China, and Somalia.

Companies throughout Europe are learning to adjust to the changing workforce. Amadeus Global Travel Distribution serves the travel industry, primarily in Europe, but its staff of 650 is composed of individuals from 32 different countries. Amadeus developed a series of workshops to teach managers how to lead multicultural teams. Such seminars also teach them how to interact better with peers, subordinates, and superiors who come from a variety of countries. Other companies experiencing much the same phenomenon in Europe and being proactive about it include Mars, Hewlett-Packard Spain, Fujitsu Spain, and BP. Companies in Asia are also encountering increasing diversity. In Thailand, where there is a shortage of skilled and unskilled workers because of rapid industrialization and slow population growth, there is a growing demand for foreign workers to fill the gap, which creates problems integrating local and foreign workers. Thus, the issue of workforce diversity is not limited to the United States.

The Value of Diversity

The United States has historically been seen as a "melting pot" of people from many different countries, cultures, and backgrounds. For centuries, it was assumed that people who came from other countries should assimilate into the existing cultural context they were entering. Although equal employment opportunity and accompanying affirmative action legislation have had significant effects on diversifying workplaces, they sometimes focused on bringing into the workplace people from culturally different groups and fully assimilating them into the existing organization. In organizations, however, integration proved difficult to implement. Members of the majority were slow to adapt and usually resistant to the change. Substantive career advancement opportunities rarely materialized for those who were "different."

The issue of workforce diversity has become increasingly important in the last few years as employees, managers, consultants, and the government finally realized that the composition of the workforce affects organizational productivity. Today, instead of a melting pot, the workplace in the United States might be regarded as more of a "tossed salad" made up of a mosaic of different flavors, colors, and textures. Rather than trying to assimilate those who are different into a single organizational culture, the current view holds that organizations need to celebrate the differences and utilize the variety of talents, perspectives, and backgrounds of all employees.

Assimilation

Assimilation is the process through which members of a minority group become socialized into learning the ways of the majority group. In organizations this entails hiring people from diverse backgrounds and attempting to mold them to fit into the existing organizational culture. One way that companies attempt to make people fit in is by requiring that employees speak only one language. For instance, Carlos Solero was fired after he refused to sign a work agreement that included a policy of English-only at a suburban manufacturing plant near Chicago. Management said the intent of the English-only policy was to improve communication among workers at the plant. In response, Solero and seven other Spanish speakers filed lawsuits against the plant. Attempts to assimilate diverse workers by imposing English-only rules can lead to a variety of organizational problems. Most organizations develop systems such as performance evaluation and incentive programs that reinforce the values of the dominant group.

(Chapter 18 discusses organizational culture as a means of reinforcing the organizational values and affecting the behavior of workers.) By universally applying the values of the majority group throughout the organization, assimilation tends to perpetuate false stereotypes and prejudices. Workers who are different are expected to meet the standards for dominant group members.

Dominant groups tend to be self-perpetuating. Majority group members may avoid people who are "different" simply because they find communication difficult. Moreover, informal discussions over coffee and lunch and during after-hours socializing tend to be limited to people in the dominant group. As a result, those who are not in the dominant group miss out on the informal communication opportunities in which office politics, company policy, and other issues are often discussed in rich detail. Subsequently, employees not in the dominant group often do not understand the more formal communications and may not be included in necessary actions taken in response. The dominant group likewise remains unaware of opinions from the "outside."

Similarly, since the dominant group makes decisions based on its own values and beliefs, the minority group has little say in decisions regarding compensation, facility location, benefit plans, performance standards, and other work issues that pertain directly to all workers. Workers who differ from the majority very quickly get the idea that to succeed in such a system, one must be like the dominant group in terms of values and beliefs, dress, and most other characteristics. Because success depends on assimilation, differences are driven underground.

Not paying attention to diversity can be very costly to the organization. In addition to blocking minority involvement in communication and decision making, it can result in tensions among workers, lower productivity, increased costs due to increasing absenteeism, increased employee turnover, increased equal employment opportunity and harassment suits, and lower morale among the workers.

Benefits of Valuing Diversity

Valuing diversity means putting an end to the assumption that everyone who is not a member of the dominant group must assimilate. This is not easily accomplished in most organizations. Truly valuing diversity is not merely giving lip service to an ideal, putting up with a necessary evil, promoting a level of tolerance for those who are different, or tapping into the latest fad. It is providing an opportunity to develop and utilize all of the human resources available to the organization for the benefit of the workers and the organization as a whole.

Valuing diversity is not just the right thing to do for workers; it is the right thing to do for the organization, both financially and economically. One of the most important benefits of diversity is the richness of ideas and perspectives that it makes available to the organization. Rather than relying on one homogeneous dominant group for new ideas and alternative solutions to increasingly complex problems, companies that value diversity have access to more perspectives on a problem. These fresh perspectives may lead to development of new products, opening of new markets, or improving service to existing customers.

Overall, the organization wins when it truly values diversity. Workers who recognize that the organization truly values them are likely to be more creative, motivated, and productive. Valued workers in diverse organizations experience less interpersonal conflict because the employees understand each other. When employees of different cultural groups, backgrounds, and values understand each other, they have a greater sense of teamwork, a stronger identification with the team, and a deeper commitment to the organization and its goals.

Technology and Business

Technology refers to the methods used to create products, including both physical goods and intangible services. Technological change has become a major driver for other forms of organization change. Moreover, it also has widespread effects on the behaviors of people inside an organization. Three specific areas of technology worth noting here are: (1) the shift toward a service-based economy, (2) the growing use of technology for competitive advantage, and (3) mushrooming change in information technology.

Manufacturing and Service Technologies

Manufacturing is a form of business that combines and transforms resources into tangible outcomes that are then sold to others. The Goodyear Tire and Rubber Company is a manufacturer because it combines rubber and chemical compounds and uses blending equipment and molding machines to create tires. Broyhill is a manufacturer because it buys wood and metal components, pads, and fabric and then combines them into furniture. And Apple is a manufacturer because it uses electronic, metal, plastic, and composite components to build smartphones, computers, and other digital products.

Manufacturing was once the dominant technology in the United States. During the 1970s, manufacturing entered a long period of decline, primarily because of foreign competition. U.S. firms had grown lax and sluggish, and new foreign competitors came onto the scene with better equipment and much higher levels of efficiency. For example, steel companies in the Far East were able to produce high-quality steel for much lower prices than large U.S. steel companies like such as Bethlehem Steel and U.S. Steel. Faced with a battle for survival, some companies disappeared, but many others underwent a long and difficult period of change by eliminating waste and transforming themselves into leaner and more efficient and responsive entities. They reduced their workforces dramatically, closed antiquated or unnecessary plants, and modernized their remaining plants. Over the last decade or so, however, their efforts have started to pay dividends as U.S. manufacturing has regained a competitive position in many different industries. While low wages continue to center a great deal of global manufacturing in Asia, some manufacturers are now thriving in the United States.

During the decline of the manufacturing sector, a tremendous growth in the service sector kept the overall U.S. economy from declining at the same rate. A **service organization** is one that transforms resources into an intangible output and creates time or place utility for its customers. For example, Merrill Lynch makes stock transactions for its customers, Avis leases cars to its customers, and your local hairdresser cuts your hair. In 1947, the service sector was responsible for less than half of the U.S. gross national product (GNP). By 1975, however, this figure reached 65 percent, and by 2006 had surpassed 75 percent. The service sector has been responsible for almost 90 percent of all new jobs created in the United States since 1990. Moreover, employment in service occupations is expected to grow 26.8 percent between 2010 and 2020.

Managers have come to see that many of the tools, techniques, and methods that are used in a factory are also useful to a service firm. For example, managers of automobile plants and hair salons each have to decide how to design their facility, identify the best location for it, determine optimal capacity, make decisions about inventory storage, set procedures for purchasing raw materials, and set standards for productivity and quality. At the same time, though, service-based firms must hire and train employees based on a different skill set than is required by most manufacturers. For instance, consumers seldom come into contact with the Toyota employee who installs the seats in their car, so that person can be hired based on technical skills. But Avis must recruit people who not only know how to do a job but who can also effectively interface with a variety of consumers. These and related service technology issues are explored throughout our book in a our new Services boxed insert.

Technology and Competition

Technology is the basis of competition for some firms, especially those whose goals include being the technology leaders in their industries. A company, for example, might focus its efforts on being the lowest-cost producer or on always having the most technologically advanced products on the market. But because of the rapid pace of new developments, keeping a leadership position based on technology is becoming increasingly challenging. Another challenge is meeting constant demands to decrease cycle time (the time that it takes a firm to accomplish some recurring activity or function from beginning to end).

Businesses have increasingly found that they can be more competitive if they can systematically decrease cycle times. Many companies, therefore, now focus on decreasing cycle times in areas ranging from developing products to making deliveries and collecting credit payments. Twenty years ago, it took a carmaker about five years from the decision to launch a new product until it was available in dealer showrooms. Now most companies can complete the cycle in less than two years. The speedier process allows them to more quickly respond to changing economic conditions, consumer preferences, and new competitor products while recouping more quickly their product-development costs. Some firms compete directly on how quickly they can get things done for consumers. In the early days of personal computers, for instance, getting a made-to-order system took six to eight weeks. Today, firms such as Dell can usually ship exactly what the customer wants in a matter of days.

Information Technology

Most people are very familiar with advances in information technology. Cellular telephones, electronic books, smart phones such as the iPhone and Blackberry, the iPad, and digital cameras, as well as technologically based social networking sites like Facebook, are just a few of the many recent innovations that have changed how people live and work. Breakthroughs in information technology have resulted in leaner organizations, more flexible operations, increased collaboration among employees, more flexible work sites, and improved management processes and systems. On the other hand, they have also resulted in less personal communication, less "down time" for managers and employees, and an increased sense of urgency vis-à-vis decision making and communication— changes that have not necessarily always been beneficial.

FOUNDATIONS OF INDIVIDUAL BEHAVIOR

Ricky W. Griffin & Gregory Moorhead

Individual Differences

As already noted, every individual is unique. Individual differences are personal attributes that vary from one person to another. Individual differences may be physical, psychological, and emotional. The individual differences that characterize a specific person make that person unique. As we see in the sections that follow, basic categories of individual differences include personality, attitudes, perception, and creativity. First, however, we need to note the importance of the situation in assessing the individual's behavior.

Are the specific differences that characterize a given person good or bad? Do they contribute to or detract from performance? The answer, of course, is that it depends on the circumstances. One person may be dissatisfied, withdrawn, and negative in one job setting but satisfied, outgoing, and positive in another. Working conditions, coworkers, and leadership are just a few of the factors that affect how a person performs and feels about a job. Thus, whenever a manager attempts to assess or account for individual differences among her employees, she must also be sure to consider the situation in which behavior occurs.

Since managers need to establish effective psychological contracts with their employees and achieve optimal fits between people and jobs, they face a major challenge in attempting to understand both individual differences and contributions in relation to inducements and contexts. A good starting point in developing this understanding is to appreciate the role of personality in organizations.

Personality and Organizations

Personality is the relatively stable set of psychological attributes that distinguish one person from another. A longstanding debate among psychologists—often expressed as "nature versus nurture"—concerns the extent to which personality attributes are inherited from our parents (the "nature" argument) or shaped by our environment (the "nurture" argument). In reality, both biological and environmental factors play important roles in determining our personalities. Although the details of this debate are beyond the scope of our discussion here, managers should strive to understand basic personality attributes and how they can affect people's behavior in organizational situations, not to mention their perceptions of and attitudes toward the organization.

The "Big Five" Personality Traits

Psychologists have identified literally thousands of personality traits and dimensions that differentiate one person from another. But in recent years, researchers have identified five fundamental personality traits that are especially relevant to organizations. These traits, illustrated in Figure 4.1, are now commonly called the "big five" personality traits.

Agreeableness refers to a person's ability to get along with others. Agreeableness causes some people to be gentle, cooperative, forgiving, understanding, and good-natured in their dealings with others. But lack of it results in others' being irritable, short-tempered, uncooperative, and generally antagonistic toward other people. Researchers have not yet fully investigated the effects of agreeableness, but it seems likely that highly agreeable people are better at developing good working relationships with coworkers, subordinates, and higher-level managers, whereas less agreeable people are not likely to have particularly good working relationships. The same pattern might extend to relationships with customers, suppliers, and other key organizational constituents.

Conscientiousness refers to the number of goals on which a person focuses. People who focus on relatively few goals at one time are likely to be organized, systematic, careful, thorough, responsible, and self-disciplined. Others, however, tend to pursue a wider array of goals, and, as a result, tend to be more disorganized, careless, and irresponsible, as well as less thorough

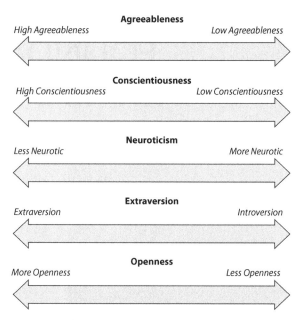

Figure 4.1 The "Big Five" Personality Framework. The "big five" personality framework is currently very popular among researchers and managers. These five dimensions represent fundamental personality traits presumed to be important in determining the behaviors of individuals in organizations. In general, experts agree that personality traits closer to the left end of each dimension are more positive in organizational settings, whereas traits closer to the right are less positive.

and self-disciplined. Research has found that more conscientious people tend to be higher performers than less conscientious people in a variety of different jobs. This pattern seems logical, of course, since conscientious people take their jobs seriously and approach their jobs in a highly responsible fashion.

The third of the "big five" personality dimensions is neuroticism. People who are relatively more neurotic tend to experience unpleasant emotions such as anger, anxiety, depression, and feelings of vulnerability more often than do people who are relatively less neurotic. People who are less neurotic are relatively poised, calm, resilient, and secure; people who are more neurotic are more excitable, insecure, reactive, and subject to extreme mood swings. People with less neuroticism might be expected to better handle job stress, pressure, and tension. Their stability might also lead them to be seen as being more reliable than their less stable counterparts.

Extraversion reflects a person's comfort level with relationships. Extroverts are sociable, talkative, assertive, and open to establishing new relationships. Introverts are much less sociable, talkative, and assertive, and more reluctant to begin new relationships. Research suggests that extroverts tend to be higher overall job performers than introverts and that they are more likely to be attracted to jobs based on personal relationships, such as sales and marketing positions.

Finally, openness reflects a person's rigidity of beliefs and range of interests. People with high levels of openness are willing to listen to new ideas and to change their own ideas, beliefs, and attitudes in response to new information. They also tend to have broad interests and to be curious, imaginative, and creative. On the other hand, people with low levels of openness tend to be less receptive to new ideas and less willing to change their minds. Further, they tend to have fewer and narrower interests and to be less curious and creative. People with more openness might be expected to be better performers due to their flexibility and the likelihood that they will be better accepted by others in the organization. Openness may also encompass a person's willingness to accept change; people with high levels of openness may be more receptive to change, whereas people with little openness may resist change.

The "big five" framework continues to attract the attention of both researchers and managers. The potential value of this framework is that it encompasses an integrated set of traits that appear to be valid predictors of certain behaviors in certain situations. Thus, managers who can both understand the framework and assess these traits in their employees are in a good position to understand how and why they behave as they do. On the other hand, managers

must be careful to not overestimate their ability to assess the "big five" traits in others. Even assessment using the most rigorous and valid measures is likely to be somewhat imprecise. Another limitation of the "big five" framework is that it is primarily based on research conducted in the United States. Thus, its generalizability to other cultures presents unanswered questions. Even within the United States, a variety of other factors and traits are also likely to affect behavior in organizations.

The Myers-Briggs Framework

Another interesting approach to understanding personalities in organizations is the Myers-Briggs framework. This framework, based on the classical work of Carl Jung, differentiates people in terms of four general dimensions: sensing, intuiting, judging, and perceiving. Higher and lower positions in each of the dimensions are used to classify people into one of sixteen different personality categories.

The Myers-Briggs Type Indicator (MBTI) is a popular questionnaire that some organizations use to assess personality types. Indeed, it is among the most popular selection instruments used today, with as many as 2 million people taking it each year. Research suggests that the MBTI is a useful method for determining communication styles and interaction preferences. In terms of personality attributes, however, questions exist about both the validity and the stability of the MBTI.

Emotional Intelligence

The concept of emotional intelligence has been identified in recent years and provides some interesting insights into personality. Emotional intelligence, or EQ, refers to the extent to which people are self-aware, can manage their emotions, can motivate themselves, express empathy for others, and possess social skills. (EQ is used to parallel the traditional term IQ, which of course stands for "intelligence quotient.") These various dimensions can be described as follows:

- *Self-awareness* This is the basis for the other components. It refers to a person's capacity for being aware of how he or she is feeling. In general, more self-awareness allows a person to more effectively guide his or her own life and behaviors.
- *Managing emotions* This refers to a person's capacities to balance anxiety, fear, and anger so that they do not interfere with getting things accomplished.
- *Motivating oneself* This dimension refers to a person's ability to remain optimistic and to continue striving in the face of setbacks, barriers, and failure.
- *Empathy* Empathy refers to a person's ability to understand how others are feeling even without being explicitly told.
- *Social skill* This refers to a person's ability to get along with others and to establish positive relationships.

Preliminary research suggests that people with high EQs may perform better than others, especially in jobs that require a high degree of interpersonal interaction and that involve influencing or directing the work of others. Moreover, EQ appears to be something that isn't biologically based but instead can be developed.

Other Personality Traits at Work

Besides these complex models of personality, several other specific personality traits are also likely to influence behavior in organizations. Among the most important are locus of control, self-efficacy, authoritarianism, Machiavellianism, self-esteem, and risk propensity.

Locus of control is the extent to which people believe that their behavior has a real effect on what happens to them. Some people, for example, believe that if they work hard they will succeed. They may also believe that people who fail do so because they lack ability or motivation. People who believe that individuals are in control of their lives are said to have an internal locus of control. Other people think that fate, chance, luck, or other people's behavior determines what happens to them. For example, an employee who fails to get a promotion may attribute that failure to a politically motivated boss or just bad luck, rather than to her or his own lack of skills or poor performance record. People who think that forces beyond their control dictate what happens to them are said to have an external locus of control.

Self-efficacy is a related but subtly different personality characteristic. A person's self-efficacy is that person's belief about his or her capabilities to perform a task. People with high self-efficacy believe that they can perform well on a specific task, whereas people with low self-efficacy tend to doubt their ability to perform a specific task. Self-assessments of ability contribute to self-efficacy, but so does the individual's personality. Some people simply have more self-confidence than others. This belief in their ability to perform a task effectively results in their being more self-assured and better able to focus their attention on performance.

Another important personality characteristic is authoritarianism, the extent to which a person believes that power and status differences are appropriate within hierarchical social systems such as organizations. For example, a person who is highly authoritarian may accept directives or orders from someone with more authority purely because the other person is "the boss." On the other hand, a person who is not highly authoritarian, although she or he may still carry out reasonable directives from the boss, is more likely to question things, express disagreement with the boss, and even refuse to carry out orders if they are for some reason objectionable.

A highly authoritarian manager may be relatively autocratic and demanding, and highly authoritarian subordinates are more likely to accept this behavior from their leader. On the other hand, a less authoritarian manager may allow subordinates a bigger role in making decisions, and less authoritarian subordinates might respond more positively to this behavior.

Machiavellianism is another important personality trait. This concept is named after Niccolo Machiavelli, a sixteenth-century author. In his book *The Prince*, Machiavelli explained how the nobility could more easily gain and use power. The term "Machiavellianism" is now used to describe behavior directed at gaining power and controlling the behavior of others. Research suggests that the degree of Machiavellianism varies from person to person. More Machiavellian individuals tend to be rational and nonemotional, may be willing to lie to attain their personal goals, put little emphasis on loyalty and friendship, and enjoy manipulating others' behavior. Less Machiavellian individuals are more emotional, less willing to lie to succeed, value loyalty and friendship highly, and get little personal pleasure from manipulating others. By all accounts, Dennis Kozlowski, the indicted former CEO of Tyco International, had a high degree of Machiavellianism. He apparently came to believe that his position of power in the company gave him the right to do just about anything he wanted with company resources.

Self-esteem is the extent to which a person believes that he or she is a worthwhile and deserving individual. A person with high self-esteem is more likely to seek higher-status jobs, be more confident in his or her ability to achieve higher levels of performance, and derive greater intrinsic satisfaction from his or her accomplishments. In contrast, a person with less self-esteem may be more content to remain in a lower-level job, be less confident of his or her ability, and focus more on extrinsic rewards (extrinsic rewards are tangible and observable rewards like a paycheck, job promotion, and so forth). Among the major personality dimensions, self-esteem is the one that has been most widely studied in other countries. Although more research is clearly needed, the published evidence suggests that self-esteem as a personality trait does indeed exist in a variety of countries and that its role in organizations is reasonably important across different cultures.

Risk propensity is the degree to which a person is willing to take chances and make risky decisions. A manager with a high risk propensity, for example, might experiment with new ideas and gamble on new products. Such a manager might also lead the organization in new and different directions. This manager might be a catalyst for innovation or, if the risky decisions prove to be bad ones, might jeopardize the continued well-being of the organization. A manager with low risk propensity might lead an organization to stagnation and excessive conservatism, or might help the organization successfully weather turbulent and unpredictable times by maintaining stability and calm. Thus, the potential consequences of a manager's risk propensity depend heavily on the organization's environment.

Customer Self-Efficacy

Imagine you lead a company that offers customers the opportunity to bungee jump off a 100-foot bridge spanning a raging river. You have employees whose jobs include hooking up customers properly, filling out legal waiver of liability forms, and ensuring that the jumps go off without errors and that customers have some scary fun. Your revenue stream and profits require that this process proceeds with a minimum of delay, as you have learned that making customers wait too long leads to many who lose their courage, run out of time, or get impatient and leave. The challenge for you is to enhance your customers' belief in their ability to make the jump—their self-efficacy—so they will take the plunge with the confidence that they are capable of success-fully performing this task.

In reviewing your knowledge of ways to enhance self-efficacy from your organizational behavior course, you realize that the same strategies you learned about for enhancing employee self-efficacy can also be used for customers. You recall that there are four ways to promote self-efficacy. These are, from most to least influential, enactive mastery, vicarious experience, verbal persuasion, and emotional (physiological) arousal. Enactive mastery is learned through repeated experiences in which a person discovers the level of performance of which he or she is capable. The second way to develop self-efficacy is through vicarious experiences or modeling, whether by self-modeling or by observing another person. The third strategy for developing self-efficacy is verbal persuasion. The final strategy for developing self-efficacy is the individual's physiological state.

With this knowledge, you quickly realize that you can use some or all of these in designing how your bungee jump is set up and in training your employees how to enhance your customers' self-efficacy and improve their ability to co-produce the value of the bungee experience. The easiest strategy to implement is to redesign the waiting line in a way that the customers waiting to jump can observe others taking the plunge. This allows you to use vicarious experiences of others to enhance the self-efficacy of the customers in line. Watching others, especially those that look like them or those who are inferior to them in some way (age, size, etc.) is an effective strategy for building self-efficacy: "If that person can do it, so can I."

You might also include a television monitor for waiting customers to observe that broadcasts footage of prior jumpers, carefully edited to include a diverse array of people similar to those typically seeking out this experience. A related physical setting strategy is to find ways to evoke a physiological response that inspires people to take on difficult challenges, such as playing the theme song from *Rocky*.

The second step is to train your employees on things they can do to enhance customer self-efficacy. Employees can be taught to observe and determine guest performance capabilities for co-producing the required tasks, to intervene in ways that enhance self-efficacy, and to provide persuasive encouragement. Disney cast members, for example, are extensively trained to train guests in the use of its FASTPASS system from a machine that is not easy for all guests to use. Cast members are trained to recognize and train those guests who need assistance to build mastery in a way similar to the training that airline desk agents must go through to teach the airline passenger how to co-produce the self-ticketing procedure.

For our bungee example, we can teach employees what to say to encourage waiting customers to jump. Another strategy is to teach your employees how to identify pairing or groupings of customers so that friends or significant others waiting can be encouraged to chant encouragement to the first person in the group. Not only will those chanting encouragement enhance the self-efficacy of the person waiting to jump, but the employee can also point out to the person about to jump that he or she will be serving as a role model for the others to follow.

The point is simple—not only does knowledge of self-efficacy and how it operates help in developing strategies for better managing your employees' perceptions of their ability to successfully perform their tasks, but the same strategies that enhance employee performance in doing their jobs will enhance your customers' ability to do their parts in the co-production of a service experience. In our bungee example, if the customer doesn't jump, that customer leaves disappointed and our revenue stream suffers.

Discussion Question: Reflect on service experiences you have had and discuss the things the organization did to enhance your self-efficacy.

Attitudes in Organizations

People's attitudes also affect their behavior in organizations. Attitudes are complexes of beliefs and feelings that people have about specific ideas, situations, or other people. Attitudes are important because they are the mechanism through which most people express their feelings. An employee's statement that he feels underpaid by an organization reflects his feelings about his pay. Similarly, when a manager says that she likes a new advertising campaign, she is expressing her feelings about the organization's marketing efforts.

How Attitudes Are Formed

Attitudes are formed by a variety of forces, including our personal values, our experiences, and our personalities. For example, if we value honesty and integrity, we may form especially favorable attitudes toward a manager whom we believe to be very honest and moral. Similarly, if we have had negative and unpleasant experiences with a particular coworker, we may form an unfavorable attitude toward that person. Any of the "big five" or individual personality traits may also influence our attitudes. Understanding the basic structure of an attitude helps us see how attitudes are formed and can be changed.

Attitude Structure

Attitudes are usually viewed as stable dispositions to behave toward objects in a certain way. For any number of reasons, a person might decide that he or she does not like a particular political figure or a certain restaurant (a disposition). We would expect that person to express consistently negative opinions of the candidate or restaurant and to maintain the consistent, predictable intention of not voting for the political candidate or not eating at the restaurant. In this view, attitudes contain three components: cognition, affect, and intention.

Cognition is the knowledge a person presumes to have about something. You may believe you like a class because the textbook is excellent, the class meets at your favorite time, the instructor is outstanding, and the workload is light. This "knowledge" may be true, partially true, or totally false. For example, you may intend to vote for a particular candidate because you think you know where the candidate stands on several issues. In reality, depending on the candidate's honesty and your understanding of his or her statements, the candidate's thinking on the issues may be exactly the same as yours, partly the same, or totally different. Cognitions are based on perceptions of truth and reality, and, as we note later, perceptions agree with reality to varying degrees.

A person's affect is his or her feelings toward something. In many ways, affect is similar to emotion—it is something over which we have little or no conscious control.

For example, most people react to words such as "love," "hate," "sex," and "war" in a manner that reflects their feelings about what those words convey. Similarly, you may like one of your classes, dislike another, and be indifferent toward a third. If the class you dislike is an elective, you may not be particularly concerned. But if it is the first course in your chosen major, your affective reaction may cause you considerable anxiety.

Intention guides a person's behavior. If you like your instructor, you may intend to take another class from him or her next semester. Intentions are not always translated into actual behavior, however. If the instructor's course next semester is scheduled for 8 a.m., you may decide that another instructor is just as good. Some attitudes, and their corresponding intentions, are much more central and significant to an individual than others. You may intend to do one thing (take a particular class) but later alter your intentions because of a more significant and central attitude (fondness for sleeping late).

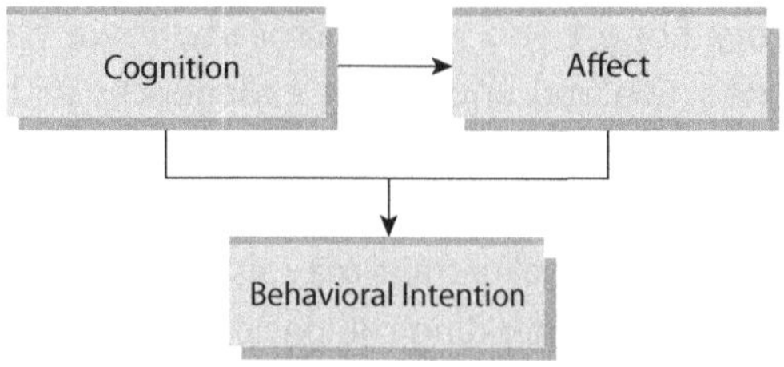

Figure 4.2 Attitude Formation. Attitudes are generally formed around a sequence of cognition, affect, and behavioral intention. That is, we come to know something that we believe to be true (cognition). This knowledge triggers a feeling (affect). Cognition and affect then together influence how we intend to behave in the future.

Cognitive Dissonance

When two sets of cognitions or perceptions are contradictory or incongruent, a person experiences a level of conflict and anxiety called cognitive dissonance. Cognitive dissonance also occurs when people behave in a fashion that is inconsistent with their attitudes. For example, a person may realize that smoking and overeating are dangerous yet continue to do both. Because the attitudes and behaviors are inconsistent with each other, the person probably will experience a certain amount of tension and discomfort and may try to reduce these feelings by changing the attitude, altering the behavior, or perceptually distorting the circumstances. For example, the dissonance associated with overeating might be resolved by continually deciding to go on a diet "next week."

Cognitive dissonance affects people in a variety of ways. We frequently encounter situations in which our attitudes conflict with each other or with our behaviors. Dissonance reduction is the way we deal with these feelings of discomfort and tension. In organizational settings, people contemplating leaving the organization may wonder why they continue to stay and work hard. As a result of this dissonance, they may conclude that the company is not so bad after all, that they have no immediate options elsewhere, or that they will leave "soon."

Attitude Change

Attitudes are not as stable as personality attributes. For example, new information may change attitudes. A manager may have a negative attitude about a new colleague because of the colleague's lack of job-related experience. After working with the new person for a while, however, the manager may come to realize that he is actually very talented and subsequently develop a more positive attitude. Likewise, if the object of an attitude changes, a person's attitude toward that object may also change. Suppose, for example, that employees feel underpaid and as a result have negative attitudes toward the company's reward system. A big salary increase may cause these attitudes to become more positive.

Attitudes can also change when the object of the attitude becomes less important or less relevant to the person. For example, suppose an employee has a negative attitude about his company's health insurance. When his spouse gets a new job with an organization that has outstanding insurance benefits, his attitude toward his own insurance may become more moderate simply because he no longer has to worry about it. Finally, as noted earlier, individuals may change their attitudes as a way to reduce cognitive dissonance.

Deeply rooted attitudes that have a long history are, of course, resistant to change. For example, over a period of years a former airline executive named Frank Lorenzo developed a reputation in the industry of being antiunion and of cutting wages and benefits. As a result, employees throughout the industry came to dislike and distrust him. When he took over Eastern Airlines, its employees had such a strong attitude of distrust toward him that they could never agree to cooperate with any of his programs or ideas. Some of them actually cheered months later when Eastern went bankrupt, even though it was costing them their own jobs!

Key Work-Related Attitudes

People in an organization form attitudes about many different things. Employees are likely to have attitudes about their salary, their promotion possibilities, their boss, employee benefits, the food in the company cafeteria, and the color of the company softball team uniforms. Of course, some of these attitudes are more important than others. Especially important attitudes are job satisfaction and organizational commitment.

Job Satisfaction

Job satisfaction reflects the extent to which people find gratification or fulfillment in their work. Extensive research on job satisfaction shows that personal factors such as an individual's needs and aspirations determine this attitude, along with group and organizational factors such as relationships with coworkers and supervisors and working conditions, work policies, and compensation.

A satisfied employee tends to be absent less often, to make positive contributions, and to stay with the organization. In contrast, a dissatisfied employee may be absent more often, may experience stress that disrupts coworkers, and may be continually looking for another job. Contrary to what a lot of managers believe, however, high levels of job satisfaction do not necessarily lead to higher levels of productivity. One survey indicated that, also contrary to popular opinion, Japanese workers are less satisfied with their jobs than their counterparts in the United States.

Organizational Commitment

Organizational commitment, sometimes called job commitment, reflects an individual's identification with and attachment to the organization. A highly committed person will probably see herself as a true member of the firm (for example, referring to the organization in personal terms such as "we make high-quality products"), overlook minor sources of dissatisfaction, and see herself remaining a member of the organization. In contrast, a less committed person is more likely to see herself as an outsider (for example, referring to the organization in less personal terms such as "they don't pay their employees very well"), to express more dissatisfaction about things, and to not see herself as a long-term member of the organization.

Organizations can do few definitive things to promote satisfaction and commitment, but some specific guidelines are available. For one thing, if the organization treats its employees fairly and provides reasonable rewards and job security, its employees are more likely to be satisfied and committed. Allowing employees to have a say in how things are done can also promote these attitudes. Designing jobs so that they are stimulating can enhance both satisfaction and commitment.

Research suggests that Japanese workers may be more committed to their organizations than are U.S. workers. Other research suggests that some of the factors that may lead to commitment, including extrinsic rewards, role clarity, and participative management, are the same across different cultures.

Affect and Mood in Organizations

Researchers have recently started to renew their interest in the affective component of attitudes. Recall from our previous discussion that the affective component of an attitude reflects our emotions. Managers once believed that emotion and feelings varied among people from day to day, but research now suggests that although some short-term fluctuation does indeed occur, there are also underlying stable predispositions toward fairly constant and predictable moods and emotional states.

Some people, for example, tend to have a higher degree of positive affectivity. This means that they are relatively upbeat and optimistic, that they have an overall sense of well-being, and that they usually see things in a positive light. Thus, they always seem to be in a good mood. People with more negative affectivity are just the opposite. They are generally downbeat and pessimistic and they usually see things in a negative way. They seem to be in a bad mood most of the time.

Of course, as noted above, short-term variations can occur among even the most extreme types. People with a lot of positive affectivity, for example, may still be in a bad mood if they have just been passed over for a promotion, gotten extremely negative performance feedback, or have been laid off or fired, for instance. Similarly, those with negative affectivity may be in a good mood—at least for a short time—if they have just been promoted, received very positive performance feedback, or had other good things befall them. After the initial impact of these events wears off, however, those with positive affectivity generally return to their normal positive mood, whereas those with negative affectivity gravitate back to their normal bad mood.

Perception in Organizations

Perception—the set of processes by which an individual becomes aware of and interprets information about the environment—is another important element of workplace behavior. If everyone perceived everything the same way, things would be a lot simpler (and a lot less exciting!). Of course, just the opposite is true: People perceive the same things in very different ways. Moreover, people often assume that reality is objective and that we all perceive the same things in the same way.

To test this idea, we could ask students at the University of Texas and the University of Oklahoma to describe the most recent football game between their schools. We probably would hear two conflicting stories. These differences would arise primarily because of perception. The fans "saw" the same game but interpreted it in sharply contrasting ways.

Since perception plays a role in a variety of workplace behaviors, managers should understand basic perceptual processes. As implied in our definition, perception actually consists of several distinct processes. Moreover, in perceiving we receive information in many guises, from spoken words to visual images of movements and forms. Through perceptual processes, the receiver assimilates the varied types of incoming information for the purpose of interpreting it.

Basic Perceptual Processes

Figure 4.3 shows two basic perceptual processes that are particularly relevant to managers—selective perception and stereotyping.

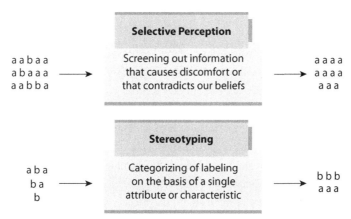

Figure 4.3 Basic Perceptual Processes. Perception determines how we become aware of information from our environment and how we interpret it. Selective perception and stereotyping are particularly important perceptual processes that affect behavior in organizations.

Selective Perception

Selective perception is the process of screening out information that we are uncomfortable with or that contradicts our beliefs. For example, suppose a manager is exceptionally fond of a particular worker. The manager has a very positive attitude about the worker and thinks he is a top performer. One day the manager notices that the worker seems to be goofing off. Selective perception may cause the manager to quickly forget what he observed. Similarly, suppose a manager has formed a very negative image of a particular worker. She thinks this worker is a poor performer who never does a good job. When she happens to observe an example of high performance from the worker, she may quickly forget it. In one sense, selective perception is beneficial because it allows us to disregard minor bits of information. Of course, the benefit occurs only if our basic perception is accurate. If selective perception causes us to ignore important information, however, it can become quite detrimental.

Stereotyping

Stereotyping is categorizing or labeling people on the basis of a single attribute. Certain forms of stereotyping can be useful and efficient. Suppose, for example, that a manager believes that communication skills are important for a particular job and that speech communication majors tend to have exceptionally good communication skills. As a result, whenever he interviews candidates for jobs he pays especially close attention to speech communication majors. To the extent that communication skills truly predict job performance and that majoring in speech communication does indeed provide those skills, this form of stereotyping can be beneficial. Common attributes from which people often stereotype are race and sex. Of course, stereotypes along these lines are inaccurate and can be harmful. For example, suppose a human resource manager forms the stereotype that women can only perform certain tasks and that men are best suited for other tasks. To the extent that this affects the manager's hiring practices, he or she is (1) costing the organization

Do You Have an Excessive Need to Be Yourself?

As manager of a restaurant supply warehouse, Harry "Hands-On" Hinderson likes to keep a close watch on how his subordinates go about the tasks he assigns them. He corrects minor errors in order to avoid rough edges on the final product, requires workers to check with him on most decisions, and reassigns unpromising projects before they turn into major disasters. The demands on his own time and energy, of course, are quite high, so Harry once decided to try the hands-off approach: He gave a couple of veteran employees projects and deadlines and then backed off. One worker broke down and asked for guidance before the deadline, and the other turned in a report that fell short of both her own standards and Harry's.

I was right in the first place, Harry concluded. *If I don't look over their shoulders, people just don't get the job done.* When he complained about his own workload, a fellow manager said, "You're micromanaging yourself into an early grave." "I'm a micromanager," replied Harry. "That's just the way I am."

Not surprisingly, some employees don't like to work with Harry. "He's one of those crazy micromanagers," they say. In a sense, they're guilty of stereotyping Harry by lumping him in the category of "crazy micromanagers" and reducing him to his micromanagerial traits, but, ironically, they're probably stereotyping him because Harry is guilty of stereotyping *himself*.

Basically, *self-stereotyping* means that people tend to identify themselves according to the characteristics of some "in group" to which they believe they belong. Whenever someone says something like "I'm always late" or "I'm not a good listener" or "I'm terrible at math," he or she is self-stereotyping. Harry has self-stereotyped himself as a micromanager, but one has to wonder: Was he always a micromanager? How (and why) did he become a micromanager? One of the most serious drawbacks of self-stereotyped assessments is the fact that they tend to become self-fulfilling prophecies. Studies show, for example, that when women are reminded that they're "no good at math," they perform worse on math tasks. In turn, they're perceived by others as a poor at math and treated accordingly—say, by teachers and employers.

Before long, says executive coach Marshall Goldsmith, we begin to define ourselves by our beliefs about ourselves, evolving into "a pile of behaviors that we define as 'me.' ... If we buy into our behavior definition of 'me' ... we can learn to excuse almost any annoying action"—or unacceptable workplace performance—"by saying, 'That's just the way I am!'"

Obviously, such an attitude is not a prescription for change and improvement.

In Harry's case, his belief that he *is* a micromanager at his core—along with his micromanagerial behavior—could have negative consequences. In particular, micromanagers aren't generally the best managers: According to MindTools, a website dedicated to enhancing career skills, *a truly effective manager sets up those around him to succeed. Micromanagers, on the other hand, prevent employees from making ... their own decisions ... . Good managers empower their employees to do well by giving [them] opportunities to excel; bad managers disempower their employees by hoarding those opportunities. And a disempowered employee is an ineffective one.*

Harry's entrenched practice of self-stereotyping may well contribute to career disappointment down the road. Like his subordinates, his superiors will eventually stereotype him as a micromanager, and if they have any managerial savvy, they'll hold micromanagers responsible for producing ineffective employees. When it comes time to reward managerial performance, Harry will probably get passed over because he'll be perceived as a member of the group known as "micromanagers." And this will probably happen regardless of Harry's *individual* strengths as a manager. That's the way stereotyping works.

References: "Avoiding Micromanagement," MindTools (1996–2012), www.mindtools.com on April 11, 2012; Marshall Goldsmith, "Do You Have an Excessive Need to Be Yourself?" *Harvard Business Review*, July 13, 2009, http://blobgs.hbr.org on April 11, 2012; Sean Silverthorne, "Self-Stereotyping Can Damage Your Career," *CBSNews.com*, July 16, 2009, www.cbsnews.com on April 11, 2012; John Grohol, "Stereotyping That Hurts, Stereotyping That Helps," *PsychCentral.com*, April 10, 2008, http://psychcentral.com on April 11, 2012; Linda Talley, "Are You Personally Stereotyping Yourself?" *Linda Talley dot Com*, February 1, 2012, www.lindatalley.com on April 11, 2012; Dave Franzetta, "Have You Stereotyped Yourself?" *Ubiquitous Wisdom*, December 26, 2011, www.ubiquitouswisdom.com on April 11, 2012.

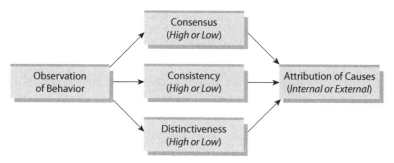

Figure 4.4 The Attribution Process. The attribution process involves observing behavior and then attributing causes to it. Observed behaviors are interpreted in terms of their consensus, their consistency, and their distinctiveness. Based on these interpretations, behavior is attributed to either internal or external causes.

valuable talent for both sets of jobs, (2) violating federal law, and (3) behaving unethically.

It's bad enough when other people subject you to stereotyping. To see what can happen when you make matters worse by stereotyping *yourself*, see the *Diversity* box entitled "Do You Have an Excessive Need to Be Yourself?"

Perception and Attribution

Attribution theory has extended our understanding of how perception affects behavior in organizations. Attribution theory suggests that we observe behavior and then attribute causes to it. That is, we attempt to explain why people behave as they do. The process of attribution is based on perceptions of reality, and these perceptions may vary widely among individuals.

Figure 4.4 illustrates the basic attribution theory framework. To start the process, we observe behavior, either our own or someone else's. We then evaluate that behavior in terms of its degrees of consensus, consistency, and distinctiveness. Consensus is the extent to which other people in the same situation behave in the same way. Consistency is the degree to which the same person behaves in the same way at different times. Distinctiveness is the extent to which the same person behaves in the same way in different situations. We form impressions or attributions as to the causes of behavior based on various combinations of consensus, consistency, and distinctiveness. We may believe the behavior is caused internally (by forces within the person) or externally (by forces in the person's environment).

For example, suppose you observe one of your subordinates being rowdy, disrupting others' work, and generally making a nuisance of himself. If you can understand the causes of this behavior, you may be able to change it. If the employee is the only one engaging in the disruptive behavior (low consensus), if he behaves like this several times each week (high consistency), and if you have seen him behave like this in other settings (low distinctiveness), a logical conclusion would be that internal factors are causing his behavior.

Suppose, however, that you observe a different pattern: Everyone in the person's work group is rowdy (high consensus); and although the particular employee often is rowdy at work (high consistency), you have never seen him behave this way in other settings (high distinctiveness). This pattern indicates that something in the situation is causing the behavior—that is, that the causes of the behavior are external.

Types of Workplace Behavior

Now that we have looked closely at how individual differences can influence behavior in organizations, let's turn our attention to what we mean by workplace behavior. Workplace behavior is a pattern of action by the members of an organization that directly or indirectly influences the organization's effectiveness. One way to talk about workplace behavior is to describe its impact on performance and productivity, absenteeism and turnover, and organizational citizenship. Unfortunately, employees can exhibit dysfunctional behaviors as well.

Performance Behaviors

Performance behaviors are the total set of work-related behaviors that the organization expects the individual to display. You might think of these as the "terms" of the psychological contract. For some jobs, performance behaviors can be narrowly defined and easily measured. For example, an assembly-line worker who sits by a moving conveyor and attaches parts to a product as it passes by has relatively few performance behaviors. He or she is expected to remain at the workstation and correctly attach the parts. Performance can often be assessed quantitatively by counting the percentage of parts correctly attached.

For many other jobs, however, performance behaviors are more diverse and much more difficult to assess. For example, consider the case of a research-and-development scientist at Merck. The scientist works in a lab trying to find new scientific breakthroughs that have commercial potential. The scientist must apply knowledge learned in graduate school and experience gained from previous research. Intuition and creativity are also important. And the desired breakthrough may take months or even years to accomplish. Organizations rely on a number of different methods to evaluate performance. The key, of course, is to match the evaluation mechanism with the job being performed.

Dysfunctional Behaviors

Some work-related behaviors are dysfunctional in nature. That is, dysfunctional behaviors are those that detract from, rather than contribute to, organizational performance. Two of the more common ones are absenteeism and turnover. Absenteeism occurs when an employee does not show up for work. Some absenteeism has a legitimate cause, such as illness, jury duty, or a death or illness in the family. At other times, the employee may report a feigned legitimate cause that's actually just an excuse to stay home. When an employee is absent, legitimately or not, her or his work does not get done at all or a substitute must be hired to do it. In either case, the quantity or quality of actual output is likely to suffer. Obviously, some absenteeism is expected, but organizations strive to minimize feigned absenteeism and reduce legitimate absences as much as possible.

Turnover occurs when people quit their jobs. An organization usually incurs costs in replacing workers who have quit, and if turnover involves especially productive people, it is even more costly. Turnover seems to result from a number of factors, including aspects of the job, the organization, the individual, the labor market, and family influences. In general, a poor person-job fit is also a likely cause of turnover. People may also be prone to leave an organization if its inflexibility makes it difficult to manage family and other personal matters and may be more likely to stay if an organization provides sufficient flexibility to make it easier to balance work and non-work considerations. One Chick-fil-A operator in Texas has cut the turnover rate in his stores by offering flexible work schedules, college scholarships, and such perks as free bowling trips.

Other forms of dysfunctional behavior may be even more costly for an organization. Theft and sabotage, for example, result in direct financial costs for an organization. Sexual and racial harassment also cost an organization, both indirectly (by lowering morale, producing fear, and driving off valuable employees) and directly (through financial liability if the organization responds inappropriately). Workplace violence is also a growing concern in many organizations. Violence by disgruntled workers or former workers results in dozens of deaths and injuries each year.

Organizational Citizenship

Managers strive to minimize dysfunctional behaviors while trying to promote organizational citizenship. Organizational citizenship refers to the behavior of individuals who make a positive overall contribution to the organization. Consider, for example, an employee who does work that is acceptable in terms of both quantity and quality. However, she refuses to work overtime, won't help newcomers learn the ropes, and is generally unwilling to make any contribution beyond the strict performance of her job. This person may be seen as a good performer, but she is not likely to be seen as a good organizational citizen.

Another employee may exhibit a comparable level of performance. In addition, however, he always works late when the boss asks him to, he takes time to help newcomers learn their way around, and he is perceived as being helpful and committed to the organization's success. He is likely to be seen as a better organizational citizen.

A complex mosaic of individual, social, and organizational variables determines organizational citizenship behaviors. For example, the personality, attitudes, and needs of the individual must be consistent with citizenship behaviors. Similarly, the social context, or work group, in which the individual works must facilitate and promote such behaviors. And the organization itself, especially its culture, must be capable of promoting, recognizing, and rewarding these types of behaviors if they are to be maintained. The study of organizational citizenship is still in its infancy, but preliminary research suggests that it may play a powerful role in organizational effectiveness.

Synopsis

Understanding individuals in organizations is important for all managers. A basic framework for facilitating this understanding is the psychological contract—people's expectations regarding what they will contribute to the organization and what they will get in return. Organizations strive to achieve an optimal person-job fit, but this process is complicated by the existence of individual differences.

Personalities are the relatively stable sets of psychological and behavioral attributes that distinguish one person from another. The "big five" personality traits are agreeableness, conscientiousness, neuroticism, extraversion, and openness. Myers-Briggs dimensions and emotional intelligence also offer insights into personalities in organizations. Other important personality traits include locus of control, self-efficacy, authoritarianism, Machiavellianism, self-esteem, and risk propensity.

Attitudes are based on emotion, knowledge, and intended behavior. Cognitive dissonance results from contradictory or incongruent attitudes, behaviors, or both. Job satisfaction or dissatisfaction and organizational commitment are important work-related attitudes. Employees' moods, assessed in terms of positive or negative affectivity, also affect attitudes in organizations.

Perception is the set of processes by which a person becomes aware of and interprets information about the environment. Basic perceptual processes include selective perception and stereotyping. Perception and attribution are also closely related.

Workplace behavior is a pattern of action by the members of an organization that directly or indirectly influences organizational effectiveness. Performance behaviors are the set of work-related behaviors the organization expects the individual to display in order to fulfill the psychological contract. Dysfunctional behaviors include absenteeism and turnover, as well as theft, sabotage, and violence. Organizational citizenship entails behaviors that make a positive overall contribution to the organization.

VALUES AND EMOTIONS

John R. Schermerhorn Jr., Mary Uhl-Bien, and Richard N. Osborn

nvolves taking action to keep stress from reaching destructive levels in the first place. Work and life stressors must be recognized before one can take action to prevent their occurrence or to minimize their adverse impacts. Persons with Type A personalities, for example, may exercise self-discipline; supervisors of Type A employees may try to model a lower-key, more relaxed approach to work. Family problems may be partially relieved by a change of work schedule; simply knowing that your supervisor understands your situation may also help to reduce the anxiety caused by pressing family concerns.

Personal Wellness To keep stress from reaching a destructive point, special techniques of stress management can be implemented. This process begins with the recognition of stress symptoms and continues with actions to maintain a positive performance edge. The term "wellness" is increasingly used these days. **Personal wellness** involves the pursuit of one's job and career goals with the support of a personal health promotion program. The concept recognizes individual responsibility to enhance and maintain wellness through a disciplined approach to physical and mental health. It requires attention to such factors as smoking, weight management, diet, alcohol use,

and physical fitness. Organizations can benefit from commitments to support personal wellness. A University of Michigan study indicates that firms have saved up to $600 per year per employee by helping them to cut the risk of significant health problems. Arnold Coleman, CEO of Healthy Outlook Worldwide, a health fitness consulting firm, states: "If I can save companies 5 to 20 percent a year in medical costs, they'll listen. In the end you have a well company and that's where the word 'wellness' comes from."

Values

Values can be defined as broad preferences concerning appropriate courses of action or outcomes. As such, values reflect a person's sense of right and wrong or what "ought" to be. "Equal rights for all" and "People should be treated with respect and dignity" are representative of values. Values tend to influence attitudes and behavior. For example, if you value equal rights for all and you go to work for an organization that treats its managers much better than it does its workers, you may form the attitude that the company is an unfair place to work; consequently, you may not produce well or may perhaps leave the company. It is likely that if the company had had a more egalitarian policy, your attitude and behaviors would have been more positive.

Sources of Values

Parents, friends, teachers, siblings, education, experience, and external reference groups are all value sources that can influence individual values. Indeed, peoples' values develop as a product of the learning and experience they encounter from various sources in the cultural setting in which they live. As learning and experiences differ from one person to another, value differences result. Such differences are likely to be deep seated and difficult (though not impossible) to change; many have their roots in early childhood and the way a person has been raised.

Personal Values

The noted psychologist Milton Rokeach has developed a well-known set of values classified into two broad categories. **Terminal values** reflect a person's preferences concerning the "ends" to be achieved; they are the goals an individual would like to achieve during his or her lifetime. Rokeach divides values into 18 terminal values and 18 instrumental values as summarized in Figure 5.1. **Instrumental values** reflect the "means" for achieving desired ends. They represent *how* you might go about achieving your important end states, depending on the relative importance you attached to the instrumental values. Look at the list in Figure 5.1. What are your top five values, and what does this say about you?

Illustrative research shows, not surprisingly, that both terminal and instrumental values differ by group (for example, executives, activist workers, and union members).[37] These preference differences can encourage conflict or agreement when different groups have to deal with each other.

A more recent values schema, developed by Bruce Meglino and associates, is aimed at people in the workplace:

Terminal Values	Instrumental Values
A comfortable life (and prosperous)	Ambitious (hardworking)
An exciting life (stimulating)	Broad-minded (open-minded)
A sense of accomplishment (lasting contribution)	Capable (competent, effective)
A world at peace (free of war and conflict)	Cheerful (lighthearted, joyful)
A world of beauty (beauty of nature and the arts)	Clean (neat, tidy)
Equality (brotherhood, equal opportunity)	Courageous (standing up for beliefs)
Family security (taking care of loved ones)	Forgiving (willing to pardon)
Freedom (independence, free choice)	Helpful (working for others' welfare)
Happiness (contentedness)	Honest (sincere, truthful)
Inner harmony (freedom from inner conflict)	Imaginative (creative, daring)
Mature love (sexual and spiritual intimacy)	Independent (self-sufficient, self-reliant)
National security (attack protection)	Intellectual (intelligent, reflective)
Pleasure (leisurely, enjoyable life)	Logical (rational, consistent)
Salvation (saved, eternal life)	Loving (affectionate, tender)
Self-respect (self-esteem)	Obedient (dutiful, respectful)
Social recognition (admiration, respect)	Polite (courteous, well mannered)
True friendship (close companionship)	Responsible (reliable, dependable)
Wisdom (mature understanding of life)	Self-controlled (self-disciplined)

Figure 5.1 Rokeach value survey.

- *Achievement*—getting things done and working hard to accomplish difficult things in life
- *Helping and concern for others*—being concerned for other people and with helping others
- *Honesty*—telling the truth and doing what you feel is right
- *Fairness*—being impartial and doing what is fair for all concerned

These four values have been shown to be especially important in the workplace; thus, the framework should be particularly relevant for studying values in OB.

Meglino and colleagues used their value schema to show the importance of value congruence between leaders and followers. **Value congruence** occurs when individuals express positive feelings upon encountering others who exhibit values similar to their own. When values differ, or are *incongruent,* conflicts over such things as goals and the means to achieve them may result. What they found was that satisfaction with the leader by followers was greater when there was congruence in terms of achievement, helping, honesty, and fairness values.

Cultural Values

Cultural values are also important in the increasingly global workplace. **Culture** is the learned, shared way of doing things in a particular society. It is the way, for example, in which its members eat, dress, greet and treat one another, teach their children, solve everyday problems, and so on. Geert Hofstede, a Dutch scholar and consultant, refers to culture as the "software of the mind," making the analogy that the mind's "hardware" is universal among human beings. But the software of culture takes many different forms. We are not born with a culture; we are born into a society that teaches us its culture. And because culture is shared among people, it helps to define the boundaries between different groups and affect how their members relate to one another.

Cultures vary in their underlying patterns of values and attitudes. The way people think about such matters as achievement, wealth and material gain, and risk and change may influence how they approach work and their relationships with organizations. A framework developed by Hofstede offers one approach for understanding how value differences across national cultures can influence human behavior at work. The five dimensions of national culture in his framework can be described as follows:

1. **Power distance** is the willingness of a culture to accept status and power differences among its members. It reflects the degree to which people are likely to respect hierarchy and rank in organizations. Indonesia is considered a high-power-distance culture, whereas Sweden is considered a relatively low-power-distance culture.
2. **Uncertainty avoidance** is a cultural tendency toward discomfort with risk and ambiguity. It reflects the degree to which people are likely to prefer structured versus unstructured organizational situations. France is considered a high uncertainty avoidance culture, whereas Hong Kong is considered a low uncertainty avoidance culture.
3. **Individualism-collectivism** is the tendency of a culture to emphasize either individual or group interests. It reflects the degree to which people are likely to prefer working as individuals or working together in groups. The United States is a highly individualistic culture, whereas Mexico is a more collectivist one.
4. **Masculinity-femininity** is the tendency of a culture to value stereotypical masculine or

feminine traits. It reflects the degree to which organizations emphasize competition and assertiveness versus interpersonal sensitivity and concerns for relationships. Japan is considered a very masculine culture, whereas Thailand is considered a more feminine culture.

5. **Long-term/short-term orientation** is the tendency of a culture to emphasize values associated with the future, such as thrift and persistence, or values that focus largely on the present. It reflects the degree to which

Types of Emotions

Researchers have identified six major types of emotions: anger, fear, joy, love, sadness, and surprise. The key question from an emotional intelligence perspective is: Do we recognize these emotions in ourselves and others, and can we manage them well? Anger, for example, may involve disgust and envy, both of which can have very negative consequences. Fear may contain alarm and anxiety; joy may contain cheerfulness and contentment; love may contain affection, longing, and lust; sadness may contain disappointment, neglect, and shame.

It is also common to differentiate between **self-conscious emotions** that arise from internal sources and **social emotions** that are stimulated by external sources. Shame, guilt, embarrassment, and pride are examples of internal emotions. Understanding self-conscious emotions helps individuals regulate their relationships with others. Social emotions like pity, envy, and jealousy derive from external cues and information. An example is feeling envious or jealous upon learning that a co-worker received a promotion or job assignment that you were hoping to get.

The Nature of Moods

Whereas emotions tend to be short-term and clearly targeted at someone or something, **moods** are more generalized positive and negative feelings or states of mind that may persist for some time. Everyone seems to have occasional moods, and we each know the full range of possibilities they represent. How often do you wake up in the morning and feel excited and refreshed and just happy, or wake up feeling grouchy and depressed and generally unhappy? And what are the consequences of these different moods for your behavior with friends and family, and at work or school?

The field of OB is especially interested in how moods affect someone's like-ability and performance at work. When it comes to CEOs, for example, a *Business Week* article claims that it pays to be likable, stating that "harsh is out, caring is in." Some CEOs are even hiring executive coaches to help them manage their affects to come across as more personable and friendly in relationships with others. If a CEO goes to a meeting in a good mood and gets described as "cheerful," "charming," "humorous," "friendly," and "candid," she or he may be viewed as on the upswing. But if the CEO goes into a meeting in a bad mood and is perceived as "prickly," "impatient," "remote," "tough," "acrimonious," or even "ruthless," the perception will more likely be of a CEO on the downslide.

Figure 5.2 offers a brief comparison of emotions and moods. In general, emotions are intense feelings directed at someone or something; they always have rather specific triggers; and they come in many types—anger, fear, happiness, and the like. Moods tend to be more generalized positive or negative feelings. They are less intense than emotions and most often seem to lack a clear source; it's often hard to identify how or why we end up in a particular mood. But moods tend to be more long-lasting than emotions. When

Watch Out for Facebook Follies

Facebook is fun, but if you put the wrong things on it-the wrong photo, a snide comment, and complaints about your boss-you might have to change your online status to "Just got fired!"

Bed Surfing Banker—After a Swiss bank employee called in sick with the excuse that she "needed to lie in the dark," company officials observed her surfing Facebook. She was fired and the bank's statement said it "had lost trust in the employee."

Angry Mascot—The Pittsburgh Pirates fired their mascot after he posted criticisms of team management on his Facebook page. A Twitter campaign by supporters helped him get hired back.

Short-changed Server—A former server at a pizza parlor in North Carolina used Facebook to call her customers "cheap" for not giving good tips. After finding out about the posting, her bosses fired her for breaking company policy.

Who's Right and Wrong? *You may know of other similar cases where employees ended up being penalized for things they put on their Facebook pages. But where do you draw the line? Isn't a person's Facebook page separate from one's work; shouldn't one be able to speak freely about their jobs, co-workers, and even bosses when outside the workplace? Or is there an ethical boundary that travels from work into one's public communications that needs to be respected? What are the ethics here-on the employee and the employer sides?*

someone says or does something that causes a quick and intense positive or negative reaction from you, that emotion will probably quickly pass. However, a bad or good mood is likely to linger for hours or even days and influence a wide range of behaviors.

How Emotions and Moods Influence Behavior

A while back, former CEO Mark V. Hurd of Hewlett-Packard found himself dealing with a corporate scandal. It seems that the firm had hired "consultants" to track down what were considered to be confidential leaks by members of HP's Board

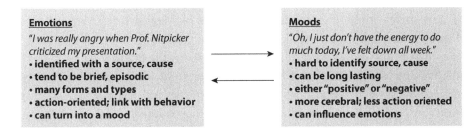

Emotions
"I was really angry when Prof. Nitpicker criticized my presentation."
• **identified with a source, cause**
• **tend to be brief, episodic**
• **many forms and types**
• **action-oriented; link with behavior**
• **can turn into a mood**

Moods
"Oh, I just don't have the energy to do much today, I've felt down all week."
• **hard to identify source, cause**
• **can be long lasting**
• **either "positive" or "negative"**
• **more cerebral; less action oriented**
• **can influence emotions**

Figure 5.2 Emotions and moods are different, but can also influence one another.

of Directors. When meeting the press and trying to explain the situation and resignation of board chair Patricia C. Dunn, Hurd called the actions "very disturbing" and the *Wall Street Journal* described him as speaking with "his voice shaking."

We can say that Hurd was emotional and angry that the incident was causing public humiliation for him and the company. Chances are the whole episode resulted in him being in a bad mood for a while. In the short run, at least, Hurd's emotions and mood probably had spillover consequences for those working directly with him and maybe for HP's workforce as a whole. Rut even further, was this just a one-time reaction on his part or was it an expected pattern that he displayed whenever things went wrong?

Emotion and Mood Contagion

Although emotions and moods are influenced by different events and situations, each of us may display some relatively predictable tendencies. Some people seem almost always positive and upbeat about things. For these optimists we might say the glass is nearly always half full. Others, by contrast, seem to be often negative or downbeat. They tend to be pessimists viewing the glass as half empty. Such tendencies toward optimism and pessimism not only influence the individual's behavior, they can also influence other people he or she interacts with—coworkers, friends, and family members.

Researchers are increasingly interested in **emotion and mood contagion**–the spillover effects of one's emotions and mood onto others. You might think this as a bit like catching a cold from someone. Evidence shows that positive and negative emotions are "contagious" in much the same ways, even though the tendency may not be well recognized in work settings. One study

found team members shared good and bad moods within two hours of being together; bad moods, interestingly, traveled person-to-person faster than good moods. Other research shows that when mood contagion is positive, followers report being more attracted to their leaders and rate the leaders more highly. The mood contagion also has up and down effects on moods of co-workers and teammates, as well as family and friends.

Daniel Goleman and his colleagues studying emotional intelligence believe leaders should manage emotion and mood contagion with care. "Moods that start at the top tend to move the fastest," they say, "because everyone watches the boss." This was very evident as CEOs in all industries–business and nonprofit alike—struggled to deal with the impact of economic crisis on their organizations and workforces. "Moaning is not a management task," said Rupert Stadler of Audi: "We can all join in the moaning, or we can make a virtue of the plight. I am rather doing the latter."

Emotional Labor

The concept of **emotional labor** relates to the need to show certain emotions in order to perform a job well. Good examples come from service settings such as airline check-in personnel or flight attendants. They are supposed to appear approachable, receptive, and friendly while taking care of the things you require as a customer. Some airlines like Southwest go even further in asking service employees to be "funny" and "caring" and "cheerful" while doing their jobs.

Emotional labor isn't always easy; it can be hard to be consistently "on" in displaying the desired emotions in one's work. If you're having a bad mood day or have just experienced an emotional run-in with a neighbor, for example, being

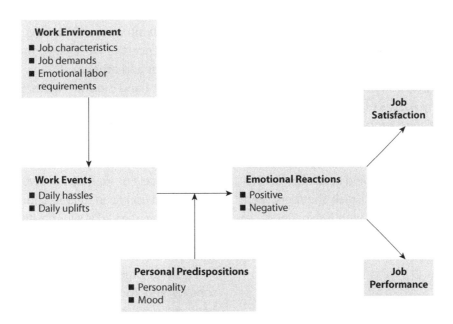

Figure 5.3 Figurative summary of Affective Events Theory.

"happy" and "helpful" with a demanding customer might seem a little much to ask. Such situations can cause **emotional dissonance** where the emotions we actually feel are inconsistent with the emotions we try to project. That is, we are expected to act with one emotion while we actually feel quite another.

It often requires a lot of self-regulation to display organizationally desired emotions in one's job. Imagine, for example, how often service workers struggling with personal emotions and moods experience dissonance when having to act positive toward customers. Scholars call it *deep acting* when someone tries to modify their feelings to better fit the situation—such as putting yourself in the position of the air travelers whose luggage went missing and feeling the same sense of loss. *Surface acting* is hiding true feelings while displaying very different ones—such as smiling at a customer even though the words they used to express a complaint just offended you.

Cultural Aspects of Emotions and Moods

Issues of emotional intelligence, emotion and mood contagion, and emotional labor can be complicated in cross-cultural situations. General interpretations of emotions and moods appear similar across cultures, with the major emotions of happiness, joy, and love all valued positively. But the frequency and intensity of emotions is known to vary somewhat. In mainland China, for example, research suggests that people report fewer positive and negative emotions as well as less intense emotions than in other cultures. Norms for emotional expression also vary across cultures. In collectivist cultures that emphasize group relationships such as Japan, individual emotional displays are less likely to occur and less likely to be accepted than in individualistic cultures.

Informal cultural standards called **display rules** govern the degree to which it is appropriate to display emotions. For example, British culture tends to encourage downplaying emotions, while Mexican culture is much more demonstrative in public. Overall, the lesson is that the way emotions are displayed in other cultures may not mean what they do at home. When Walmart first went to Germany, its executives found that an emphasis on friendliness embedded in its U.S. roots didn't work as well in the local culture. The more serious German shoppers did not respond well to Walmart's friendly greeters and helpful personnel. And along the same lines, Israeli shoppers seem to equate smiling cashiers with inexperience, so cashiers are encouraged to look somber while performing their jobs.

Emotions and Moods as Affective Events

Figure 5.3 presents the Affective Events Theory as a summary for this discussion of emotions, moods, and human behavior in organizations. The basic notion of the theory is that our emotions and moods are influenced by events involving other people and situations. Emotions and moods, in turn, influence the work performance and satisfaction of us and others.

The left-hand side of Figure 5.3 shows how the work environment, including the job and its emotional labor requirements, and daily work events create positive and negative emotional reactions. These influence job satisfaction and performance. For example, everyone experiences hassles and uplifts on the job, sometimes many of these during a workday. Our positive and negative emotional reactions to them influence the way we work at the moment and how we feel about it.

Personal predispositions in the form of personality and moods also affect the connection between work events and emotional reactions. Someone's mood at the time can exaggerate the emotions experienced as a result of an event. If you have just been criticized by your boss, for example, you are likely to feel worse than you would otherwise when a colleague makes a joke about the length of your coffee breaks.

A MENU OF MORAL ISSUES

One Week in the Life of the *Wall Street Journal*

J. Owen Cherrington & David J. Cherrington

Our lives are filled with moral issues; almost everything we do has a moral component. Issues of right and wrong are inherent in almost every business decision and for some decisions they represent the central concern. It is our observation that very few people appreciate how prevalent moral issues are.

When we are asked to present ethics seminars, several organizations specifically ask us to interview their members so we can focus the seminar on the specific moral issues their members face. Although every organization thinks its ethical problems are unique because it is a heavy manufacturer, a bank, a school, a church, or some other industry, our interviews with their members indicate that all of them face similar moral issues. The specific applications may differ slightly, but the core issues are the same. As a result of our interviews, we have developed a list of twelve common ethical concerns that we call a menu of moral issues. We have heard employees in every organization describe numerous illustrations of all twelve moral issues.

Our interviews and seminars also indicate that moral questions arise much more frequently than most people expect. Although some moral issues are very blatant, others are subtle and easily overlooked. At the beginning of an ethics seminar, for example, when we ask participants to describe a moral issue they have faced the previous week, most of them struggle to remember something other than a highly publicized event. After reviewing the menu of moral issues, however, most participants can identify numerous situations where ethical issues are involved. Once they recognize how frequently they face these moral issues, they also report that they often struggle with questions of where they should draw the line between moral and immoral conduct.

The purpose of this article is to summarize the most prominent moral issues that seem to be universal in every organization and illustrate them. Our menu contains twelve issues; although it may not be complete, we have found that it provides a useful foundation to make people more aware of moral issues and more sensitive to situations that lead to immoral behavior.

Menu of Moral Issues

1. *Taking things that do not belong to you. (Stealing)*

Air is free and you can take all you want; but taking an employer's cash is stealing. What about taking office supplies, making personal long distance phone calls, and using company time for personal business? What about cutting firewood in the canyon, picking flowers in a public park, hunting out of season, and keeping items found on the sidewalk?

2. *Saying things that you know are not true. (Lying)*

Telling lies that mislead others and distort the truth is wrong. But, is it acceptable to tell "white lies," to overstate compliments, to give false praise, or to understate your credentials on a job application? Are there times when tact is better than honesty? Is lying alright when you are protecting someone?

3. *False impressions. (Fraud and Deceit)*

When is it wrong to pretend you are someone you aren't? Are you responsible for correcting others' false impressions such as not accepting unearned praise or not letting others take the blame for your mistakes? If you receive something by mistake are you obligated to return it? Are you being deceitful when you dress for success or pretend to be successful so clients will have confidence in you?

4. *Conflict of interest and influence buying. (Bribes, payoffs, and kickbacks)*

Can you make an objective decision involving two or more parties if one party has given you anything of value, regardless of the party's motive? What are the differences between bribes, tips, and facilitating payments? What is the motive behind giving and when is it appropriate to accept a gift?

5. *Hiding versus divulging information.*

When do you have a responsibility to divulge information that another party has an interest in knowing, such as flaws in something you are selling, negative recommendations for former employees, and advantages of competing products? When do you have a responsibility to protect information that is personal or proprietary, such as information about someone's lifestyle and habits, trade secrets, and client lists? What is the critical difference between disloyal tattling and ethical whistle-blowing?

6. *Unfair advantage. (Cheating)*

When is it wrong to take advantage of a situation? How unfair must the situation be before it is wrong, such as using inside information to make investment decisions, charging higher prices where customers have limited options, granting privileges to friends or family, crowding in line, or registering early? Is it fair to use your position in an organization to obtain a settlement more favorable than could be obtained by an outsider? Is an increase in pay to top corporate officers justified when the pay and benefits of lower level employees are being cut?

7. *Personal decadence.*

Individuals set their own standards of excellence, but some are content to aim far below excellence. Where should the line of immorality be drawn regarding such acts as performing slow or sloppy work, extravagant expense account spending, losing your temper when angry, using alcohol and other stimulants, and accepting worker's compensation when you are capable of working?

8. *Interpersonal abuse.*

What kinds of interpersonal behaviors are abusive of others, such as physical violence, sexual harassment, emotional abuse, abuse of one's position, racism, and sexism?

9. *Organizational abuse.*

What organizational practices are abusive of members, such as inequity in compensation, misusing power or position, high stress jobs, performance appraisals that destroy self-esteem, transfers or time pressures that destroy family life, terminating people through no fault of their own, encouraging loyalty and not rewarding it, and creating the myth that the organization will benevolently protect or responsibly direct an employee's career?

10. *Rule violations.*

We are expected to obey countless rules, including laws, social conventions, organizational rules, and religious commandments. Are they all equally important or are some rule violations more serious than others? Should individuals feel a moral obligation to obey rules?

11. *Accessory to unethical acts.*

If you discover something unethical, are you obligated to report it? If you say nothing about it, are you an accessory to the misdeed? To what extent are you responsible for the acts of others? Do you have a responsibility to "investigate" the acts of associates prior to your involvement? Are you responsible or accountable for the acts of others through association?

12. *Moral balance. (Ethical dilemmas)*

Moral dilemmas often involve choosing between two equally desirable or undesirable options, only one of which can be selected. Which of two moral choices is most right or most wrong? Is it right to help one group at the detriment of another group?

Illustrations of Moral Issues

To illustrate the prevalence of these moral issues, we selected articles that appeared in *The Wall Street Journal* during the week of April 8–12, 1991. These five publications included more than sixty articles illustrating different moral issues. The majority of the articles described immoral actions and the negative consequences they produced; however, some articles reported efforts by companies to behave morally. Since we selected this week arbitrarily, we assume that a similar number of moral issues would be found any other week.

1. *Taking things that do not belong to you. (Stealing)*

Stealing refers to taking things that belong to others and it is almost universally considered wrong. Since *The Wall Street Journal* only reports business news, common robberies and thefts are not reported unless the amounts are sizable and they have an impact on a company. Nevertheless, during the survey week, there were several references to people taking money or merchandise that belonged to someone else. Two articles were especially informative because they described legal methods of "stealing" through broker commissions and bankruptcies.

An article on April 12 described a stockbroker who "took" money from his clients by investing their money and collecting commissions. He profited from the brokerage fees he charged while his trades were described as unauthorized, excessive, and unsuitable for his clients. For example, he used an investment of $447,667 from one of his clients to make $6.1 million in trades over a period of 21 months that reduced the client's investment to $112,000. His commissions on these trades was $140,000. Another client's investment dwindled from $114,000 to $8 800 while he earned $47,000 in commissions from numerous unprofitable and unauthorized transactions. His clients lost money even though he technically did not steal it. Although he was not indicted for theft, the New York Stock Exchange permanently barred him from ever working for a Big Board-brokerage firm again.

An April 9 article described the economic problems of companies in the apparel industry and explained how some manufacturers lose money when their retail clients declare bankruptcy. For example, Bullfrog Knits, a manufacturer of moderately priced children's clothing, lost money in 1990 for the first time in its nine year history. The losses resulted from clients who declared bankruptcy. In 1990, 150 of its retail accounts filed for protection under Chapter 11 of the bankruptcy code, and an additional 40 accounts in 1991. Bullfrog Knits' survival is threatened because so many retail stores are failing to pay for the merchandise they order. Some stores apparently continued to order merchandise after it was evident they could not pay for it. In other cases, however, the "theft" was unintentional because the retailers had their own financial problems. Retailers rely on bank loans to finance their inventories and the banks were unable or unwilling to extend more credit. But even when it is not intentional stealing, the result is similar: Bullfrog Knits is losing money because

its clients are taking merchandise without paying for it.

Although commissions and bankruptcies are legal actions and they usually serve a valuable business function, they are immoral if they are obtained unfairly and result in taking things that belong to others. Just because something is legal does not make it moral.

2. *Saying things that you know are not true. (Lying)*

Lying is almost always considered wrong when there is a legitimate expectation of hearing the truth. Some lies are very subtle and excused because no one is hurt. An April 8th article describes how employers are encouraged to lie to job applicants to obtain free consulting advise. According to the article, this practice is encouraged by *Executive Strategies Newsletter* as a means for companies to obtain creative ideas, such as a new marketing plan or a sales campaign. The companies advertise a fictitious job opening, and as part of the hiring process applicants are asked to prepare a financial overview of ten targeted companies, a customized turnaround plan for the company itself, or a presentation on how the company should position itself competitively.

The company sifts through the applicants' presentations and selects the best ideas. The companies would have paid several thousand dollars to consultants for this advice. The newsletter justified this practice by saying it would help the applicants sharpen their job-seeking skills. The applicants reported, however, that they felt lied to and abused.

False advertising is a prominent moral issue in business and it was the topic of an article that described the exaggerated claims of several companies which sell bottled water. The Food and Drug Administration has found that rather than being fresh, pure, spring water as advertised, some bottled water is less pure than ordinary tap water. Knowing where to draw the line on misleading advertising is a difficult moral issue. Advertisers often make exaggerated claims regarding their products but they resist calling this lying because they say consumers expect advertising to contain overstated claims. Therefore, they say these exaggerations are not lying since they are consistent with normal business practices and do not violate the customers' expectations of hearing the truth. Nevertheless, the claims are false and misleading. An April 8th article describes the Federal Trade Commissions' crackdown on several national advertisers for false and misleading claims. But, many advertisements are not prohibited even though they do not tell the truth.

Insurance companies are apparently the victims of extensive lying, which people use to get what they think they deserve. Insurance is a program of shared risk, where the fortunate are expected to pay more in premiums than they receive in services, while the unfortunate receive more than they pay. This concept is inconsistent with such attitudes as "everyone deserves to get back as much as they paid" or "let the insurance company pay for elective repairs or medical services since they are free." Three articles described cases of lying to insurance companies. The first one explained how Value Rent-a-Car overcharged customers and insurance companies for premiums and accidents. Customers were induced to purchase unnecessary duplicate insurance coverage and insurance companies were billed multiple times for damages that were not repaired. The second article reported that Blue Shield's fraud detection efforts saved subscribers $9.2 million in 1990. The third article reported that Medicaid expected to recover $1 billion from companies that charged it for health care expenses that should have been paid by their own insurance first. Overstating expenses and misrepresenting accidents are growing problems for insurance

companies and these three articles show the enormity of insurance fraud.

3. *False impressions. (Fraud and deceit)*

False impressions designed to mislead others are wrong. When they lead to fraud, they are also illegal. Financial investors expect investment opportunities to be as they appear and misrepresentation is considered illegal. An April 8th article described an FBI sting operation against brokerage houses that use false impressions to manipulate penny stocks in shell companies with little or no assets. Fictitious financial statements and false regulatory filings are used to create the impression of business activity which increases the stock price from a few cents to as much as 50 cents within a few weeks. The brokers profit from the appreciated value of the stock they buy and sell, from commissions on the stock they sell, from finders fees for identifying shell companies, and from payoffs for falsifying documents. The results of the sting operation netted indictments against 18 brokers and four brokerage firms across the country.

International business transactions are often clouded by suspicions of distrust because cultural differences make it easy to create false impressions. An article illustrating false impressions in an international transaction (April 11) described Mitsubishi's purchase of Value Rent-a-Car. Mitsubishi officials claim that information provided to them before the sale misled them about the company's assets and liabilities. They also claim that electronic eavesdropping equipment was used to overhear their private conversations during the negotiations.

Correcting false impressions is just as important as not intentionally creating them. Knowingly allowing a false impression to persist would be deceitful, especially when it would be seriously misleading to others. Companies generally benefit from being honest and forthright with their customers. Avoiding false impressions was the topic of an April 10th article describing U.S. Bancorp's efforts to caution its customers about the hazards of credit card purchases. Quite unlike the typical "buy now—pay later" theme of other credit card ads, U.S. Bank's ads warn their customers that they can get into debt with amazing speed and if they fail to pay their entire balance they will be charged a very expensive interest rate. According to the article, the ad is so popular that disk jockeys for at least six radio stations announce when it will be played next.

4. *Conflict of interest and influence buying. (Bribes, payoffs, and kickbacks)*

A conflict of interest exists when a person who is expected to make an impartial decision has a vested interest in one of the parties that could benefit from the decision. It is unrealistic for decision makers to think they can make unbiased decisions after they have accepted anything of material worth from one of the parties. Decision makers should be sensitive to conflict of interest situations and avoid them, either by not participating in the decision process or by removing their vested interests. Several illustrations of conflicts of interest were reported during the survey week.

An April 9th article suggests that conflicts of interest along with other forms of theft and fraud are destroying Poland's economy and threatening its transition from communism to a free market. Many joint ventures between private and public companies are managed by one group who manipulate sales and markups to bleed the state while lining their own pockets. This account dramatically illustrates how free-market systems rely on the assumption that people and organizations are honest and ethical in their business dealings.

An April 9th article described a subtle and even controversial form of conflict of interest

among Wall Street brokerage firms. Many brokerage firms buy large issues of stocks they plan to recommend to their clients. The firms argue that such a stockpile allows them to meet investor's sudden demands for recommended stocks without causing the stock prices to jump. The New York Stock Exchange, however, claims that this practice, known as "front running" is illegal. The Big Board announced that it will take disciplinary action against any brokerage firms that buy stocks ahead of their customers' orders. Although the brokerage firms object to this ruling, it should be clear that the integrity of their recommendations is compromised by the fact that they have purchased a large issue of stocks that must now be sold.

An April 12th article described a conflict of interest in the Rhode Island Motor Vehicle Dealers License commission which licenses dealers to sell cars in the state. This commission is comprised largely of the car dealers who are regulated by it. The commissioners have refused to grant a license to the AAA South Central New England auto club which has a car-buying service that sells cars below the price of other dealers. The American Automobile Association has decided to fight the commission to preserve its car-buying service and the case will go before the Rhode Island Supreme Court. Regardless of how the court rules, everyone should recognize that the commissioners have a clear conflict of interest as they regulate their own dealerships and the applications of competitors.

Gifts, including campaign contributions, should be recognized as a source of influence buying that creates a conflict of interest. Three articles described illustrations of improper conduct as a result of campaign contributions. One article was an editorial discussing the thrift crisis and the light prosecution of a leading player who made sizable campaign contributions to congressmen. The editorial argued that the light sentencing resulted partly from the congressmen's acceptance of the contributions and the incongruent position this created for assigning responsibility for the savings and loan fiasco. The other two articles described an investigation into an Alaskan representative's role in the sinking of a fishing ship. The ship's owner, Arctic Alaska Fisheries Corporation, had made sizable campaign contributions to the representative. The representative sent a memo to the Coast Guard asking them to ease enforcement of certain safety requirements. If these requirements had been strictly followed, the ship would not have sunk. The representative denies a connection between the campaign giving and this memo. But even if there was no formal agreement, the fact that he accepted the contribution necessarily influences his thinking and prevents him from being neutral and unbiased.

5. *Hiding versus divulging information.*

Information is power and the misuse of information typically occurs in one of three ways: revealing information that should not be revealed, not revealing information that should be revealed, and acting on information that has not been publicly announced.

The April 12th issue contained a small announcement that CBS and one of its anchor-women were being sued for $100 million for reporting on a child custody dispute involving alleged molestation. CBS would not comment on the case, and perhaps others should also be more discrete in reporting information that could damage a person's reputation, especially when the charges are alleged but not confirmed.

Even true information can be an invasion of privacy. An April 10th article reported that improper IRS publicity caused $10.9 million of damages to an insurance executive who was demoted after the IRS announced that he pleaded guilty to tax evasion and was put on probation for failing to

pay $3,500. In granting this large award, the tax court said the IRS, in its effort to advertise the consequences of cheating, negligently ignored a plea bargain agreement to maintain confidentiality.

A critical moral issue is whether personal information should be published, even if it is true, when it serves to damage individuals and inhibit rebuilding their lives. An April 11th article described the efforts of lawmakers and civil liberties groups to regulate the encroachment of computer files into the privacy of individuals. Limiting access to computer data bases is a complex decision because it pits the property rights of marketers against the privacy rights of people.

Making appropriate information available to the public often serves as an effective deterrent against fraud. Four articles described illustrations of information that should be open to the public, such as who owns the stock of Independence Bank in Encino, California, who holds the controlling interest in First American Bankshares Incorporated, how an Atlanta-based branch of an Italian bank made $3 billion of illicit loans to Iraq, and why investor complaints with brokerage firms should be disclosed. Each article claimed that the release of timely information would have reduced the likelihood of fraud.

Although most companies resist reporting adverse publicity, especially when the potential problem is not certain, an April 11th article described how many electric utilities are taking an active role in warning their customers of the potential hazards of electromagnetic fields. Even though the dangers are not clear and there are no established standards for unacceptable levels of exposure to electricity, some utilities have published bulletins explaining the mysteries of electricity and health, and they offer to visit consumers' homes to measure the electromagnetic emissions.

6. *Unfair advantage. (Cheating)*

There are countless ways to take unfair advantage of people and organizations usually without violating the law. A useful question for assessing whether a situation is unfair is to ask if everyone would be equally satisfied regardless of which side of the transaction they were given. If the answer is no, then it is probably unfair. Another useful question to ask is how you would feel if the complete facts of the situation were accurately reported on the front page of *The Wall Street Journal*. If you would feel uncomfortable having the transaction reported, then it is probably unfair.

Executive compensation is often criticized as unfair. An April 10th article questioned the excessive severance pay (totaling $11.7 million) given to five executives who left Equitable Life Assurance Society while the company was being restructured. Likewise, an April 12th article described the exorbitant salaries being paid to Drexel executives even though Drexel is in bankruptcy reorganization. Drexel's creditors have good reason to be upset. Drexel's chief executive officer will receive close to a million dollars and other executive salaries will also be high. Shortly before declaring bankruptcy, Drexel distributed $350 million in bonuses to executives, and in 1987 it paid $550 million to Michael Milken, its former junk bond chief.

Insider trading is a unique moral problem in business because the temptations are so great, the opportunities are so prevalent, and the line determining what is acceptable is not always clear. Two articles described instances of illegal insider trading and a third article discussed the controversy surrounding insider trading in the bond market. Detecting insider trading is more difficult in the bond and commodities markets since prices are not recorded hourly, and some even argue that the rules governing insider trading in the stock market should not apply to bond and commodities markets. It seems obvious, however, that if inside information in the stock market creates an uneven playing field for investors, then inside information would be just as unfair in other markets.

Monopolies and price-fixing are business practices that are considered unfair. One article described how DuPont was being sued for monopolizing the materials for making bullet-proof vests and another article claimed that four other companies were guilty of collusion and price fixing, including Nintendo Company, Mitsubishi Electric Corporation, Minolta Corporation, and Panasonic Company. Because they are considered unfair, monopolies and price fixing have been prohibited by law.

An illustration of an unfair advantage that may be immoral but not illegal is Intel's dominance in the computer chip industry. An April 8th article describes how Intel's competitors are combining to fight what they perceive is an unfair advantage. Intel computer chips became the standard in the early 1980s when IBM chose Intel's chip over their competitors. In 1986, Intel decreed that no other chip suppliers could sell Intel's newest 386 chip. Since then, Intel chips have dominated over eighty percent of the PC market.

Three unfair advantages have angered Intel's customers: their profit margins (estimated at eighty percent) are unreasonably high, they compete unfairly by providing chips their customers need while at the same time manufacturing complete computer systems to compete directly against their customers, and they restrict the production of chips to increase prices.

Whether Intel's actions were unfair or legitimate attempts to protect its competitive advantage is open for debate. Intel tried to hide the design of its new chip to prevent competitors from designing clone chips. When competitors succeeded, Intel used legal proceedings in an ethically questionable way to delay them from marketing a similar chip. Intel launched a barrage of law suits against NEC when NEC released a clone of Intel's 386 chip. These suits took several years for the courts to litigate, and by the time NEC obtained the right to sell the chip, the business opportunity was gone.

The coalition against Intel illustrates how people feel incensed when they observe an unfair advantage and try to fight it. Conditions that are unfair violate one's feelings of fundamental fairness.

7. *Personal decadence.*

People define their own standards of right and wrong and decide how they will respond to such issues as substance abuse, work habits, personal health, and contributing to society. Three articles were related to these issues. One article mentioned a person who was charged with the possession of cocaine; another article explained how thrift funds were misused to pay for prostitutes and a beach house; and a third article explained how General Electric saves over $1 million annually with an employee fitness center.

The work habits of American workers have frequently been questioned because they increasingly demand more pay for less work. Some companies have found that the work habits of their work force are threatening their competitive position. An April 8th article described the changes Ford Motor Company is making to improve its efficiency. Ford's salaried employees seem to be less efficient than competing Japanese firms and Ford is discharging 500 to 1,000 salaried employees in an attempt to cut salary costs and bring their expenses in line with leaner Japanese auto makers. Ford has also cut merit pay of white-collar workers by twenty-five percent, reduced their medical benefits, and eliminated their cost-of-living increases. Ford's changes reflect a growing concern about the deteriorating work ethic of American workers.

Supporting people who are unemployed or injured presents a difficult moral concern that requires balancing compassion for those who truly need help versus contempt for those who could work but are abusing the assistance. Two articles touched on this issue: one was an editorial by a disabled person criticizing government-mandated entitlement programs for making recipients increasingly dependent on them. This editorial advocates more self-reliance and less government assistance. The other article describes efforts to make government assistance more accessible through electronic welfare because it reduces the social stigma of receiving welfare. Rather than receiving food stamps or checks, welfare recipients use a credit card in an automated teller machine to withdraw cash. Electronic welfare, however, is not expected to change the incidence of welfare fraud by those who chose to abuse the system.

Individuals must decide for themselves about their work values: whether they are committed to pursue excellence and take pride in their work or whether they are content to perform careless and sloppy work or no work at all. Those who choose to build society and contribute to the common good receive moral approbation, while those who destroy society or try to live off the efforts of others receive moral blame.

8. *Interpersonal abuse.*

Interpersonal abuse occurs when an individual intentionally mistreats another person or shows favoritism to some at the expense of others. Racial slurs, derogatory nicknames, disparaging sarcasm, and other forms of personal harassment are illustrations of interpersonal abuse. Behavior that serves to destroy another person's safety, self-esteem, or mental health or to deprive people of their free agency or opportunities for advancement is generally considered immoral. Most instances of interpersonal abuse are unmistakably wrong; however, moral questions may occasionally arise such as what is the difference between office romances and sexual harassment, which jokes are acceptable, and when does humor become offensive.

The Wall Street Journal frequently reports court cases of race and sex discrimination. During the survey week, three articles mentioned problems caused by sexual harassment, hate crimes, and race norming. Problems of racism and sexism stem from a failure to treat individuals with dignity and respect. Race norming is a difficult moral issue that has divided the personnel testing profession and forced the Department of Labor to discontinue administering the General Aptitude Test Battery, a popular test that has been extensively validated. For reasons that are not clear, certain racial groups score significantly lower than others on various aptitude tests in spite of efforts to eliminate cultural bias from the test items. Should an individual's percentile score be relative to other members of that person's racial group or relative to the entire population? Race norming is inconsistent with efforts to eliminate race and sex as considerations in employment.

Racism and sexism are typically viewed as manifestations of undesirable prejudice and stereotypes. An April 11th article described some female entertainers who are criticized for perpetuating negative female stereotypes in their rap music. The lyrics to their songs, and even some group names, are described as explicit, steamy, pornographic, raunchy, and risque. In an interview, some of the women said they intentionally try to be as rude and nasty as possible and rely on blatant raunchy sex to sell their records. Although magazine reviews and even student groups have been outraged at the stage performances and records of these female rappers, their concerts are sold out and their records are extremely profitable.

Because their raps are degrading to both men and women, their songs are considered demeaning to all humanity. But efforts to curtail their songs raise moral issues of censorship, legislating morality, and social decency.

9. *Organizational abuse.*

Every organization has the capacity to abuse people. Even benign organizations that have socially responsible goals and are led by kind and ethical leaders can have a destructive impact on the lives of their members. Some forms of abuse are clear and intentional while other forms of abuse are subtle and unintentional—no one ever intended for people to be harmed.

Several articles described layoffs and why they were necessary. Layoffs are usually traumatic experiences, even when companies make every effort to minimize the harm to terminated employees. Nevertheless, some of these layoffs involved long term employees who probably feel betrayed because they expected to continue until retirement and will have difficulty finding new employment. An April 10th article reported that a Pulitzer prize was awarded for an earlier article describing the human cost of Safeway's leveraged buy-out. That article described the devastating human suffering in terms of suicide, divorce, alcoholism, and family abuse that occurred after 63,000 employees were terminated because of a leveraged buy-out.

Numerous occurrences of organizational abuse are not accidental. Employees are abused whenever they are asked to do something dishonest or immoral. In some situations employees are faced with moral dilemmas because their jobs require them to perform unethical or illegal acts. Even relatively minor episodes, such as a secretary having to tell people that a manager is out when the manager is really in, can create an uncomfortable situation for the secretary who may feel forced to compromise his or her personal integrity.

An article on April 8th, describes how Mexican youth are being abused in factory jobs. Children as young as ten years old work with dangerous machines and chemicals in shoe factories and other industries. Although Mexican law prohibits hiring children under age 14, an estimated five to ten million children are in the work force.

Although much needs to be done to reduce organizational abuse, the best solution lies in teaching people how to protect themselves from organizations.

10. *Rule violations.*

Most firms have rules, and most executives expect employees to abide by these rules even if they disagree with them. Rule violations are often viewed as an indication of immoral behavior. However, some rules seem arbitrary and unnecessary, which raises the question of whether some rule violations are more serious than others. Some of the most well-recognized rules include laws, social conventions, organizational rules, and religious commandments:

(a) *Laws:* Wearing seat belts, obeying speed limits, avoiding illicit drugs, and not copying computer software.

(b) *Social conventions:* Not talking in libraries, not spitting on sidewalks, not cutting across lawns, and not smoking in public buildings.

(c) *Organizational rules:* Charging office expenses as travel expenses, manipulating budget accounts to make operations look better, punching in/out for other employees, submitting false production reports, and violating dress and grooming standards.

(d) *Religious commandments:* Extramarital affairs, Sabbath day observance, alcoholism, and eating unapproved food.

Most of the articles describing moral issues identified at least one rule violation that contributed to other unethical actions. The most frequently mentioned violations concerned the Securities and Exchange Commission's rules. An April 10th article, for example, described how the former chairman of Singer Company concealed the true ownership of stock and filed false statements to the Securities and Exchange Commission. For this deceit he was sentenced to a four-year prison term.

People usually accept a moral obligation to follow legitimate rules and uphold the laws of the land. The problem is that many rules are arbitrary, irrational, and unworthy of support and obedience. For example, some organizations impose seemingly absurd rules regarding dress codes, parking privileges, expense reporting, and performance measurement. People will only adhere to irrational rules when there is adequate surveillance and punishment. A greater problem with irrational rules, however, is that they tend to destroy moral internalization. People do not internalize rules and feel a moral obligation to follow them if they are senseless. Rules need to improve the quality of life or contribute to organizational effectiveness and leaders have a responsibility to explain the importance of the rules.

11. *Accessory to unethical acts.*

Deciding how to respond when you observe something immoral can be a critical moral dilemma itself. On one hand, it is argued that you should only get involved when it directly concerns you. On the other hand, it is argued that we all have a moral responsibility to act morally ourselves, encourage others to act morally, and report all immoral conduct. Three articles describe incidents that endorse the latter view.

In an April 8th article describing the Federal Reserve Board's investigations of bank fraud, the

Fed acknowledges that it can not prevent all fraud and needs the cooperation of others. In explaining its failure to uncover $3 billion in illicit loans to Iraq, the Fed described the problem as a massive fraud in which a large number of employees acted together to conceal the operation and deceive auditors and examiners. Rather than concealing the problem, the Fed expected employees to report it.

In an April 8th article the Environmental Protection Agency also makes it clear that several parties share the responsibility for disposing of wastes. Waste haulers are expected to know what they are hauling rather than deferring responsibility for the contents to the companies for whom they haul. But, how far does the responsibility extend? An April 11th article describes how courts are holding lending institutions responsible for the cleanup of hazardous waste sites. Under the federal Superfund law, those who own or operate contaminated sites are responsible for cleaning them. Although the law shields lenders from liability if they hold a security interest and do not participate in management, a federal appeals court found a commercial financing company liable for the cleanup of hazardous wastes created by a business to which it loaned money. These three cases suggest that when individuals know about something immoral, society expects them to take appropriate action to report or prevent it.

12. *Moral balance.*

Moral dilemmas are sometimes difficult to resolve and ethics texts explain the classical methods of ethical analysis for deciding what is right. During the survey week, there were at least 10 ethical dilemmas:

- Buying Mexican products to help their struggling economy versus refusing to buy products to support child labor laws.

- Using taxol to treat women with ovarian cancer versus saving the endangered forests of Pacific Yew trees from which the taxol chemical is extracted.
- Financing bank insurance from the Federal Reserve Board versus from the Treasury.
- Requiring companies to make greater accommodations for the handicapped versus spending money to create more jobs.
- Providing tax credits to stimulate business research versus increasing taxes to pay for the credits.
- Increasing the documentation requirements to prevent penny stock fraud versus making the reporting requirements so difficult that the penny stock funding is eliminated.
- Saving the historic Fourth Ward in Houston and its Black neighborhoods versus renovating the area with malls and condominiums.
- Enlarging Japan's airport versus destroying surrounding farmlands.
- Reducing Social Security and increasing taxes versus funding the Treasury's budget deficits with excess Social Security funds
- Requiring fleet vehicles to run on non-gasoline versus failing to reduce air pollution.

The most popular forms of ethical analysis involve either a utilitarian or deontological analysis. Both types of analysis have their strengths and weaknesses and individuals ought to know how to competently perform each. Unfortunately, people may fail to recognize ethical dilemmas and the need for moral balance because their thinking is biased by a vested interest or personal preference.

The moral issues described above seem to be common to all organizations and analyzing them should help individuals in two ways: to increase their sensitivity to the kinds of moral issues that occur in every organization, and to help them recognize the situations when they occur. Finding so many articles in just one week of the *Wall Street*

Journal clearly demonstrates that moral issues are very pervasive in business. Individuals are more likely to behave ethically if they recognize the moral issues inherent in the decisions they are making.

COMMUNICATION PROCESSES

Joseph E. Champoux

The word *communication* will be used here in a very broad sense to include all of the procedures by which one mind may affect another. This, of course, involves not only written and oral speech, but also music, the pictorial arts, the theatre, the ballet, and in fact all human behavior.

This quotation comes from the opening of a classic work describing a communication theory. The heart of the definition is in the first sentence. All communication tries to affect the behavior of at least one other person. Communication can change the way a person perceives his environment and lead to behavior change.

Organizational communication includes the purpose, flow, and direction of messages and the media used for those messages. Such communication happens within the complex, interdependent social systems of organizations. Think of organizational communication as another view of behavior in organizations. This chapter calls such behavior "message behavior"—behavior that includes sending, receiving, and giving meaning to messages.

Communication processes in organizations are continuous and constantly changing. They do not have a beginning or an end, nor do they follow a strict sequence. During communication, the sender creates messages from one or more symbols to which he attaches meaning. Messages can be oral, written, or nonverbal; they can also be intentional or unintentional. Messages deal with tasks to be done, maintenance of organizational policies, or information about some state of the organization. They can go to people inside the organization or outside the organization.

Organizational communication happens over a pathway called a **network**, a series of interconnected positions in an organization. The network can be formal, as defined by organizational positions and relationships among them. It can also be informal, as defined by informal patterns of social interaction and the informal groups. Communication over the network goes in any direction: downward, upward, or horizontally. Communication networks in organizations are interdependent, interlocking, and overlapping systems of human interaction. They involve relationships among individuals, within and among groups, or dispersed almost randomly throughout an organization.

The Basic Communication Process

Figure 7.1 shows the basic communication process. The **sender** decides what message to send and encodes it using symbols that he assumes the receiver will understand. The sender converts the message to a signal and transmits the message over a communication channel to the receiver. The **channel** can be a person's voice, an electronic device, a written medium, or a video medium. The **receiver** decodes the received message and interprets its meaning. The receiver responds to the message by acting consistently with that interpretation. You use the basic communication process whenever you send an e-mail to a friend. You are the sender, your friend is the receiver, and the channel is the electronic method of transmission.

Modern **communication media** provide senders many choices. Senders can choose to use telephones, e-mail, letters or memoranda, videoconferencing, and face-to-face meetings. The criteria for choosing a medium vary. Senders can use written media for formality and a clear message and face-to-face meetings to convey a sense of teamwork. E-mail use, however, is largely based on availability and ease of use.

The **feedback loop** at the bottom of the figure implies interdependence between the sender and receiver during the communication process. The sender interprets the receiver's response and can send an additional message for clarification.

Noise surrounds the entire communication process in organizations and can make communication less effective. Various distortions, errors, and foreign material often affect the quality of the signal. The noise shown in the model represents these distortions; they are additions to the signal not intended by the sender. You can illustrate this for yourself by tuning a radio to a distant station. The static you hear is noise in the communication channel. The static makes it hard for you to understand the radio message. A later section discusses communication dysfunctions that result from the presence of noise.

Workforce diversity introduces other forms of noise. The different worldviews that come from the backgrounds of a diverse workforce can prove troublesome to some people. If the receiver stereotypes a sender as ignorant because of the way he speaks, the receiver likely will distort the message. Senders with English as a second language also might not speak like native speakers, causing some receivers to distort or ignore the message.

A person's accent can also add noise to a communication interaction. The large regional

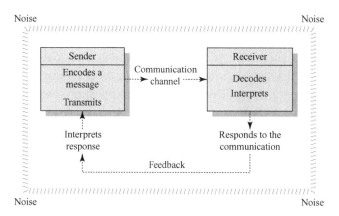

Figure 7.1 The Basic Communication Process

differences in accents throughout the United States can distort communication for some receivers. The same is true for people interacting with call center technicians who are outside the United States. Noise from accents also appears in languages other than English. Telemundo, the Spanish-language television network, trains its telenovela (soap opera) actors to speak an accent-free Spanish. The actors come from all over Latin America and normally speak Spanish with regional accents. Telemundo's accent-free approach reduces noise for its largely Mexico-born and Mexican American audience (receivers).

International diversity can also add noise. Korean culture, for example, values a stern, strict demeanor. This cultural value makes it difficult for Koreans to smile when providing service. The Korean Air Service Academy in Seoul, South Korea, offers smile training to companies that want to present a warm, friendly service experience.

Types of Communication

Verbal and nonverbal communication are the two major types of communication found in organizational communication processes. **Verbal communication** includes oral, written, and electronic forms of communication. **Nonverbal communication** includes eye movements, gestures, facial expressions, tone of voice, and the like.

Both verbal and nonverbal communication can appear together in a communication process and interact to create meaning for a receiver. Nonverbal communication adds much of the feeling and emotion that a sender wants to give to a message. Nonverbal communication often has more effect than verbal communication on the meaning receivers give a message.

Verbal Communication

Oral and written messages are the two major forms of verbal communication. The following paragraphs discuss many characteristics of the different forms of verbal communication you will likely find in today's organizations.

Oral communication includes all forms of speech between a sender and receiver. Oral communication can occur during face-to-face interaction or by telephone, radio, or television. Although oral communication usually has the immediate attention of the receiver, sometimes the message can be recorded and played later; cassette recordings, telephone answering devices, and computer-recorded voice-mail are examples.

Unless the interaction is transcribed or recorded, oral communication leaves no retrievable record of the message and response. When the sender wants to affect the receiver's opinion on some matter, oral communication is more effective than written. Nonverbal communication by both the sender and the receiver, however, can affect the final interpretation of the message.

American Sign Language (ASL), the language that deaf and hearing-impaired people use, is a form of verbal communication. Although it is a visual language, communication theorists classify it as mainly verbal. Deaf and hearing-impaired people use ASL's patterns of hand and finger movements to communicate. ASL includes patterns of facial expression and body movements to express emotions and distinguish sentence types. The United States and Canada use ASL. French Canadians use a different form of signing. Country and regional differences in signing systems vary greatly.

Written communication is any form of handwriting, printed memo, report, or message sent over an electronic medium such as a computer network. The receiver's response is more delayed in written communication than in oral communication, because the receiver must first read the message before interpreting and responding to it.

Written communications compete with each other for the time and attention of the receiver. They also compete with oral communication, a form with the advantage of at least the sender's vocal presence. Written communication can interact with nonverbal communication. The way a sender gives a memo or report to a receiver, for example, can affect the receiver's perception of the message when he reads it.

Written communication has some advantages over oral communication. First, it is a retrievable and almost permanent recording of a message. Second, comprehension often is greater with written than with oral communication, because the receiver can reread a written communication to be sure he understands the sender's intended meaning. Therefore, managers commonly use memoranda to document agreements.

As modern technology develops, **electronic** and **video communications** are becoming increasingly important. Such communication includes the use of e-mail, computer networks, fax machines, computer conferencing, and videoconferencing. Those methods offer the advantages of speed, accuracy, easy dispersal to many locations, direct interaction, and quick feedback. Videoconferencing also allows people in different places to see each other while they talk. A later section discusses emerging technologies and their effects on communication in detail.

Nonverbal Communication

Nonverbal communication is behavior that communicates without written or spoken words. Examples include gestures, posture, seating position, voice tone and inflection, speed of speech, and the physical environment of the communication interaction. People use these nonverbal cues to communicate explicitly or implicitly with each other. Individuals combine verbal and nonverbal communications to create unique communication styles.

Nonverbal communication can contradict, amplify, or complement verbal communication. Subordinates might perceive a supervisor who does not maintain eye contact during a conversation as insincere. Some people might perceive a person with a relaxed facial expression as having more power than a person with a nervous facial expression. A professor who tells you to ask questions when you do not understand something and then leaves time for questions reinforces your perception that he wants you to understand.

The rest of this section describes four aspects of nonverbal communication: (1) physical aspects of the person, (2) the physical environment of communication, (3) time, and (4) communication with signs and signals. The interpretations given here are North American. A later section, "International Aspects of Organizational Communication," gives interpretations from other cultures. See that section's citations for a description of the almost endless forms of nonverbal communication in different cultures.

Physical Aspects of the Person

Physical aspects of the person, such as voice, facial expressions, gestures, body movements, and posture, are all forms of nonverbal communication. Each can regulate, add to, or detract from the intended meaning of the sender.

Receivers infer meaning from how a sender vocalizes a verbal message. Receivers often can sense that a sender has positive feelings about the receiver when the sender speaks fast, fluently, and with few references to himself. A sender who increases the volume and rate of his speech can also persuade a receiver to accept a message. A receiver might perceive deceit when the sender makes many speech errors and talks slowly.

Facial expressions tell much about feelings, especially when the person is unwilling or unable to express his feelings. A smile while speaking can show affection for the receiver. A frown can suggest disgust or despair, feelings the sender might not want to mention.

Senders can use gestures, such as punctuated hand and arm movements, to emphasize parts of their message. Senders who look away from the receiver imply uncertainty about their message. A shift in posture, such as leaning forward, implies the sender is about to make a new and possibly important point.

Physical Environment of Communication

The physical setting of a communication interaction is the second major type of nonverbal communication. The environment includes all aspects of using space, including the distance between the sender and the receiver.

A person who remains seated behind a desk puts a barrier between himself and a visitor. Such an arrangement might unintentionally tell the visitor that the seated person is cold, distant, and even uninterested in the visitor. Increasingly, U.S. managers place tables and comfortable chairs in an open area of the office. Coming out from behind the desk makes a guest feel more comfortable, and the arrangement gives a feeling of openness.

North Americans normally hold business conversations with a distance of 5½ to 8 feet between speakers. Any closer distance can make the receiver uncomfortable and cause the person to move away. As a later section will explain, this North American custom does not hold in many other countries. The difference in the distance between speakers is an especially difficult cross-cultural issue in communication.

Time

The third type of nonverbal communication is a person's orientation to and use of time. North American businesspeople consider it rude to arrive late for an appointment or a meeting. They interpret lateness as disrespect for themselves and for the organization they represent.

North Americans are also distinctly future oriented. They consider the long term to be about five to ten years. You will find later that time orientations and the meaning of time vary among cultures.

Communication with Signs and Signals

Communication with signs and signals is a pervasive part of our lives. Turn signals on vehicles, traffic control signals, and caution flags used by highway workers are all common examples. A handshake is an important and almost everyday physical sign. Some people in North America believe a firm handshake suggests confidence and a weak handshake shows uncertainty.

Functions of Organizational Communication

The **functions of organizational communication** include sharing information, providing performance feedback, integrating and coordinating parts of the organization, persuading others, expressing emotion, and innovating. Figure 7.2 summarizes these functions.

Communication processes help **share information** with people inside and outside the organization. The information includes descriptions of the organization's mission, strategy, policies, and tasks. Descriptions of the organization's mission go to organization members, stockholders, and, through advertising and other media, to people outside the organization. Information about task direction and feedback on task performance mainly goes to members of the organization.

The **performance feedback** function of organizational communication lets people know about the quality of their job performance. Feedback can reduce uncertainty, give people important cues about levels of performance, and act as a motivational resource. Reducing uncertainty is especially important during the early stages of learning a task. Giving the right behavioral cues early lets people know which behaviors will lead to valued rewards and which will not. Feedback can be given orally face to face or provided more formally through the organization's performance appraisal system.

An organization's communication process helps **integrate and coordinate** the many parts of an organization. Communication among design engineering, manufacturing, and marketing departments helps coordinate successful new product development. The performance of project groups, for example, can benefit from

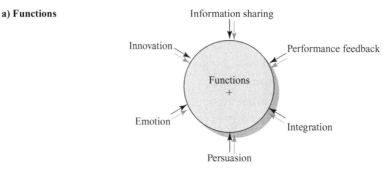

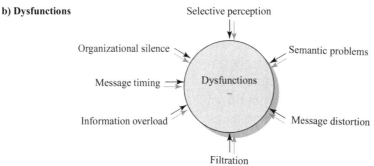

Figure 7.2 Function and Dysfunction of Organizational Communication

cross-functional team members communicating with colleagues they know outside the group.

A key part of the definition of communication is its role in affecting the behavior of someone else. People in organizations use communication processes to persuade other people to behave in a way the communicator desires. The **persuasion** function of communication often plays a key role in large-scale organizational change.

The **emotional** function of communication focuses on the human side of the organization. People often need to express their feelings of satisfaction or dissatisfaction with their tasks, supervision, and the context within which they work. An organization's communication process can play a useful function for its members by letting them express their feelings.

Modern organizations feel they must turn out a continuous stream of **innovative** services and products to compete in both domestic and world markets. The communication process lets an organization gather information from its external environment and move it to key decision points within the organization. As managers make innovative decisions, they can move information about those decisions to people both inside and outside the organization. By supporting innovation, the communication process plays a major role in how the organization adapts to its ever-changing external environment.

Dysfunctions of Organizational Communication

Figure 7.1 showed the basic model of communication surrounded by noise. Noise includes all forms of error that can happen during communication. Errors can come from the sender, the receiver, the message, and the medium of communication. Such noise or errors lead to **dysfunctions of organizational communication**. Other dysfunctions come from powerful organizational processes that pressure employees to keep silent about events they see or experience. Figure 7.2 summarizes these dysfunctions. A later section, "Improving Communication Effectiveness," describes ways of decreasing these dysfunctions to improve communication effectiveness.

Selective perception lets receivers block out information they do not want to hear in a message. Receivers might block out threatening information or information that disagrees with their beliefs. They might also block some information to reduce the amount they need to process. Despite the sender's intended meaning, the receiver "selectively listens" to the communication. The receiver then uses the perceived information in the message to develop his meaning of it. Selective perception can also affect the information the sender gets from the receiver about the receiver's interpretation of the sender's message. The sender's assessment of the accuracy of the receiver's interpretation can affect the sender's reaction to the receiver. For example, the sender might repeat the message several times if he believes the receiver did not understand it correctly.

Semantic problems are communication dysfunctions that occur when the receiver's interpretation of a message differs from the sender's intended message. Some words have different meanings for different people. For example, words or phrases such as *good*, *average*, and *do your best* can have widely varying interpretations. Such words often are at the center of semantic problems in oral and written performance appraisals. Other semantic problems stem from the jargon used by professional or technical groups and the in-group language of different functional groups in an organization.

Accountants talk about "burden," manufacturing engineers discuss "metrology," computer specialists worry about "upload and download," and Harry Potter fans chant "Expecto patronum, expecto patronum" just before a major business presentation. Further semantic problems come from the international context of globally operating firms. One case study of five Russian companies with Western participation showed the immense difficulties in communication because of different meanings given to words. For example, the concept of feedback in an organization meant "top-down control" to the Russian managers and "continuous involvement of employees" to their Western counterparts.

Message distortion can occur when the sender and receiver do not have the same frame of reference. We all have had different experiences that give different meanings to our present experiences. The attributes, background, organizational position, and culture of the sender and receiver might differ, causing them to interpret messages differently. Receivers can distort messages by making assumptions about the sender and what his message means. Such assumptions can cause the receiver to begin decoding and taking action before hearing the entire message. Both the meaning and the action might not be what the sender intended.

Senders can filter (subtract from) the content of a message either intentionally or unintentionally. **Message filtration** reduces a message's information content, possibly leading to misinterpretation by the receiver. The sender might intentionally filter a message because of fear of the receiver's reaction. The sender might unintentionally filter a message if he does not understand the problem or issue he wants to communicate. Both types of message filtration produce messages without enough information to let the receiver interpret them accurately.

Information overload is a communication dysfunction that happens when a person gets more information than he can process effectively. Receivers can react to information overload in several ways. They might ignore or screen out some messages to prevent overwhelming themselves with incoming information. Sometimes, receivers delay their responses to incoming messages to a later, less busy time. An overloaded sender or receiver might not immediately pass on information needed to understand a message, or he might duplicate a message already sent. In either case, the receiver asks questions to help him understand the intended meaning. These are especially dangerous reactions, because the duplication and questioning increase information overload throughout a communication system.

Message timing affects whether communication dysfunctions will happen. Messages with short deadlines do not leave enough time for accurate interpretation. The action taken by the receiver might not be the sender's intended action. Dysfunctions can also happen when a sender transmits a message well ahead of the time for action. Receivers do not always remember such messages, so no action takes place.

Senders get the action they want from a message only if the receiver accepts it. The sender's credibility and power play a central role in the acceptance. Such factors are important in organizational communication because the sender's position often gives him power over the receiver. This relationship is a central feature of superior–subordinate communication. If the subordinate does not consider the sender to be a credible source of a message, he is unlikely to accept the message.

Organizational silence, the absence of communication, is a serious communication dysfunction proposed by some contemporary researchers. Employees are unwilling to voice their views of organizational events. Organizational silence is not affected by noise, as are the other dysfunctions. Employees withhold their opinions about organizational matters because they believe it is futile or they will experience reprisal. The areas noted for organizational silence include pay inequity, decision procedures, unethical behavior, poor customer service, and the negative effects of organizational change.

Listening

Many communication professionals consider listening a primary skill for success in almost any activity. It is the first skill a person learns as a child, followed by speaking, reading, and writing. Listening is also a big part of human communication activities. Estimates suggest people spend about 50 percent of their time listening.

Listening is different from hearing. Hearing is a physiological process of detecting and processing sounds. **Listening** is the mental process of assigning meaning to sounds. The **listening process** includes both intrapersonal and interpersonal activities. A person receives a message from another person (interpersonal), tries to interpret it (intrapersonal), and responds to the other person to show the meaning given to the message (interpersonal). The process repeats during a communication interaction as both parties try to reach mutual understanding.

Active Listening

With **active listening**, the listener is responsible for the completeness of a speaker's message. A listener's role in the communication process is not to passively absorb a spoken message and derive meaning from it. With active listening, the listener is responsible for hearing a speaker's message correctly by accurately hearing the facts in a message and understanding the speaker's feelings about the message. An active listener makes a deliberate effort to understand a message from the speaker's viewpoint.

A message's meaning includes its content and the sender's feelings. In active listening, a listener attends to all verbal and nonverbal cues to get the total meaning. Verbal cues include message content, speed of speech, body movements, and the like. A listener asks questions to get the speaker to clarify a point. He might also rephrase the message until the speaker is satisfied that the listener understands. A manager can use active listening to help positively manage conflict. Active listening helps the manager understand the true wants of the parties to the conflict episode.

Active listening can have positive effects on the speaker, because the speaker knows that an active listener cares about the message, respects the speaker's opinion, and wants to understand the speaker. Active listening gives speakers the sense that their message is important and that the listener is sincerely interested.

Improving Communication Effectiveness

Improving communication effectiveness is possible throughout the communication process. The previous discussion of communication dysfunctions implied many of the following improvements.

Sender

Senders who understand the receiver's background and culture are more effective than senders who do not understand. A receiver's background includes education, social status, and professional or technical training. The last is important because of the special meaning such training can give to many words. Senders avoid using jargon to avoid communication dysfunctions. What a sender knows about the receiver helps him send messages with enough content to communicate as intended.

Knowing the receiver's culture is important when communicating across national boundaries. Senders must take special care when communicating (oral, written, or nonverbal) with people from other cultures.

Asking for oral or written feedback to a message helps a sender improve his communication effectiveness. The feedback gives the sender some observations on how the receiver perceived and interpreted the message. The sender can then adjust the message as needed for clearer understanding.

Formal training in written and oral communication can improve a sender's effectiveness. Training in written communication skills can focus on basic writing skills such as sentence structure and the right level of complexity for various audiences. Senders can also use software tools such as WhiteSmoke™ and RightWriter® to analyze their written communication. Although neither tool automatically makes a person a more effective writer, they offer observations on a person's writing that can improve effectiveness.

Receiver

A receiver can improve communication effectiveness by knowing and understanding the sender. If the sender is in an organization subunit that uses its own language, then the receiver needs to learn that language or ask the sender to clarify the message. The same suggestion applies to jargon used by senders with a professional or technical background. In both situations, the receiver is at a disadvantage in the communication process because he does not understand the sender's language.

The receiver's knowledge of himself can also improve communication effectiveness. If the receiver uses jargon or in-group language, he will interpret messages with that jargon in the background. The jargon introduces noise into the communication process and can distort the messages received. The receiver's perceptual process can also make the communication process less effective. Being aware of how jargon and his own perceptual process can alter the meaning of messages helps a receiver improve his communication effectiveness.

Receivers can use the feedback loop of the communication process to improve their role in that process. A receiver can ask a sender to clarify a message, especially if the sender typically uses jargon or in-group language. The receiver can also state his understanding of the message, so the sender can react to that interpretation. Both feedback activities require close interdependence between the sender and receiver to improve communication.

Message

The construction of the message can play a key role in communication effectiveness. Long messages with complex language are often difficult to understand. Messages using language that is highly different from the receiver's language can also be misinterpreted. Differences in language include jargon, in-group language, and languages of different cultures. Simple, concise messages, in language shared by the sender and receiver, are more effective than long, complex messages riddled with jargon.

Electronic message systems such as e-mail, voice-mail, local area networks, and computer conferencing systems let a sender transmit the same message quickly to many people. Such computer-based messages lack the feelings and emotional information that can come from non-verbal communication. To add nonverbal communication, Internet users developed emoticons ("smileys") to put some emotion into their text messages.

Medium

The message transmission medium should have little noise for the communication process to be effective. A sender can overcome or reduce noise in communication by using multiple channels. A manager can follow an oral message, such as instructions to a subordinate, with a written memo summarizing the conversation. The manager can also meet with a subordinate to discuss a memo sent earlier. In both cases, the manager is using multiple channels to improve communication effectiveness.

An earlier chapter's discussion of perception emphasized that people perceive high-contrast objects faster than low-contrast objects. A sender can introduce high contrast into messages by using a different color paper or ink than is normal for written communications. A sender can also change the setting in which he sends oral messages. Sitting behind a desk can imply formality and distance from the receiver. Sitting next to the receiver can imply informality and closeness.

Technology and Communication

Some forecasters predict that **technology and communication** will combine and lead to major changes in organizational communication processes in the future. Although these technologies are available to almost any organization, if they are to improve an organization's communication processes they must be used in various combinations. Existing and expected combinations of these technologies will cause nearly revolutionary changes in the way people will communicate in the future. These emerging technologies encourage the development of the "virtual groups" and "virtual organizations."

The telephone will remain a major communication device in developed nations. Major changes will come from fiber optics and new satellites. Digital cellular telephones allow communication among cellular users in most parts of the world. Laptop, notepad, and tablet personal computers (PCs) will include digital cellular facsimile devices and wireless Internet connectors. Combine these devices with digital communication satellites, and you can quickly see the flexibility and mobility of future communication.

Distributed computing technology exists now and will grow in use. An organization's members will continue to communicate directly on a computer network. Digital technology lets all forms of text, images, audio, video, and numeric data move over a network. Satellites and fiber optics allow high-speed connections among networks at any of an organization's locations. An organization with global operations, for example, could move all forms of information quickly to distant places. All of these factors combine to contribute to the growing phenomenon of "multicommunicating"—synchronous conversations that overlap.

Distributed computing also affects communication among organizations. The Internet links millions of people in more than 100 countries and is a fast-growing source of commerce. The Internet also lets students in different countries interact to complete their course work.

Social networking sites can link people in widely dispersed locations. Facebook, Twitter, MySpace, and LinkedIn help people interact worldwide. The Instant Messenger feature of AOL allows quick links among people. Such sites have an almost addictive quality, bonding people to the site and to each other.

A significant transformation of communication has happened, and will continue into the future, because of "social software." This software features Internet-based applications that help people communicate from almost anywhere. The following are the prominent forms of social software:

- Blogs: Web log; personal online journals
- Wikis: Collaborative Web sites that anyone can edit
- Social tagging: Online services that let people bookmark Web content

- Podcasting: Audio and video distributed over the Internet; can download to personal computers and iPods

PCs will continue to grow in use as communication tools. PCs equipped with modems, faxes, and wireless communication cards let people in an organization quickly communicate with each other. Satellite and fiber optic links enable them to transmit media, such as text, numeric data, graphic images, audio, and video images. By communicating with their PCs, people in different countries can lessen the effects of time zone differences. For example, someone in Calgary, Canada, can send an e-mail or fax to someone in Bucharest, Romania, before the latter person arrives at work.

Videoconferencing allows face-to-face communication over almost any distance. People in a videoconference can see each other, speak to each other, show graphic images, and send documents over the Internet. Such systems are a substitute for traveling to distant sites for meetings.

Existing technology also allows desktop videoconferencing in which a small camera mounted on a computer monitor sends the video image to the receiving computer. The other party has the same configuration, making two-way video and audio interaction possible. A window containing the video image opens on each person's computer. Other parts of the screen can show the text of a report the two parties are revising or graphics for an upcoming joint business presentation. Fiber optics, wireless technology, and new satellite technology allow desktop videoconferencing between locations almost anywhere in the world.

Multimedia PCs help users manage any form of information media. Such computers feature scanners, soundboards, business presentation software, CD-ROMs, and, for advanced users, animation software. Business presentations can include full-color three-dimensional graphics, photographs, video images, background sound, and text. Properly designed, such presentations can have dramatic effects on an audience. The overhead projector with black-and-white celluloid slides is giving way to multimedia business presentations controlled by a presenter and his PC. Such presentations make large audience communication not only possible, but also dramatic.

Communication Roles in Organizations

Individuals in organizations play different **communication roles** and serve different functions in the communication process. The five roles are initiator, relayer, liaison, terminator, and isolate. The following descriptions emphasize the relative frequency of communication behaviors of each role.

Initiators start communications and send more messages than they receive or pass on to someone else. **Relayers** receive and pass on more messages than they start or end. The liaison role is more complicated than either the initiator or relayer. **Liaisons** connect two parts of an organization but are not a members of either part. A liaison helps coordinate organizational functions by getting messages from one part of an organization to another. Liaisons can hinder message flow, however, if they become bottlenecks in a communication network. Managers can have all of these roles in organizations. Nonmanagers will most typically have relayer and liaison roles. Highly specialized nonmanagement employees, such as an Internet specialist, can have an initiator role because of a need to send critical information to other employees.

The last two roles involve more passive communication behavior. **Terminators** are at the end of a communication network and mainly receive messages. They infrequently send messages or relay information to others in the organization. **Isolates** are usually outside the normal communication process. They send, receive, or relay only a few messages.

Communication Networks

Communication in organizations takes place within a structured system called a **communication network**. Some networks form from an organization's design. Others emerge from informal social interaction within organizations.

Figure 7.3 shows several possible communication networks, using lines to show communication channels between nodes. Communication over a network is often bidirectional. The following discussion of communication networks applies to all communication forms, whether face-to-face, by electronic media, or by video media.

Pair-wise communication is any form of oral or written communication between two people. It occurs between superiors and subordinates, between individuals of different status with no direct reporting relationship, between peers, and between friends. Whenever you chat with a friend, for example, you are involved in pair-wise communication. Each person in a pair focuses attention on the other person. This feature distinguishes pair-wise communication from the other forms of communication described in this section. The direction of pair-wise communication can be top down, bottom up, or lateral.

Small group communication networks involve three or more people directly interacting during the communication. The groups can be face to face or widely dispersed if the communication process uses an audio, video, or computer-based medium. Small group communication occurs within an organization's departments, work units, and teams, and within an organization's informal groups. Communication interaction within small groups rotates among group members in either a structured or a random pattern. Whether the group is in one location or dispersed, communication occurs within either a centralized or a decentralized communication network.

Centralized communication networks have a single person as a key figure in sending and receiving messages, no matter where they go in the network. In centralized networks, only one or a few parts of the network have the potential to get information. Branch managers of banks often have this communication role between their branch and other parts of the bank organization.

Decentralized communication networks feature freely flowing communication with no person playing a central or controlling role. Decentralized networks spread the potential to get information throughout the network, so that

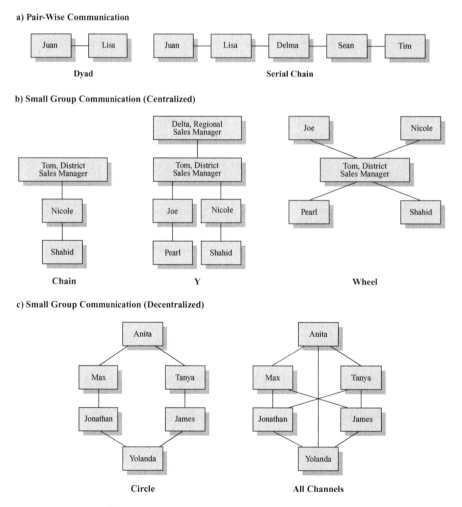

Figure 7.3 Communication Networks

all parts have about equal information status. No person in the network depends exclusively on anyone else. For example, many insurance companies let their claims processors make almost all decisions about a claim without referring to anyone else in the company.

Centralized and decentralized communication networks have different advantages and disadvantages. Centralized networks are faster and have fewer errors when solving simple problems or tasks, but are less effective with complex problems or tasks. Decentralized networks are faster and more accurate with complex problems than with simple problems. They also process more messages and yield higher satisfaction among network members, whatever the type of problem or task.

Large audience communication gets a message from one person or a few people and delivers it to many people. The sender designs a message before sending it to the audience. Such messages usually are sent continuously with no interruption from the audience. The audience can include 20, hundreds, thousands, or, with the help of radio and television, millions of people. Some typical organization examples are department meetings, briefing sessions, training programs, orientation meetings, and new product or service introductions.

International Aspects of Organizational Communication

This chapter alluded several times to cross-cultural issues in communication. Those issues go beyond the spoken and written language of another country. Although English is widely spoken when doing business in non-English-speaking countries, nonnative speakers will not always understand your message correctly, owing to nonverbal communication differences.

Nonverbal communication often has different meanings in different countries. North Americans ordinarily stand 5½ to 8 feet apart while speaking. In Latin American cultures, people stand much closer. When a North American speaks to a Latin American in that person's home country, the Latin American moves close to the North American, who then feels uncomfortable and backs away. The Latin American might perceive the North American as cold and distant, an unintended communication of the nonverbal behavior.

Time orientation and the meaning of time also differ widely among cultures. Latin Americans view time more casually than North Americans. North Americans value promptness in keeping appointments, a nonverbal behavior that the Swiss even more strongly emphasize. A North American or a Swiss might feel insulted if someone is late for an appointment, even though no insult was intended.

Egyptians usually do not look to the future, which they define as anything more than a week away. South Asians think of the long term as centuries, not the typical five- or ten-year view of North Americans. The Sioux Indians of the United States do not have words for "time," "wait," or "waiting" in their native language. You can readily see that misunderstandings about time could arise in a face-to-face business meeting of people from different countries or among people in a culturally diverse workforce.

CONFLICT IN ORGANIZATIONS

Joseph E. Champoux

Conflict is doubt or questioning, opposition, incompatible behavior, controversy, or antagonistic interaction. Conflict in organizations includes interactions in which (1) one party opposes another party or (2) one party tries to block another party from reaching his goals. The range of events considered conflict is deliberately broad. It includes disagreements, debates, disputes, and active efforts to prevent a party from getting what he wants. Critical elements of conflict are interdependence with another party and the perception of incompatible goals. The parties in conflict can be individuals, entire groups within the organization, or members of virtual teams at scattered locations.

Conflict is a basic organizational process that needs managing. Some conflict scholars argue that conflict is vital to continuous improvement in organizations and that conflict management is crucial to its successful use. Many managers, however, believe they should eliminate conflict from their organizations. Social scientists who have studied conflict have usually focused on its negative results. Although this chapter's observations are supported by the results of much conflict research, you will find parts of this chapter unsettling if you have a negative view of conflict.

Conflict in organizations is a fascinating subject in its own right and something that any manager needs to understand thoroughly.

Later, this chapter describes conflict as happening in episodes. As the conflict episodes rise and fall, periods of cooperation might occur. Task groups where members must work together to reach their goals often display a common pattern. At some point, especially in the group's early stages of development, the members can fiercely disagree about how to reach the group's goals. Conflict develops at this point as discussions and disagreements. If the members of the group eventually agree about how to reach the goals, the conflict recedes and cooperation returns.

The chapter's perspective does not view conflict as bad for an organization or suggest that managers should remove all conflict. This perspective views conflict as an inevitable part of organization life and as necessary for organizational growth and survival. The latter is especially true if the organization is in an environment requiring innovation and change.

Conflict management, including both increasing and decreasing conflict, is a basic responsibility of any manager. The goals of this chapter are to (1) help you develop an understanding about conflict processes in organizations and (2) show you how to diagnose conflict situations. This knowledge can help you do a better job of conflict management.

Functional and Dysfunctional Conflict

Functional conflict works toward the goals of an organization or a group. **Dysfunctional conflict** blocks an organization or a group from reaching its goals. Conflict is dysfunctional when it is either higher than needed by a group to reach its goals or so low that a group is less effective than it could be in reaching its goals. Because the boundary between functional and dysfunctional conflict is often fuzzy, deciding what level of conflict is functional requires a manager to understand both the positive and the negative results of conflict. A knowledgeable manager then tries to manage conflict to keep it within functional bounds.

Conflict that is functional in one group can be dysfunctional in another group. A process analysis team that is trying to solve a difficult quality problem, for example, might need more conflict than a group doing routine tasks. The conflict requirements of a group or an entire organization can also change with time. Conflict that is functional at one point can be dysfunctional at another point. Organizations or groups that have enjoyed an unchanging environment might need more conflict to help adapt to a turbulent environment.

Dysfunctionally high conflict can produce excessive levels of tension, anxiety, and stress. It can drive out people who could be valuable to the group but cannot tolerate such a high level of conflict. Dysfunctionally high conflict can also reduce trust, leading to continual antagonistic interactions. As a result, one or more parties to the conflict might withhold or distort information. Poor-quality decision making can result when conflict reaches a dysfunctional level. The conflict can also absorb management's attention, diverting valuable resources from other tasks.

Dysfunctionally low conflict is the opposite of dysfunctionally high conflict. The organization or group does not encourage new ideas or tolerate different points of view. Decisions are made with poor information. The organization encourages traditional approaches, although the external environment requires innovation and change. This description of dysfunctional conflict might strike you as strange because of the widespread idea that conflict is bad for organizations.

Conflict management involves maintaining conflict at a level that is functional for the group. If the conflict level is dysfunctionally high, managers should reduce the conflict. If the conflict level is dysfunctionally low, managers should increase the conflict. Much of the rest of this chapter will show you how to manage conflict to get functional results.

Levels and Types of Conflict in Organizations

Organization conflict occurs at several levels and appears in different forms. The various levels and types of conflict often have different sources and roots.

Understanding the levels and types of conflict can help a person diagnose a conflict episode and effectively manage conflict.

Intraorganization Conflict

Intraorganization conflict includes all types of conflict occurring within an organization. This type of conflict occurs at the interfaces of organization functions created by the design of the organization. Such conflict can occur along the vertical and horizontal dimensions of the organization. Vertical conflict develops between managers and subordinates. Horizontal conflict occurs between departments and workgroups. Two department managers, for example, might be in conflict because the organization has not clearly defined their areas of authority. Their decision-making areas overlap, and each wants the other to give up some authority.

Other types of intraorganization conflict are intragroup conflict and intergroup conflict. **Intragroup conflict** is conflict among members of a group. Conflict within a group is likely to be highest during the early stages of group development when there are strong differences among members. The conflict can be about ways of doing tasks or reaching the group's goals. **Intergroup conflict** is conflict between two or more groups in an organization. This type of conflict often has its roots in the organization's design.

Interpersonal conflict happens between two or more people, such as between a customer and a sales clerk or between two people within an organization. Interpersonal conflict is the most basic form of conflict behavior in organizations. Although the previous discussions focused on the interfaces at which intraorganization conflict can happen, the conflict behavior actually occurs at the interpersonal level.

Interpersonal conflict happens for many reasons, including basic differences in views about what should be done, efforts to get more resources to do a job, or differences in orientation to work and time in different parts of an organization. Interpersonal conflict can also arise because of intrapersonal conflict. A person might release the internal tension of intrapersonal conflict by lashing out at someone during an interpersonal interaction.

Intrapersonal Conflict

Intrapersonal conflict happens within an individual. The conflict arises because of a threat to the person's basic values, because of a feeling of unfair treatment by the organization, or from multiple and contradictory sources of socialization. Cognitive dissonance describes how people react to intrapersonal conflict. People will feel internally uncomfortable and try to reduce the discomfort. Another form of intrapersonal conflict is negative inequity. Individuals who perceive themselves as getting less for their contributions to the organization than they believe they deserve experience intrapersonal conflict.

Intrapersonal conflict can also arise when an employee sees actions within an organization that he considers illegal or unethical. Individuals base such judgments on their personal values and ethics. The tension created by the intrapersonal conflict can lead the individual to act directly against the organization. This act of "whistle blowing" pits the individual against other members of the organization in what can become extremely heated conflict behavior.

Interorganization Conflict

Interorganization conflict is conflict between two or more organizations that results from relationships between them. For example, an organization might become highly dependent on its suppliers or distributors, increasing the potential for conflict over delivery times or other agreements. The hostile takeover of one organization by another is also a form of interorganization conflict.

Interorganization conflict differs from competition between organizations. Two organizations can compete in the same market without engaging in conflict behavior. Burger King and McDonald's are competitors in the fast-food business, but neither organization tries to prevent the other from doing business.

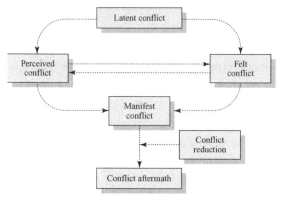

Figure 8.1 Conflict Episode Model

Conflict Episodes

Conflict processes in organizations occur as a series of **conflict episodes** that rise, fall, and vary in duration. The episode model used in this chapter is one of several such models in the research literature. Although the models vary in specific features, they have common elements. Each sees antecedents to conflict (latent conflict) that lead to conflict behavior. An episode ends with an aftermath that links it to a later episode. Figure 8.1 shows the stages of a conflict episode.

Latent Conflict

Latent conflict includes factors in the person, group, or organization that might lead to conflict behavior. These conditions are conflict antecedents and are a potential for conflict in an organization.

Think of latent conflict as lurking in the background waiting for the right conditions to emerge as conflict behavior. Just as a latent image on a piece of exposed film becomes visible in the presence of certain chemicals, latent conflict

rises to the level of awareness under certain conditions. Some basic forms of latent conflict are scarce resources, such as limited budgets or equipment, and incompatible goals of both individuals and groups. More than one form of latent conflict can be present at the same time. A later section, "Latent Conflict: Sources of Conflict in Organizations," describes several types of latent conflict found in organizations.

Perceived Conflict

Even when latent conflict factors are present, conflict might not be perceived by those potentially in conflict. **Perceived conflict** is the moment when the parties to a conflict become aware of the conflict. Two mechanisms limit perceived conflict. People can block out mild conflict by suppressing their awareness of it. If many conflict conditions exist in an organization, individuals might focus selectively on them, letting them successfully manage the conflict. All the perceptual mechanisms operate for perceived conflict.

Latent conflict does not always precede the perception of conflict. People can perceive themselves in conflict when no latent conditions exist.

A common example is misunderstanding another person's position on an issue. The misperception substitutes for the antecedent.

Felt Conflict

Felt conflict is the emotional part of a conflict episode. At least one individual personalizes the conflict and focuses on the parties involved, losing sight of the underlying issues. Some conflict episodes never enter the felt conflict stage. Two individuals disagree, but neither feels any hostility toward the other. They treat the disagreement as an issue to settle that has nothing to do with them personally.

Other conflict episodes have a strong felt conflict element. Feelings between the two parties can become intense. They express hostility orally and in extreme cases physically. This type of conflict episode is what you likely recall if you have strong negative feelings about conflict. The arrow from perceived conflict to felt conflict in Figure 8.1 shows the possibility of personalizing conflict after the parties perceive the presence of the conditions for conflict. Conflict episodes with strong felt conflict are among the more difficult to manage well.

Felt conflict also includes the values and attitudes the parties to a conflict episode hold about each other. High levels of trust and a value orientation of interpersonal cooperation can lead to lower perceived conflict. The opposite attitudes and values can lead to high perceived conflict. The arrow from felt conflict to perceived conflict in Figure 8.1 shows that felt conflict can lead to perceived conflict.

Manifest Conflict

Manifest conflict is the actual conflict behavior between the parties to the conflict episode. It includes oral, written, or physical aggression. Oral manifestations are the arguments often seen either between the parties or between other people. Written manifest conflict is the exchange of memoranda or other documents designed to make a point or win an argument. Physical aggression is strongly negative conflict behavior intended to injure an opponent.

Some research notes that any party in a conflict episode can involve others outside the episode. The other people include coworkers or friends. The person who engages another person can share perceptions of the conflict, trying to make sense of an episode. Such sensemaking behavior is likely to happen when a conflict episode continues for an extended period.

Conflict Aftermath

Conflict episodes end with a **conflict aftermath**. If the conflict episode is settled to the satisfaction of the parties involved, the conflict aftermath will be clear of any potential latent conflict for a new episode. When the conflict ends, but the basis of the conflict is still present, the aftermath holds the latent conflict for a new conflict episode. For example, disputes over the allocation of scarce resources often are settled by compromise. No one gets exactly what they want, so the aftermath contains the latent desires for more resources. A new episode might start later because of the latent conflict left in the aftermath of a previous episode. As you will see later, each method of reducing conflict leaves a different conflict aftermath.

Relationships Among Conflict Episodes

Figure 8.2 shows the relationships among conflict episodes. Each conflict episode links to the next by the connection between the conflict aftermath and the latent conflict. Breaking that connection is the challenge of effective conflict management. Effective long-term reduction of dysfunctionally high conflict requires discovering the latent conflict and removing it from the conflict aftermath. You will discover that it is not always possible to completely clear the aftermath of a conflict episode. In this sense, conflict is a fact of organization life.

Conflict Frames and Orientations

People approach conflict episodes with different perceptual frames. They also have different conflict orientations that can affect their behavior during an episode. If you must manage conflict, understanding these frames and orientations can help you diagnose conflict.

Conflict frames are the perceptual sets that people bring to conflict episodes. They act as perceptual filters, removing some information from the episode and emphasizing other information. Research has identified conflict frames that vary along three dimensions:

- **Relationship–task:** A **relationship** emphasis focuses on the parties' interpersonal relationship. A **task** emphasis focuses on the material aspects of an episode, such as a budget.
- **Emotional–intellectual:** An **emotional** emphasis focuses on feelings in the episode (felt conflict). An **intellectual** emphasis focuses on observed behavior (manifest conflict).
- **Cooperate–win:** A **cooperation** focus emphasizes the role of all parties to the conflict. A party with a **winning** focus wants to maximize personal gain.

Some limited research shows the different frames' effects in conflict episodes. People can start an episode with different conflict frames, but end the episode with the same frame. Those who end an episode with a relationship or intellectual

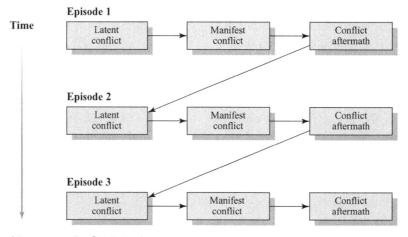

Figure 8.2 Relationships among Conflict Episodes

frame feel good about their relationship with the other party. Cooperation-focused people end an episode with more positive results than those focused on winning.

Conflict orientations are different behavioral patterns that people bring to a conflict episode. Understanding your orientation and the possible orientations of others can help you understand behavior in the episode. Some conflict orientations overlap with some conflict frames.

The five conflict orientations are dominance, collaborative, compromise, avoidance, and accommodative:

- **Dominance:** Person wants to win the conflict episode and overwhelm the other party; views conflict episodes as battles to fight and win.
- **Collaborative:** Person wants to satisfy the desires of all parties to the conflict and sincerely wants to find a solution that satisfies everyone.
- **Compromise:** Person splits the difference so each party gets part of what it wants.
- **Avoidance:** Person backs away from a conflict episode, possibly because of low tolerance for conflict.
- **Accommodative:** Person focuses on the other party's needs and desires, ignoring his own needs and desires.

A person's orientation toward conflict can change as the conflict episode unfolds. Whether a change in orientation occurs depends on how firmly the person holds to the orientation, the importance of the issues to the person, and his perception of an opponent's power. A dominance-oriented person presses to win important issues, but can shift to a compromise orientation. The shift can happen if the person perceives that the other party's power and potential to win the conflict episode are stronger.

Each orientation affects the conflict episode aftermath differently. Avoidance, accommodative, and dominance orientations leave well-defined aftermaths that can result in later conflict. A collaborative orientation can leave the cleanest aftermath when it successfully identifies and satisfies the desires of all parties to the conflict. A clean aftermath reduces the chance of future conflict over the same issues. Compromise is a middle ground, leaving some aftermath, but not as much as the first three orientations.

Research evidence strongly shows that a collaborative orientation to conflict yields more positive long-term benefits for organizations than the other four orientations. Benefits include better-quality decisions, increased trust, and increased satisfaction with the results of a conflict episode.

Latent Conflict: Sources of Conflict in Organizations

Recall that latent conflict is the antecedent to a conflict episode. Many natural conditions of organizations act as latent conflict. Such latencies lurk in the background and trigger conflict when the right conditions occur. The presence of latent conflict does not always lead to manifest conflict, although the latencies create high conflict potential. It is also important to understand latent conflict because the latencies provide clues about how to reduce dysfunctionally high conflict.

The types of latent conflict described in this section are major sources of organizational conflict. They are representative, but not exhaustive, of conflict sources. Creative diagnosis of organizational conflict requires identifying conflict latencies. Any specific conflict episode can have variations in latent conflict.

Dependence on **scarce resources** is a common latent conflict in organizations. The scarce resources can be tangible—such as money, equipment, and facilities—or intangible—such as knowledge and expertise. Individuals or groups often find themselves dependent on the same facility to do their work. The resource is finite and cannot be expanded quickly. The dependence on the single facility can bring individuals into conflict. A common example is a single copying machine within a department. Several people could want to use the machine simultaneously, and an argument could erupt between two potential users. The single machine as a scarce resource is the latency for the conflict episode.

Organizational differentiation produces groups and work units with different goals, time horizons, views of the world, and languages. For example, research and development people typically think in the long term and have their own scientific jargon. Production people want to get tasks done now according to a specific schedule. The various orientations produced by this differentiation form a latency that can lead to a conflict episode when members of the different units must interact.

Organizations have many **rules, procedures, and policies** to guide decision making about recurring events. The rules, procedures, and policies that can help produce a smooth-functioning organization also can act as a latent conflict. This type of latent conflict could be lurking in your college or university. Each school usually has policies governing when a new section of a class can be opened. For example, your school might say 100 students must be enrolled in a section of a course before the school opens a new section. A professor, however, might prefer that his classes not exceed 60 students. The professor closes the class at 60. Students complain to an administrator. The administrator and the professor begin a conflict

episode, the latency for which was a previously existing policy.

Cohesive groups develop a culture of their own. The members of such groups strongly identify with the group and care about what it represents. Groups also can differ in what they value. Conflict can start when members of such groups interact with each other.

High **interdependence** among people at work is another source of conflict in organizations. Interdependence can come from job design, with jobs linked to each other. It also can be found where work is designed around groups and not individuals. Whatever its source, interdependence in organizations forces people to interact with each other. The required interaction increases the potential for conflict within the organization.

Communication barriers are another source of latent conflict in organizations. If individuals or groups do not interact frequently with each other, misunderstandings can develop between the groups. This type of latent conflict is common in organizations with shift work. The day shift does not interact with the evening shift except briefly at a shift change. Members of each shift develop opinions about the quality of the other shift's work. As those opinions become diverse, the potential for conflict during the shift change increases.

Ambiguous jurisdictions occur when the organization has not clearly defined areas of decision authority. "Turf battles" erupt when two people or groups believe they have responsibility for the same activity. This type of latent conflict is common in a matrix organization, if the organization has not clearly defined the areas of jurisdiction. Many people in such organizations work for more than one person. Conflict can arise when those people receive conflicting orders from their multiple bosses.

The reward system of the organization is another area of latent conflict. **Reward systems** that encourage different and incompatible behavior are a significant source of latent conflict. A common example is the design of reward systems for sales and manufacturing people. Salespeople receive a commission for selling. Manufacturing managers get rewards for keeping costs down. Salespeople can make more sales by offering early delivery dates, but those dates might not fit into manufacturing's production schedule. The conflict potential is high and can lead to a conflict episode when sales and manufacturing interact.

Conflict Management

Conflict management focuses on maintaining conflict at functional levels for a department, work unit, or entire organization. Conflict management does not mean the elimination of conflict, nor does it refer only to conflict reduction. It means maintaining conflict at the right level to help the department, work unit, or organization reach its goals.

Basic to the process of conflict management is the choice of a **desired conflict level**. The desired conflict level varies according to the **perceived conflict requirements** of the unit. Several factors affect the choice of the desired conflict level. Organizational cultures place differing values on debate, disagreement, and conflict. Managers in organizational cultures that support debate, doubt, and questioning might perceive a higher desired conflict level than managers in cultures that do not. The nature of the organization's product or service also affects the desired conflict level. Creative and innovative products or services require a higher level of conflict than more routine and predictable products and services. Organizations facing fast-changing external environments require higher conflict levels for successful adaptation than organizations facing stable external environments.

Desired conflict levels for an organization, department, or work unit can vary from one group to another and for the same group over time. If an organization's environment shifts from stable to turbulent, then the right level of conflict can become higher. A shift in the opposite direction can cause the right level of conflict to become lower.

The preceding paragraphs emphasized a manager's perception of the desired conflict level. The manager's **tolerance for conflict** affects his perception of a unit's conflict requirements. A manager who avoids conflict likely has a lower tolerance for conflict than a manager who actively engages in functional conflict behavior. Even when a work unit requires a specific conflict level, a manager's tolerance for conflict affects his perception of the desired level.

Figure 8.3 shows the conflict management process. The figure shows the process as a thermostat, emphasizing a manager's monitoring of conflict levels. If conflict levels are at a functional level, the manager (thermostat) does nothing. If the conflict level is **dysfunctionally high**, the

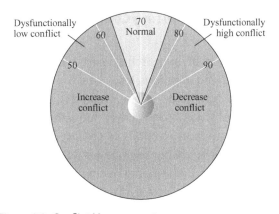

Figure 8.3 Conflict Management

manager tries to reduce the conflict. If the conflict level is **dysfunctionally low**, the manager tries to increase the conflict. In the same way that a thermostat maintains a desired room temperature, conflict management maintains a desired conflict level.

What are the symptoms that a manager can read to decide whether the conflict level is dysfunctionally high or low? Low trust in a work unit, deliberate distortion of information, high levels of tension during interpersonal interactions, and antagonism between parties are all signs of dysfunctionally high conflict. In extreme cases, dysfunctional conflict can take the form of sabotage of the organization's products or services or violence against other parties.

Suppression and withdrawal are two symptoms of dysfunctionally low conflict. Suppression includes denial of differences and a desire to perceive similarities between parties that do not exist. Repressing controversial information and prohibiting disagreements about legitimate issues also are signs of suppression. Withdrawal includes reduced communication to avoid interactions that could lead to controversy, the belief in "peace at any price," and walking away from a disagreeable interaction.

Reducing Conflict

Three types of approaches exist for **reducing conflict** in organizations: lose–lose, win–lose, and win–win. Although these approaches usually are called methods of conflict resolution, this chapter refers to them as methods of conflict reduction, because many do not remove conflict. Managers should use caution when reducing conflict to ensure it does not fall to a dysfunctionally low level.

U.S. organizations are increasingly convinced of the effectiveness of conflict reduction training.

Training programs are now widely used. Some research points to their effectiveness in successfully reducing conflict.

Lose–lose methods of conflict reduction do not try to deal directly with the conflict. None of the parties to the conflict episode get what they want. These methods of conflict reduction leave a conflict aftermath that can start a new conflict episode about the same issues. Sometimes the lose–lose approaches ignore the conflict and do not try to reduce it. Typical lose–lose methods include avoidance, compromise, and third-party intervention.

Avoidance is an obvious way to reduce conflict in the short run, but it does not permanently reduce the conflict. A conflict episode can recur when the parties meet again. Withdrawal can happen because one party to the conflict has a low tolerance for conflict or because one party has an avoidance orientation to conflict. The conflict episode is stressful, and the party simply wants to avoid the confrontation. Anyone trying to manage conflict must be aware of the prospect of avoidance. Although manifest conflict levels will not be high, the latent conflict is still there. Later conflict episodes can arise and surprise those managing conflict.

Compromise uses bargaining and negotiation to reduce conflict. Each party to the conflict gives up something to get something he values. Although manifest conflict drops, there is no clear conflict aftermath. The parties to the conflict have not completely resolved the underlying issues. When the latent conflict is scarce resources, compromise is a common reduction method, because resources often cannot be expanded quickly. The conflict over the copying machine described earlier offers an opportunity for compromise. Let each party copy part of what he needs and return later to copy the rest. The manifest conflict behavior subsides, but the latent conflict stays.

Third-party intervention often asks a neutral person for a solution to a conflict episode. Arbitration of labor disputes is a common example of third-party intervention. The third party might try to reduce the conflict by giving something to each party in the conflict episode. In this respect, it is much like compromise, with the third party suggesting the compromise. Also, as with compromise, a conflict aftermath follows the episode. The issues often are not satisfactorily settled for all concerned. A manager can also act as the third party, but managers are rarely neutral in their view of the conflict episode.

Win–lose conflict reduction methods make one party to the conflict a clear winner and the other party a clear loser. Such techniques leave a conflict aftermath that can result in a new conflict episode about the same issues. The techniques include dominance, authoritative command, and majority rule.

Dominance happens when one party to a conflict overwhelms the other. Dominance can occur because one party has higher organization status or more power. It can also happen when one party to the conflict has a low tolerance for conflict. You can think of dominance as the other side of avoidance. If one party has an appeasement or avoidance conflict orientation, the other party can easily dominate the episode. Dominance leaves a conflict aftermath because it does not try to discover why the conflict occurred.

Organizations widely use **authoritative command** for conflict reduction, partly because of the formal authority relationships found there. Two people in conflict refer their conflict to a common superior who decides the solution to the conflict. Manifest conflict stops, but the conflict episode ends with a conflict aftermath.

Decision-making groups faced with conflict over issues can use **majority rule** to reduce the conflict. Each issue is put to a vote, letting some members of the group win and others lose. If the

alternatives are acceptable to all concerned, this method can work effectively. If the same people lose repeatedly and personalize the loss, majority rule leaves a potentially destructive aftermath.

With **win–win** conflict reduction methods, parties to the conflict episode get what they want. These methods include problem solving, integration, and a superordinate goal. Win–win approaches do not leave a conflict aftermath, because they directly address the causes of the conflict and try to remove them. Although these techniques do not strongly differ, they have some useful distinctions.

Problem solving tries to find the true basis of a conflict episode. This method tries to fully expose all differences among the parties. All parties to the conflict encourage and support minority views to ensure they get full expression. Minority views often positively contribute to group performance. The parties view differences as important sources of information leading to creative solutions to the conflict. Organizations and managers that use problem solving do not view conflict negatively. They see conflict episodes as constructive opportunities for creative solutions to problems. Properly done, problem solving leaves little or no conflict aftermath.

Integration seeks solutions that are in the best interests of all parties. It assumes that people's deeply held interests and desires are the basis of conflict. This approach tries to find a solution that fully meets the goals of each party.

A **superordinate goal** is a goal desired by all parties to the conflict but unattainable by any party alone. Superordinate goals compel cooperation even if the parties otherwise do not want to cooperate. Organizations using group-based incentive programs are using a form of superordinate goal. Everyone in the group wants to get the reward, but no one can do it alone.

Superordinate goals should work well where the latent conflict is high interdependence. The superordinate goal operates in the background, forcing the members of the group to cooperate. Later conflict episodes are less likely in the presence of a continually operating superordinate goal.

Increasing Conflict

Conflict management includes **increasing conflict** when it is dysfunctionally low. The goal of increasing conflict is to get the functional qualities of conflict described earlier, such as more information for decisions and creative solutions to problems. Increasing conflict must be done skillfully and cautiously so conflict levels do not become dysfunctionally high. The manager's role is to structure situations as described in this section and not express opinions or take positions on issues. This role is especially important, because it can encourage subordinates to express their views.

Groups with members of different social backgrounds, education, expertise, organization positions, and opinions have high conflict potential. By deliberately forming **heterogeneous groups** to find creative solutions to problems, a manager tries to use the functional qualities of conflict. Organizations with a diverse workforce have an especially rich resource for forming groups with high conflict potential.

A manager of a decision-making group can ask one group member to play the **devil's advocate** role. This person deliberately criticizes a position that has emerged as dominant within the group. Alternatively, the manager can ask each person in the group to critique the alternatives under consideration. Each approach recognizes the information-generating function of conflict.

Dialectical inquiry is a structured debate of opposing views about solutions to a decision problem. Two people or groups prepare arguments and debate the question in the presence of the person who makes the final decision. One argument presents the prevailing opinion about a decision. The other argument presents a believable and plausible alternative. The decision maker forms a final decision by drawing upon information presented by both sides.

Managers can also try to **develop an organizational culture** with a set of values and norms that support openness about debate and opinions. They must devote time to building this type of culture. Searching for quick solutions to problems can lead to pressure to reduce differences and emphasize similarities.

International Aspects of Conflict in Organizations

The research and conceptual models underlying this chapter are mainly of North American origin. They likely require modification when considering cross-cultural differences in the meaning of conflict and its related concepts. Cultures of various countries place differing values on conflict. Cultures that emphasize individualism and competition among people likely positively value conflict. English-speaking countries, the Netherlands, Italy, and Belgium are examples. Cultures that emphasize collaboration, cooperation, and conformity likely negatively value conflict. Examples include many Asian and Latin American countries, Portugal, Greece, and Turkey. Although there is no direct research evidence, such cultural differences imply that different conflict levels are functional for organizations in different countries.

As noted in the previous chapter, cross-cultural research has studied intergroup processes, the processes within which intergroup conflict happens. The research implies that collaborative and cooperative cultures expect little conflict during intergroup interactions. They favor suppression of conflict with little discussion about people's feelings during a conflict episode. Felt conflict will likely be part of some conflict episodes, but hidden from public view.

Managers from an individualistic country face some dilemmas when managing conflict in a less individualistic country. Because they believe that expression of feelings during a conflict episode is acceptable, the suppression of feelings could baffle them. The idea that increasing conflict in such countries can be good might confuse local people. A manager might believe that more conflict will produce more information, better ideas, and innovation, but the local culture might not support that behavior. The result could be almost immediate dysfunctional results.

Ethical Issues About Conflict in Organizations

Potential differences in people's tolerance for conflict suggest some ethical issues. Experiencing conflict levels that are much higher than a person's tolerance level can lead to stress. A manager with a high tolerance for conflict might deliberately keep conflict levels higher than subordinates want. The ethical question pivots on whether such managers should reveal their intentions about desired conflict levels. Full disclosure would let subordinates leave the group if they found the conflict levels dysfunctionally stressful. Disclosure would be needed when new people are considered for employment or when a new manager takes over an existing group.

Managers can create conditions that increase conflict potential in an organization. Deliberately increasing conflict is an effort to guide behavior in a desired direction. Some methods, such as using a devil's advocate in a decision-making group, often are obvious to group members. Other methods, such as building a group with heterogeneous members, are less obvious. Subtle methods of increasing conflict connote manipulation of people's behavior, raising an ethical issue. Full disclosure by managers can help. Managers can openly state their intention to use conflict to generate ideas and innovation. If people are then free to join a group or not, the ethical issue likely subsides.

People in organizations might experience intrapersonal conflict from requests to act against their moral values, or from observing behavior they consider unethical. In both cases, the people might feel compelled to act, such as reporting unethical acts, seeking a transfer to another part of the organization, or quitting the organization altogether.

Optimal conflict levels can vary among countries. The ethical issue centers on whether managers should honor such values even if their home country values support higher conflict levels.

Summary

Conflict in organizations is opposition, incompatible behaviors, or antagonistic interaction. It includes interactions in which one party opposes another party, or one party tries to prevent or block another party from reaching his goals. Conflict can have both functional and dysfunctional effects on an organization.

Conflict behavior happens within interpersonal interactions, between groups (intergroup), within groups (intragroup), and between organizations (interorganization). Other conflict behavior starts because people experience strong conflicts within themselves (intrapersonal).

Conflict in organizations has an episodic quality. Many aspects of organizations act as the conflict latencies that can start an episode. Latent conflict lies dormant until conditions are right for the conflict to emerge as manifest conflict. The latter is the actual conflict behavior between the parties in a conflict episode. Managers can try to reduce the conflict by using a conflict reduction method. Conflict episodes often end with a conflict aftermath that can become the latent conflict for a later episode.

There are many methods for reducing and increasing conflict. Most methods of conflict reduction leave a conflict aftermath. A few, such as integration and resource expansion, do not. Managers must carefully use the methods for increasing conflict so conflict levels do not become dysfunctionally high.

Countries differ in the levels of conflict that are functional. For example, collectivistic countries have a lower level of functional conflict than.

GROUPS AND INTERGROUP PROCESSES

Joseph E. Champoux

Groups, group dynamics, and intergroup processes are inevitable and critical aspects of organizations and their management. This chapter builds upon premises that emphasize the inevitability of groups in organizations. Those premises view groups as having both good and bad effects for organizations and their members. The chapter also examines the growing use of virtual groups and self-managing teams.

A **group** is an interdependent set of people doing a task or trying to reach a common goal. Group members regularly interact with each other and depend on each other to do their tasks. Job and organizational design can affect the degree of mutual dependence. A group is a complex, adaptive system that can change its membership, goals, and structure over time.

Groups can powerfully affect people's behavior. Knowledge of how and why groups form, and an understanding of their dynamics, can help you function better within a group or manage group activities. The following classic statement captures this chapter's orientation toward groups in organizations: "[G]roups exist; they are inevitable and ubiquitous; they mobilize powerful forces having profound effects upon individuals; these effects may be good or bad; and through a knowledge of group dynamics there lies the possibility of maximizing their good value."

Formal and Informal Groups

Formal groups are either functional groups within an organization or task groups. Functional groups are clusters of people formed by the organization's design, such as divisions, departments, sections, and work units. They are a product of the organization's division of labor, the way the organization has divided its total work to reach its goals. Such groups are often permanent, but can change if the organization redesigns its structure.

Organizations form task groups as temporary groups to carry out specific duties, usually special projects. Committees, project teams, and task forces are examples of task groups. Other examples from quality management are process-action teams and continuous-improvement teams. Temporary task groups do not have the enduring qualities of permanent groups, because they usually disband when they finish their assignment.

Virtual groups and self-managing teams are emerging types of formal groups. Networked computers and workstations link members of virtual groups. Self-managing teams typically have high internal autonomy and decision authority about work scheduling, team member assignments, and the choice of a team leader. Later sections examine both virtual groups and self-managing teams in detail.

Interaction patterns within organizations can affect the formation of informal groups within and across formal groups. **Informal groups** can form along interest lines, such as the task specialization of individuals, hobbies, or other concerns. They might be friendship groups whose members associate with each other both at work and away from work. Outsiders and newcomers cannot readily see informal groups, which are part of an organization's background. These informal groups form a "shadow organization" that applies good and bad powerful forces to the organization.

Basic Concepts for Understanding Groups in Organizations

Several basic concepts will help you understand the dynamics of groups in organizations. Group members take on specific roles within the group. A **role** is a set of activities, duties, responsibilities, and required behaviors. It is also a set of shared expectations about how a person ought to behave in a group. Both the organization and the group help define a person's role.

Group **norms** are unwritten rules that define acceptable role behavior of group members. Norms include performance levels valued by the group, teamwork within the group, and relationships with managers and other aspects of the formal organization. New members learn a group's norms from its socialization process, a process described in the later section "Workgroup Socialization."

A **cohesive group** has members who are attracted to the group's task, to its prestige, and to other members of the group. Members of cohesive groups like to be together, care about each other, and typically know each other well. A cohesive group can also pressure a new member to conform to its norms. Some research suggests that cohesive groups can perform better than noncohesive groups.

Two types of **conformity** to group norms are possible: compliance and personal acceptance. **Compliance** means a person goes along with the group's norms but does not accept them. A person might comply to help the group appear united to outsiders or to prevent conflict within the group. **Personal acceptance** means an individual's beliefs and attitudes are congruent with group norms. Personal acceptance is the more powerful of the two types of conformity. A person might strongly defend the group's norms and try to socialize new members to them, because she has internalized those norms. Conformity to group norms is not necessarily bad; it can bring order to a group's activities. Because members know what to expect from each other and share performance expectations, conformity often leads to more effective group performance. A later section in the chapter discusses the dysfunctions of excessive conformity.

Behavior in groups falls into two major classes: required and emergent. **Required behavior** is what a person must do because of organization membership and as part of the person's role in the formal group. Required behaviors include being at work at a specific time, performing job duties in a certain way, and interacting with specific people in another department to complete a task. **Emergent behavior** grows out of the interactions among group members. Such behavior can focus on work tasks or be purely social. The norms of a group can define emergent behavior. Organizations do not prescribe emergent behaviors and often do not formally acknowledge that such behavior happens. The newcomer to an existing cohesive group will not immediately understand the function and meaning of many emergent behaviors.

Functions of Groups in Organizations

Groups have several **functional effects** on organizations. Groups can be an important source of socialization of organization members. Whether the result of the socialization will be functional for the organization depends on the group's orientation to management.

Groups can be a source of rewards for members, serving as an important motivational system. Praise and other rewards offered by the group can reinforce member behavior. Groups also provide support for their members while they work. This function of groups is especially important to those doing hazardous work, where the cooperation of all members of the group is necessary to do a job safely.

Cohesive groups with norms supportive of management can have several other functional results. If tasks are interdependent, the cooperative behavior of cohesive group members helps them complete tasks. A cohesive group can produce innovative work behavior that has value for the organization. Cohesive groups are self-policing and can stamp out deviant behavior. Control over individual behavior in cohesive groups is more immediate than controls used by managers.

Dysfunctions of Groups in Organizations

Groups sometimes have **dysfunctional consequences** for either the group member or the organization. Groups can take more time to do some tasks than individuals. The group structure takes time to develop. Conflict in the early stages of group development takes time to settle.

People who are members of cohesive groups often experience some loss of their individual identity. Groups give individuals a degree of anonymity, causing some people to behave in atypical ways. Responsibility for negative results of the group's actions can become diffused among group members. Because no single person takes responsibility for a bad decision, people in groups can escape accountability for their behavior.

Virtual groups (discussed more fully in the later section "Virtual Groups") can experience negative effects that are unique to such groups. The absence of social cues because of little or no face-to-face interaction removes important communication information that humans use. Nonverbal communication such as eye contact and emotional gestures can tell people in the group that the speaker feels passionately about her views. Their absence in electronic communication can reduce the effect of minority positions (see the section "Majority and Minority Influences in Groups") on group results, perhaps leading to poor decisions or ineffective problem solving.

Virtual groups can take longer to make decisions than other types of groups. If the decision or problem has a time-critical element, then a virtual group is not a likely optimal approach.

Other dysfunctional consequences can appear in all types of groups. **Social loafing**, or the free-rider effect, can develop when a person perceives her effort in the group as unimportant or as not easily seen by others. **Sucker effects** happen when other group members perceive a member as a free rider, someone not pulling her weight, and reduce their efforts to remedy feelings of inequity. In both cases, group members reduce their efforts toward the group's goals, often lowering overall group performance.

A cohesive group can put strong pressure on its members to conform to its norms. Such **conformity** can lead to high levels of uniformity of behavior within the group. It also can lead to close monitoring of member behavior to ensure compliance with the group's norms. The amount of control a group exerts over its members can exceed the control of individual managers or supervisors. The almost continual interaction among group members keeps them under the watchful "eye of the norm."

Uniformity in decision-making groups can also lead to groupthink. **Groupthink** is a major dysfunction of cohesive decision-making groups. Groups suffering from groupthink strive for consensus, typically consider only a few alternatives before making a decision, and do not periodically reexamine the assumptions underlying their decisions. The obvious results for an organization are a less effective decision-making process and poor-quality decisions.

Model of Cohesive Group Formation

This section builds a conceptual model that you can use to analyze how and why cohesive groups form in an organization. The model applies to both formal and informal groups. Central to the model are the concepts of activities, interactions, and sentiments.

Figure 9.1 shows a model of cohesive group formation. Required work activities lead to social interaction when the factors allowing it exceed those restricting it. The bases of attraction affect the formation of sentiments during the interactions. If individuals are attracted to each other, mutually positive sentiments can develop. A cohesive group then forms, with norms governing group member behavior.

Activities, Interactions, and Sentiments

Activities are the formal organizational requirements, such as job duties and responsibilities. Activities follow from formal group membership and the organization's division of labor. The

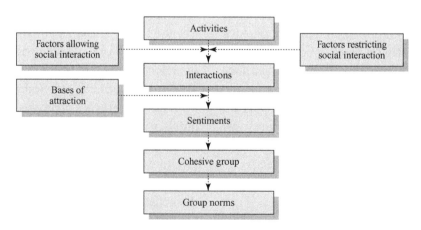

Figure 9.1 Model of Cohesive Group Formation

physical layout of the work area and the technical process of the organization can also demand certain activities. Activities are the same as required behaviors. They are behaviors a person must do because of organizational membership.

Interaction refers to social interaction between two or more people. The interaction can be face to face, with two people talking to each other, or interaction through memoranda and reports. Interaction can also occur using telecommunications devices, televideo devices, personal computers (PCs), e-mail, and the World Wide Web (WWW).

Sentiments are attitudes, beliefs, and feelings about the person or persons with whom an individual interacts. Sentiments develop from social interactions and are feelings of like or dislike for one another.

Required behavior can lead to social interaction. People are required to do certain things as employees of the organization (activities). Those required activities bring a person into contact with other people (interaction). The following is an example of an activities, interactions, and sentiments pattern:

Valerie has just joined a cross-functional team that has the task of analyzing the complex procurement processes of her company. The team is large, with 15 members. Valerie comes from the Human Resources function; other team members come from Accounting, Finance, Marketing, and Manufacturing. During the team's discussions (activities), Valerie must interact with Jessica from Manufacturing. She learns from their conversations that she and Jessica share a common interest in restoring older Vespa motor scooters.

Notice that the interactions are part of required work behavior. During the interaction, Valerie and Jessica learn about each other's background and interests and discover they have a common interest. From this information, they can develop positive or negative feelings (sentiments) about each other.

Work activities lead to patterns of social interaction that let people sort out their sentiments. If they find they share similar interests, likes, and dislikes, they can be attracted to each other. A cohesive group can form if the interactions involve several people.

Organizational Factors that Affect Cohesive Group Formation

Several **factors** in the physical layout of work areas, work processes, organizational design, and job design affect the **formation of cohesive groups**. Those factors will either allow social interaction or restrict it. If the factors allowing social interaction exceed those that restrict it and positive sentiments emerge among those who interact, a cohesive group should form. A manager who understands those factors can use them to encourage the formation of a cohesive group or to build barriers against its formation.

The proximity of people affects social interaction. If people are physically close together, the potential for social interaction is high. If they are widely separated, the potential is low. The physical separation of formal groups forms clear boundaries between groups. A clearly defined boundary increases the potential for social interaction within the formal group. A less well-defined boundary decreases that potential. Fuzzy boundaries can also increase social interaction among members of different groups, decreasing the possibility of a cohesive group forming. The ambient noise level affects whether people can talk easily to each other while working. A high noise level decreases the chance of oral communication; a low noise level increases that chance.

Job activities requiring interaction among workers increase the potential of cohesive group formation. Similarly, incomplete job descriptions can require an individual to go to a coworker for help. The presence of complete job descriptions decreases the likelihood of such social interaction.

Free time at work during rest periods and the ability to move around while working increase the probability of social interaction. A job that does not require close attention lets the worker interact with other nearby workers. The opposite characteristics decrease the potential for social interaction.

Absenteeism and turnover within a formal group also affect social interaction. High absenteeism decreases the chance of the same group of people interacting with each other. Low absenteeism has the opposite effect. High turnover increases the instability of group membership. The continual presence of new people causes the group to focus on socializing the new people, decreasing the likelihood of a stable pattern of social interaction.

Bases of Attraction

Physical factors alone do not fully explain cohesive group formation. **Bases of attraction** explain why people who can potentially interact are sufficiently attracted to each other to form a cohesive group.

Similarities in attitudes, beliefs, gender, ethnic background, age, social status, and education can be the bases of people's attraction to each other. Individuals are attracted to each other because they share common experiences. Membership in a group can also satisfy a person's desire for social interaction, causing the person to be attracted to group members. Individuals might perceive group memberships as helping them to reach a goal. For example, you might join a college sorority or fraternity because you believe that companies like to hire college graduates who have been involved in such organizations.

When people form mutually positive sentiments about each other, they move toward the formation of a cohesive group. Such groups have norms that guide the behavior of group members.

Stages of Group Development

All types of groups (face-to-face, virtual, and self-managing teams) can develop in a series of stages, with each stage emphasizing something different. Early aspects of development focus on the social structure of the group: norms, social status, roles, and role relationships. Each stage has different implications for member behavior and group performance. The stages are not discrete, clearly identifiable states. They are plateaus in the group's evolution from beginning to end. Groups of strangers that have not done the group's task before are most likely to experience all stages of development.

The **stages of group development** are a controversial area of group and group dynamics research. Little research has examined the stages in organizational settings. A conservative conclusion from the research evidence says the stages apply only to newly formed groups. That conclusion suggests that knowledge about group development could be especially important in an organization that deliberately uses groups to do work.

During the **group formation stage (forming)**, group members meet each other for the first time and learn about the group's tasks. The group defines its social and task boundaries. People who have never been together before introduce themselves to each other. They reveal their characteristics and abilities to other group members, sometimes slowly. The members also discuss preliminary ideas about how to do the group's task.

The **intragroup conflict stage (storming)** begins to evolve. Discussions focus on behavior, roles, and social relationships that are right for doing the group's task. Informal leaders begin to emerge, even if a formal leader exists, as is often true for a formal task group. Power struggles might erupt between competing informal leaders. Conflict arises about how the group should do its tasks. People often struggle to keep their identity and autonomy as the group tries to give an identity to the individual. New members entering an existing cohesive group experience the power and force of the group's socialization process at this stage.

By the **group cohesion stage (norming)**, the group has defined its roles and role relationships. The group agrees about correct member behavior. Members accept each other, and an identifiable group culture emerges. Conflict is less intense at this stage than during the preceding stage. If conflict is accepted as part of the group's norms, the group defines acceptable conflict behavior. The conflict at this stage focuses less on the social structure of the group than on different ways of doing the group's task. The way group members perform their tasks might be evaluated. Conflict can arise if an individual sharply deviates from the group's norm about task behavior.

Group members become comfortable with each other at the **task orientation stage (performing)** and have accepted the group's norms. Members have settled upon their goals and worked out their division of labor. The task or tasks are now defined, and energy focuses on doing the group's work.

Some groups reach their goals, disband, and end their existence as an identifiable group (**termination or adjourning stage**). Other groups redefine their task and membership. If either event happens, the group returns to the first stage of development and restarts the process.

Functional groups and cohesive informal groups reach the task orientation stage of development and plateau there. Under certain conditions, such groups repeat the stages and experience redevelopment. When newcomers join an established group, the group's social structure and ways of doing its task often are altered. Established members of the group, especially formal or informal leaders, socialize the new member to the group's norms. All the forces and dynamics of socialization processes come into play for the newcomer.

Organizations that undergo a major redesign often redistribute existing organization members into new formal groups. The people are not new to the organization, but they are new to the groups in which they find themselves. The stages of group development repeat as groups affected by the reorganization try to redevelop.

Social Structure of Groups

All mature groups have a **social structure** with several dimensions. These dimensions include group member roles, role relationships, the group's communication network, and influence patterns within the group. Knowing the social structure of a group will help you understand its members' behavior and your behavior.

Each role within a group is a major dimension of its structure. Group norms partly define each member's role and expected behavior. Individuals can change their roles, adding to and taking away from them. Each member learns a role in a group during early socialization to the group's norms. Each role has a specific position within the group's status structure. The **status structure** defines the relative position of each role and the relationships among the roles.

Table 9.1 describes some typical roles found in groups. The roles cluster into the broad classes of task roles, maintenance roles, and individual roles. **Task roles** focus on the group's tasks, issues, or problems. **Maintenance roles** focus on behavioral processes within the group with the intent of reaching the group's goals. **Individual roles** focus on member needs and behavior that often have little to do with the group's task.

Each group member holds a position in the group's **communication network**. Some members have a central position in the network, with connections to all group members. They play a central role in the group because of their connections to other group members. Other people play peripheral roles; they are distant from other group members and are not highly involved in its communication network. The degree of centrality or marginality of an individual varies from one group to another. Another possible position in a group's communication network is between two other members. Communication must go through a person who has such a connecting role. That person can impede or enhance communication within the group depending on how well she handles the communication requirements of this role.

Power and influence patterns within a group follow from a person's role in the group. Formal groups often have appointed leaders with authority over other members of the group. Informal leaders develop within informal and formal

Table 9.1 Typical Roles Found in Groups

Task Roles	
Initiator	Offers new ideas about how to do the group's task or resolve its problems.
Information seeker/giver	Seeks clarifying information or adds new information to the group's discussions.
Elaborator	Extends the information used by the group by offering examples or trying to show the expected results of the group's effort.
Coordinator	Helps pull together the activities of group members.
Recorder	Keeps a written record of the group's activities
Maintenance Roles	
Encourager	Motivates other members to contribute ideas to the group.
Harmonizer	Referees conflict among group members.
Compromiser	Reduces conflict within the group by finding ways of splitting differences.
Gatekeeper	Tries to keep communication links open with important parties outside the group.
Follower	Accepts the direction of the group, usually passively.
Individual Roles	
Aggressor	Acts hostilely toward other group members.
Blocker	Resists the group's direction and opposes the views of others.
Joker	Engages in horseplay; tells stories and jokes unrelated to group activities.
Dominator	Tries to give direction to other group members and assert own higher status over others.

Source: Benne, K., and P. Sheats. 1948. Functional Roles of Group Members. *Journal of Social Issues* 2: 43–46. This classic source also describes other roles in groups.

groups. Those individuals take on the social power other group members give them.

A group's structure can affect its members and the performance of the group. A person's position and role in a group can lead to the satisfaction or frustration of the person's needs. An individual with a strong need for dominance or power can satisfy that need by assuming a leadership role within a group. If forced into a subordinate role, that person's needs will be frustrated.

People often are members of many groups in an organization and play different roles in different groups. A person can hold a leadership position in one group and a subordinate position in another. The different roles require the person to behave differently in the two groups. Such differences can lead to conflict among the roles people play within an organization.

Factors That Affect Group Effectiveness

Many factors can affect a group's effectiveness. **Effectiveness** includes member satisfaction and reaching group and organization goals. These factors are important considerations when managers and organizations deliberately use groups to get work done.

A group's **physical environment** affects interaction within the group. People at the ends of a rectangular table participate more in group activities than those in other positions. People who know each other well often sit next to each other. People interact more with those seated across from them than with those in other seats. Leaders often emerge from the head of a rectangular table, but it is more difficult to predict the emergence of leaders in a circular arrangement.

The **size and type of area** in which a group works can affect its effectiveness. Large groups feel crowded when they do not have enough space to work comfortably. Groups with physical boundaries can become more cohesive than groups whose boundaries are diffused or blurred.

Compatibility of group members in both needs and personality can lead to higher group productivity. Individuals who have a high need for dominance, for example, are more compatible with people who can play a subordinate role. Conflict within a group increases when members are not compatible with each other.

Although compatibility can lead to high performance, groups with members of diverse abilities who apply those abilities to the group's task also are effective. Group tasks requiring variations in people's performance call for differences in member characteristics. If the tasks require similarities in people's performance, similarities in member characteristics lead to higher performance. Members with special skills who apply those skills to the group's task will often actively participate and can strongly affect the group's decisions.

Group goals have strong effects on group performance. Groups with specific, clear goals outperformed those with less specific goals. The research evidence is unclear about whether involvement in goal setting has positive effects. Feedback also likely plays an important role in group performance. Other evidence suggests that interdependent groups should receive group, not individual, rewards.

Productivity typically is lower in large groups than in small ones. **Group size** has several specific effects, including the following:

- Satisfaction with the group's activities decreases as size increases.
- Participation of members drops as size increases.

- The strength of bonds among group members decreases as group size increases.
- Large groups have more resources such as information for doing the group's task.
- Reaching agreement about a group's activities or making decisions is more difficult in large groups than in small ones.
- A leader more likely emerges as group size increases.
- Large groups make communication and co-ordination of group members more difficult.
- People in large groups have difficulty learning about each other. For example, in a three-person group the number of possible relationships is 6, in a four-person group 25, and in a six-person group 301!

Small groups work well for tasks with high cooperation requirements. People working on difficult tasks do better when the group allows feedback while doing the task. A group norm of letting people know how they are doing will help such feedback. Keeping the group size small enough also can encourage feedback so that people will know the performance of other group members.

Virtual Groups

Virtual groups are human groups using computer systems to link group members. They feature an information technology environment using PCs or workstations connected over a network. The network can be in a single room, over an organization's intranet, or over the Internet. Such connections allow different temporal and physical patterns ranging from meeting in a single room simultaneously or at dispersed locations asynchronously. Figure 9.2 shows one virtual group configuration. Software within the system supports problem-solving and decision-making groups. The system's goal is to support group processes that increase decision effectiveness and quality.

A single-room layout has individuals or small groups seated at individual PCs. Some physical interaction is possible within this pattern. Another pattern lets people work from their offices either within the same building or at scattered locations. This design typically does not allow direct physical interaction. Another design links people over the Internet either within rooms equipped for virtual

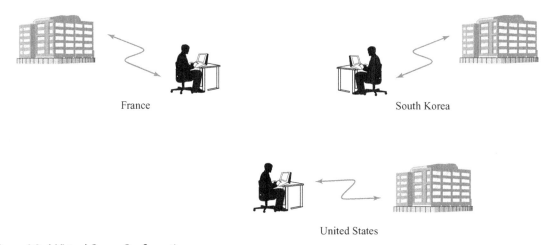

France

South Korea

United States

Figure 9.2 A Virtual Group Configuration

groups or at individual computers. The people in this pattern can be at scattered locations anywhere in the world. This type of group becomes part of the virtual organization.

Electronic meeting systems or **group decision support systems** are underlying technologies for virtual groups. Several such systems exist from different sources. Two examples are GroupSystems (www.groupsystems.com) and Cisco Systems WebEx (www.webex.com).

Virtual group technologies have the following features and characteristics:

- Decision tools software supports a problem-solving or decision-making task.
- Process tools software supports a particular approach to a group's task. An example is an electronic brainstorming tool.
- Parallel communication allows group members to communicate with everyone in the group. Members input ideas and observations and simultaneously receive other members' ideas and observations, with little domination by a few people.
- Anonymous communication attaches no identification to a person's message. Some virtual groups allow identification of the person who originated a message.
- Shared software is available equally to all group members. Such sharing lets group members work on joint tasks.
- Shared view gives all group members the same view of the group's work.
- Communication within the virtual group is either synchronous (real time) or asynchronous (any time). Synchronous communication happens in chat rooms, with e-mail, and with other direct computer conferencing. The latter can include videoconferencing on a PC or workstation. Asynchronous communication uses e-mail or bulletin boards for threaded discussions.

Virtual groups present organizations and managers with the following challenges:

- Building trust among group members
- Building group cohesiveness
- Reducing feelings of member isolation and detachment from the group
- Balancing interpersonal and technical skill requirements of group members
- Managing potential conflict among geographically dispersed group members
- Recognizing the performance of groups and group members

Some research has given guidelines on how to meet these challenges. Timeliness and consistency of interactions among members bring trust to the group. Training in conflict management, meeting management, and virtual group leadership helps build cohesiveness. Periodic face-to-face meetings of group members help reduce feelings of isolation. Selecting people with the right interpersonal and technical skills helps ensure a balance in these skills among members. Fair performance assessments come from peer reviews and using interaction information available from virtual group software. All these factors help reduce the challenges and increase virtual group effectiveness.

Self-Managing Teams

Self-managing teams are increasingly part of modern organizational life. These teams also are called self-directed teams, self-leading teams, self-regulating teams, or empowered teams. If properly designed, such groups adopt the good features of face-to-face workgroups and use knowledge about groups and their dynamics. Modern technology lets people work at remote locations connected to each other over the Internet or over an organization's intranet.

A **self-managing team** is a group of people doing interdependent tasks to produce a product or deliver a service. Team members manage most aspects of their work, including making member work assignments, choosing a leader, and assessing their work quality. Managers should not use self-managing teams when people should work independently or when they want to work independently.

Sports teams have many examples of task independence and task interdependence in team success. Swimming, track, and gymnastics rely on individual athletic performance, not a group of them in an interdependent relationship. Hockey, soccer, and basketball depend on closely coordinated interdependent athletes for success. Successful self-managing work teams in organizations depend on these same factors.

An organization that relies on self-managing teams moves decisions to the teams. Managers authorize the teams to decide about product design, process design, and customer service. Decentralization and self-managing teams flatten organizations by removing one or more layers of management. The result is often a nimble organization poised to meet changing opportunities and constraints in the external environment.

Managers assume team members have more knowledge about the technical aspects of their work and specific tasks than do other people. Team members share their technical knowledge among themselves and help train new members. Teams usually have specific quantity and quality goals to reach. Managers hold the team accountable for reaching these goals, but let the team decide how to reach them.

Team size and composition can affect team performance. Large groups typically perform worse than smaller groups. Some experts recommend teams of five to seven members. Managers need to balance the heterogeneity and homogeneity of the team and select team members based on skills and abilities required by technical tasks. Teams with members who have experience in many functional areas of an organization can perform higher than teams with members from few functional areas. Managers also need to consider the social skills of team members. They should choose those who are comfortable interacting with other people and who believe they can perform effectively in a team environment.

Team processes include cooperative behavior, interdependence, and conflict management. The interaction, activities, and sentiments view described earlier applies to self-managing teams. Organizations use self-managing teams to maximize the benefit of the technical and social abilities of team members. Well-managed teams guide themselves through the inevitable conflict and emerge as cohesive teams with widely shared goals of quality work performance.

Team leader selection varies widely among self-managing teams. Some teams choose their leader without management approval. In other cases, management appoints the leader or approves a team's recommendation. In still other situations, a team will not have an appointed leader. Leadership responsibilities and duties rotate among team members.

Organizations that use self-managing teams often use group-based performance rewards. They base the rewards on team performance, not individual performance. The reward goes to the team and is distributed to team members as either a percentage of base pay or a fixed amount. Research evidence shows positive performance effects of such rewards.

Self-managing teams can directly interact with suppliers and customers inside and outside the organization. Direct interaction with customers gives teams quick, accurate feedback. Such feedback can play an important role in sustaining member motivation.

Interactions with suppliers let information flow quickly in both directions. Suppliers can inform a team of any changes in what they supply; the team can inform suppliers about quality or scheduling problems so the supplier can quickly correct the problem.

Managers in organizations using self-managing teams have many roles that can help team performance. Typically, several teams report to a manager. The manager plays a supportive role for the teams by getting needed resources and managing conflict between teams and other parts of the organization. She also plays an informative role, getting critical information to the team. Such information can focus on team performance, the team's contribution to the larger organization, or the organization's direction.

Several empirical studies show the positive effects of properly designed self-managing teams that have the management support described earlier. Such teams have higher work performance and higher levels of customer service than either individuals or other types of workgroups. Team members report higher job satisfaction and higher team and organizational commitment than people working under other systems. Research results also show decreased absenteeism and turnover.

Other research shows the failure of poorly designed or poorly supported teams. Managers who want to move their organizations toward self-managing teams face difficult tasks. The use of such teams often requires large-scale organizational change and many changes in management behavior. Employees also can respond to such changes with resistance to the change effort. Some research shows that employee belief of possible unfair treatment within the new teams was associated with resistance to the change effort.

The unfair treatment included perceptions of undesirable task assignments and conflicts with other team members over preferred days off.

Workgroup Socialization

This section discusses socialization at the group level. The two processes have similar features and dynamics, but also differ in some significant ways.

Most past empirical socialization research focused on socialization processes and effects at the organization or individual level. Little empirical research focused on workgroup socialization. This section presents current conceptual and theoretical thinking about workgroup socialization and its probable effects on you.

Workgroup socialization processes likely unfold in the following three related phases:

- **Phase I: Anticipation:** A potential newcomer to a group develops an image of participation in the group. That image includes expectations about a work role in the group and the character of interactions with group members. Existing group members develop expectations about the newcomer's behavior and conformity to group norms.
- **Phase II: Encounter:** The new group member enters the group, learns her role in it, and meets the reality of the workgroup's social processes. Both the newcomer and the group members experience simultaneous processes of acceptance.
- **Phase III: Adjustment:** The new group member has successfully adapted to the workgroup's requirements, and the workgroup has successfully adapted to the new member.

The phase names and process descriptions might look familiar. Workgroup socialization phases, however, have a distinctly reciprocal quality in the interaction between the newcomer and the group members.

Some workgroup socialization dynamics distinguish it from organizational socialization processes. A new member's entry into an existing group can strongly affect its processes and structure. Because workgroups are smaller than the organization to which they belong, newcomers come into closer contact with workgroup processes than organizational processes. For example, a gifted athlete joins an existing team and profoundly affects the team's dynamics and playing ability. A major distinguishing characteristic of workgroup socialization from organizational socialization is this process of mutual adjustment and adaptation.

Another distinguishing feature of workgroup socialization occurs in the formation of new workgroups, whether they are face-to-face groups, virtual groups, or self-managing teams. Forming new groups starts the process of socializing the entire workgroup. Note the wording of the last phrase. It implies that an entire group of people concurrently passes through the workgroup socialization phases described in the previous list. This process features complex interactions during a frenzied mutual adjustment period.

Any group member can want to leave a group or a group can decide it wants an individual to leave. In either case, a withdrawal process starts with the person becoming a marginal group member. Other group members might try to reattract or resocialize the person. If they are unsuccessful, the person leaves, keeping a memory of group membership and becoming part of the group's history.

Empirical and theoretical research continues on workgroup socialization. You will likely experience many dynamics discussed in this section as you enter and leave workgroups during your work career.

Majority and Minority Influences in Groups

Cohesive groups feature an attachment to a group's norm or position by most group members. **Majority group members** can pressure minority or deviant members to conform to a group's norm or position. Majority group members outnumber **minority group members** and often hold negative views of minority or deviant members.

Although minority group members are outnumbered in groups, research shows positive group performance effects of their influence. A group could perform at a low level because members ignore information from one or more nonconforming members. Minority group members do not accept prevailing group opinion on an issue, problem, or decision. Minority members bring alternative views to a problem or decision faced by the group. They actively increase conflict within the group (to promote broad-ranging discussion. Minority members promote divergent thinking among majority members. The result is new information that can lead to better decisions or problem solutions.

Minority group members affect majority opinion by three methods. They present consistent, confident statements of their position. They repeat statements of opinion showing persistence and commitment to their position. They also can time their statements for maximum effect. For example, a minority member may notice an increase in workplace accidents and push for better health insurance coverage.

Effects of Workforce Diversity

Workforce diversity has both positive and negative effects on group development and functioning. People of different backgrounds and orientations view problems and issues differently. Potentially, their diverse outlooks can help them create more solutions to problems and find better ways of doing the group's work. This feature of diverse groups is especially useful to organizations that use teams to analyze work processes to achieve continuous improvement. Successful management of diverse groups requires knowledge of group dynamics and conflict management and an understanding and acceptance of differences among people.

Workforce diversity can also have negative effects on groups. Group members' intentions can be misinterpreted because of their different ways of viewing the world. Such problems are especially likely when members hold stereotypes about other members. Communication difficulties can arise if group members do not have a common first language or do not speak English in a smooth, polished way. Distrust might exist because group members fear the new and unknown. Diversity can also create high conflict potential, leading to inefficiencies in the group's processes.

These aspects of workforce diversity can introduce confusion and complexity to a group's processes. Diverse groups will take longer to pass through the early stages of group formation and become cohesive. Recall that some bases of attraction are people's personal qualities. Workforce diversity introduces wide variation in those qualities, making the process of becoming cohesive longer, more complex, and more difficult.

Empirical research directed at the effects of workforce diversity and group dynamics has shown mixed results. Heterogeneous groups can take longer to match the performance of homogeneous groups. The emerging evidence from continued research points to positive effects within groups that effectively manage their differences.

Intergroup Processes in Organizations

Intergroup processes happen when members of two or more groups must interact to complete a task. Such processes feature interactions among members of different groups in an organization, such as manufacturing, quality assurance, finance, marketing, and design engineering. Although behavior at group interfaces is called intergroup behavior, groups do not interact directly. Members of groups interact with each other, representing their group's interests. The basic management issue is the effective coordination of activities that require contributions of people from different groups.

People from different groups can have different task, time, and goal orientations. Marketing people might have a strong customer focus; manufacturing people usually are cost and schedule conscious; research and development people often take a long-term view. These different orientations can affect the quality of social interaction among members of different groups.

Several forces affect intergroup interactions. People typically view their group as composed of members with differing characteristics and other groups as having homogeneous members. People also tend to favor people from their own group and to place positive value on its purpose. Groups with poor interpersonal relations (low cohesiveness) often experience high intergroup conflict. Such social psychological responses can lead to categorization, stereotyping, and perceptual distortion of members from other groups.

Intergroup behavior often leads to conflict between groups, partly because of these social psychological forces. That conflict must be managed to keep it at a functional level so people can reach their work goals. Conflict management is an almost inevitable and key part of managing intergroup processes.

The intergroup processes described here apply to both formal and informal groups. As organizations become increasingly affected by workforce diversity, formal groups likely will have more diverse members. Not only will diversity have positive and negative effects on intragroup processes, but it can have similar effects on intergroup processes.

Workforce diversity could have important effects on the behavior between members of informal groups. Because informal groups form around bases of attraction, cohesive informal groups could form based on workforce demography. Characteristics such as gender, race, country of origin, and age could be the basis of such groups. Stereotyping and perceptual distortion of people from such informal groups can affect the quality of intergroup behavior among group members.

International Aspects of Groups in Organizations

Cross-cultural factors affect groups, group dynamics, and intergroup processes in several ways. Although forming and participating in groups are natural human characteristics, their functions vary in different cultures.

The tendency to accept group pressure for conformity to a group's norms, for example, varies among cultures. The Japanese encourage high conformity to the norms of a group, which has the person's primary loyalty. Experimental research with German students showed a low tendency to conform. Conformity was moderate among people in Hong Kong, Brazil, Lebanon, and the United States. Such evidence suggests caution in carrying your home country view of conformity into other cultures.

All societies pressure deviates to conform to norms, but the strength of the pressure and the intensity with which deviates are rejected vary from culture to culture. Some limited experimental evidence showed that French, Swedish, and Norwegian groups were highest in pressuring members to conform and in the intensity with which they rejected deviates. German and British groups were much lower in those pressures. Other research suggests that collectivistic cultures usually have higher levels of conformity than individualistic cultures. These research results imply that understanding cultural differences in conformity is important for managers in organizations operating in different countries.

Acceptance of self-managing teams and some of their features likely varies across cultures. Such teams fit the low power distance, high individualistic cultures of Australia and the United States. Countries that emphasize collectivism and strongly emphasize social status (high power distance) would accept teams, but possibly resist their self-managing feature. Group-oriented work activities likely will work, but supervisors should continue with their authority for hiring and firing and other areas of customary decision making.

Some research shows that team effectiveness is high in collectivistic systems. One possible reason is the likely absence of social loafing, the group dysfunction discussed earlier. It appears more strongly within groups in individualistic cultures than within groups in collectivistic cultures. Collectivistic cultures also expect little expression of conflict during intergroup interactions. They favor suppressing conflict, with little discussion about the feelings of different group members.

Ethical Issues About Groups in Organizations

The major ethical issues about groups in organizations center on conformity to group norms and the question of informed free choice. Cohesive groups develop powerful forces of socialization to their norms. If their socialization efforts are unsuccessful, such groups reject deviant members. A person can expect assignment to a formal group as a regular part of an employment contract, but can have little knowledge of the presence of informal groups and their norms before joining the organization. The ethical question becomes: Are managers required to inform recruits about all cohesive groups in the organization?

A second ethical issue centers on the selection of members for self-managing teams. People with weak affiliation needs usually do not enjoy high levels of interpersonal interaction. Self-managing teams require extensive interaction among members for success. Do managers have an ethical duty to screen people for membership based on the strength of their social needs? Should managers make membership on such teams voluntary, so people can choose whether to join a team?

Conflict levels within groups, especially heterogeneous groups, can be high and continuous. Such heterogeneity can come from the deliberate selection of members or can mirror the diversity of an organization's workforce. Some people find high conflict stressful. Do managers have an ethical duty to screen people for group membership based on the amount of conflict they can tolerate?

DECISION-MAKING AND PROBLEM-SOLVING PROCESSES

Joseph E. Champoux

The **decision-making process** defines a decision problem, creates alternative courses of action, and chooses among them using decision criteria. The criteria for choosing among alternatives can include the cost, profit, danger, or pleasure of each alternative. Although decision making focuses on choice, it also intends to reach a goal.

Decision making fits within the larger context of problem-solving activities in organizations. Individuals in organizations, especially managers, face problems, opportunities, and events that require action. The **problem-solving process** identifies the problem, tries to find root causes, and creates options that become input to a decision-making process. Decision making is the part of the problem-solving process that chooses a course of action.

Both individuals and groups can make decisions. Individuals do a good job with well-structured problems that have several tightly coupled parts. Groups do a better job with ill-defined problems with loosely coupled parts. They work well with problems too complex for a single person to solve. Such decisions include those affecting multiple constituencies and decisions needing the commitment of those affected to get effective execution.

Although decision making is a basic function of a manager's role, nonmanagers also make decisions. Organizations that embrace quality management or use self-managing teams involve many nonmanagers in decision processes. Throughout this chapter, the term decision maker refers to a person at any organizational level who chooses a course of action when faced with a decision situation.

Decision Strategies

The two major **decision strategies** are programmed and unprogrammed. Three dimensions define the characteristics of each strategy. The **routine–nonroutine dimension** describes whether the decision is common or unusual. The **recurring–nonrecurring dimension** describes whether the decision happens often or infrequently. The **certainty–uncertainty dimension** describes the degree of predictability of the decision. Risk embraces a large part of the certainty–uncertainty dimension. Situations with complete certainty or uncertainty are not as common as risky situations. When making decisions under risk, the decision maker assesses the probability of the alternatives during the decision process.

Decision makers use a **programmed decision strategy** for routine, recurring, and predictable decisions. This strategy relies on existing rules and standard procedures, uses well-known decision criteria, and applies uniform processing to a decision problem. Examples include handling exchanges and returns after Christmas and recording and processing accrued vacation and sick leave time.

Decision makers use an **unprogrammed decision strategy** for nonroutine, nonrecurring, and unpredictable decisions. Decision makers use this strategy when faced with novel or unusual events that they have not encountered in the past. Such unstructured events require creative problem solving for effective decision making.

The Decision-Making Process

The decision-making process is much more than choosing from alternative courses of action. The process involves several interrelated phases, only one of which is choice. Figure 10.1 shows those phases.

Decision processes are dynamic. They can unfold linearly or restart at an earlier phase. A decision maker can also repeat or restart the entire process, depending on the conditions that unfold during the process. Decision makers can move in both directions in the sequence and even stop for an extended time at one phase.

The first phase is **problem identification and diagnosis**. The organization faces an issue or problem that needs a solution. The issue or problem could be as simple as a request by a customer

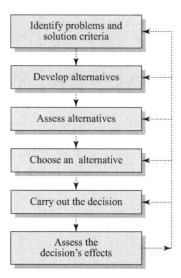

Figure 10.1 The Decision-Making Process

or an employee to do something not covered by existing policies or as major as widespread unethical behavior in the organization. Whether the problem is simple or difficult, its presence starts the decision process.

The first phase includes **identification of criteria** that will show that the issue is resolved or the problem is solved. This element is important, because it ties directly to the last phase, which is assessing the decision's effects. The criteria should be as explicit and as measurable as possible so managers can determine the success or failure of the decision.

The second phase focuses on **developing alternatives** for dealing with the issue or solving the problem. The decision maker searches for alternatives and information about the alternatives. The search can be informal, such as a telephone call for advice on a simple but unusual issue, or formal, such as a marketing survey to find out why the company's product is losing market share.

When faced with a complex problem, the decision maker might look at many different alternatives and consider them simultaneously. During the search, the decision maker often faces time and cost constraints, which can lead to imperfect or incomplete information about each alternative.

Decision makers discard alternatives they view as unacceptable solutions to the problem or issue, based on the criteria developed in the first phase. Acceptability, of course, is a judgment based on the decision maker's perception of the alternatives. Acceptable alternatives then become part of the decision maker's set of possible alternatives that move to the assessment phase of the decision process.

The decision maker now **assesses the alternatives** in the feasible set. She examines each alternative to see what desirable and undesirable results it is likely to have. The decision maker considers whether those affected by an alternative are likely to accept it. How well the decision is accepted can affect its success. The decision maker also considers the amount of risk each alternative involves and the certainty of its results.

After the decision maker completes the assessment, she must **choose an alternative**. Although people commonly associate decision making only with this phase, the decisions are actually made by means of the entire dynamic and interdependent process just described.

Decision makers may face several dilemmas, including the following:

- Two or more alternatives appear equally good. If the decision maker is truly indifferent, a random process such as a coin toss can make the choice.
- No one alternative can solve the issue or problem. Here the decision maker can use a set of alternatives to solve the problem or restart the decision process to search for better alternatives.
- No alternatives offer enough positive results to offset expected negative effects. The decision maker can restart the process to see if better alternatives exist. Note that, in both

this and the previous dilemma, a decision has been made—the decision not to decide.
- The decision maker perceives many alternatives as acceptable. The decision maker can go back to the previous phase to get more information about the alternatives and then try to make a choice.

The decision maker is ready to **carry out the decision** after she has chosen an alternative. Moving the decision to action is often as complicated as making the decision. Those asked to carry out the decision may accept decisions about simple issues but resist tough decisions about complex problems. The major issues in this phase go beyond the quality of the decision. They focus squarely on managing a successful implementation.

The last phase in the decision process **assesses the decision's effects**. The criteria for assessing the decision come from the first phase. The people asked to carry out the decision measure the results and compare them to the criteria. If the results are not as desired, corrective action may be required. If it becomes clear that the criteria need revision, the entire process begins again.

Decision-Making Models

Problem-solving and decision-making processes can follow several models. Each model describes variations in the decision process and includes different assumptions. These assumptions imply that the models apply to different types of decisions in modern organizations.

The Rational Model

The **rational model** of decision making has its roots in the classical economic theory of the firm and statistical decision making. According to this model, a decision maker approaches a decision problem in the following way:

1. The decision maker has a goal she wants to maximize or minimize. That goal can be profit, revenue, market share, cost, and so on.
2. The decision maker knows all alternatives and their results. She has complete information about each alternative. The decision maker is also fully knowledgeable about the degree of risk and uncertainty associated with each alternative.
3. The decision maker uses some function to give a preference ordering to the alternatives under consideration. The decision maker knows that function at the beginning of the decision process.
4. The decision maker applies the preference ordering function to the set of alternatives and chooses the alternative that maximizes the goal.

The rational model sees decision making as proceeding sequentially from beginning to end. This model does not have dynamic properties such as revising the goal or extending the search for new alternatives.

The Bounded Rationality Model

The **bounded rationality model** assumes decision makers have limitations that constrain rationality in the decision process. Those limits include the absence of complete information about alternatives and their results, cost constraints, time constraints, and limitations in dealing with complex problems.

Because of these limitations, decision makers might not consider all possible alternatives and therefore might not choose the alternative that maximizes a goal. Instead, the decision maker picks an alternative that is good enough to reach the goal. Selecting a satisfactory, but not optimal, alternative is known as **satisficing behavior**, a term that emphasizes the decision maker's search for satisfactory, not optimal, solutions. The following classical analogy shows the distinction between optimizing and satisficing: "An example is the difference between searching a haystack to find the sharpest needle in it and searching the haystack to find a needle sharp enough to sew with."

The bounded rationality model is both open and dynamic. Decision makers attend to forces and constraints imposed by the environment of the decision. As new information comes into the decision process, they can change both the goal of the decision problem and the set of alternatives. If the decision maker does not find a satisficing alternative in the set under consideration, she broadens the search for more alternatives.

Unstructured Decision-Making Models

Unlike the two models just described, many decisions do not have a structure that allows orderly progression from identifying the decision problem to selecting an alternative. **Unstructured decisions** often are unprecedented, significant, and complex events that defy program-like decision processes. To put it more dramatically, unstructured decision making is a

process characterized by novelty, complexity, and openendedness, by the fact that the organization usually begins with little understanding of the decision situation it faces or the route to its solution, and only a vague idea of what the solution might be and how it will be evaluated when it is developed.

Decision makers solve such complex, unstructured, and ambiguous problems by breaking them into manageable parts to which they apply more structured approaches to decision making. The novelty of such problems usually does not allow an optimizing approach to selecting an alternative. Decision makers rely on satisficing approaches for finding solutions to unstructured problems.

Unstructured decisions are especially vulnerable to factors that can disturb orderly movement through the decision process. The process can encounter political forces trying to stop a decision, make false starts because of inadequate information about the problem, or run into blank walls when an alternative does not solve the unstructured problem. The decision maker assesses many alternatives simultaneously using a series of cycles for finding and assessing them. During the process of finding and assessing alternatives, one alternative can emerge as the preferred choice. Such an "implicitly favored" alternative emerges during the decision process, not just at the end of the process. During the search for alternatives, the decision maker rejects those alternatives that are unacceptable and adds those that are acceptable to the set, even though she has already identified a preference.

The decision maker then moves to a stage of confirming the implicitly chosen alternative. During this stage, she tries to arrive at the belief that her implicit preference was the right choice. Many aspects of selective perception, distortion, and attribution operate during this phase. The task for the decision maker is to believe that her implicit favorite is better than at least one alternative to which it is compared.

The Garbage Can Model of Decision Making

The **garbage can model** of decision making was developed to explain decision making under highly ambiguous conditions. Ambiguous conditions arise in organizations when goals are not clear, organizational participants change fast, and the technologies of the organization are either poorly understood or swiftly change. The fast-changing global environments of many organizations also add ambiguity.

Decision making under ambiguity does not lend itself to the more rational, structured approaches described earlier. In ambiguous situations, a decision maker might not know all the alternatives available and the results of each alternative. She also might not have a clear set of rules to guide her as she chooses from the alternatives.

The garbage can model sees decision making under ambiguity as a time-sensitive process of four almost independent streams or flows: problem streams, solution streams, participant streams, and choice opportunity streams. These streams are constantly moving through an organization. The convergence of the streams at some point results in a decision.

Problem streams are the issues or problems facing the organization or part of the organization at a particular time. **Solution streams** are the solutions available to a decision maker, even though these solutions might have no direct connection to the problems. **Participant streams** are the decision makers and others who are available to decide. The **choice opportunity streams** are the chances to decide.

The garbage can metaphor was chosen deliberately and is not an attempt at humor. The contents of a real garbage can consist of whatever people have tossed into the can. A decision-making garbage can is much the same. The four streams flow toward the garbage can. Whatever is in the can when a decision is needed contributes to that decision. The garbage can model sees decision making in organizations as chaotic: Solutions look for problems to solve, and decision makers make choices based on the arbitrary mix of the four streams in the garbage can.

Political Decision-Making Models

Political decision-making models assume that individuals and groups in organizations pursue their self-interests and try to reach decisions that serve those interests. These models see decision making as a power- and conflict-based process featuring bargaining and compromise as ways of reducing conflict. The decisions that emerge from this process usually do not satisfy everyone involved.

Political decision-making models view power as a central feature of the decision process. Such models define power as the ability or capacity of an individual or group to overcome an opponent. According to the model, individuals or groups try to gain power and affect decisions by developing strategies such as controlling information that is critical to a decision and building coalitions within the organization to gain support for a position. Political forces within an organization are most likely to affect resource allocation decisions, such as budget decisions.

Assets and Liabilities of Group Decision Making

Group decision-making processes have both **assets and liabilities**. Recognizing these assets and liabilities can help you understand what group decision making can and cannot do.

Assets

Groups of people can bring more knowledge, information, skills, and abilities to a problem than individuals working alone. The heterogeneity of a decision-making group can stimulate discussion and debate about how to solve the problem. Each person contributes a piece of information or knowledge to the decision process. Some research shows that groups with goals of cooperation manage their discussions more effectively than groups with goals of competition.

When groups make decisions, everyone in the group understands more about the decision. Participants in the process know which alternatives were reviewed and why one was selected and others rejected.

Participation in a decision-making group can lead to increased acceptance of the decision. If they perceive their participation as legitimate, participants can develop a sense of ownership of decisions, reducing resistance while carrying out the decision.

Group decision making also helps the personal development of participants, letting them work on more complex problems in the future. Group decision making can improve collaborative problem-solving skills, develop trust among those who participate, enhance interpersonal skills, and increase job satisfaction.

Liabilities

Group decision making also has liabilities. Individuals who participate in group decision making might feel strong social pressures to conform to an emerging norm. Pressure is placed on those who disagree to get them to accept the favored alternatives.

Often one person dominates a group, especially if the group had no appointed leader from the start. Such people become dominant by participating more, being particularly persuasive, or persisting in their position.

As the group uncovers alternatives, individuals can develop strong preferences for a particular alternative. Although that alternative might not be the best solution to the problem, attention may shift to converting those who do not agree with the favored alternative.

Group decision making takes time and is ill suited for problems that require quick decisions. The time liability of group decision making includes not only the time of the principal decision maker, but also the time of everyone involved in the process.

Choosing Between Individual and Group Decision Making

Managers can choose from several **alternative social processes for decision making**. This section describes the approaches and briefly discusses a normative model that guides choices among them.

Alternative Social Processes for Decision Making

Table 10.1 shows several approaches to decision making. The table identifies the approaches with a combination of letters and Roman numerals. The letters represent the major characteristics of a process; the Roman numerals are variants of a process. The approaches labeled with an "A" are **authoritative** in character, which means the decision maker alone makes the decision. The "C" approaches are **consultative**, with the decision maker getting information and advice from others before deciding. The "G" approach uses **group** processes for decision making and tries to get consensus among group members.

You can view the approaches as social processes for decision making. These approaches have several characteristics as you move from the "A" approaches to the "G" approaches:

- Social interaction increases between the decision maker and others involved in the decision.
- Participants in the decision process have increased involvement, which can lead to more influence on the decision and increased commitment to the decision. They also have a better understanding of the problem because of their involvement in making the decision.
- The social processes for making a decision become increasingly complex and feature increased potential for conflict.
- The time to make a decision increases.

The Vroom–Yetton Model

A normative decision-making model has been proposed that guides a person's choices among

Table 10.1 Different Approaches to Decisions Affecting Individuals and Groups

Symbol	Definition
AI	You solve the problem or make the decision yourself using information available to you at the present time.
AII	You obtain any necessary information from subordinates, then decide on a solution to the problem yourself. You may or may not tell subordinates the purpose of your questions or give information about the problem or decision on which you are working. The input provided by them is clearly in response to your request for specific information. They do not play a role in the definition of the problem or in generating or evaluating alternative solutions.
CI	You share the problem with relevant subordinates individually, getting their ideas and suggestions without bringing them together as a group. Then you make the decision. This decision may or may not reflect your subordinates' influence.
CII	You share the problem with your subordinates in a group meeting in which you obtain their ideas and suggestions. You make the decision, which may or may not reflect your subordinates' influence.
GII	You share the problem with your subordinates as a group. Together you generate and evaluate alternatives and attempt to reach agreement (consensus) on a solution. Your role is much like that of [a] chairperson, coordinating the discussion, keeping it focused on the problem, and making sure that the critical issues are discussed. You can provide the group with information or ideas you have, but you do not try to "press" them to adopt "your" solution, and you are willing to accept and implement any solution that has the support of the entire group.

Source: Table 2.1. "Decision Methods for Group and Individual Problems" from *Leadership and Decision-Making*, by Victor H. Vroom and Philip W. Yetton, © 1973. There is no GI approach for decisions affecting groups.

the alternative approaches to decision making just described. The **Vroom–Yetton model** uses a set of rules that protects a decision's acceptance and quality. The model picks the approach indicated by the rules as best for the decision problem under consideration.

The Vroom–Yetton model considers decision problems to have certain characteristics. The decision maker assesses the characteristics of the decision problem by asking some diagnostic questions. The answers to those questions guide the decision maker to the model's recommended approach for that decision problem. For example, if the decision maker has enough information to decide, the model selects AI. If high conflict about decision alternatives is likely, the model selects CII or GII.

The model has received broad general support from several research efforts. No one suggests the model guarantees perfect decisions; however, research evidence says that decisions made by processes that the model selects are consistently higher-quality than decisions made by processes the model does not select. The decision's effectiveness, quality, and acceptance decline as the number of rule violations increases. One study focused on the model's prescription of group processes (CII and GII) when conflict is likely to occur among subordinates and acceptance of the decision is important. That study showed that subordinates were more likely to accept a decision from a group decision process than an individual one.

Judgment Biases

The description of decision-making models started with models that see the process as rational and ended with models that have a less rational view. Those models see decision makers using less than optimal judgment. Many factors can affect human judgment during the decision-making process.

Heuristics

Decision makers use several **heuristics** or guidelines to simplify the task of processing an often bewildering array of information developed during decision making. These strategies let them move quickly through the process, but also limit the information to which they attend. Although heuristics can lead to accurate decisions, they often introduce biases in human judgment. People are not always aware that they use heuristics. The next paragraphs describe three heuristics. Which do you tend to use when faced with a decision?

The **availability heuristic** is the tendency to recall and use information that is easily retrieved from memory. Such information usually is vivid, emotional, specific, and recent. Information without those characteristics might apply to the decision problem, but is less available to the decision maker. For example, managers who do performance appraisals often recall recent events better than earlier events. As a result, they do not have a continuous stream of information for the entire performance period. The result could be an unbalanced and possibly unfair performance appraisal.

The **representativeness heuristic** leads a decision maker to compare a current event to past events about which the person has knowledge or beliefs. If the current and past events are not comparable or if the decision maker's beliefs are incorrect, the decision might not be accurate. This heuristic includes stereotypes. Using stereotypes with an increasingly diverse workforce can lead to inaccurate or discriminatory hiring and promotion decisions.

Anchoring and adjustment is a heuristic decision makers use to get a starting point for a decision and then adjust beyond that point. This heuristic can play a big role in setting a person's hiring salary or developing a budget. For example, a manager might set a new employee's salary by increasing the person's present salary by some percentage. The salary offer will not necessarily reflect the new employee's true value to the organization. The anchoring and adjustment heuristic is tenacious, tying the decision maker to the original anchor even when other information indicates that the behavior is irrational.

Judgment Biases

When heuristics are right for the decision problem, they can help managers make good decisions. They help the person process information and simplify complex decisions. When the heuristic is not right for the decision, it can introduce systematic **judgment biases** that lead to wrong or irrational decisions. Heuristics can work alone or in combination to bias a person's judgment.

The availability heuristic leads to judgment biases that adversely affect the accuracy of the information used in a decision process. Inaccuracies come from the recalled information, estimates of the frequencies of events, and errors in association. The **ease of recall bias** occurs when people recall vivid, recent events more easily than other events. A person perceives easily recalled events as happening more often than less easily recalled events. This bias can affect a supervisor's judgment in a performance appraisal. Recent, dramatic events can have more effect on a performance appraisal than older, less remarkable events.

The representativeness heuristic yields judgment biases that affect estimates of events that occur and misperceptions about whether a series of events is random or not. A **misconception of chance bias** occurs when people judge the randomness of a sequence of events from its appearance, although the number of events is statistically too small for that conclusion. A manufacturing manager could question the randomness of a sampling process that resulted in good, good, good, good, bad, good, bad, bad, bad, good. Statistical theory says that one sequence is equally likely as any other sequence when drawn randomly.

The anchoring and adjustment heuristic affects a decision maker's ability to make accurate estimates that can affect project completions or budgets. An **overconfidence bias** can lead to inaccurate judgments when answering questions about which the person has little knowledge. For example, a manager firmly believes her sales estimate for Gillie's Hatch Valley Chile Company in Hatch, New Mexico, is accurate. Gillie's is a real, but little known, company that does not publish sales figures.

Some judgment biases stem from multiple heuristics. A **confirmation trap bias** can lead to behavior that avoids disconfirming and uncomfortable information. People tend to search for information that supports what they believe is true. They tend not to seek information that challenges their views. For example, a manager tentatively decides to introduce a product and seeks only confirming evidence to reach a decision.

Framing Effects

The presentation of a decision problem can lead to **framing effects**, a form of judgment bias that affects decision makers. Differences in presentation or framing of the problem affect their choices. As an illustration, read Decision Problems 1 and 2 in Table 10.2 and choose an alternative for each.

Psychological research on decision making has consistently shown that people prefer Program A for Decision Problem 1 and Program D for Decision Problem 2. Perhaps you did the same. Now look closely at the problems. The only difference between them is the wording. The programs in Problem 1 are phrased as gains and those in Problem 2 as losses. People prefer to avoid risks (**risk-averse** behavior) when facing decisions involving gains. They prefer to take risks (**risk-seeking** behavior) in decisions involving losses.

Framing decisions as losses can contribute to excessively risky decision behavior. Hoping to regain losses through the risky alternative, decision makers might engage in excessive and possibly inappropriate risky decision behavior. Such decision behavior can be associated with high levels of decision failures.

Decision makers also should view a decision problem from different frames to see whether they get contradictory results. Some research points to success from reframing decision problems. Although such efforts add time to the decision process, better decisions can result.

Escalation of Commitment

Decision makers face a common dilemma: Should they end a losing course of action or increase

Table 10.2 Framing Effects and Decision Problems

Problem 1

Assume you are a plant manager faced with the prospect of laying off 600 workers. You are considering two programs to reduce the number of people laid off:

- If you choose Program A, you will save 200 jobs.
- If you choose Program B, a 33 percent chance exists to save the jobs of all 600 workers and a 67 percent chance exists to not save any workers' jobs.

Problem 2

Assume that you are a plant manager faced with the prospect of laying off 600 workers. You are considering two alternative programs to reduce the number of people laid off:

- If you choose Program C, you will lay off 400 workers.
- If you choose Program D, you have a 33 percent chance of no layoffs and a 67 percent chance of laying off all 600 workers.

Source: Tversky, A., and D. Kahneman. 1981. The Framing of Decisions and the Psychology of Choice. *Science* 211: 453–58. Problems 1 and 2 are based on page 453. Problem 3 comes from page 454.

their commitment to it in the hope of getting future positive results and recovering past losses? Research evidence suggests they are likely to commit more resources, a process called **escalation of commitment**, to a losing course of action. Some evidence suggests this result varies among cultures. Managers from low uncertainty avoidance cultures such as Singapore are less likely to follow a losing course of action.

Commitment escalation typically happens when decisions can have strong effects on an organization. Such decisions include capital investments, major research and development investments, plant expansions, and the like. Decision makers watch the effects of their decisions to see whether intended results occur. Some decisions succeed and others fail—it is when they fail that irrational decision behavior happens.

Rational decision theory emphasizes using future costs and benefits, not past or sunk costs, to assess alternatives. Economists argue that sunk costs should play no role in a present decision, but decision makers often do not see them as psychologically sunk. As a result, past decisions can have negative effects on present ones.

Several factors contribute to escalating commitment. The decision maker might feel a need to justify past actions to self for ego protection or to others who assess her performance. Pressures for decision behavior consistency and the desire to appear as a rational decision maker can result in irrational escalation. Decision makers with confidence in their skills and abilities appear more likely to escalate commitment than those with less confidence.

Recall from the framing effects discussion that decision makers tend to avoid risk for positively framed problems and seek risk for negatively framed problems. The latter tendency can contribute to commitment escalation, which leads to failure. A failing project appears to the decision maker as a choice between losses. The first choice is to stop the project and accept the sunk costs. That option has a 100 percent chance of happening if the action is taken. The second choice is to consider an option with some probability of loss and some probability of success. This is the risky choice a decision maker will likely take when she frames the problem as a loss.

Groupthink

Groups can make bad, even disastrous, decisions. A major example is the space shuttle Challenger tragedy. Despite evidence of safety hazards, senior managers at the National Aeronautics and Space Administration (NASA) pressed for the launch. Why do group decision processes go awry?

One prominent and popular explanation is the groupthink phenomenon, an ugly disease presumed to infect cohesive decision-making groups. Members of such groups have worked closely together for some time and share a common set of values. These groups often operate during times of crisis, putting stress on their members to reach a commonly agreed-upon decision.

Groupthink involves excessive conformity to a group norm that supports agreement among group members. Decision-making groups with groupthink have lost their ability to critically assess alternative solutions to a problem. They also have lost the ability to examine the effects of past decisions critically, especially decisions that have become dysfunctional for the organization. Another major feature of groupthink is the absence of ethical concerns for the effects of the group's decisions.

Groupthink does not affect decision-making groups simply because they are cohesive. The nature of the norms of such groups is the key to groupthink. If those norms have the qualities just described, then the decision process becomes seriously dysfunctional. If those norms support continuously and critically examining alternatives, the decision-making group will not suffer from groupthink.

The group leader can head off the dysfunctional effects of groupthink in several ways. She can encourage critical appraisals of issues, ideas, and alternatives that the group considers. She should deliberately stimulate conflict during the decision process to get the information the group

needs for a quality decision. The group leader can assign one member to play devil's advocate for each group meeting. It also helps to invite knowledgeable outsiders to the group's meetings and to encourage them to analyze and comment on the group's deliberations.

Groupthink theory has received extensive research attention since its introduction in the early 1970s. Existing research evidence does not support all parts of the theory. Despite its lack of clear empirical research support, it remains an intuitive explanation of group decision-making failure.

Improving Decision Making in Organizations

Many methods exist to **improve decision making** in organizations. Some are human-based methods; others use computers and related technologies.

Human-Based Methods

The human-based methods for improving decision making are designed to generate more decision alternatives or to increase the criticism of the alternatives. Some methods also increase conflict in a decision-making group to offset the liabilities of such groups.

Brainstorming is a method of improving decision making that involves spontaneously generating ideas while deferring critical evaluation of those ideas. Its role in the decision process is to create a set of decision alternatives, not to pick the final alternative.

Four rules guide brainstorming. First, group members generate ideas in a freewheeling fashion. Wacky ideas are welcome. Second, at this stage there is no criticism of any idea, no matter how bizarre or bland. Third, many ideas are desired. The assumption is that, if people suggest many ideas, some will be good ones. Fourth, after ideas are presented, group members suggest ways to combine or improve them. At the end of a brainstorming session, decision makers should have many alternative solutions to a problem or issue.

A new approach to brainstorming uses computer technology to improve the results of the process. Some research has shown that face-to-face brainstorming does not always yield as many good alternatives as people working alone. The lack of anonymity in a face-to-face group inhibits some people from offering their ideas. **Electronic brainstorming** links people by computers so they do not interact directly. Participants behave anonymously in the process, letting them offer ideas without fear of social pressure from a dominant person. Electronic groups are the broader example of using technology in decision-making groups.

The **nominal group technique (NGT)** is a procedure for generating large amounts of information about a decision problem. The NGT uses a structured approach to decision making that is useful for generating, evaluating, and choosing alternative courses of action. It is a special case of brainstorming that does not include direct interaction. Research evidence shows NGT as outperforming the interactive brainstorming just described. NGT usually creates more ideas of at least equal quality.

During the early stages of the NGT, members of the decision-making group do not interact or talk with each other. Instead, they write their ideas about the decision problem on paper. After about 20 minutes, each person reads one idea from her list. Another person records each idea on a flip-chart in full view of all members of the group. The reading and recording continue with each member presenting one idea at a time, until all ideas are recorded.

During the reading and recording phase, no discussion takes place. By the end of this phase, the group has generated its set of ideas for the decision problem. The group then discusses the ideas on the flip-chart. After the discussion, each group member votes privately on the ideas. Finally, the individual votes are pooled to arrive at a decision about the problem.

The **Delphi method** is a structured technique for making decisions that are surrounded by uncertainty or that are conflicting values laden. This method also is used when group members are geographically scattered. Forecasting future events and determining public policy are examples of the types of decisions that can use the Delphi method.

Several people anonymously contribute to a group's decision when made by the Delphi method. Such people often are experts in their fields. They do not have any face-to-face contact. Members of a Delphi group interact through paper-and-pencil questionnaires or through computers.

The Delphi method follows a sequence of interrelated steps. The person managing the Delphi summarizes the outcomes of those steps using frequency distributions, the median, the quartile, or other appropriate statistics. The summary then becomes the input to the next step.

The Delphi method avoids some liabilities of group decision making. The lack of face-to-face interaction decreases the chance of one person becoming dominant. The controlled feedback from the summaries of each stage helps ensure the information accuracy passed from step to step.

The **devil's advocate technique** starts with one decision maker, or a group of decision makers, advocating and arguing forcefully for a decision alternative. Another person or group plays the role of critic, finding fault with the alternative and arguing for its rejection. The devil's advocate technique assumes a good decision alternative will withstand harsh criticism. Research evidence suggests the technique helps in reaching high-quality decisions.

Dialectical inquiry is a structured, logical, and analytical method of examining decision alternatives. The process begins by describing the favored decision alternative and the data used to select it. The process analyzes the assumptions held by the decision makers when choosing the alternative. Another decision alternative is then selected for consideration. That alternative could be a new one or one rejected earlier in the decision process. The assumptions underlying the choice of the counter-alternative are also derived logically. Research evidence suggests this technique can also help in reaching high-quality decisions.

Other human-based methods exist for improving group decision making. These diverse methods have many names, including "appreciative management" and "Technology of Participation." They recognize that decision-making groups are increasingly diverse, with many different viewpoints. The goal of these methods is to harness differences, decrease dysfunctional conflict, and focus diverse members on the organization's goals.

Computer-Based Methods

Computer-based methods of improving decisions in organizations include management information systems, decision support systems, and expert systems. The rapid spread of computer-based methods means you will likely encounter some of these systems in your work career.

Management information systems are information processing systems used by organizations to support their daily operating activities and decision-making functions. The systems can be manual, but are most powerful when they are computer based. Management information systems integrate different subsystems according to a general information management plan. Data within the subsystems conform to the specifications of the integrated system, allowing easy sharing throughout the system. Multiple users reach the management information system with terminals or personal computers (PCs). Users get a wide range of data, decision models, and database querying methods. Management information systems strongly support the analytical, strategic planning, and decision activities of an organization.

Decision support systems are computer-based systems designed to aid human decision makers' judgment. These systems do not automate an organization's decision processes; instead, they support those processes and help decision makers arrive at better decisions. Decision support systems are dynamic systems that change and evolve as a decision maker uses them. They can also be tailored to a decision maker's way of making decisions. An organization could have several decision support systems for different decision makers and classes of decisions. Contemporary uses of such systems include sales forecasting, cargo aircraft flight schedules, and medical decisions.

Expert systems support decision making by simulating an expert's knowledge and decision process. An expert system designed to help medical diagnosis, for example, has a database of symptoms and a set of decision rules that guide a user through a diagnosis. Users access the interactive systems through a terminal or a PC. The users do not need to be experts in the area covered by the expert system.

International Aspects of Decision Making And Problem Solving

The earlier description of the decision process phases applies most directly to decision making in the United States, Canada, and some European countries. The behavior of a single decision maker, or those participating in each phase, varies depending on the culture in which the decision process happens. Because behaviors vary, decision makers from different cultures who must interact to reach decisions often have difficulty understanding each other's behavior.

Decision makers from different cultures bring different orientations to the problem identification and diagnosis phase of decision making. Some cultures focus on solving problems. Other cultures accept their situation and rely on providence to take care of the future. U.S. decision makers, for example, often see problems as something to attack and solve. Malaysian, Thai, and Indonesian decision makers usually try to adjust to the problem and accept situations presented to them.

Evaluating and choosing alternatives differ dramatically across cultures. The person who makes the decision, the speed of the decision process, and the risk allowed in choosing alternatives all vary from culture to culture. Decision making is more centralized in Philippine and Indian organizations than in Swedish and Austrian organizations. Decision making proceeds slowly in Egyptian organizations, but quickly in U.S. organizations. Decision makers in Singapore and Denmark are more likely to take bigger risks than decision makers in Portugal and Greece. Cultures also vary in the order in which decision makers assess alternatives. Decision makers in Japan and China usually consider all alternatives before choosing. Decision makers in the United States, Germany, and Canada typically use a serial process, rejecting alternatives along the way to a final choice.

Ethical Issues in Decision Making and Problem Solving

Decision-making and problem-solving processes in organizations raise several ethical concerns. Ethical questions can arise not only when choosing among alternatives, but also when setting the goal for a decision, creating a set of alternatives, and assessing them. Other ethical questions arise when carrying out the decision.

An ethical decision maker willingly engages in an open and fair dialogue with all parties potentially affected by the decision. The decision maker's responsibilities include giving information freely without deceiving others involved. The moral decision maker likely does not know the right answer for every ethical issue, but freely discusses all issues with affected parties.

A model of decision making and ethics has been proposed that tries to explain why unethical decisions happen. The model proposes that decision makers who face ethical issues in a decision proceed in two phases. The first phase applies a decision rule that states a minimum cutoff for each dimension. An ethical rule in this phase could state, "We reject any alternative that creates a conflict of interest." When an alternative passes that rule, the decision maker then assesses it further by considering its benefits or costs weighted by its importance.

Research underlying this model suggests decision makers consider the ethical dimension with other dimensions when assessing alternatives. Positive benefits of dimensions other than the ethical one can overwhelm an undesirable ethical dimension. The ethical dimension also can have negative effects with little likelihood of happening. For example, the penalty is a large fine, but the organization is unlikely to be caught, which might lead decision makers to an unethical decision.

TEAM PRODUCTIVITY THROUGH MANAGEMENT OF AGREEMENT

The Abilene Paradox

Uchora Udoji

On a very hot Sunday afternoon in Coleman, Texas in the United States, a young man, his wife and his wife's parents were at leisure on a porch. They played dominoes and sipped lemonade. It was not the best of afternoons but it was tolerable. Suddenly the wife's father suggested that they all drive down to Abilene—about 53 miles from Coleman—to have lunch. The young man knew for certain it was a bad idea. They would be making this trip—with the dust storm and heat—in an old, un-airconditioned car. But the young man's wife said, "Sounds like a great idea—I would like to go". The young man replied, "It sounds good to me too—if your mother wants to go". His wife's mother said, "Of course I want to go—I haven't been to Abilene in a long time".

As was expected, the heat was cruel and by the time they got to Abilene, they were coated with dust and sweat. To crown it all, the meal was mediocre. Four hours later, they were back in Coleman hot, exhausted and unhappy. To be convivial and to break the uncomfortable silence, the young man said, "Great trip wasn't it?" The mother-in-law blurted out "Quite frankly, I would rather have stayed here. I went along because I didn't want to be the party pooper—I went because the three of you wanted to go". The young man said "Well

… I didn't want to go. I just went along because my wife wanted to". The young man's wife raised her voice "don't make me the culprit—you, dad and mum were the ones who wanted to go". The father-in-law cut in, "The truth is I didn't want to go; I just thought you all were bored. You young people don't visit much … I suggested it because I thought you would enjoy it. On a hot day like this, I really prefer to stay at home playing dominoes … "

They had all done just the opposite of what they wanted and the reason was that they all assumed the other person wanted to go.

When teams march into the Abilene paradox they take actions different from what they really want to do. Professor Jerry B. Harvey (George Washington University), in 1971, developed a concept from the above real-life experience to show how group members make decisions which **they believe** they have all agreed upon. In real terms, there is no consensus. He avers that *the inability to manage agreement, not the inability to manage conflict*, is the main indicator that a group is caught in the web of the Abilene Paradox.

The Abilene paradox is a major source of team dysfunction. Productivity should increase through teamwork; but when all the members of a team go along with a decision not because a consensus has been reached, but because each person assumes every one else is in agreement, the performance of the team is likely to decline.

Characteristics of the Abilene Paradox

1. Team members individually, but in private, recognize the *problem/issue* facing the team.
2. Team members individually, but in private, know *what it would take to deal with the problem/issue*.
3. The members *do not communicate what they truly believe* to one another. In meetings, they soften their positions or state them in ambiguous language. In extreme cases some members will even communicate the very opposite of their beliefs—what they communicate to others (as their belief) is based on what they assume or perceive to be the opinions of others.
4. *The opinions communicated based on inaccurate perceptions* lead members to make a collective decision that leads to action. It is in carrying out the action or after the action has been carried out that they realize that the decision runs contrary to individual desires.
5. Usually when the decision backfires, the members feel anger, frustration and dissatisfaction with the team. This feeling could lead members to take warring or blaming positions towards each other.
6. If the team members do not understand that the root of their disagreement is *mismanaged agreement*, this dysfunctional behaviour is likely to repeat itself. In extended cases, it becomes a norm and could eventually evolve as culture.

The Source of Abilene Paradox

Why would team members do something that is bound to result in both individual dissatisfaction and team failure even when it is obvious?

Human beings have a fundamental need to get along with others—"to stay connected". This is natural. However, a disordered desire "to belong" will typically induce the acceptance of decisions and actions with which a person fundamentally disagrees.

Harvey suggests that the general view is that *the individual's fear of the UNKNOWN* lies at the core of the paradox; but he disagrees with this view. He suggests that *fear of the KNOWN*—the fear of what people know is sure to happen—is at the core of the paradox. For example, people fear that if they do not "go along", they will likely face separation, alienation, ostracism. Ostracism is a powerful punitive tool. It is for this reason that solitary confinement exists in prisons as a corrective or punitive tool. Most people will rather go along with the group (be a part of something) than face any form of victimization.

Sometimes, a team member would rather concur with popular suggestions than take the risk of making a suggestion that may lead to a flawed decision. This happens when there exists an unwillingness to accept risk as a reality of life that must be confronted. Some people will not make a suggestion if there are certain risks involved; risks such as project setback, project failure, injury to self-esteem, dent to career, lifetime blaming, etc. that may arise if the suggestion leads to a trip (decision) that is worse than a trip to Abilene.

Action anxiety could also lead to mismanaged agreement. It occurs when people think that any decision or action—no matter how irrational—would be better than no decision or action at all. It results when the need to be seen as being "part of the team" takes priority over the need to be open about beliefs, opinion, desires and even facts. This could lead to an open acceptance of decisions and action taken by the group even when the decision is absurd and the action, senseless. Action anxiety is found on teams when time schedules are tight, when there is pressure from management for "action", etc.

Negative fantasies are products of the imagination; they occur when the member thinks of all the terrible things that "*will*" happen if he speaks his mind, states his beliefs, desires or facts. It does not matter to him that the probability of the fantasy occurring is low. He works himself to a state where he equates what "may happen" to what "will surely happen". Because his thought process has twisted a fantasy to "reality", he takes a decision based on this "reality" which is only a fantasy. This prevents the victim from sharing his true thoughts.

Dealing with Abilene Paradox

Fortunately, with commitment and discipline, the Abilene paradox can be prevented and controlled. However like every habit, the more entrenched it is in an individual or a team, the more the time, the effort and the commitment required to end it.

The first challenge facing the affected team is breaking the cycle of wrong assumptions and fear which forms the basis for thinking one thing and saying another. Working on the fear factor as well as developing sound communication skills can accomplish this.

Left-Hand/Right-Hand Column Exercise

Developed by Chris Argyris, Harvard University Professor, this exercise uncovers the reasons for meaning one thing and saying another. The apparatus is quite simple—a sheet of paper and a pen/pencil! The person under assessment draws a line down the middle of the sheet of paper. At the top of the sheet of paper, to the right, the person writes "WHAT I SAID" and to the left, "WHAT I AM THINKING" and makes the listings accordingly. When the listings are made after a meeting, it helps see clearly *what he thinks* versus *what he says*. When listings are made on reflecting over a couple of situations, he may notice a recurring pattern that clearly suggests he is a "victim of Abilene". Much information on why he is a victim is available on answering the following questions:

- What was my objective?
- Why didn't I say what was on the left hand column?
- Why did I say what was on the right hand column?
- What caused me to think and feel this way?
- What did I assume other members were thinking?
- How did the comments I made contribute to the decision and action of team members? Did my comments cause some confusion or difficulty and it what way?

The Ladder of Inference

The ladder of inference explains why different people given the same variables—the same data, the same environment, etc.—think differently, behave differently, arrive at differing conclusions, etc.?

As shown in Figure 24.1, we begin our reasoning with **True Data and Experience**—unadulterated and coming in "as is". Over time, beclouded by influences, we use **Selected Data and Experience**, which is only a subset of the former. We Attach Meaning to the Selected Data and Experience and from here, we grow **Assumptions**, arrive at **Conclusions** which form our new **Beliefs** or support our old **Beliefs**. Our **beliefs** lead us to behave the way we do and our behaviour—our **Action**—creates further data and experience.

The link between our **Actions** and **True Data and Experience** creates a loop (see Figure 24.1).

Over time, we tend to select more data that support or confirm our beliefs. At some point, our **Selected Data and Experience** becomes to us, synonymous with **True Data and Experience**. This situation develops because our actions, driven by our beliefs, create results which when interpreted, support or fuel our *selected data and experience* causing us to equate *true data* with *selected data*; thus, to us, they become one and the same thing. This creates a new loop that short circuits reality (Figure 24.2). The challenge is to discontinue short circuiting reality—to see reality for what it truly is—because select data and experience is only a small subset of reality.

Understanding the *Ladder of Inference*, (also developed by Argyris) and the ability to trace one's own thinking around the loop it forms provides a basis for understanding why we (and even others) think one thing and say or do another.

There are many similarities in the way we each take in true data and experience, but there are significant differences in our interpretations and the resulting behaviour. For this reason, even though we live in the same world and are exposed to the same data, we make differing deductions that form the different beliefs, opinions and perceptions that exist on teams. These varying views can be a positive force providing the diversity that adds value to teamwork or a negative force that leads to the suppression of views that in turn reduces the value that normally would be gained from teaming. This negative force can cause varying levels of factioning, conflicts, etc.

Balancing Advocacy with Inquiry

When a team member puts out a suggestion or position, it helps if a genuine inquiry into the position or opinion by other team members is

Figure 24.1 The Ladder of Inference

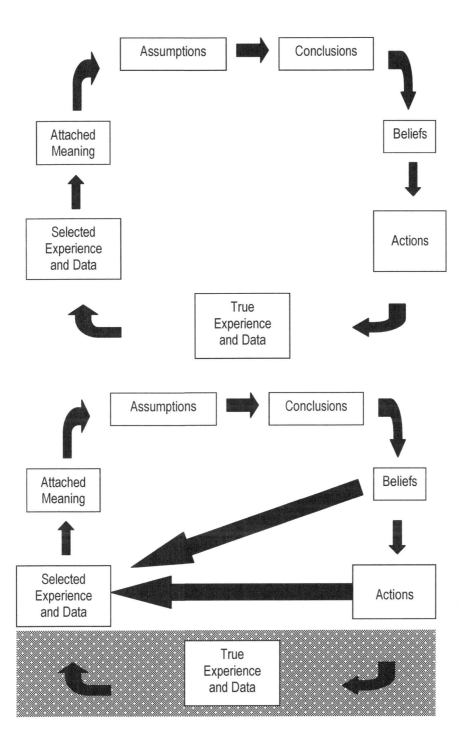

Figure 24.2

encouraged. Blending advocacy and inquiry promotes collaborative learning. In pure advocacy, the aim is "winning the argument". When two advocates argue, very little is learnt. The reason is that in trying to "win the argument" they tend to use select data—data that supports their perspective. Typically, they would deliberately hold back information that could support the other party's argument.

When a combination of inquiry and advocacy is used, the aim is to find the *best line of reasoning*. When everyone on a team makes his reasoning available for team examination, it creates an atmosphere of idea abandonment or surrender to the team that fosters team spirit. It means a member does not just question the reasoning behind other's views; he, in the process, presents his views, clarifies his thought process stating his assumptions and practically calls on others to question his views.

It may be worth mentioning that uncontrolled inquiry wastes time and kills initiative; therefore, team members must monitor inquiry closely. This way, the right balance between advocacy and inquiry is achieved and the possibility of "travelling to Abilene" is greatly reduced.

For best results, in advocating one's views and inquiring into the views of others:

1. State clearly your thought process—state how you arrived at your conclusions, make references to data and present sources upon which the data is based.
2. Invite others to criticize and/or build on your views—ask for opinions, possible loopholes, flaws, etc.
3. Challenge others to come up with differing opinions even when it appears unavailable.
4. Actively question other opinions that differ from your own—for example, ask questions like "how did you come to this conclusion?" "Have you considered so and so information?" "Did you read the comment made by so and so?"
5. State opinions, assumptions, suspicions and perceptions as what they are (not as facts).
6. Don't fake interest in the response of others.
7. Don't be patronizing or condescending.
8. Don't work hard at "showing the idiocy" of others.
9. When in an impasse situation, suggest that you all put heads together to come up with logic or information or an experiment that may change views or provide other options.
10. Allow yourself and your views to be criticised and encourage others to do the same. Where a criticism is not given constructively and the recipient is getting sensitive, one can rephrase the criticism in such a way that a message is clearly passed to the recipient that the important thing is the substance, and to the giver, a message that criticisms can be better phrased.

Dialogue

Dialogue involves two or more persons, exploring issues from varying perspectives. The participants present their assumptions but in a detached manner. We appreciate the dialogue technique when we understand that sometimes, when we disagree with others it is basically because our thoughts stand between us. When we detach ourselves from our suggestions or opinions we are more likely to see things from a different perspective. During dialogue, people watch their own thinking; they begin to see the defective and superior parts of their point of view as well as the defective and superior parts of the point of view of others. Creativity takes place in the blending of the superior parts of all sides of the argument in an effort to achieve the best line of reasoning and therefore, the best decision. Dialogue focuses more on understanding the issue, the data available, the assumptions present, the resources, etc. The "best line of reasoning" evolves during the creative process. Dialogue involves:

- The application of listening skills.
- Criticizing issues not persons.
- Managing emotions to ensure minimum attachment to opinions.
- Probing for information that oils the process.
- Understanding and appreciating that people with whom we dialogue interpret issues differently because they may not share our "frame of reference".

Successful dialoguing causes the participants to *think in unison* in an effective manner—this means there is a voluntary ownership of whatever decisions arrived at.

The techniques of Balancing Advocacy with Inquiry and Dialogue work best under the following conditions:

1. Team members are not afraid to express their views or challenge the views of others when they possess the data to do so reasonably.
2. Changing one's mind after new information or argument is put forward is not seen as a sign of weakness but rather of strength and self-confidence.
3. Members are not punished for making legitimate suggestions that lead to project setback or failure.
4. Openly expressed disagreement, if backed-up with data and analysis does not cause

a member to be ostracized or branded a "go-alone" or someone who is not a team player; rather it is recognized as a professional responsibility and rewarded.
5. Attainment of objectives, rather than being a "yes man" is the basis for reward and advancement of team members.

None of the techniques discussed takes precedence over the other in battling the Abilene paradox. Each technique may be used in isolation or with one or more of the other techniques (in the right blend) as it may be appropriate.

Fundamentally, the team leader should encourage team members to fight their fears as well as develop the requisite communication skills to enable them express their true opinions. This way, the team does not travel to Abilene unless there is a consensus based on a true belief that there is a need to take a chance even if the trip should eventually take the team to Abilene.

Mutual recrimination is a major feature in teams caught in the paradox. It is always easy to point accusing fingers at others, particularly at the team leader. The reality is that when a team goes to Abilene, all the members are victims; and blaming, arguments, accusations and counter-accusations do not solve anything. If anything, they consume time that would otherwise be productively used to beat a speedy retreat. Team leadership in a performing team rotates; the onus lies on all members to ensure trips to Abilene are prevented and where the trip has happened, to suggest ways to get out of Abilene, fast.

Collusion is also a feature of the paradox. A team does not get caught without the collusion of its members. An autocratic boss thrives when subordinates are willing to collude with his autocracy and obsequious subordinates exist when a boss is willing to collude with their obsequiousness.

It is easier and safer to keep quiet and hop on a bandwagon; but this is not teamwork. Nobody ever said teamwork was easy. Team members have roles—the challenge is to create the enabling atmosphere for the roles to be put to good use to create generative learning.

Consensus takes place when a decision is made, truly accepted and supported by all team members, even though the decision may not be the first preference of each individual member. Consensus is not about everyone's acceptance of a decision based on the ability of the one to influence the other through fear, intimidation or other means that may border on coercion or manipulation. It is not about voting. It is about arriving at a decision through group learning which produces the "best line of reasoning" which in turn produces more group learning. It is by this process that the level of productivity of a team grows—through the growth of the productivity of the individual team members who grow because they learn from each other.

References

1. Harvey, Jerry B., *"The Abilene Paradox and Other Meditations on Management"*, Jossey-Bass, 1988.
2. Senge, Peter M., *"The Fifth Discipline: The Art and Practice of the Learning Organization"*, Doubleday, 1994.
3. Senge, Peter M. et al, *"The Fifth Discipline Fieldbook: Strategies and Tools for Building a Learning Organization"*, Doubleday, 1994.

MOTIVATION AND WORK BEHAVIOR

Debra L. Nelson & James Campbell Quick

otivation is the process of arousing and sustaining goal-directed behavior. The word motivation comes from the Latin root word *movere*, which means "to move." Because motivation concerns creating a psychological state, it is one of the more complex topics in organizational behavior.

Motivation theories attempt to explain and predict observable behavior. The wide range and variety of motivation theories result from the great diversity of people and the complexity of their behavior in organizations. Motivation theories may be broadly classified into three theories of motivation: internal, process, and external. Internal theories of motivation give primary consideration to variables within the individual that impact motivation and behavior. The hierarchy of needs theory exemplifies the internal theories. Process theories of motivation emphasize the nature of the interaction between the individual and the environment. Expectancy theory exemplifies the process theories. External theories of motivation focus on the elements in the environment, including the consequences of behavior as the basis for understanding and explaining people's behavior at work. Any single motivation theory explains only a small portion of the variance in

human behavior. Therefore, alternative theories have developed over time in an effort to account for the unexplained portions of the variance in behavior.

Internal Needs

Philosophers and scholars have theorized for centuries about human needs and motives. During the past century, attention narrowed to understanding motivation in businesses and other organisations. Max Weber, an early German organizational scholar, argued that the meaning of work lay not in the work itself but in its deeper potential for contributing to a person's ultimate salvation. From this Calvinistic perspective, the Protestant ethic was the fuel for human industriousness. The Protestant ethic said people should work hard because those who prospered at work were more likely to find a place in heaven. The "Protestant Ethic" box lets you evaluate how strongly you have a pro-Protestant versus a non-Protestant ethic. Although Weber, and later M. R.

Protestant Ethic

Rate the following statements from 1 (for disagree completely) to 6 (for agree completely).

_____ 1. When the workday is finished, people should forget their jobs and enjoy themselves.

_____ 2. Hard work makes us better people.

_____ 3. The principal purpose of people's jobs is to provide them with the means for enjoying their free time.

_____ 4. Wasting time is as bad as wasting money.

_____ 5. Whenever possible, a person should relax and accept life as it is rather than always striving for unreachable goals.

_____ 6. A good indication of a person's worth is how well he or she does his or her job.

_____ 7. If all other things are equal, it is better to have a job with a lot of responsibility than one with little responsibility.

_____ 8. People who do things the easy way are the smart ones.

_____ Total your score for the pro-Protestant ethic items (2, 4, 6, and 7).

_____ Total your score for the non-Protestant ethic items (1, 3, 5, and 8).

A non-Protestant ethic score of 20 or over indicates you have a strong nonwork ethic; 15–19 indicates a moderately strong nonwork ethic; 9–14 indicates a moderately weak nonwork ethic; 8 or less indicates a weak nonwork ethic.

A pro-Protestant ethic score of 20 or over indicates you have a strong work ethic; 15–19 indicates a moderately strong work ethic; 9–14 indicates a moderately weak work ethic; 8 or less indicates a weak work ethic.

Source: M. R. Blood, "Work Values and Job Satisfaction," *Journal of Applied Psychology* 53 (1969): 456–459. Copyright © 1969 by the American Psychological Association.

Blood (see "Protestant Ethic"), both used the term *Protestant ethic,* many see the value elements of this work ethic in the broader Judeo-Christian tradition. We concur.

A more complex motivation theory was proposed by Sigmund Freud. For him, a person's organizational life was founded on the compulsion to work and the power of love. He saw much of human motivation as unconscious by nature. *Psychoanalysis* was Freud's method for delving into the unconscious mind to better understand a person's motives and needs. Freud's psychodynamic theory offers explanations for irrational and self-destructive behavior, such as suicide or workplace violence. The motives underlying such traumatic work events may be understood by analyzing a person's unconscious needs and motives. The psychoanalytic approach also helps explain workplace deviance behavior (WDB), which can have a negative impact on business unit performance. Freud's theorizing is important as the basis for subsequent need theories of motivation. Research suggests that people's deeper feelings may transcend culture, with most people caring deeply about the same few things.

Internal needs and external incentives play an important role in motivation. Although extrinsic motivation is important, so too is intrinsic motivation, which varies by the individual. Four drives or needs underlie employee motivation: to acquire, to bond, to comprehend, and to defend; organizations that meet these needs can improve performance. Intrinsic work motivation is linked to spillover effects from work to home, with mothers transmitting the emotions of happiness, anger, and anxiety from work to home. Interestingly, fathers who have high intrinsic work motivation tended to report greater overall anxiety at home after the workday. Therefore, it is important for managers to consider both internal needs and external incentives when attempting to motivate their employees. Managers elicit more intrinsic motivation and engagement from their employees when they support them to make progress in meaningful work, as Graham demonstrates in"A Model Manager Motivational Style."

A Model Manager Motivational Style

Graham is a model manager whose style of motivation was observed as he led a small team of chemical engineers in the multinational European firm Kruger-Bern.* He excelled in four ways. First, Graham established a positive work climate, one event at a time, which set positive behavioral norms for his team. He did this by focusing on the positive in contrast to communicating unrealistic positivity. Second, Graham stayed attuned to the everyday work and progress of his team. This flowed naturally from the positive, nonjudgmental climate that he established. Third, Graham targeted his support based on recent project events and team activity. Each day he anticipated what he might do to make the most positive impact on team members' inner work lives and progress, from being a catalyst to removing an inhibitor or from being a nurturer to being an antidote to toxic events or emotions. Fourth, Graham positioned himself as a resource for team members rather than as a judge, micro-manager, or disciplinarian. He did this by checking in with the team and its members, not checking up on them. By being a model manager, Graham recognized the natural internal motivation that people have to do meaningful work and make a positive contribution. His motivational style and behaviors helped his team members see small wins and daily progress versus a cycle of setbacks and inhibiting frustrations.

*Kruger-Bern is a pseudonym to protect the company's confidentiality.
Source: T. M. Amabile and S. J. Kramer, "The power of small wins," Harvard Business Review (May 2011): 70–80.

External Incentives

Early organizational scholars made economic assumptions about human motivation and developed differential piece-rate systems of pay that emphasized external incentives. They assumed that people were motivated by self-interest and economic gain. The Hawthorne studies confirmed the positive effects of pay incentives on productivity and also found that social and interpersonal motives were important. However, there are those who raise the question about where self-interest ends and the public interest begins. For example, public service employees may respond more positively to perceptions of the benefit their agencies provide to the public than to self-interest economic incentives such as merit pay.

Those who made economic assumptions about human motivation emphasized financial incentives for behavior. The Scottish political economist and moral philosopher Adam Smith argued that a person's *self-interest* was God's providence, not the government's. More recently, executives have focused on enlightened self-interest. Self-interest is what is in the best interest and benefit to the individual; enlightened self-interest additionally recognizes the self-interest of other people. Adam Smith laid the cornerstone for the free enterprise system of economics when he formulated the "invisible hand" and the free market to explain the motivation for individual behavior. The "invisible hand" refers to the unseen forces of a free market system that shape the most efficient use of people, money, and resources for productive ends. Smith's basic assumption was that people are motivated by self-interest for economic gain to provide the necessities and conveniences of life. Thus, employees are most productive when motivated by self-interest.

Technology is an important concept in Smith's view because he believed that a nation's wealth is primarily determined by the productivity of its labor force. Therefore, a more efficient and effective labor force yields greater abundance for the nation. Technology is important as a force multiplier for the productivity of labor.

Frederick Taylor, the founder of scientific management, was also concerned with labor efficiency and effectiveness. His central concern was to change the relationship between management and labor from one of conflict to one of cooperation.

Taylor believed the basis of their conflict was the division of the profits. Instead of continuing this conflict over the division of profits, labor and management should form a cooperative relationship aimed at enlarging the total profits.

Employee Recognition and Ownership

Modern management practices—such as employee recognition programs, flexible benefit packages, and stock ownership plans—build on Smith's and Taylor's original theories. These practices emphasize external incentives, which may take a strictly economic form such as money or a more material form, such as Outstanding Employee awards, gold watches, and other organizational symbols of distinction. Whataburger, a fast food chain with 700 stores in the Southwest, has developed the WhataGames, in which the best employees compete for bragging rights as well as cash, prizes, and even medals. This corporate Olympics is a training and loyalty exercise that helps significantly reduce turnover and build commitment. One bridge approach to employee motivation that considers both psychological needs and external incentives is psychological ownership. An increasing number of scholars and managers emphasize the importance of feelings of ownership for the organization. One study of 800 managers and employees in three different organizations found that psychological ownership increased organizational citizenship behavior, a key contextual performance beyond the call of duty.

Maslow's Need Hierarchy

Psychologist Abraham Maslow proposed a theory of motivation emphasizing psychological and interpersonal needs in addition to physical needs and economic necessity. Maslow's theory was based on a hierarchy of needs. This theory was later applied through Theory X and Theory Y, which were two sets of assumptions about people at work. Maslow's hierarchy was again reformulated in an Existence, Relatedness, Growth (ERG) theory of motivation using a revised, three-tiered classification scheme for basic human needs. The

three are Existence needs, Relatedness needs, and Growth needs.

The Hierarchy of Needs

The core of Maslow's theory of human motivation is a hierarchy of five need categories. Although he recognized that there were factors other than one's needs (e.g., culture) that contributed to determining behavior, he focused his theoretical attention on specifying people's internal needs. Maslow labeled the five hierarchical categories as physiological needs, safety and security needs, love (social) needs, esteem needs, and the need for self-actualization. Maslow's *need hierarchy* is depicted in Figure 11.1, which shows how the needs relate to Douglas McGregor's assumptions about people, which will be discussed next.

Maslow conceptually derived the five need categories from the early thoughts of William James and John Dewey, coupled with the psychodynamic

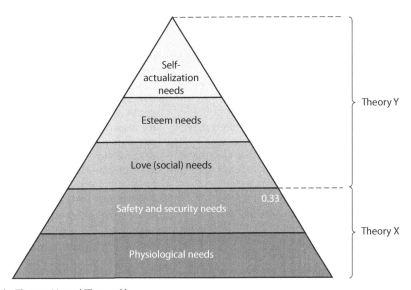

Figure 11.1 Human Needs, Theory X, and Theory Y

thinking of Sigmund Freud and Alfred Adler. Maslow's need theory was later tested in research with working populations. For example, one study reported that middle managers and lower-level managers had different perceptions of their need deficiencies and the importance of their needs. One distinguishing feature of Maslow's need hierarchy is the following progression hypothesis. Although some research has challenged the assumption, the theory says that only ungratified needs motivate behavior. Further, it is the lowest level of ungratified needs in the hierarchy that motivates behavior. As one level of need is met, a person progresses to the next higher level of need as a source of motivation. Hence, people progress up the hierarchy as they successively gratify each level of need.

Theory X and Theory Y

One important organizational implication of the need hierarchy concerns how to manage people at work (see Figure 11.1). Douglas McGregor understood people's motivation using Maslow's need theory. He grouped the physiological and safety needs as "lower order" needs and the social, esteem, and self-actualization needs as "higher order" needs, as shown in Figure 11.1. McGregor proposed two alternative sets of assumptions about people at work based on which set of needs were the motivators. His *Theory X* and *Theory Y* assumptions are included in Table 11.1. McGregor saw the responsibility of management as the same under both sets of assumptions. Specifically, "management is responsible for organizing the elements of productive enterprise—money, materials, equipment, people—in the interest of economic ends."

McGregor believed that Theory X assumptions are appropriate for employees motivated

Table 11.1 McGregor's Assumptions about People

Theory X	Theory Y
• People are by nature indolent. That is, they work as little as possible. • People lack ambition, dislike responsibility, and prefer to vbe led. • People are inherently self-centered and indifferent to organizational needs. • People are by nature resistant to change. • People are gullible, not very bright, and the ready dupes of the charlatan and the demagogue. • With respect to people, management's task is a process of directing their efforts, motivating them, controlling their actions, and modifying their behavior to fit the needs of the organization. • Without the active intervention of management, people would be passive—even resistant—to organizational needs. They must therefore be persuaded, rewarded, punished, controlled—their activities must be directed.	• People are not by nature passive or resistant to organizational needs. They have become so as a result of experience in organizations. • The motivation, the potential for development, the capacity for assuming responsibility, and the readiness to direct behavior toward organizational goals are all present in people. Management does not put them there. It is a responsibility of management to make it possible for people to recognize and develop these human characteristics for themselves. • The essential task of management is to arrange conditions and methods of operation so that people can achieve their own goals best by directing their own efforts toward organizational objectives.

by lower-order needs. Theory Y assumptions, by contrast, are appropriate for employees motivated by higher-order needs. Employee participation programs are one consequence of McGregor's Theory Y assumptions. Therefore, Fortune 1000 corporations use employee involvement as one motivation strategy for achieving high performance. Whole Foods Market founder and CEO John Mackey relies on Maslow's hierarchy of needs in leading the company.

Gordon Forward, founding CEO of world-class Chaparral Steel Company, considered the assumptions made about people central to motivation and management. He viewed employees as resources to be developed. Using Maslow's need hierarchy and Theory Y assumptions about people, Gordon cultivated and developed a productive, loyal workforce that was later acquired by Brazilian steelmaker Gerdau Ameristeel and become Midlothian, Texas Steel Mill.

ERG Theory

Clayton Alderfer recognized Maslow's contribution to understanding motivation, but he believed that the original need hierarchy was not quite accurate in identifying and categorizing human needs. As an evolutionary step, Alderfer proposed the ERG theory of motivation, which grouped human needs into only three basic categories: existence, relatedness, and growth. Alderfer classified Maslow's physiological and physical safety needs in an existence need category; Maslow's interpersonal safety, love, and interpersonal esteem needs in a relatedness need category; and Maslow's self-actualization and self-esteem needs in a growth need category.

In addition to the differences in categorizing human needs, ERG theory added a regression hypothesis to go along with the progression hypothesis originally proposed by Maslow. Alderfer's regression hypothesis helped explain people's behavior when frustrated at meeting needs at the next higher level in the hierarchy. Specifically, the regression hypothesis states that people regress to the next lower category of needs and intensify their desire to gratify these needs. Hence, ERG theory explains both progressive need gratification and regression when people face frustration.

McClelland's Need Theory

A second major need theory of motivation focuses on personality and learned needs. Henry Murray developed a long list of motives and manifest needs in his early studies of personality. David McClelland was inspired by Murray's early work. McClelland identified three learned or acquired needs, called *manifest needs*. These were the needs for achievement, power, and affiliation. Some individuals have a high need for achievement, whereas others have a moderate or low need for achievement. The same is true for the other two needs. Hence, it is important to emphasize that different needs are dominant in different people.

For example, a manager may have a strong need for power, a moderate need for achievement, and a weak need for affiliation. Each need has quite different implications for people's behavior. The Murray Thematic Apperception Test (TAT) was used as an early measure of the achievement motive, and McClelland and his associates developed it more. The TAT is a projective test.

Need for Achievement

The *need for achievement* concerns issues of excellence, competition, challenging goals, persistence, and overcoming difficulties. A person with a high need for achievement seeks excellence in performance, enjoys difficult and challenging goals, and is persevering and competitive in work activities. Example questions that address the need for achievement are as follows: Do you enjoy difficult, challenging work activities? Do you strive to exceed your performance objectives? Do you seek out new ways to overcome difficulties?

McClelland found that people with a high need for achievement perform better than those with a moderate or low need for achievement, and he has noted national differences in achievement motivation. Individuals with a high need for achievement have three unique characteristics. First, they set goals that are moderately difficult yet achievable. Second, they like to receive feedback on their progress toward these goals. Third, they do not like having external events or other people interfere with their progress toward the goals. Need for achievement a strong predictor of success in business, especially entrepreneurship and sales roles where control is high, but may actually lead to failure in politics because personal control is low. How individuals interpret goal performance may depend on whether the goal is personal or societal. When evaluating goal progress, especially when failure occurs, feedback should minimize triggering a negative mood and frustration.

High achievers often hope and plan for success, as we saw in Thinking Ahead with the passion and persistence of James Dyson. High achievers may be content to work alone or with other people, whichever is more appropriate to their task. They like being very good at what they do, and they develop expertise and competence in their chosen endeavors. Research shows that need for achievement generalizes well across countries with adults who are employed full-time. In addition, international differences in the tendency for achievement have been found. Specifically, achievement tendencies are highest for the United States, an individualistic culture, and lowest for Japan and Hungary, collectivistic societies.

Need for Power

The *need for power* is concerned with the desire to make an impact on others, influence others, change people or events, and make a difference in life. The need for power is interpersonal because it involves influence with other people. Individuals with a high need for power like to control people and events. McClelland makes an important distinction between socialized power, which is used for the benefit of many, and personalized power, which is used for individual gain. The former is a constrictive force, whereas the latter may be a very disruptive, destructive force.

A high need for power was one distinguishing characteristic of managers rated the best in McClelland's research. Specifically, the best managers had a high need for socialized power, as opposed to personalized power. These managers are concerned about others; have an interest in organizational goals; and have a desire to be useful to the larger group, organization, and society. For example, on the McClelland need profile, Management Sciences for Health CEO Jonathan D. Quick, M.D., displayed a high need for interactive power, or socialized power, which is positive. This contrasts with the need for imperial power, a need in which he was very low, which is again positive.

Though successful managers have the greatest upward velocity in an organization and rise to higher managerial levels more quickly than their contemporaries, they benefit their organizations most if they have a high socialized power need.

Need for Affiliation

The *need for affiliation* is concerned with establishing and maintaining warm, close, intimate relationships with other people. Those with a high need for affiliation are motivated to express their emotions and feelings to others while expecting them to do the same in return. They find conflicts and complications in their relationships disturbing and are strongly motivated to work through any such barriers to closeness. The relationships they have with others are, therefore, close and personal, emphasizing friendship and companionship. We see in the "Academic Motivation and Interpersonal Attachment" box that academic motivation and interpersonal attachment styles interact such that when there is congruence, the best grade point average (GPA) and academic well-being outcomes result.

Over and above these three needs, Murray's manifest needs theory included the need for autonomy. This is the desire for independence and freedom from any constraints. People with a high need for autonomy prefer to work alone and to control the pace of their work. They dislike bureaucratic rules, regulations, and procedures. The need for relationships is important in each theory. A study of 555 nurses in specialized units found that intrinsic motivation increased with supportive relationships on the job. Figure 11.2 summarizes

Academic Motivation and Interpersonal Attachment

Academic motivation is not the same for everyone. Some individuals are academically motivated to be with family and friends, and other individuals are motivated to study as a way to establish their independence and autonomy. Similarly, everyone does not have the same style of interpersonal attachment. Some individuals grow up with secure attachments and become paradoxically securely attached interpersonally and autonomous at the same time. Other individuals do not have histories of secure attachments and, therefore, grow up to be more somewhat avoidant or fiercely independent. In two studies of 314 people, the researchers found that the congruence of academic motivation and interpersonal attachment style led to the best GPA and academic well-being results. Specifically, for individuals whose academic motivation was relational in nature (i.e., family and friends), they did better academically if their interpersonal attachment style was secure versus avoidant or fiercely independent. For individuals whose academic motivation was to establish their independence, they did better academically if their interpersonal attachment style was avoidant, or fiercely independent, versus secure. The results indicate that individual differences, needs, motivations, and interpersonal styles are important considerations when looking at the relationships between goals and performance outcomes. Studying for classes is goal-directed behavior that requires people to consider their own interest and the interests of others close to them while studying. The degree to which these reasons stimulate effective studying depends upon the person.

Source: J.S. Gore and M.J. Rogers, "Why do I study? The moderating effect of attachment style on academic motivation," *The Journal of Social Psychology* (2010), 150(5): 560–578.

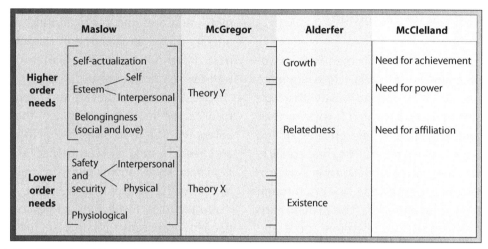

Figure 11.2 Need Theories of Motivation

Maslow's hierarchy of needs with its two extensions in the work of McGregor and Alderfer. The figure also includes McClelland's need theory of motivation and shows the parallel structures of these four motivational theories.

Herzberg's Two-Factor Theory

Frederick Herzberg departed from the need theories of motivation and examined the experiences that satisfied or dissatisfied people at work. This motivation theory became known as the two-factor theory. Herzberg's original study included 200 engineers and accountants in western Pennsylvania during the 1950s. Herzberg asked these people to describe two important incidents at their jobs: one that was satisfying and made them feel exceptionally good at work and another that was dissatisfying and made them feel exceptionally bad at work.

Herzberg and his colleagues argue that people have two sets of needs: one related to the avoidance of pain and the other related to the desire for psychological growth. Conditions to the work environment would affect one or the other of these needs. Work conditions related to satisfaction of the need for psychological growth are labeled *motivation factors*. Work conditions related to dissatisfaction caused by discomfort or pain are labeled *hygiene factors*. Each set of factors relates to one aspect of what Herzberg identified as the human being's dual nature regarding the work environment. Thus, motivation factors relate to job satisfaction, and hygiene factors relate to job dissatisfaction, as shown in Table 11.2.

Motivation Factors

Job satisfaction is produced by building motivation factors into a job, according to Herzberg. This process is known as job enrichment. In the original research, the motivation factors were identified as responsibility, achievement, recognition, advancement, and the work itself. When these

Table 11.2 Herzberg's Motivation-Hygiene Theory

Hygiene Factors: Job Dissatisfaction	Motivation Factors: Job Satisfaction
• Company policy and administration	• Achievement
• Interpersonal relations	• Recognition of achievement
• Supervision	• Work itself
• Working conditions	• Responsibility
• Salary	• Advancement
• Status	• Salary
• Security	• Growth

factors are present, they lead to superior performance and effort on the part of job incumbents.

Figure 11.3 shows that salary is a motivational factor to some studies. Many organizational reward systems now include other financial benefits, such as stock options, as part of an employee's compensation package. A long-term study of young men in the United States and the former West Germany found job satisfaction positively linked to earnings and changes in earnings, as well as voluntary turnover.

Motivation factors lead to positive mental health and challenge people to grow, contribute to the work environment, and invest themselves in the organization. According to the theory and original research, the absence of these factors does not lead to dissatisfaction. Rather, it leads to the lack of satisfaction. The motivation factors are the more important of the two sets of factors

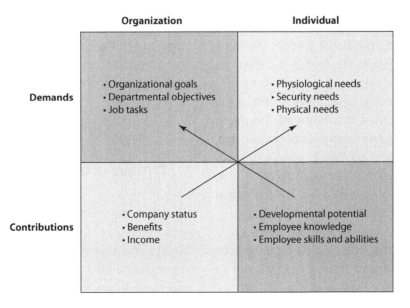

Figure 5.3 The Individual–Organizational Exchange Relationship. *Source*: J. P. Campbell, M. D. Dunnette, E. E. Lawer III, and K. E. Weick, Jr., *Managerial Behavior, Performance, and Effectiveness* (New York McGraw-Hill, 1970).

because they directly affect a person's motivational drive to do a good job. When they are absent, the person is demotivated to perform well and achieve excellence. The hygiene factors are a completely distinct set of factors unrelated to the motivation to achieve and do excellent work.

Hygiene Factors

Job dissatisfaction occurs when the hygiene factors are absent or insufficient. In the original research, the hygiene factors were company policy and administration; technical supervision; salary; interpersonal relations with one's supervisor; working conditions; and status. These factors relate to the job context and may be considered support factors. They do not directly affect a person's motivation to work but influence the extent of the person's discontent. They cannot stimulate psychological growth or human development but may be thought of as maintenance factors. Excellent hygiene factors result in employees' being not dissatisfied and contribute to the absence of complaints about these contextual considerations. Organizational justice might he considered a hygiene factor. Justice climates can yield positive responses, such as good organizational citizenship though that is influenced by the quality of the employee-supervisor relationships.

When these hygiene factors are poor or absent, the person complains about poor supervision, poor medical benefits, or whatever hygiene factor is poor. Employees experience a deficit arid are dissatisfied when the hygiene factors are absent. Many companies have initiated formal flextime policies as a way to reduce dissatisfaction and persuade women leaders to return to work. Even in the absence of good hygiene factors, employees may still be motivated to perform their jobs well if the motivation factors are present. Although this may appear to be a paradox, it is not. Because motivation and hygiene factors are independent of each other, it is possible to be simultaneously dissatisfied and motivated.

The combination of motivation and hygiene factors can result in one of four possible job conditions. First, a job high in both motivation and hygiene factors leads to high motivation and few complaints among employees. Second, a job low in both factors leads to low motivation and many complaints among employees. Third, a job high in motivation factors and low in hygiene factors leads to high employee motivation to perform coupled with complaints about aspects of the work environment. Fourth, a job low in motivation factors and high in hygiene factors leads to low employee motivation to excel but few complaints about the work environment.

Two conclusions can be drawn at this point. First, hygiene factors are of importance up to a threshold level. Once this threshold is reached, however, there is little value in improving them. For example, once workers feel that their working conditions are safe and secure, there is little value in making them safer and more secure. Second, the presence of motivation factors is essential to enhancing employee motivation to excel at work. The "What's Important to Employees?" box asks you to rank a set of ten job reward factors in terms of their importance to the average employee, supervisors, and you.

Critique of the Two-Factor Theory

Herzberg's two-factor theory has been critiqued on a number of grounds. One criticism concerns the classification of the two factors. Data have not shown a clear dichotomization of incidents into hygiene and motivator factors. For example, employees almost equally classify pay as a hygiene factor and a motivation factor. A second criticism

What's Important to Employees?

There are many possible rewards that employees may receive. Listed below are ten possible job reward factors. Rank these factors three times. First, rank them as you think the average employee would rank them. Second, rank them as you think the average employee's supervisor would rank them for the employee. Finally, rank them according to what you consider important.

Your instructor has normative data for 1,000 employees and their supervisors that will help you interpret your results and put them in the context of Maslow's need hierarchy and Herzberg's two-factor theory of motivation.

Employee	Supervisor	You	
			1. Job security
			2. Full appreciation of work done
			3. Promotion and growth in the organization
			4. Good wages
			5. Interesting work
			6. Good working conditions
			7. Tactful discipline
			8. Sympathetic help with personal problems
			9. Personal loyalty to employees
			10. A feeling of being in on things

Source: "Crossed Wires on Employee Motivation," *Training and Development* 49 (1995): 59–60. American Society for Training and Development.

is the absence of individual differences in the theory. Specifically, individual differences such as age, sex, social status, education, or occupational level may influence the classification of factors. A third criticism is that intrinsic job factors, such as the workflow process, may be more important in determining satisfaction or dissatisfaction on the job. Psychological climate can impact job satisfaction as well though it is important to consider both organizational and individual level referents.

Finally, almost all of the supporting data for the theory come from Herzberg and his students using his peculiar critical incident technique. These criticisms challenge and qualify, yet do not invalidate, the theory. Independent research found his theory valid in a government research and development environment. Herzberg's two-factor theory has important implications for the design of work.

Two New Ideas in Motivation

While executives like Whole Foods Market's CEO John Mackey value traditional motivation theories such as Maslow's, others like PepsiCo's CEO Steve Reinemund use new motivational ideas with their employees. Two new ideas in motivation have emerged in the past decade. One centers on eustress, strength, and hope. This idea comes from the new discipline of positive organizational behavior. A second new idea centers on positive energy and full engagement. This idea translates what was learned from high-performance athletes for Fortune 500 executives and managers, such as those at PepsiCo. Both new ideas concern motivation, behavior, and performance at work.

Eustress, Strength, and Hope

The positive side of stress concerns its value as a motivational force, as in eustress. *Eustress* is healthy, normal stress. Aligned with eustress in the new discipline of positive organizational scholarship are investing in strengths, finding positive meaning in work, displaying courage and principled action, and drawing on positive emotions at work. This new, positive perspective on organizational life encourages optimism, hope, and health for people at work. Rather than focusing on the individual's needs, or alternatively, on the rewards or punishment meted out in the work environment, this new idea in motivation focuses on the individual's interpretation of events.

Eustress is one manifestation of this broad, positive perspective. People are motivated by eustress when they see opportunities rather than obstacles, experience challenges rather than barriers, and feel energized rather than frustrated by the daily experiences of organizational life. Thus, eustress is a healthy and positive motivational force for individuals who harness its energy for productive work and organizational contributions.

Positive Energy and Full Engagement

The second new idea in motivation takes lessons learned from professional athletes and applies them in order to develop corporate athletes. Jim Loehr's central tenets are the management of energy rather than time and the strategic use of disengagement to balance the power of full activity engagement. This approach to motivation suggests that individuals do not need to be activated by unmet needs but are already activated by their own physical, emotional, mental, and spiritual energy. A manager's task is to help individuals learn to manage their energy so that they can experience periodic renewal and recovery and thus, build positive energy and capacity for work. That is what Dyson aims to do in stirring creative passions. One UK public service provider categorizes its employees by engagement level as we see in the "Engaging Your 'Pole Vaulters.'"

A key to positive energy and full engagement is the concept that energy recovery is equally important to, if not more important than, energy expenditure. Individuals may be designed more as sprinters than long-distance runners, putting forth productive energy for short periods and then requiring time for recovery to reenergize. This approach to motivation and work is based on a balanced approach to the human body's potential to build or enhance its capacity, enabling the individual to sustain a high level of performance in the face of increasing work demands. Organizations with high levels of employee engagement perform well financially, even in volatile economic times.

Engaging Your "Pole Vaulters"

Strongly engaged employees are called "Grand Prix Drivers" and compose the largest group of employees in most organizations. Insuring that they do not burn out is the central leadership challenge for these valuable employees. "Flatliners" are often a substantial group of disengaged employees whose negative energy can be difficult to reverse or turn around. "Pole Vaulters" are an intriguing group of employees who practice on-again, off-again enthusiasm. They may be the group with the best opportunity for investing leadership effort for a nice return. Amey is a UK leading public services provider who has a best practice approach to engaging its "Pole Vaulters." The company manages the vital infrastructure and business services that nearly everyone, everywhere relies on. To engage their "Pole Vaulters," Amey assigns them to its Engagement Champions network of 150 select employees.

The Engagement Champions promote companywide engagement. Assigning "Pole Vaulters" encourages them to deepen and broaden their enthusiasm toward all of the company initiatives. The "Pole Vaulters" may be the minority group of employees with the highest payoff once they become more consistently and fully involved in company activities. By focusing on this group, Amey aims to get leveraged payoffs from limited effort. The smallest group of employees in most organizations is the "Long Distance Runners" who are reliable and consistent though not as engaged as the "Grand Prix Drivers." Low energy investment in keeping them involved is the right way to go for this small group of employees.

Source: K. Truss and E. Soane., "Engaging the 'Pole Vaulters' in your staff" *Harvard Business Review* (March 2010): 24.

Social Exchange and Equity Theory

Equity theory is a social exchange process theory of motivation that focuses on the individual-environment interaction. In contrast to internal needs theories of motivation, equity theory is concerned with the social processes that influence motivation and behavior. According to Peter Blau, power and exchange are important considerations in understanding human behavior. In the same vein, Amitai Etzioni developed three categories of exchange relationships people have with organizations: committed, calculated, and alienated involvements. Etzioni characterized committed relationships as moral ones with high positive intensity, calculated relationships as ones of low positive or low negative intensity, and alienated relationships as ones of high negative intensity. Committed relationships may characterize a person's involvement with a religious group, and alienated relationships may characterize a person's incarceration in a prison. Social exchange theory may be the best way to understand effort-reward relationships and the sense of fairness at work as seen in a Dutch study. Moral principles in workplace fairness are important because unfairness leads to such things as theft, sabotage, and even violence.

Demands and Contributions

Calculated involvements are based on the notion of social exchange in which each party in the relationship demands certain things of the other and contributes accordingly to the exchange. Business partnerships and commercial deals are excellent examples of calculated involvements. When they work well and both parties to the exchange benefit, the relationship has a positive orientation. When events like losses occur or conflicts arise, the relationship has a negative orientation. Single significant events, or anchor events, can throw a calculated exchange relationship out of equilibrium and move the relationship to competition or altruism. A model for examining these calculated exchange relationships is set out in Figure 11.3. We use this model to examine the nature of the relationship between a person and his or her employing organization. The same basic model can be used to examine the relationship between two individuals or two organizations.

Demands

Each party to the exchange makes demands upon the other. These demands express the expectations that each party has of the other in the relationship. The organization expresses its demands on the individual in the form of goal or mission statements, job expectations, performance objectives, and performance feedback. These are among the primary and formal mechanisms through which people learn about the organization's demands and expectations of them.

The organization is not alone in making these demands of the relationship. As we have previously discussed, the individual has needs to be satisfied as well. These satisfaction needs form the basis of the expectations or demands placed on the organization by the individual. Employee need-fulfillment and the feeling of belonging are both important to healthy social exchange and organizational membership. These needs may be conceptualized from the perspective of Maslow, Alderfer, Herzberg, or McClelland.

Contributions

Just as each party to the exchange makes demands upon the other, each also has contributions to make to the relationship. These contributions are the basis for satisfying the demands expressed by the other party in the relationship. Employees can satisfy organizational demands through a range of contributions, including their skills, abilities, knowledge, energy, professional contacts, and native talents. As people grow and develop over time, they increasingly able to satisfy the range of demands and expectations placed upon them by the organization.

In a similar fashion, organizations have a range of contributions available to the exchange relationship to meet individual needs. These contributions include salary, benefits, advancement opportunities, security, status, and social affiliation. Some organizations are richer in resources and better able to meet employee needs than others. Thus, one concern that individuals and organizations share is whether the relationship is a fair deal or an equitable arrangement for both members. Social exchange relationship perceptions are influenced by executive leadership style, organizational culture, and employment approach, which in turn have an effect on commitment and performance but not organizational citizenship behavior.

Adams's Theory of Inequity

Blau's and Etzioni's ideas about social process and exchange provide a context for understanding fairness, equity, and inequity in work relationships. Stacy Adams explicitly developed the idea that *inequity* in the social exchange process is an important motivator. Adams's theory of inequity suggests inequity or unfairness motivates people more than equity or fairness. Inequity occurs when a person receives more, or less, than the person believes is deserved based on effort and/or contribution Inequity leads to the experience of tension, and tension motivates a person to act in a manner to resolve the inequity.

When does a person know that the situation is inequitable or unfair? Adams suggests that people examine the contribution portion of the exchange relationship discussed above. Specifically, individuals consider their inputs (their own contributions to the relationship) and their outcomes (the organization's contributions to the relationship). Next, they calculate an input/outcome ratio. Then, they compare this ratio to another case. This other case, the comparison other, could be a specific case of which they are aware or a generalized or idealized notion of fairness Figure 11.4 shows one equity situation and two inequity situations, one negative and one positive. For example, inequity in (b) could occur if the comparison other earned a higher salary, and inequity in (c) could occur if the person had more vacation time, in both cases all else being equal. Although not illustrated in this example, nontangible inputs, like emotional investment, and nontangible outcomes, like job satisfaction, may well enter into a person's equity equation.

Pay inequity has been a particularly thorny issue for women in some professions and companies. Eastman Kodak and other companies have made real progress fan addressing the problem through pay equity. As organizations become increasingly globalized, determining pay and benefit equity/inequity across national borders may be difficult.

Adams would consider the inequity in Figure 11.4(b) to be a first level of inequity. A more severe, second level of inequity would occur if the comparison other's inputs were lower than the person's. Inequalities in one (inputs or outcomes) coupled with equality in the other (inputs or outcomes) are experienced as a less severe inequity than inequalities in both inputs and outcomes. Adams's theory, however, does not provide a way of determining if some inputs (such as effort or experience) or some outcomes are more important or weighted more than others, such as a degree or certification.

The Resolution of Inequity

Once a person establishes the existence of an inequity, a number of strategies can be used to restore equity to the situation. Adams's theory provides seven basic strategies: (1) alter the person's outcomes, (2) alter the person's inputs, (3) alter the comparison other's outcomes, (4) alter the comparison other's inputs, (5) change who is used as a comparison other, (6) rationalize the inequity, and (7) leave the organizational situation.

	Person		Comparison other
(a) Equity	$\dfrac{\text{Outcomes}}{\text{Inputs}}$	$=$	$\dfrac{\text{Outcomes}}{\text{Inputs}}$
(b) Negative Inequity	$\dfrac{\text{Outcomes}}{\text{Inputs}}$	$<$	$\dfrac{\text{Outcomes}}{\text{Inputs}}$
(c) Positive Inequity	$\dfrac{\text{Outcomes}}{\text{Inputs}}$	$>$	$\dfrac{\text{Outcomes}}{\text{Inputs}}$

Figure 11.4 Equity and Inequity at Work

Within each of the first four strategies, an employee can employ a wide variety of tactics. For example, if an employee has a strategy to increase his or her income by $11,000 per year to restore equity, the tactic might be a meeting between the employee and his or her manager concerning the issue of salary equity. The person would present relevant data on the issue. Another tactic would be to work with the company's compensation specialists. A third tactic would be to bring the matter before an equity committee in the company. A fourth tactic would be to seek advice from the legal department.

The selection of a strategy and a set of tactics is a sensitive issue with possible long-term consequences. In this example, a strategy aimed at reducing the comparison other's outcomes may have the desired short-term effect of restoring equity while having adverse long-term consequences in terms of morale and productivity. Similarly, the choice of legal tactics may result in equity but have the long-term consequence of damaged relationships in the workplace. Therefore, as a person formulates the strategy and tactics to restore equity, the range of consequences of alternative actions must be taken into account. Hence, not all strategies or tactics are equally preferred. Equity theory does not include a hierarchy predicting which inequity reduction strategy a person will or should choose.

Field studies on equity theory suggest that it may help explain important organizational behaviors. For example, one study found that workers who perceived compensation decisions as equitable displayed greater job satisfaction and organizational commitment. In addition, equity theory may play an important role in labor-management relationships with regard to union-negotiated benefits.

New Perspectives on Equity Theory

Since the original formulation of the theory of inequity, now usually referred to as equity theory, a number of revisions have been made in light of new theories and research. One important theoretical revision proposes three types of individuals based on preferences for equity. *Equity sensitives* are those people who prefer equity based on the originally formed theory. Equity sensitivity contributes significantly to variations in free time spent working. Females and minorities have not always been equitably treated in business and commerce. *Benevolents* are people who are comfortable with an equity ratio less than that of their comparison other, as exhibited in the Calvinistic heritage of the Dutch. These people may be thought of as givers. One study of 465 adults found that Benevolents value work outcomes such as benefits because of how the benefits help their family members. Another example of giving is the James Dyson Foundation for philanthropy, as we see in Looking Back. *Entitleds* are people who are comfortable with an equity ratio greater than that of their comparison other; as exhibited by some offspring of the affluent who want and expect more. These people may he thought of as takers.

Research on organizational justice has a long history. One study suggests that a person's organizational position influences self-imposed performance expectations. Specifically, a two-level move up in an organization with no additional pay creates a higher self-imposed performance expectation than a one-level move up with modest additional pay. Similarly, a two-level move down in an organization with no reduction in pay creates a lower self-imposed performance expectation than a one-level move down with a modest decrease in pay. In addition, procedural justice can predict task performance though this effect may be influenced by intrinsic motivation.

One of the unintended consequences of inequity and organizational injustice is dysfunctional behavior. Organizational injustice caused by payment inequity can even lead to insomnia though training in interactional justice reduces these effects. More seriously, workplace injustice can trigger aggressive reactions or other forms of violent and deviant behavior that do harm to both individuals and the organization. Fortunately, only a small number of individuals respond to such unfairness through dysfunctional behavior.

Although most studies of equity theory take a short-term perspective, one should consider equity comparisons over the long term as well. Increasing, decreasing, or constant experiences of inequity over time may have very different consequences for people. For example, do increasing inequity experiences have a debilitating effect on people? In addition, equity theory may help companies implement two-tiered wage structures, such as the one used by American Airlines in the early 1990s. In a two-tiered system, one group of employees receives different pay and benefits than another group. A study of 1,935 rank-and-file members in one retail chain using a two-tiered wage structure confirmed the predictions of equity theory. The researchers suggest that unions and management may want to consider work location and employment status (part-time versus full-time) prior to the implementation of a two-tiered system.

Expectancy Theory of Motivation

Whereas equity theory focuses on a social exchange process, V.H. Vroom's expectancy theory of motivation focuses on personal perceptions of the performance process. His theory is founded on two basic notions. First, people desire certain outcomes of behavior and performance which may be thought of as rewards or consequences of behavior. Second, people believe that there are relationships among the effort they put forth, the performance they achieve, and the outcomes they receive. Expectancy theory is a cognitive process theory of motivation.

The key constructs in the expectancy theory of motivation are the *valence* of an outcome, *expectancy*, and *instrumentality*. Valence is the value or importance one places on a particular reward. Expectancy is the belief that effort leads to performance (e.g., "If I try harder, I can do better").

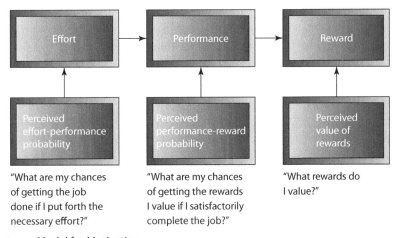

Figure 11.5 An Expectancy Model for Motivation

Instrumentality is the belief that performance is related to rewards, (e.g., If I perform better, I will get more pay").

A model for the expectancy theory notions of effort, performance, and rewards is depicted in Figure 11.5.

Valence, expectancy, and instrumentality are all important to a person's motivation. Expectancy and instrumentality concern a person's beliefs about how effort, performance, and rewards are related. For example, a person may firmly believe that an increase in effort has a direct, positive effect on performance, and that a reduced amount of effort results in a commensurate reduction in performance. Another person may have a very different set of beliefs about the effort-performance link. The person might believe that regardless of the amount of additional effort put forth, no improvement in performance is possible. Therefore, the perceived relationship between effort and performance varies from person to person and from activity to activity.

In a similar fashion, people's beliefs about the performance-reward link vary. One person may believe that an improvement in performance has a direct, positive effect on the rewards received, whereas another person may believe that an improvement in performance has no effect on the rewards received. Again, the perceived relationship between performance and rewards varies from person to person and from situation to situation. Where people attach symbolic meaning to monetary rewards, a positive effect occurs over and above the reward's economic value. From a motivation perspective, the person's subjective belief about the relationships between these constructs is what is important rather than the objective nature of the relationship. During volatile times in business, the performance-reward linkage may be confusing.

Managers and companies have used expectancy theory to design motivation programs.

Sometimes called *performance planning and evaluation systems,* these motivation programs are designed to enhance a person's belief that effort would lead to better performance and that better performance would lead to merit pay increases and other rewards. Valence and expectancy are particularly important in establishing priorities for people pursuing multiple goals when using this approach.

The third key idea of expectancy theory concerns valence. Valence is the value that people place on various rewards. Assuming individuals want rewards, their motivation increases along with their belief that effort leads to performance and performance leads to rewards. One person might prefer salary to benefits, whereas another person prefers the reverse. People place different values on each reward. In fact, employees vary notably with respect to the link between work and pay as well as in how they value money. Expectancy theory has been studied in a wide variety of organizational contexts. One study found that students were more motivated to study when they believed their effort would lead to higher grades.

Motivational Problems

Within the expectancy theory framework, motivational problems stem from three basic causes: disbelief in a relationship between effort and performance, disbelief in a relationship between performance and rewards, and lack of desire for the rewards offered. Interestingly, defensive pessimism may motivate if the act of worrying triggers an active planning process that reduces anxiety and prevents performance problems.

If the motivational problem is related to the person's belief that effort will not result in performance, the solution lies in altering this belief. The person can be shown how an increase in effort or an alteration in the kind of effort put forth can be converted into improved performance. For example, the textbook salesperson who does not believe more calls (effort) will result in greater sales (performance) might be shown how to strong prospects with higher probability sales from weaker prospects with lower probability sales. When calling upon strong prospects, more calls (effort) could be converted into greater sales (performance).

If the motivational problem is related to the person's belief that performance will not result in rewards, the solution lies in altering this belief. The person can be shown how an increase in performance or a somewhat altered form of performance will he converted into rewards. For example, the textbook salesperson who does not believe greater sales (performance) will result in higher commissions (rewards) might be shown computationally or graphically that a direct relationship does exist. Hence, greater sales (performance) are directly converted into higher commissions (rewards).

If the motivational problem is related to the value the person places on, or the preference the person has for, certain rewards, the solution lies in influencing the value placed on the rewards or altering the rewards themselves. For example, the textbook salesperson may not particularly want higher commissions, given the small incremental gain he would receive at his tax level. In this case, the company might establish a mechanism for sheltering commissions from befog taxed or alternative mechanisms for deferred compensation.

Although, the theory has been shown to predict job satisfaction accurately, research results on expectancy theory have been mixed and best by several difficulties. The theory's complexity makes it difficult to test the full model especially because the measures of instrumentality, valence, and expectancy have only weak validity. Additionally, measuring the expectancy constructs is time-consuming; the values for each construct can change over time for each individual. Finally, the theory assumes the individual is rational and acts as a minicomputer, calculating probabilities and values. In reality, human calculations are more complex as they include psychological, emotional, and social factors.

WORK MOTIVATION AND PERFORMANCE

John A. Wagner III & John R. Hollenbeck

Instrumentality: Learning Theories

The understanding of valence contributed by need theories provides only one piece of the motivational puzzle—what people want. To understand behavior, we need to know not just what people want but what they believe will lead to the attainment of what they want. As noted earlier, these beliefs are referred to as *instrumentalities*. Learning theories help clarify how relationships between behaviors and rewards come to be perceived. They also provide information that allows us to estimate the character, permanence, and strength of these relationships.

The notion that people generally behave so as to maximize pleasure and minimize pain was first formulated by the ancient Greek philosophers and captured in the concept of **hedonism**. Virtually all modern theories of motivation incorporate this concept. It is especially conspicuous in learning theories, all of which attempt to explain behavior in terms of the associations that people use to link some behavior and some outcome. Two types of learning theories are discussed here:

operant learning (reinforcement theory) and social learning.

Reinforcement Theory

Reinforcement theory proposes that a person engages in a specific behavior because that behavior has been reinforced by a specific outcome. A simple example of positive reinforcement can be seen in a recent study that examined ways to reduce absenteeism. In this study, several locations of a garment factory that had been experiencing attendance problems served as the backdrop for an intervention that was designed around public recognition. The idea was to give positive attention to workers who were absent less than three days each quarter. Employees who managed this were given (a) personal attention in the form of a letter from the CEO thanking them for their diligence, (b) a public celebration party where they were wined and dined along with other winners, and (c) small symbolic mementos (a gold necklace for women and a gold penknife for men) to highlight their accomplishments. Within a year, plants that had adopted the recognition program experienced a 50 percent reduction in absenteeism compared to control plants.

A more complex example of how to link organizational strategy, technological advances, and positive reinforcement can be seen with MBNA, a company that produces Visa and MasterCard credit cards. MBNA's strategy is to market credit cards to "affinity groups," that is, groups with strong loyalties. Thus, they produce cards that incorporate anything from the Dallas Cowboys logo to personal pet photos (for Ralston Purina). Members of these affinity groups are lucrative customers, with incomes 20 percent above the national average and balances close to $2,000 above the industry average. Not surprisingly, however, these high-profile customers also demand high levels of service and, above all, they hate to wait.

To make sure that service is provided, MBNA relies heavily on an integrated system of technology and incentives. For example, one goal they have is to make sure that 98.5 percent of phone calls get picked up on fewer than two rings. They measure this electronically, and at any moment on a given day it is possible to get a reading that shows that employees are achieving "two-ring pickup" 98.4 percent of the time, and to show that this is 1.2 percent higher than average, a 1 percent fall-off from the previous day, and 0.1 percent shy of the goal. Results for this and 14 other goals (such as processing a request to increase a credit line in 15 minutes or less) are then posted daily on 60 scoreboards at MBNA facilities around the country.

Incentives are then wrapped around these electronic measures. For example, every day the 98.5 percent standard is met, money is thrown into an employee pool. Money from this pool is then handed out at regular intervals—as much as $1,000 per employee—depending on the percentage of times the goal is met. Similar incentives are tied to the other 14 goals. The effect on

employees is evident in the words of manager Janine Marrone, who notes, "If you're an MBNA employee and go to a restaurant and hear a phone ring more than twice, it drives you nuts—you have to stop yourself from going behind the counter and answering it." Indeed, the term *operant learning* derives from the fact that the person must perform some *operation* to receive the reinforcing outcome.

Operant learning is especially good for reinforcing simple or well-learned responses. In some cases, however, managers may want to encourage a complex behavior that might not occur on its own. In this instance, the process of shaping can be helpful. **Shaping** means rewarding successive approximations to a desired behavior, so that "getting close counts." For example, someone who has never played golf is highly unlikely to pick up a club and execute a perfect drive with his or her first swing. Left alone to try repeatedly with no instruction, a novice golfer probably will never exhibit the correct behavior.

In shaping, rather than waiting for the correct behavior to occur on its own, close approximations win rewards. Over time, rewards are held back until the person more closely approaches the right behavior. Thus a golf instructor might at first praise a novice golfer for holding the club with the right grip. To obtain a second reward, the novice may be required not only to display the correct grip but also to stand at the appropriate distance from the ball. To obtain additional rewards, the novice may have to do both of these things and execute the backswing correctly, and so on. In this way, simple initial behaviors become shaped into a complex desired behavior. Over time, increasingly difficult behaviors have to be mastered, and this kind of "deliberate practice" can eventually lead to high levels of expertise. Indeed, studies of experts in many different fields suggest that this kind of hard work and dedication directed at learning new details about a specific task is what underlies the success of many great performers in sports, business, science, and medicine. Across many different disciplines, the research seems to suggest that it takes at least ten years to truly develop expertise with any complex task.

Extinction is a second form of reinforcement. In extinction, a weakened response occurs because the desired outcome is no longer paired with some positive reinforcer. Indeed, one problem with reinforcement systems is that they often focus attention so exclusively on the reinforced behavior that other non-reinforced behaviors languish. For example, in attempting to process a credit application more quickly, an employee may sacrifice quality (and perhaps issue credit to a poor risk) if no reinforcement exists for making good decisions as well as fast ones.

Negative reinforcement and punishment are two other types of reinforcement used to influence behavior. In **negative reinforcement**, the likelihood that a person will engage in a particular behavior increases because the behavior is followed by the removal of something the person dislikes. In **punishment**, the likelihood of a given behavior decreases because it is followed by something that the person dislikes. Figure 12.1 illustrates the distinctions drawn among positive reinforcement, extinction, negative reinforcement, and punishment. As shown in the figure, reinforcement theory can be used to promote or inhibit behaviors, as can employing both positive and negative rewards.

Managers in organizations sometimes contend that they cannot use reinforcement theory because they do not have enough resources to give positive reinforcements. For example, they cannot always raise salaries or award bonuses as they might like. Behavioral management programs that rely on positive reinforcement often need to go beyond money to truly be effective. Moreover, as Figure 12.1 makes clear, positive reinforcement is merely one of a number of possible ways to

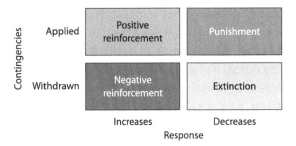

Figure 12.1 Effects of Methods of Reinforcement on Behavioral Response

increase the frequency of a desired behavior. For instance, managers can employ negative reinforcement to increase a response. They can find something about the job that people do not like and, when employees engage in desired behaviors, remove it. A sales manager who wants to increase sales and who knows that salespeople hate to complete paperwork associated with their work, for example, might offer to shift the responsibility for completing paperwork to others if these employees increase their productivity. The sales force's enthusiasm for selling might increase noticeably as a result.

Although it is sometimes difficult to come up with ideas for positive rewards, most organizations can easily envision a wide variety of ways to punish people. Indeed, managers often instinctively react in this manner when confronted with a behavior that they wish to eliminate. This is somewhat problematic because research shows that, when approached the right way, people can learn a great deal from their errors, and in some training contexts the *best* way for people to learn is to force them to make certain types of errors. If the errors occur in a supportive training context that minimizes the negative emotional reactions that come with failure, this promotes both learning and risk taking.

As Figure 12.1 shows, however, by itself punishment can only suppress undesired behaviors but not promote desired behaviors. In many instances, some other undesirable behavior may simply spring up in place of the old, bad behavior. For example, taking away access to the Internet may simply transform a cyberslacker into a slacker. Moreover, punishment tends to have short-lived effects, and it can produce side effects such as negative emotional reactions among those who are punished. Finally, one important side effect of punishment is that it often leads to cover-ups of information that needs to get out in order to improve systems. For example, the Federal Aviation Authority (FAA) and the airline pilots unions had an agreement on voluntary information sharing that protected any pilot who made an error from prosecution if he or she reported the error within 24 hours of the incident. The purpose of this protection was to perfect the entire airline system and make sure no other pilot made the same mistake. However, owing to strained labor relations between the pilots unions and the airlines, the airlines were increasingly using such reports as a pretext to fire pilots, which led the union to threaten to suspend the program in 2008. Many observers felt the negative effects of punishing pilots for errors (cover-ups) were much worse than the gain that might come from firing one or two pilots who made a mistake.

Despite these dangers, many organizations continue to mete out punishment, because some behaviors are so damaging to the firm that stopping them is crucial. Moreover, failure to take action may imply acceptance of the offending behavior, and the organization may be held liable for the employee's actions. For example, if a cyberslacking employee downloads and transmits pornography over the company's Internet connection, this practice could be viewed as creating a hostile work environment—opening up the organization to sexual harassment charges. Thus, rather than eliminating punishment altogether, organizations need to strive to punish employees

more effectively. A company can take several steps to move in this direction.

First, effective discipline programs are *progressive*—that is, they move in incremental steps. A program might start with a simple oral warning, followed by a written formal notice and then some actual disciplinary action that falls short of termination (such as suspension). Second, punishment should be *immediate* rather than delayed. This characteristic maximizes the perceived contingency between the offending behavior and the punishment, and it minimizes the perception that the offending behavior represents a pretext to punish the person for something else. Third, punishment should be *consistent*, so that the punishment is the same no matter who commits the offense. Fourth, punishment should be *impersonal*— that is, directed at the behavior rather than at the individual as a person. Finally, punishment should be *documented* to construct a "paper trail" of physical evidence that supports the contention that the punishment meted out was progressive, immediate, consistent, and impersonal.

In addition to implementing these five steps, in organizations that employ self-managing teams, it is important to have team members join in this decision. As individuals, group members are often more lenient than hierarchical supervisors. When allowed to discuss the offense as a group and reach consensus, however, the group as a whole tends to show much less leniency. Indeed, group-based decisions regarding discipline often resemble the decision that would be made by supervisors working alone. Recognition of this fact is important, because supervisors armed with the support of the work group they represent enjoy a much stronger position when it comes to doling out punishment.

Although the steps described previously may seem like simple and rational procedures that do not need to be spelled out, this perception is not always accurate. The types of offenses that call for punishment often generate strong emotional reactions from managers that short-circuit rationality. Indeed, these disciplinary procedures may seem excruciatingly slow to the offended manager, and they may frustrate his or her need for quick and satisfying retribution. Managers need to be assured that the process is slow but sure. In the end, if the problem employee must be fired, the procedures ensure that the company can prove the action was justified. Otherwise, the company might be sued for "wrongful discharge" and be unable to terminate the offending party.

Social Learning

Social learning theory, as proposed by Albert Bandura, encompasses a theory of observational learning that holds that most people learn behaviors by observing others and then *modeling* the behaviors perceived as being effective. Such observational learning is in marked contrast to the process of learning through direct reinforcement, and it better explains how people learn complex behavioral sequences.

For example, suppose a worker observes a colleague who, after giving bad news to their manager, is punished. Strict reinforcement theory would suggest that, when confronted with the same task, the observing worker will be neither more nor less prone to be the bearer of bad tidings because that person has not personally been reinforced. Social learning theory suggests otherwise. Although the worker may not have directly experienced the fate of a colleague, he or she will nonetheless learn by observation that this manager "shoots the messenger." The employee will probably conclude that the best response in such situations is to keep quiet. Even though the manager might not agree that problems should be covered up, his or her behavior may send

precisely this message. Indeed, "fearing the boss more than the competition" has been cited as one of the top ten reasons companies fail.

Besides focusing on learning by observation, social learning theory proposes that people can reinforce or punish their own behaviors; that is, they can engage in *self-reinforcement*. According to Bandura, a self-reinforcing event occurs when (1) tangible rewards are readily available for the taking, (2) people deny themselves free access to those rewards, and (3) they allow themselves to acquire the rewards only after achieving difficult self-set goals. For example, many successful writers, once alone and seated at their workstations, refuse to take a break until they have written a certain number of pages. Obviously, the writers can leave any time they wish. They deny themselves the reward of a rest, however, until they have accomplished their self-set goals. Research indicates that this type of self-reinforcement can be used to help people stop smoking, overcome drug addiction, cure obesity, improve study habits, enhance scholastic achievement, and reduce absenteeism.

Valence and instrumentality, the first two parts of our model of motivation, combine to influence the desire to perform (Figure 12.2). People will be motivated to perform at a high level as long

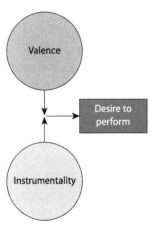

Figure 12.2 Step 1: The Desire to Perform as a Function of Valence and Instrumentality

as they perceive that receiving high-valence outcomes is contingent upon giving a strong personal performance. Our understanding of the process depicted in Figure 12.2 partly depends on need theories, which explain which outcomes individuals will perceive as having positive valences. In addition, reinforcement theories explain how people learn about contingencies, so they provide insight into the process that makes people want to perform.

Expectancy: Self-Efficacy Theory

Self-Efficacy and Behavior

Although actually part of Bandura's social learning theory, self-efficacy constitutes an important topic in its own right. **Self-efficacy** refers to the judgments that people make about their ability to execute courses of action required to deal with prospective situations. Individuals high in self-efficacy believe that they can master (or have mastered) some specific task. Self-efficacy determines how much effort people will expend and how long they will persist in the face of obstacles or stressful experiences. When beset with difficulties, people who entertain serious doubts about their capabilities tend to slacken their efforts or give up altogether. In contrast, those who have a strong sense of efficacy tend to exert greater effort to master the challenges, and the positive effects for this characteristic seem to manifest themselves even if one controls for cognitive ability and various other personality traits. Indeed, if high levels of self-efficacy have a downside, it is the fact that these people will often confidently persist even in the face of consistent feedback indicating that they should change their tactics or lower their self-image. This overconfidence effect

also leads people who are high in self-efficacy to underestimate the amount of resources needed to accomplish some difficult goal. However, for the most part, the positive aspects of high self-efficacy seem to outweigh these negative side effects.

Sources of Self-Efficacy

Given that feelings of self-efficacy can greatly influence behavior, it is important to identify the sources of those feelings. Bandura identified four sources of self-efficacy beliefs. First, self-efficacy can reflect a person's *past accomplishments*. Past instances of successful behavior increase personal feelings of self-efficacy, especially when these successes seem attributable to unchanging factors such as personal ability or a manageable level of task difficulty.

The link between self-efficacy theory and social learning theory is made clear in Bandura's second source of self-efficacy beliefs: *observation of others*. Merely watching someone else perform successfully on a task may increase an individual's sense of self-efficacy with respect to the same task. Note, however, that characteristics of the observer and model can influence the effects of observation on feelings of self-efficacy. For instance, the observer must judge the model to be both credible and similar to the observer (in terms of personal characteristics such as ability and experience) if the observation is to influence the individual's efficacy perceptions.

A third source of self-efficacy is *verbal persuasion*. Convincing people that they can master a behavior will, under some circumstances, increase their perceptions of self-efficacy. The characteristics of the source and the target of the communication, however, can affect how the verbal persuasion influences self-efficacy perceptions. Again, people who are perceived as credible and trustworthy are most able to influence others' self-efficacy perceptions in this manner.

Logical verification is another source of self-efficacy perceptions. With logical verification, people can generate perceptions of self-efficacy at a new task by perceiving a systematic relationship between the new task and an already-mastered task. For example, if an experienced employee is apprehensive about his or her ability to learn some new software program, the manager should emphasize how many other changes in work procedures this person has successfully managed in the past, and then argue that there is no logical reason why learning this new program will be any different.

Self-efficacy theory is particularly useful for explaining how expectancies are formed and suggesting how they might be changed. Of course, as Figure 12.3 suggests, a person's beliefs will not necessarily translate into motivation unless the person truly desires to excel. Similarly, simply wanting to excel will not bring about high levels of effort unless the person has some belief that such performance is possible.

Accuracy of Role Perceptions: Goal-Setting Theory

Role perceptions are people's beliefs about what they are supposed to accomplish on the job and how they should achieve those goals. When these beliefs are accurate, people facing a task know what needs to be done, how long it should take, and who will have the responsibility to carry out the task at hand. Such role accuracy guarantees that the energy devoted to task accomplishment will be directed toward the right activities and outcomes. At the same time, it decreases the amount of energy wasted on unimportant goals

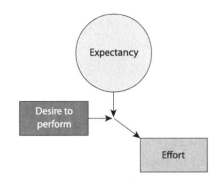

Figure 12.3 Step 2: Level of Effort as a Function of Desire and Expectancy

and activities. Goal-setting theory can help us understand how to enhance the accuracy of role perceptions.

Important Goal Attributes

Employees are often told, "Do your best." Although this axiom is intended to guide job performance in everyday situations, research has consistently demonstrated that such vague instructions can actually undermine personal performance. In contrast, more than 100 studies support the assertion that performance is enhanced by goals that are both *specific and difficult*. Indeed, setting specific goals has improved performance in a wide variety of jobs (Table 12.1). Specific and difficult goals appear to promote greater effort and to enhance persistence, especially when combined with timely feedback and incentives. Specific and difficult goals are especially effective when incorporated into a continuous improvement cycle in which future goals consist of reasonable increments on past goals. They also encourage people to develop effective task strategies and sharpen their mental focus on the task. Their primary virtue, however, is that they direct attention to specific desired results, clarifying priorities and perceptions of both what is important and what level of performance is needed.

Table 12.1 Jobholders Who Have Improved Performance in Goal-Setting Programs

Telephone servicepersons	Loggers
Baggage handlers	Marine recruits
Typists	Union bargaining representatives
Salespersons	Bank managers
Truck loaders	Assembly line workers
College students	Animal trappers
Sewing machine operators	Maintenance technicians
Engineering researchers	Dockworkers
Scientists	Die casters

As we saw in the Whirlpool example at the beginning of this chapter, however, difficult goals can also lead to unethical behaviors. For example, Bernard Ebbers, CEO of World-Com, stated, "Our goal is not to capture market share or be global, but instead our goal is to be the Number 1 stock on Wall Street." Of course, achieving the latter goal was going to be very difficult if one ignored the first two goals, and Ebbers tried to achieve this by acquiring more and more unrelated businesses. This made it look as though the company was experiencing ever greater revenues in the short term, but, without the knowledge of how to achieve market share or expand their markets, this could not be sustained over the long term—resulting in one of the largest bankruptcies ever recorded in U.S. history. Thus, although the motivational power of goals is often impressive, one has to be very careful of exactly how goals are expressed, how difficult they will be to achieve, and what exact behaviors they will motivate.

Goal Commitment and Participation

The extent to which a person feels committed to a goal can also affect performance. As depicted in Figure 12.4, specific and difficult goals tend to lead to increased performance only when there is high goal commitment. The requirement that people be committed to goals means that goals must be set carefully, because when they are too difficult they are typically met with less commitment. People may view a goal that is set too high as impossible; thus, they reject it altogether.

Fortunately, research has examined several ways to increase commitment to difficult goals. One important factor is the degree to which the goals are public rather than private. In one study, students for whom difficult goals for GPA were made public (posted on bulletin boards) showed higher levels of commitment to those goals relative to students with private goals. This study also found a significant positive relationship between need for achievement and goal commitment. Moreover, the positive relationship between need for achievement and goal commitment was especially strong when the goals were set by the students themselves, as opposed to being assigned by an outside party. If the employee is not allowed to set his or her own goals, the next best thing for instilling commitment is to at least let the employee participate in the goal-setting process. Participation promotes commitment, especially in certain cultures (low power distance). We will have more to say about cultural differences in Chapter 15, but for now we will simply note that, in some cultures (high power distance), people do not expect to participate, and hence will often show more commitment to assigned goals than those they set for themselves.

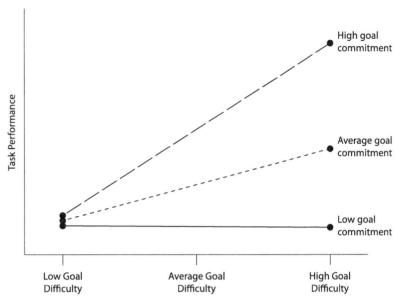

Figure 12.4 Conceptual Interactive Relationship between Goal Difficulty and Goal Commitment

Goals and Strategies

As shown in Table 12.1, goal setting can increase performance on a variety of jobs. Nevertheless, most early research on goal setting consisted of studies that focused attention on relatively simple tasks. More recent research has extended goal-setting theory into more complex task domains. In these situations, however, the links between goals, effort, and performance are less clear. A review of these studies indicates that, while goals have positive effects on all tasks, the magnitude of the effect is stronger for simple tasks than for complex tasks. Figure 12.5 illustrates how the effect of goal difficulty on performance decreases as task complexity increases.

In fact, focusing on narrow goals related to performance may discourage people from experimenting with new strategies and developing new skills, which as we noted earlier is the key to developing expertise on complex tasks. A performance drop-off often occurs when people switch from well-learned strategies to new and different ones. For example, if a person has gained a great deal of proficiency with one word-processing program,

that individual may express reluctance to upgrade to a new and improved program; while learning the new program, the employee fears that he or she will not work as quickly as was possible with the old program. Indeed, even if the worker is convinced that in the long run he or she will be able to work more rapidly with the new program, the employee may still be unwilling to pay the short-term performance costs of learning the new program.

The term **goal orientation** has been coined to distinguish between people who approach a task with the goal of learning how to improve and people whose goals focus strictly on performing at a certain level. Goal orientation is sometimes construed as an individual difference variable, but it can also be manipulated by attention-focusing instructions. Although people with a strict performance orientation often perform best on simple, stable, short-term tasks, people with a learning orientation often perform better on complex, dynamic, long-term tasks. Thus, the objectives of any managerially inspired goal-setting program must account for the need to perform at a high level as well as the need to create enough slack

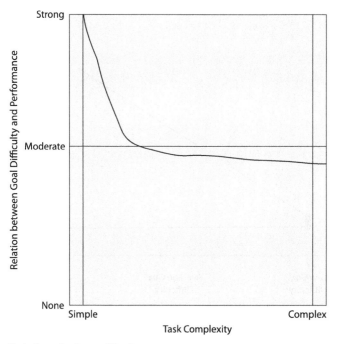

Figure 12.5 Goal Difficulty, Task Complexity, and Performance

in the system to allow people to experiment with new and potentially improved task strategies. This seems to be particularly the case for workers who are high in intelligence and hence derive more from potential learning experiences.

Although research on performance strategies has yielded findings that sometimes conflict with the results of other goal-setting studies, it is nevertheless helpful in delineating the specific, role-clarifying effects of goals. In simple tasks, where the *means* to perform a task are clear, specific and difficult goals lead to higher performance because they clarify the *ends* toward which task effort should be directed. In complex tasks, however, the means are not clear. Individuals performing such tasks do not know how to proceed in the best way, so merely clarifying the ends sought is unlikely to enhance performance.

MANAGING STRESS AND THE WORK-LIFE BALANCE

Ricky W. Griffin & Gregory Moorhead

The Nature of Stress

Many people think of stress as a simple problem. In reality, however, stress is complex and often misunderstood. To learn how job stress truly works, we must first define it and then describe the process through which it develops.

Stress Defined

Stress has been defined in many ways, but most definitions say that stress is caused by a stimulus, that the stimulus can be either physical or psychological, and that the individual responds to the stimulus in some way. Therefore, we define **stress** as a person's adaptive response to a stimulus that places excessive psychological or physical demands on him or her.

Given the underlying complexities of this definition, we need to examine its components carefully. First is the notion of adaptation. As we discuss presently, people may adapt to stressful circumstances in any of several ways. Second is the role of the stimulus. This stimulus, generally called a *stressor*, is anything that induces stress. Third, stressors can be either psychological or physical. Finally, the demands the stressor places on the individual must be excessive for stress to actually result. Of course, what is excessive for one person may be perfectly tolerable for another. The point is simply that a person must perceive the demands as excessive or stress will not actually be present.

There has been a marked increase in stress reported by airline workers in the last few years. A combination of increased pressure for salary and benefit reductions, threats to pensions, demotions, layoffs, and heavier workloads have all become more pronounced since September 11. And today's rising energy prices are likely to increase these pressures. As a result, more airline workers than ever before are seeking counseling services; turnover and absenteeism are also on the rise.

The Stress Process

Much of what we know about stress today can be traced to the pioneering work of Dr. Hans Selye. Among Selye's most important contributions were his identification of the general adaptation syndrome and the concepts of *eustress* and *distress*.

General Adaptation Syndrome

Figure 13.1 offers a graphical representation of the **general adaptation syndrome (GAS)**. According to this model, each of us has a normal level of resistance to stressful events. Some of us can tolerate a great deal of stress and others much less, but we all have a threshold at which stress starts to affect us.

The GAS begins when a person first encounters a stressor. The first stage is called "alarm." At this point, the person may feel some degree of panic and begin to wonder how to cope. The individual may also have to resolve a "fight-or-flight" question: "Can I deal with this, or should I run away?" For example, suppose a manager is assigned to write a lengthy report overnight. Her first reaction may be, "How will I ever get this done by tomorrow?"

If the stressor is too extreme, the person may simply be unable to cope with it. In most cases, however, the individual gathers his or her strength (physical or emotional) and begins to resist the negative effects of the stressor. The manager with

the long report to write may calm down, call home to tell her kids that she's working late, roll up her sleeves, order out for dinner, and get to work. Thus, at stage 2 of the GAS, the person is resisting the effects of the stressor.

Often, the resistance phase ends the GAS. If the manager completes the report earlier than she expected, she may drop it in her briefcase, smile to herself, and head home tired but happy. On the other hand, prolonged exposure to a stressor without resolution may bring on phase 3 of the GAS: exhaustion. At this stage, the person literally gives up and can no longer fight the stressor. For example, the manager may fall asleep at her desk at 3 a.m. and fail to finish the report.

Distress and Eustress

Selye also pointed out that the sources of stress need not be bad. For example, receiving a bonus and then having to decide what to do with the money can be stressful. So can getting a promotion, making a speech as part of winning a major award, getting married, and similar "good" things. Selye called this type of stress **eustress**. As we will see later, eustress can lead to a number of positive outcomes for the individual. Of course,

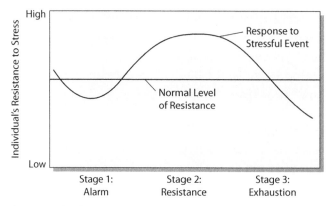

Figure 13.1 The General Adaptation Syndrome. The general adaptation syndrome (GAS) perspective describes three stages of the stress process. The initial stage is called alarm. As illustrated here, a person's resistance often dips slightly below the normal level during this stage. Next comes actual resistance to the stressor, usually leading to an increase above the person's normal level of resistance. Finally, in stage 3, exhaustion may set in, and the person's resistance declines sharply below normal levels.

there is also negative stress. Called **distress**, this is what most people think of when they hear the word *stress*. Excessive pressure, unreasonable demands on our time, and bad news all fall into this category. As the term suggests, this form of stress generally results in negative consequences for the individual. For purposes of simplicity, we will continue to use the simple term *stress* throughout this chapter. But as you read and study the chapter, remember that stress can be either good or bad. It can motivate and stimulate us, or it can lead to any number of dangerous side effects.

Individual Differences and Stress

We have already alluded to the fact that stress can affect different people in different ways. Of course, this should come as no surprise. The most fully developed individual difference relating specifically to stress is the distinction between Type A and Type B personality profiles.

Type A and B Personality Profiles

Type A and Type B profiles were first observed by two cardiologists, Meyer Friedman and Ray Rosenman. They first got the idea when a worker repairing the upholstery on their waiting-room chairs commented on the fact that many of the chairs were worn only on the front. After further study, the two cardiologists realized that many of their heart patients were anxious and had a hard time sitting still—they were literally sitting on the edges of their seats!

Using this observation as a starting point, Friedman and Rosenman began to study the phenomenon more closely. They eventually concluded that their patients were exhibiting one of two very different types of behavior patterns. Their research also led them to conclude that the differences were based on personality. They labeled these two behavior patterns Type A and Type B.

The extreme **Type A** individual is extremely competitive, very devoted to work, and has a strong sense of time urgency. Moreover, this person is likely to be aggressive, impatient, and highly work oriented. He or she has a lot of drive and motivation and wants to accomplish as much as possible in as short a time as possible.

The extreme **Type B** person, in contrast, is less competitive, is less devoted to work, and has a weaker sense of time urgency. This person feels less conflict with either people or time and has a more balanced, relaxed approach to life. He or she has more confidence and is able to work at a constant pace.

A commonsense expectation might be that Type A people are more successful than Type B people. In reality, however, this is not necessarily true—the Type B person is not necessarily any more or less successful than the Type A. There are several possible explanations for this. For example, Type A people may alienate others because of their drive and may miss out on important learning opportunities in their quest to get ahead. Type B's, on the other hand, may have better interpersonal reputations and may learn a wider array of skills.

Friedman and Rosenman pointed out that most people are not purely Type A or Type B; instead, people tend toward one or the other type. For example, an individual might exhibit marked Type A characteristics much of the time but still be able to relax once in a while and even occasionally forget about time. Likewise, even the most laid-back Type B person may occasionally spend some time obsessing about work.

Friedman and Rosenman's initial research on the Type A and Type B profile differences yielded some alarming findings. In particular, they suggested that Type A's were much more likely to get coronary heart disease than were Type B's. In recent years, however, follow-up research by other scientists has suggested that the relationship between Type A behavior and the risk of coronary heart disease is not all that straightforward.

Although the reasons are unclear, recent findings suggest that Type A's are much more complex than originally believed. For example, in addition to the characteristics already noted, they are also more likely to be depressed and hostile. Any one of these characteristics or a combination of them can lead to heart problems. Moreover, different approaches to measuring Type A tendencies have yielded different results.

Finally, in one study that found Type A's to actually be less susceptible to heart problems than Type B's, the researchers offered an explanation consistent with earlier thinking: Because Type A's are relatively compulsive, they may seek treatment earlier and are more likely to follow their doctors' orders!

Hardiness and Optimism

Two other important individual differences related to stress are hardiness and optimism. Research suggests that some people have what are termed *hardier* personalities than others. **Hardiness** is a person's ability to cope with stress. People with hardy personalities have an internal locus of control, are strongly committed to the activities in their lives, and view change as an opportunity for advancement and growth. Such people are seen as relatively unlikely to suffer illness if they experience high levels of pressure and stress. On the other hand, people with low hardiness may have more difficulties in coping with pressure and stress.

Another potentially important individual difference is optimism. **Optimism** is the extent to which a person sees life in positive or negative terms. A popular expression used to convey this idea concerns the glass "half filled with water." A person with a lot of optimism will tend to see it as half full, whereas a person with less optimism (a pessimist) will often see it as half empty. Optimism is also related to positive and negative affectivity. In general, optimistic people tend to handle stress better. They will be able to see the positive characteristics of the situation and recognize that things may eventually improve. In contrast, less optimistic people may focus more on the negative characteristics of the situation and expect things to get worse, not better.

Cultural differences are also important in determining how stress affects people. For example, research suggests that American executives may experience less stress than executives in many other countries, including Japan and Brazil. The major causes of stress also differ across countries. In Germany, for example, major causes of stress are time pressure and deadlines. In South Africa, long work hours more frequently lead to stress. And in Sweden, the major cause of stress is the encroachment of work on people's private lives.

Other research suggests that women are perhaps more prone to experience the psychological effects of stress, whereas men may report more physical effects. Finally, some studies suggest that people who see themselves as complex individuals are better able to handle stress than people who view themselves as relatively simple. We should add, however, that the study of individual differences in stress is still in its infancy. It would therefore be premature to draw rigid conclusions about how different types of people handle stress.

Common Causes of Stress

Many things can cause stress. Figure 13.2 shows two broad categories: organizational stressors and life stressors. It also shows three categories of stress consequences: individual consequences, organizational consequences, and burnout.

Organizational Stressors

Organizational stressors are various factors in the workplace that can cause stress. Four general sets of organizational stressors are task demands, physical demands, role demands, and interpersonal demands.

Task Demands

Task demands are stressors associated with the specific job a person performs. Some occupations are by nature more stressful than others. Table 13.1 lists a representative sample of relative high- and low-stress jobs, based on one study. As you can see, the jobs of surgeon and commercial airline pilot are among the most stressful, while the jobs of actuary and dietitian are among the least stressful jobs.

Beyond specific task-related pressures, other aspects of a job may pose physical threats to a person's health. Unhealthy conditions exist in occupations such as coal mining and toxic waste handling. Lack of job security is another task demand that can cause stress. Someone in a relatively secure job is not likely to worry unduly about losing that position; however, threats to job security can increase stress dramatically. For

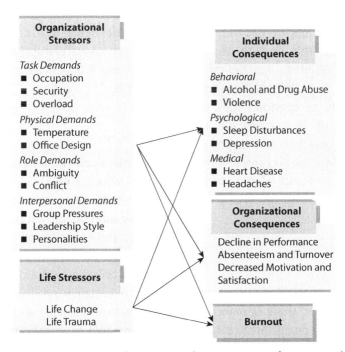

Figure 13.2 Causes and Consequences of Stress. The causes and consequences of stress are related in complex ways. As shown here, most common causes of stress can be classified as either organizational stressors or life stressors. Similarly, common consequences include individual and organizational consequences, as well as burnout. *Reference:* Adapted from James C. Quick and Jonathan D. Quick, *Organizational Stress and Preventive Management* (McGraw-Hill, 1984) pp. 19, 44, and 76.

Table 13.1 Most and Least Stressful Jobs

Top Most Stressful Jobs	Top Least Stressful Jobs
1. Surgeon	1. Actuary
2. Commercial airline pilot	2. Dietitian
3. Photojournalist	3. Computer systems analyst
4. Advertising account executive	4. Statistician
5. Real estate agent	5. Astronomer
6. Physician (general practice)	6. Mathematician
7. Reporter (newspaper)	7. Historian
8. Physician assistant	8. Software engineer

Source: www.careercast.com/jobs/content/StressfulJobs_page1, accessed on April 5, 2010.

example, stress generally increases throughout an organization during a period of layoffs or immediately after a merger with another firm. This has been observed at a number of organizations, including AT&T, Safeway, and Digital Equipment.

A final task demand stressor is overload. Overload occurs when a person simply has more work than he or she can handle. The overload can be either quantitative (the person has too many tasks to perform or too little time to perform them) or qualitative (the person may believe he or she lacks the ability to do the job). We should note that the opposite of overload may also be undesirable. As Figure 13.3 shows, low task demands can result in boredom and apathy just as overload can cause tension and anxiety. Thus, a moderate degree of workload-related stress is optimal, because it leads to high levels of energy and motivation.

Physical Demands

The **physical demands** of a job are its physical requirements on the worker; these demands are a function of the physical characteristics of the setting and the physical tasks the job involves. One important element is temperature. Working outdoors in extreme temperatures can result in stress, as can working in an improperly heated or cooled office. Strenuous labor such as loading heavy cargo or lifting packages can lead to similar results. Office design can be a problem, as well. A poorly designed office can make it difficult for people to have privacy or promote too much or too little social interaction. Too much interaction may distract a person from his or her task, whereas too little may lead to boredom or loneliness. Likewise, poor lighting, inadequate work surfaces, and similar deficiencies can create stress. And shift work can cause disruptions for people because of the way it affects their sleep and leisure-time activities.

Role Demands

Role demands can also be stressful to people in organizations. A **role** is a set of expected behaviors associated with a particular position in a group or organization. As such, it has both formal (i.e., job-related and explicit) and informal (i.e., social and implicit) requirements. People in an organization or work group expect a person in a particular role to act in certain ways. They transmit these expectations both formally and informally. Individuals perceive role expectations with varying degrees of accuracy and then attempt to enact that role. However, "errors" can creep into this process, resulting in stress-inducing problems called role ambiguity, role conflict, and role overload.

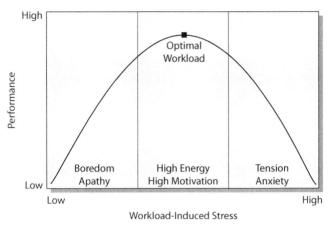

Figure 13.3 Workload, Stress, and Performance. Too much stress is clearly undesirable, but too little stress can also lead to unexpected problems. For example, too little stress may result in boredom and apathy and be accompanied by low performance. And although too much stress can cause tension, anxiety, and low performance, for most people there is an optimal level of stress that results in high energy, motivation, and performance.

Role ambiguity arises when a role is unclear. If your instructor tells you to write a term paper but refuses to provide more information, you will probably experience ambiguity. You do not know what the topic is, how long the paper should be, what format to use, or when the paper is due. In work settings, role ambiguity can stem from poor job descriptions, vague instructions from a supervisor, or unclear cues from coworkers. The result is likely to be a subordinate who does not know what to do. Role ambiguity can thus be a significant source of stress.

Role conflict occurs when the messages and cues from others about the role are clear but contradictory or mutually exclusive. One common form is *interrole conflict*—conflict between roles. For example, if a person's boss says that to get ahead one must work overtime and on weekends, and the same person's spouse says that more time is needed at home with the family, conflict may result. *Intrarole conflict* may occur when a person gets conflicting demands from different sources within the context of the same role. A manager's boss may tell her that she needs to put more pressure on subordinates to follow new work rules. At the same time, her subordinates may indicate that

they expect her to get the rules changed. Thus, the cues are in conflict, and the manager may be unsure about which course to follow.

Intrasender conflict occurs when a single source sends clear but contradictory messages. This might occur if the boss says one morning that there can be no more overtime for the next month but after lunch tells someone to work late that same evening. *Person-role conflict* results from a discrepancy between the role requirements and the individual's personal values, attitudes, and needs. If a person is told to do something unethical or illegal, or if the work is distasteful (for example, reprimanding or firing a close friend), person-role conflict is likely. Role conflict of all varieties is of particular concern to managers. Research has shown that conflict may occur in a variety of situations and may lead to a variety of adverse consequences, including stress, poor performance, and rapid turnover.

A final consequence of a conflicting role structure is **role overload**, which occurs when expectations for the role exceed the individual's capabilities. When a manager gives an employee several major assignments at once while increasing the person's regular workload, the employee will probably experience role overload. Role overload may also result when an individual takes on too many roles at one time. For example, a person trying to work extra hard at his job, run for election to the school board, serve on a committee in church, coach Little League baseball, maintain an active exercise program, and be a contributing member to his family will probably encounter role overload.

Interpersonal Demands

A final set of organizational stressors consists of three **interpersonal demands**: group pressures, leadership, and interpersonal conflict. Group pressures may include pressure to conform to the group's norms, and so forth. For instance, as we have noted before, it is quite common for a work group to arrive at an informal agreement about how much each member will produce. Individuals who produce much more or much less than this level may be pressured by the group to get back in line. An individual who feels a strong need to vary from the group's expectations (perhaps to get a pay raise or promotion) will experience a great deal of stress, especially if acceptance by the group is also important to him or her.

Leadership style also may cause stress. Suppose an employee needs a great deal of social support from his leader. The leader, however, is quite brusque and shows no concern or compassion for him. This employee will probably feel stressed. Similarly, assume an employee feels a strong need to participate in decision making and to be active in all aspects of management. Her boss is very autocratic and refuses to consult subordinates about anything. Once again stress is likely to result.

Conflicting personalities and behaviors may cause stress. Conflict can occur when two or more people must work together even though their personalities, attitudes, and behaviors differ. For example, a person with an internal locus of control—that is, who always wants to control how things turn out—might get frustrated working with a person with an external locus who likes to wait and just let things happen. Likewise, an employee who likes to have a quiet and peaceful work environment may experience stress if the adjacent office is assigned to someone whose job requires him or her to talk on the telephone much of the day.

Fries with That?

How many times can you ask "Would you like fries with that?" before you go out of your mind? Service scholars have been wrestling with this question for some time. The answer lies in understanding that laboring in a service job can be not only physically tiring but emotionally tiring as well. Not only is it tiring to say the same thing over and over again with a big smile and a sincere hello, but it is even more difficult for most people to smile at a customer when they just found out that their mortgage is overdue or that their mammogram reveals a potential problem or some other unpleasant news. It is also hard to focus on doing your job when you are a nurse caring for a young child with a terminal illness, an emergency medical technician on the scene of a bad traffic crash, or a call center employee asking the next person for a generous donation to the alma mater after the last one called yelled obscenities. All of these are examples of people doing work that has more than just a physical element to it. Smiling, caring, focusing, and staying consistent require the ability to perform tasks that have emotional aspects along with the physical.

Managing people who perform jobs with emotional labor components requires awareness of and sensitivity to the demands made upon employees by their interaction with customers. Coping strategies can help those who are faced with demands that tax their emotions. One strategy is to invent roles for employees to play. If the work of a street sweeper at a theme park is demeaning to a person who wondered why he went through four years of college to pick up spilled popcorn and trash, the manager can explain the importance of the role of a street sweeper as a cast member in a theatrical production designed to promote a fun customer environment. Thus, the supervisor would explain, the task is to see how well you can act by playing the role of the excellent street sweeper in a theatrical production. The employee now can see himself as an actor playing a role that requires skill, training, and dedication to the role as opposed to simply being a street sweeper. The ability to "play the role" is a skill that elevates the person performing it above the actual task in ways that protect egos and themselves while enhancing their performance of the role. This is surface acting, and it is similar to the smile you get when the fast food employee asks whether you "would like fries with that."

Sometimes employees become so committed to their roles in surface acting that they take on the behaviors and attitudes associated with those roles. This is called deep acting. It is when the employee acts in the role so convincingly that the displayed emotion becomes authentic. Thus, we have employees in customer contact jobs who may not have started their careers caring that much about how authentically interested and concerned they were with the customers but over time began to really feel that way. People also use surface acting to protect themselves from emotional involvement, which can detract from their ability to perform their jobs. A nurse, an emergency tech, and even a chef all have professional roles to play that allow them to use their professional norms to protect themselves against getting so deeply involved in the pain, suffering, or boredom that they can't perform their jobs with the necessary attention and focus, or even burn out when the emotional labor of doing their jobs gets to them.

Discussion Question: What ideas do you have as a manager of employees performing jobs with emotional labor content in them to help them cope? Using a telephone solicitor employee as an example, what might you do to help that person to deal with the frequent hang-ups and abusive calls that they will inevitably encounter when calling people?

Finally, we should also note that in today's world many job holders experience stress from a variety of sources simultaneously. One clear example is an airport security screener. These individuals must deal with myriad carry-on articles, some of them potentially dangerous. They face pressure from travelers to perform their job as quickly as possible but also are constantly reminded of the potential consequences of an error. Indeed, many individuals involved in security-related jobs face higher stress levels today than ever before.

Life Stressors

Stress in organizational settings also can be influenced by events that take place outside the organization. Life stressors can be categorized in terms of life change and life trauma.

Life Change

Holmes and Rahe first developed and popularized the notion of life change as a source of stress. A **life change** is any meaningful change in a person's personal or work situation. Holmes and Rahe reasoned that major changes in a person's life can lead to stress and eventually to disease. Table 13.2 summarizes their findings on major life change events. Note that several of these events relate directly (fired from work or retirement) or indirectly (change in residence) to work.

Each event's point value supposedly reflects the event's impact on the individual. At one extreme, a spouse's death, assumed to be the most traumatic event considered, is assigned a point value of 100. At the other extreme, minor violations of the law rank only 11 points. The points themselves represent life change units, or LCUs. Note also that the list includes negative events (divorce and trouble with the boss) as well as positive ones (marriage and vacations).

Holmes and Rahe argued that a person can handle a certain threshold of LCUs but that beyond that level, problems can set in. In particular, they suggest that people who encounter more than 150 LCUs in a given year will experience a decline in their health the following year. A score of between 150 and 300 LCUs supposedly carries a 50 percent chance of major illness, while the chance of major illness is said to increase to 70 percent if the number of LCUs exceeds 300. These ideas offer some interesting insights into the potential cumulative impact of various stressors and underscore our limitations in coping with stressful events. However, research on Holmes and Rahe's proposals has provided only mixed support. Moreover, the work context for many people has changed since this early work was published.

Life Trauma

Life trauma is similar to life change, but it has a narrower, more direct, and shorter-term focus. A **life trauma** is any upheaval in an individual's life that alters his or her attitudes, emotions, or behaviors. To illustrate, according to the life change view, a divorce adds to a person's potential for health problems in the following year. At the same time, the person will obviously also experience emotional turmoil during the actual divorce process itself. This turmoil is a form of life trauma and will clearly cause stress, much of which may spill over into the workplace.

Major life traumas that may cause stress include marital problems, family difficulties, and health problems initially unrelated to stress. For example, suppose a person learns she has developed arthritis that will limit her favorite activity, skiing. Her dismay over the news may translate into stress at work. Similarly, a worker coping with the traumatic aftermath of the death of her or his child will almost certainly go through difficult periods, some of which will affect her or his job performance. And millions of individuals experienced traumatic stress in the wake of the September 11th terrorist attacks.

Table 13.2 Life Changes and Life Change Units

Rank	Life Event	Mean Value	Rank	Life Event	Mean Value
1	Death of spouse	100	23	Son or daughter leaving home	29
2	Divorce	73	24	Trouble with in-laws	29
3	Marital separation	65	25	Outstanding personal achievement	28
4	Jail term	63	26	Spouse beginning or ending work	26
5	Death of close family member	63	27	Beginning or ending school	26
6	Personal injury or illness	53	28	Change in living conditions	25
7	Marriage	50	29	Revision of personal habits	24
8	Fired at work	47	30	Trouble with boss	23
9	Marital reconciliation	45	31	Change in work hours or conditions	20
10	Retirement	45	32	Change in residence	20
11	Change in health of family member	44	33	Change in schools	20
12	Pregnancy	40	34	Change in recreation	19
13	Sex difficulties	39	35	Change in church activities	19
14	Gain of new family member	39	36	Change in social activities	18
15	Business readjustment	39	37	Small mortgage or loan	17
16	Change in financial state	38	38	Change in sleeping habits	16
17	Death of close family friend	37	39	Change in the number of family get-togethers	15
18	Change to different line of work	36	40	Change in eating habits	15
19	Change in number of arguments with spouse	35	41	Vacation	13
20	Large mortgage	31	42	Christmas or other major holiday	12
21	Foreclosure of mortgage or loan	30	43	Minor violations of the law	11
22	Change in responsibilities of work	29			

The amount of life stress that a person has experienced in a given period of time, say one year, is measured by the total number of life change units (LCUs). These units result from the addition of the values (shown in the right-hand column) associated with events that the person has experienced during the target time period.

Reference: From *Journal of Psychosomatic Research*, vol. 11, Thomas H. Holmes and Richard H. Rahe, "The Social Adjustment Rating Scale."

Consequences of Stress

Stress can have a number of consequences. As we already noted, if the stress is positive, the result may be more energy, enthusiasm, and motivation. Of more concern, of course, are the negative consequences of stress. Referring back to Figure 13.2, we see that stress can produce individual consequences, organizational consequences, and burnout.

We should first note that many of the factors listed are obviously interrelated. For example, alcohol abuse is shown as an individual consequence, but it also affects the organization the person works for. An employee who drinks on the job may perform poorly and create a hazard for others. If the category for a consequence seems somewhat arbitrary, be aware that each consequence is categorized according to the area of its primary influence.

Individual Consequences

The individual consequences of stress, then, are the outcomes that mainly affect the individual. The organization also may suffer, either directly or indirectly, but it is the individual who pays the real price. Stress may produce behavioral, psychological, and medical consequences.

Behavioral Consequences

The behavioral consequences of stress may harm the person under stress or others. One such behavior is smoking. Research has clearly documented that people who smoke tend to smoke more when they experience stress. There is also evidence that alcohol and drug abuse are linked to stress, although this relationship is less well documented. Other possible behavioral consequences are accident proneness, aggression and violence, and appetite disorders. The box entitled "A Disturbance in the Work Force," discusses the possible role of the current economic downturn as a contributing factor in recent incidents of workplace violence.

A Disturbance in the Work Force

In November 2009, Jason Rodriguez, a former employee of an engineering firm in Orlando, Florida, entered the company's offices and opened fire with a handgun, killing one person and wounding five others. Rodriguez had been fired from Reynolds, Smith and Hills less than two years earlier and told police that he thought the firm was hindering his efforts to collect unemployment benefits. "They left me to rot," he told a reporter who asked him about his motive.

According to the U.S. Department of Labor, the incidence of workplace violence has actually been trending down over the past few years, in part because employers have paid more attention to the problem and taken successful preventive measures. More and more companies, for example, have set up *employee assistance programs (EAPs)* to help workers deal with various sources of stress, but EAP providers report that, in the current climate of economic uncertainty, they're being asked to deal with a different set of problems than the ones they've typically handled in the past.

In particular, financial problems have replaced emotional problems as employees' primary area of concern, and with unemployment totals having hit nearly 30-year highs, American workers appear to be more worried about the future than about such conventional stressors as pressing deadlines and demanding bosses. Today, says Sandra Naiman, a Denver-based career coach, "off- and on-the-job stresses feed into one another" to elevate stress levels all around, and workplace stress during the current recession may reflect this unfamiliar convergence of stressors.

There are as of yet no hard data to connect workplace violence with economic downturns, but many professionals and other experts in the field are convinced that the connection is real. ComPsych Corp., an EAP provider in Chicago, reports that calls are running 30 percent above normal, and according to Rick Kronberg of Perspectives Ltd., another Chicago-based EAP provider, "with the layoffs and the general financial picture, we're getting a lot of reaction … [from] people with a high degree of stress." Adds Tim Horner, a managing director at Kroll Inc., a security consulting firm: "There are signs out there that something's going on. It's not unusual that somebody snaps." Kenneth Springer, another security specialist whose job now includes keeping an eye on potentially dangerous ex-employees for their former employers, agrees: "Tough times," he says, "will cause people to do crazy things."

By the same token, says Laurence Miller, a forensic psychologist and author of *From Difficult to Disturbed: Understanding and Managing Dysfunctional Employees*, economic stress alone won't turn someone into a killer, nor is the average coworker likely to turn violent without warning. "People shouldn't be sitting around wondering if someone they've been working with for years who's been a regular guy [with] no real problems is going to suddenly snap and go ballistic on them," says Miller. "It's usually somebody," he warns, "that's had a long streak of problems." Unfortunately, that profile fits Jason Rodriguez, who'd been struggling for years with marital and mental health problems, unemployment, debt, and smoldering anger. "He was a very, very angry man," reports his former mother-in-law.

In January 2012, a judge ruled that Rodriguez was not yet fit to stand trial. His attorney cited his client's conviction that any proceedings should be a forum for exposing the people who'd been "brain-hacking" him since 2005.

References: Mark Trumbull, "Orlando Shooting Comes as Trend in Workplace Violence Drops," *Christian Science Monitor*, November 7, 2009, www.csmonitor.com on April 13, 2012; Ellen Wulhorst, "Recession Fuels Worries of Workplace Violence," Reuters, April 22, 2009, www.reuters.com on April 13, 2012; Scott Powers and Fernando Quintero, "Jason Rodriguez Profile: 'He Was a Very, Very Angry Man,'" *OrlandoSentinel.com*, November 6, 2009, www.orlandosentinel.com on April 14, 2011; Laurence Miller, *From Difficult to Disturbed: Understanding and Managing Dysfunctional Employees* (New York: AMACOM, 2008), http:// books.google.com on April 13, 2012; Jeff Weiner, "Jason Rodriguez: Accused Downtown Shooter Not Competent, Judge Says," *Orlando Sentinel*, January 11, 2012, http://articles.orlando-sentinel.com on April 13, 2012.

Psychological Consequences

The psychological consequences of stress relate to a person's mental health and well-being. When people experience too much stress at work, they may become depressed or find themselves sleeping too much or not enough. Stress may also lead to family problems and sexual difficulties.

Medical Consequences

The medical consequences of stress affect a person's physical well-being. Heart disease and stroke, among other illnesses, have been linked to stress. Other common medical problems resulting from too much stress include headaches, backaches, ulcers and related stomach and intestinal disorders, and skin conditions such as acne and hives.

Organizational Consequences

Clearly, any of the individual consequences just discussed can also affect the organization. Other results of stress have even more direct consequences for organizations. These include decline in performance, withdrawal, and negative changes in attitudes.

Performance

One clear organizational consequence of too much stress is a decline in performance. For operating workers, such a decline can translate into poor-quality work or a drop in productivity. For managers, it can mean faulty decision making or disruptions in working relationships as people become irritable and hard to get along with.

Withdrawal

Withdrawal behaviors also can result from stress. For the organization, the two most significant forms of withdrawal behavior are absenteeism and quitting. People who are having a hard time coping with stress in their jobs are more likely to call in sick or consider leaving the organization for good. Stress can also produce other, more subtle forms of withdrawal. A manager may start missing deadlines or taking longer lunch breaks. An employee may withdraw psychologically by ceasing to care about the organization and the job. As noted above, employee violence is a potential individual consequence of stress. This also has obvious organizational implications, especially if the violence is directed at another employee or at the organization in general.

Attitudes

Another direct organizational consequence of employee stress relates to attitudes. As we just noted, job satisfaction, morale, and organizational commitment can all suffer, along with motivation to perform at high levels. As a result, people may be more prone to complain about unimportant things, do only enough work to get by, and so forth.

Burnout

Burnout, another consequence of stress, has clear implications for both people and organizations. **Burnout** is a general feeling of exhaustion that develops when a person simultaneously experiences too much pressure and has too few sources of satisfaction.

People with high aspirations and strong motivation to get things done are prime candidates for burnout under certain conditions. They are especially vulnerable when the organization suppresses or limits their initiative while constantly demanding that they serve the organization's own ends.

In such a situation, the individual is likely to put too much of himself or herself into the job. In other words, the person may well keep trying to meet his or her own agenda while simultaneously trying to fulfill the organization's expectations. The most likely effects of this situation are prolonged stress, fatigue, frustration, and helplessness under the burden of overwhelming demands. The person literally exhausts his or her aspirations and motivation, much as a candle burns itself out. Loss of self-confidence and psychological withdrawal follow. Ultimately, burnout may be the result. At this point, the individual may start dreading going to work in the morning, may put in longer hours but accomplish less than before, and may generally display mental and physical exhaustion.

Managing Stress in the Workplace

Given that stress is widespread and so potentially disruptive in organizations, it follows that people and organizations should be concerned about how to manage it more effectively. And in fact they are. Many strategies have been developed to help manage stress in the workplace. Some are for individuals, and others are geared toward organizations.

Individual Coping Strategies

Many strategies for helping individuals manage stress have been proposed. Figure 13.4 lists five of the more popular.

Exercise

Exercise is one method of managing stress. People who exercise regularly are less likely to have heart attacks than inactive people. More directly, research has suggested that people who exercise regularly feel less tension and stress, are more self-confident, and show greater optimism. People who do not exercise regularly feel more stress, are more likely to be depressed, and experience other negative consequences.

Relaxation

A related method of managing stress is relaxation. We noted at the beginning of the chapter that coping with stress requires adaptation. Proper relaxation is an effective way to adapt. Relaxation can take many forms. One way to relax is to take regular vacations. One study found that people's attitudes toward a variety of workplace characteristics improved significantly following a vacation. People can also relax while on the job. For example, it has been recommended that people take regular rest breaks during their normal workday. A popular way of resting is to sit quietly with closed eyes for ten minutes every afternoon. (Of course, it might be necessary to have an alarm clock handy!)

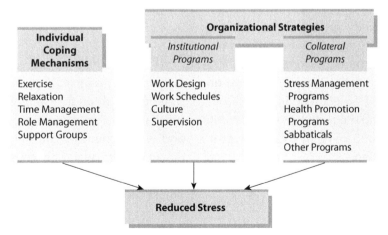

Figure 13.4 Individual and Organizational Coping Strategies Just as individual and organizational factors can cause stress, there are individual and organizational strategies for coping with stress. This figure shows the individual coping mechanisms most experts recommend and several institutional and collateral organizational programs.

Time Management

Time management is often recommended for managing stress. The idea is that many daily pressures can be eased or eliminated if a person does a better job of managing time. One popular approach to time management is to make a list every morning of the things to be done that day. Then you group the items on the list into three categories: critical activities that must be performed, important activities that should be performed, and optional or trivial things that can be delegated or postponed. Then, of course, you do the things on the list in their order of importance. This strategy helps people get more of the important things done every day. It also encourages delegation of less important activities to others.

Role Management

Somewhat related to time management is the idea of role management, in which the individual actively works to avoid overload, ambiguity, and conflict. For example, if you do not know what is expected of you, you should not sit and worry about it. Instead, ask for clarification from your boss. Another role management strategy is to learn to say "no." As simple as saying "no" might sound, a lot of people create problems for themselves by always saying "yes." Besides working in their regular jobs, they agree to serve on committees, volunteer for extra duties, and accept extra assignments. Sometimes, of course, we have no choice but to accept an extra obligation (if our boss tells us to complete a new project, we will probably have to do it). In many cases, however, saying "no" is an option.

Support Groups

A final method for managing stress is to develop and maintain support groups. A support group is simply a group of family members or friends with whom a person can spend time. Going out after work with a couple of coworkers to a basketball game, for example, can help relieve the stress that builds up during the day. Supportive family and friends can help people deal with normal stress on an ongoing basis. Support groups can be particularly useful during times of crisis. For example, suppose an employee has just learned that she did not get the promotion she has been working toward for months. It may help her tremendously if she has good friends to lean on, be it to talk to or to yell at.

Organizational Coping Strategies

Organizations are also increasingly realizing that they should be involved in managing their employees' stress. There are two different rationales for this view. One is that because the organization is at least partly responsible for creating the stress, it should help relieve it. The other is that workers experiencing lower levels of harmful stress will function more effectively. Two basic organizational strategies for helping employees manage stress are institutional programs and collateral programs.

Institutional Programs

Institutional programs for managing stress are undertaken through established organizational mechanisms. For example, properly designed jobs and work schedules can help ease stress. Shift work, in particular, can cause major problems for employees, because they constantly have to adjust their sleep and relaxation patterns. Thus, the design of work and work schedules should be a focus of organizational efforts to reduce stress.

The organization's culture also can be used to help manage stress. In some organizations, for example, there is a strong norm against taking time off or going on vacation. In the long run, such norms can cause major stress. Thus, the organization should strive to foster a culture that reinforces a healthy mix of work and nonwork activities.

Finally, supervision can play an important institutional role in managing stress. A supervisor can be a major source of overload. If made aware of their potential for assigning stressful amounts of work, supervisors can do a better job of keeping workloads reasonable.

Collateral Programs

In addition to institutional efforts aimed at reducing stress, many organizations are turning to collateral programs. A *collateral stress program* is an organizational program specifically created to help employees deal with stress. Organizations have adopted stress management programs, health promotion programs, and other kinds of programs for this purpose. More and more companies are developing their own programs or adopting existing programs of this type. For example, Lockheed Martin offers screening programs for its employees to detect signs of hypertension.

Many firms today also have employee fitness programs. These programs attack stress indirectly by encouraging employees to exercise, which is presumed to reduce stress. On the negative side, this kind of effort costs considerably more than stress management programs because the firm must invest in physical facilities. Still, more and more companies are exploring this option. L. L. Bean, for example, has state-of-the-art fitness centers for its employees. And many technology companies such as Google and Facebook provide on-site massages and gyms for their employees.

Finally, organizations try to help employees cope with stress through other kinds of programs. For example, existing career development programs, such as the one at General Electric, are used for this purpose. Other companies use programs promoting everything from humor to massage to yoga as antidotes for stress. Of course, little or no research supports some of the claims made by advocates of these programs. Thus, managers must take steps to ensure that any organizational effort to help employees cope with stress is at least reasonably effective.

For example, the Republic of Tea is a small, privately held company that promotes healthy lifestyles centered around the consumption of tea. The firm recently added a comprehensive program called the Health Ministry to help its employees live healthier lives. A nutritionist provides free counseling to employees about their diet and weight, employees get a $500 credit for gym memberships, and a workday walking program encourages all employees to take 10- to 15-minute walks on company time. Employees were even provided with high-quality walking shoes. The firm says that its health management efforts have boosted its order processing efficiency by 11 percent, increased order accuracy by 7 percent, and decreased employee absenteeism.

Work-Life Linkages

At numerous points in this chapter we have alluded to relationships between a person's work and life. In this final brief section we will make these relationships a bit more explicit.

Fundamental Work-Life Relationships

Work-life relationships can be characterized in any number of ways. Consider, for example, the basic dimensions of the part of a person's life tied specifically to work. Common dimensions would include such things as an individual's current job (including working hours, job satisfaction, and so forth), his or her career goals (the person's aspirations, career trajectory, and so forth), interpersonal relations at work (with the supervisor, subordinates, coworkers, and others), and job security.

Part of each person's life is also distinctly separate from work. These dimensions might include the person's spouse or life companion, dependents (such as children or elderly parents), personal life interests (hobbies, leisure-time interests, religious affiliations, community involvement), and friendship networks.

Work-life relationships, then, include any relationships between dimensions of the person's work life and the person's personal life. For example, a person with numerous dependents (a nonworking spouse or domestic partner, dependent children, dependent parents, etc.) may prefer a job with a relatively high salary, fewer overtime demands, and less travel. On the other hand, a person with no dependents may be less interested in salary and more receptive to overtime, and enjoy job-related travel.

Stress will occur when there is a basic inconsistency or incompatibility between a person's work and life dimensions. For example, if a person is the sole care provider for a dependent elderly parent but has a job that requires considerable travel and evening work, stress is likely to result.

Balancing Work-Life Linkages

Balancing work-life linkages is, of course, no easy thing to do. Demands from both sides can be extreme, and people may need to be prepared to make trade-offs. The important thing is to recognize the potential trade-offs in advance so that they can be carefully weighed and a comfortable decision made. Some of the strategies for doing this were discussed earlier. For example, working for a company that offers flexible work schedules may be an attractive option.

Individuals must also recognize the importance of long-term versus short-term perspectives in balancing their work and personal lives. For example, people may have to respond a bit more to work demands than to life demands in the early years of their careers. In mid-career, they may be able to achieve a more comfortable balance. And in later career stages, they may be able to put life dimensions first by refusing to relocate, working shorter hours, and so forth.

People also have to decide for themselves what they value and what trade-offs they are willing to make. For instance, consider the dilemma faced by a dual-career couple when one partner is being transferred to another city. One option is for one of the partners to subordinate her or his career for the other partner, at least temporarily. For example, the partner being transferred can turn the offer down, risking a potential career setback or the loss of the job. Or the other partner may resign from his or her current position and seek another one in the new location. The couple might also decide to live apart, with one moving and the other staying. The partners might also come to realize that their respective careers are more important to them than their relationship and decide to go their separate ways.

POWER AND POLITICAL BEHAVIOR

Joseph E. Champoux

Power and political behavior pervade organizational life, affecting everyone, not only senior executives. Of these two constructs, political behavior has the more divisive intellectual history. Some researchers describe political behavior as an important way to understand and explain much of the behavior that occurs in organizations. Other researchers view political behavior as a necessary evil of organizational life. The formal organization often does not recognize this social influence process, but it is essential to much of managerial work. Political behavior processes can serve organizational goals for some managers and the self-interest of others.

This chapter focuses on the development and use of power in organizations and the role political behavior plays in building and using that power. You can decide for yourself whether political behavior is a necessary or essential evil in organizations.

Power

Power is a person's ability to get something done the way he wants it done. Power lets a person affect other people's behavior, get people to do what they otherwise might not do, overcome resistance to changing direction, and overcome opposition. Someone with power also can prevent controversial issues from surfacing, especially during decision-making processes. Power includes the ability to gather and use physical and human resources to reach the person's goals. Although power has a negative meaning for many people, it can have positive effects in organizations.

Power is essential to the functions of leadership and management. More than simply dominance, power is the capacity to get things done in an organization. Powerful managers and leaders can achieve more, get more resources for their subordinates, and give their subordinates more chances to develop and grow. Power is also a necessary part of controlling your fate and building self-esteem.

Power in organizations has the distinct facets of potential power, actual power, and the potential for power. **Potential power** exists when one party perceives another party as having power and the ability to use it. **Actual power** is the presence and use of power. The use of power may or may not successfully reach desired results. Use of power, whether successful or unsuccessful, is actual power. **Potential for power** is the chance that individuals or groups have to build a power base with resources they control. The facets of power imply a perceptual basis of power. Power exists when one party perceives that another party has potential power, actual power, or the ability to build a power base.

A **power relationship** is a moment of social interaction where power shows itself in organizations. Three dimensions define power relationships. The **relational** dimension is the social interaction part of power. Power in organizations happens during social interactions between people and groups. The **dependence** dimension views power as how much one party relies on the actions of another. Dependence is high when valued results are unavailable from another source. High power follows from high dependence. The **sanctioning** dimension refers to one party's ability to affect the results of the other party by using rewards, penalties, or both. This power dimension has both actual and potential aspects. Actual sanctioning arises because of observations of sanctioning behavior. Potential sanctioning arises from expected sanctions or from the person's reputation for using sanctions.

Power and authority are different concepts, although a person can have both power and authority. Authority is the right to make decisions and to give direction to other people in an organization. Such authority comes to a person because of his position in the organization. It often is formally recognized in writing so people know their authority relationships. Look back at the definition of power given earlier. That definition associated power with a person's ability to get things done, not with the person's position in an organization. A person with power can be at any level in an organization, not just at the senior levels.

Power flows in all directions in organizations. It flows along the vertical dimension of organizations within superior–subordinate relationships. Power can also flow upward within superior–subordinate relationships. Here the subordinate influences his superior, a process some call "managing the boss." The third direction of power is lateral. Managers usually are highly dependent on others at the same level for cooperation and resources. A manager needs to influence people and groups outside his direct reporting relationships. Such influence extends to people and groups in other departments, in other work units, and outside the organization.

Power is dynamic, not static. As the organization's external environment changes, different subsystems of the organization, different individuals, and different coalitions may emerge as seats of power. Individuals, departments, and work units that are powerful at one point in the organization's history may not be powerful at another point. For example, individuals and units responsible for marketing a successful new product are likely to develop power, but, if the product's market share drops, their power will likely subside.

Bases of Power

Much of a manager's success in an organization depends on the influence he has over others. A manager's power decides the amount of influence he has over a subordinate. A manager can draw on several sources or **bases of power** that come from both his formal management position and his personal characteristics.

Figure 14.1 shows the organizational and personal bases of power as accumulating to a total power base. The amount of power a leader or

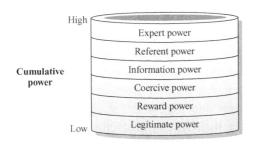

Figure 14.1 The Cumulative Effects of the Bases of Power

manager has depends on the number of bases he has available. Some research is beginning to add to the bases shown in Figure 14.1. The six shown remain the most common ones investigated in organizational research.

Some managers have only the organizational bases of power to influence people. Other managers have both organizational and personal bases. These people are in the enviable position of having many bases of power at their disposal.

Organizational Bases of Power

The **organizational bases of power** are legitimate power, reward power, coercive power, and information power. **Legitimate power** derives from the manager's position. The organization gives the manager decision authority that he uses to affect the behavior of subordinates. Assigning tasks and setting goals for completing them are examples of legitimate power.

Reward power derives from the manager's ability to tie positive outcomes to a subordinate's behavior. A manager has high reward power if he can give positive outcomes for desirable behavior. Positive outcomes can include praise, pay increases, or time off. The use of reward power to provide positive outcomes makes the manager more attractive to the subordinate. You will see later in

this chapter that understanding the subordinates' desires for various outcomes is an important part of leadership.

Coercive power derives from efforts to affect the behavior of another person through the fear of punishment. A manager has high coercive power if he has the authority to penalize subordinates. A manager has low coercive power if he has no such authority. The spoken or unspoken threat of a poor evaluation of a subordinate's performance is an example of coercive power.

Information power derives from the control and distribution of information in an organization. Deliberately controlling the receipt and distribution of information increases a manager's information power. People who hold central positions in communication networks (for example, relayer and liaison) can often build this power base. When information is scarce, others become more dependent on the manager for information.

Each management position in an organization has certain amounts of organization-based power. The amount of power in a position varies, depending on the organization's policies about rewards and punishments. The person who takes that position has some organization-based power available to affect the behavior of subordinates. When the person leaves the position, the power stays behind and does not travel with the person to a new position.

Personal Bases of Power

The **personal bases of power** flow from the manager's qualities or attributes. Those bases also depend on how subordinates attribute those qualities to the manager. The personal bases of power available to a manager with one group of subordinates will not be available to the same manager with a different group of subordinates.

The personal bases of power are referent power and expert power.

Referent power is based on the personal liking a subordinate has for a manager. The more the subordinate identifies with the manager, the stronger the referent power. A manager who is disliked by a subordinate has low referent power.

Expert power derives from the manager's technical knowledge and expertise. A manager with the knowledge and skills needed for group success has high expert power. A manager with little knowledge has low expert power. The source of the manager's influence is the subordinates' dependence on the manager for the information that they need to do their job successfully.

Power, Leadership, and Management

Powerful leaders and managers delegate decision authority to subordinates and view their subordinates' talents as a resource. Such leaders and managers can more easily change their subordinates' working conditions than powerless leaders and managers can. The powerful can get the resources and information that subordinates need to be effective. They take risks and press for innovations in their organizations. Subordinates of powerful leaders and managers can develop from the new experiences and increase their promotional opportunities. Powerful leaders and managers often share their power with their subordinates, creating more total power for the entire workgroup. A leader who uses power fairly has stronger positive effects on subordinates than one who uses power unfairly.

Because having and using power are key characteristics of a leader, powerlessness is more a feature of managers and supervisors than of leaders. Those with little or no power use close supervision and do not delegate authority to subordinates. They often distrust their subordinates

and view talented subordinates as threatening. Such managers and supervisors stick to the rules and do not take risks. Subordinates who work for the powerless do not have the chance to develop from involvement in new activities. Powerless managers and supervisors strongly focus on the work of their group, protecting it from outside interference. Their workgroup becomes "their" territory, a symbol they use to try to increase their significance in the organization.

Building Power

The task of **building power** identifies the power sources shown in Figure 14.2. Leaders and managers can use these sources to build their power base. An important step in building power is a political diagnosis. A later section of this chapter describes how to do a diagnosis.

A person can build power from his **knowledge, reputation, and professional credibility**. People with specialized knowledge have power if other people depend on that knowledge to do their jobs. A person's reputation builds from a series of successes. Power grows as a manager or leader develops a positive reputation. Giving talks at professional meetings and serving on committees

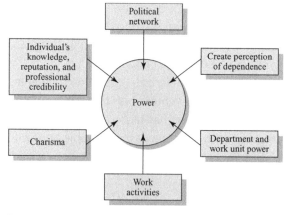

Figure 14.2 Sources of Power in Organizations

of professional associations, for example, can increase a person's professional credibility, which can lead to influence both outside and inside the organization.

A person can create a strong power base by building a **political network** within an organization. A political network depends on the person's communication channels in the organization. The communication can follow the formal organizational design or be informal in character. Forming alliances with other peer leaders and managers adds to a person's power base in an organization.

Creating a perception of dependence is still another way to build power in an organization. The perception comes from the belief that the leader or manager controls scarce resources, including people, equipment, money, information, and rewards, and can use these resources to help or impede other people. Note that the leader or manager does not need to actually control the resources. The perception of control is the key to this method of building power.

The **power base of the work unit** headed by the manager or leader depends on the department's capability to cope with uncertainty, its unique functions, changes in the external environment, and its centrality to the organization's workflow. The movement of power among departments is part of its dynamic character.

Departments that reduce uncertainty for an organization can have high power. For example, human resource management departments that become expert in affirmative action, equal employment opportunity, and workforce diversity can increase their power in their organizations. Departments offering a service available from few other sources in the organization have high power as well. Departments at key points in the workflow of an organization also enjoy considerable power. Managers or leaders whose departments hold a central position or perform a unique function in an organization can build a strong power base for themselves.

Work activities can also be another source of power. Work activities that are extraordinary, visible, and appropriate to the organization's goals are important sources of power. Extraordinary work activities usually are risky activities successfully done. Other people in the organization notice the results and develop positive feelings about the successful person. A person who is continuously successful at high-risk work activities may be regarded as charismatic.

Charisma as an important quality of leadership. Its importance comes from the power a charismatic person has over others. Those who attribute charisma to a manager or leader feel inspired by his ideas and become committed to carrying them out. Although charisma is mainly a personality quality, managers and leaders can learn to make effective and influential appeals to others. Charisma is especially important as a source of power in lateral relationships, where the manager or leader has no direct authority.

Attribution of Power

Attribution processes also operate when power is ascribed to people at all levels in an organization. The power a person assigns to another person may not be the same as the actual power of the other person.

Both personal characteristics and the context in which the person works can lead to the **attribution of power**. **Personal characteristics** include the person's formal position in the organization, technical knowledge, and position within a communication network. A person whose formal position has high status and authority will have high formal authority. Others who interact with that person will ascribe to him high power and potential influence. An attribution of power can flow to a person with high technical knowledge, especially in a technical organization. Holding a central position in a communication network might lead others to perceive the person as having high power because of his information access.

The formal and informal **contexts of the person** also affect how people attribute power to the person. The formal context includes membership in a powerful group or project. A member of such a group can mirror the power of the group and have high power attributed to him. A similar attribution process works for members of informal coalitions and social networks, if an observer believes the coalition or network is powerful.

Political Behavior

Political behavior in organizations focuses on getting, developing, and using power to reach a desired result in ambiguous, uncertain, or conflict-filled situations. Such behavior often happens outside accepted channels of authority. You can view political behavior as unofficial, unsanctioned behavior to reach a goal. Such goals often are individual goals, not organizational.

A person can use political behavior to build his bases of power. People also use political behavior to affect decisions, get scarce resources, and earn the cooperation of people outside their direct authority. Political behavior rises and falls with the dynamics of power. A person's need for power also can affect his willingness to become involved in an organization's inevitable political processes.

An organization's political processes have two characteristics that distinguish them from other organizational processes: power and influence. Behavior that uses power, builds power, or tries to influence others is political. Such behavior tries to control a result and can feature high levels of conflict. Political behavior can be directed at reaching organizational goals

or individual goals that do not benefit the organization. An example of the latter is a manager who drives his work unit to high performance levels to enhance his reputation. His demands could increase the stress on people in the work unit and have long-term dysfunctional effects, such as damaged equipment.

People at different organizational levels hold different perceptions of political behavior and react differently to it. People's perceptions tend to focus on reward practices, the presence of dominant groups, and their coworkers' political behavior. Reward practices that are not performance based are associated with negative reactions to supervisors. Favoring influential groups can yield high levels of dissatisfaction. High levels of perceived coworker political behavior are related to high levels of dissatisfaction with coworkers. Nonsupervisory personnel perceive more political behavior, and have stronger negative reactions, than supervisory personnel.

Political behavior is especially important in managing lateral relationships. Three lateral relationships in particular feature political behavior. Line–staff relationships put a staff person in a position of influencing someone else in the organization to approve an important project. Managers of human resources and finance departments usually do not have line authority over those who approve a project and carry it out. They often use their bases of power and political tactics to influence others to adopt the project.

The second type of lateral relationship is competition for resources. Managers use political behavior when competing for resources, such as money, people, equipment, and office space. They compete with other managers at the same organizational level for those resources, but none of the managers can decide the resource allocations directly.

The third type of lateral relationship is interdependence in the workflow. Managers of some work units are often dependent on other work units. Earlier stages in the workflow must be successfully completed for the success of the dependent work unit. Managers must negotiate with the managers of earlier work units to ensure an efficient workflow. Such interdependence is common in serially interdependent manufacturing (assembly lines) and service processes. Processing insurance claims is an example of a service process.

Political behavior and the political processes of organizations can institutionalize the current power holders. Political processes can become part of the organization's cultural fabric, forming a context for daily political behavior. Institutionalization is the product of a mature political process. Those in power build an organizational structure, develop policies, and create information systems that support their power bases. Once in place, these structures prevent people with little power from gaining power against the established coalition.

Political Strategies

A **political strategy** is a written or unwritten plan to reach a goal using specific political tactics. The strategy specifies the goal to reach and the political means to reach that goal. A well-designed political strategy includes a plan for dealing with changes in the political context within which the person works. The plan explicitly recognizes that political events in organizations do not always happen as expected. A political strategy specifies political tactics in various combinations and sequences for dealing with different political events as the strategy unfolds.

Executives, managers, and supervisors are not the only ones who use political strategies. Strategies are available to people at all levels of an organization. This aspect of political strategies is one reason political behavior is so pervasive in

organizations. It also helps explain the intrigue organizational politics brings to organizational life.

Researchers have documented political strategies in the following areas:

- Decisions about resource allocations, such as budgets, choice of senior executives, and the design of the organization
- Career development and enhancement
- Performance appraisals prepared by a supervisor or manager
- Pay increase decisions
- Major organizational change

Political Tactics

Political tactics are specific political influence behaviors used to reach a goal. The tactics involve either building power or using power unobtrusively. A political strategy can use a mix of tactics, moving from one to another as the political landscape changes.

Decision-making processes can have a distinctly political dimension. Politically oriented decision makers can affect the choice of alternatives that favor themselves or their organizational units. A decision maker can use his power to affect the process by **selectively emphasizing a favored decision alternative**. The alternative he wants will enhance or increase the power of the decision maker or his unit.

A politically oriented decision maker can also call upon an **outside expert or consultant**. Because the consultant is an outsider, he can bring an aura of objectivity and legitimacy to the decision alternatives under consideration. Decision makers call in consultants when power within the decision-making process is about equally dispersed and the issue is critical to either the organization or the individual. When power is well balanced, the decision maker needs another lever to increase his power within the process.

An unobtrusive way of using power in an organization is to **control the decision-making agenda**. People who want matters to stay as they are often use this tactic. By controlling the agenda, they can decide both whether an issue or problem is considered at all and, if considered, where it will appear on the agenda. Items toward the end of an agenda may get less attention than those presented earlier. Decisions made about earlier issues on the agenda can affect later decisions.

People **build coalitions** when they want to create a power base to reach the goals of their political strategy. The coalition can be internal, formed around people and groups within the organization, or external, formed around people and groups outside the organization. In both cases, the decision maker believes the individuals or groups are important to his position.

A person uses **co-optation** as a political tactic to persuade outsiders or insiders to favor his position. Through co-optation, he tries to lure people to his side. The targets of co-optation are potential opponents or people whose help can smooth the way to reaching his goals. Placing outsiders on boards of directors, advisory councils, or task forces can give them information that persuades them that a particular issue or position is important. A politically savvy person can use committees to co-opt insiders. Issues or problems that require information from many sources and the commitment of those sources to a decision can benefit from a committee approach.

Impression management is a highly manipulative political tactic. People use this tactic to control the image they project to another person. Behaviors such as looking busy and asking for more tasks and responsibilities can build positive impressions. Supervisors who want to convey an impression of impartiality during performance

feedback can begin with positive commentary before moving to any negative feedback.

Other political tactics include a repertoire of eight **influence tactics** People can use these tactics to influence others' behavior in the three power flow directions described earlier. The following summarizes the eight tactics:

- **Assertiveness:** Using threats, demands, and intimidation to affect behavior, especially with someone of lower status and power; similar to coercive power, described earlier.
- **Ingratiation:** Using flattery and creating goodwill with another person to affect his behavior; an element of impression management, described earlier.
- **Rationality:** Using a logical argument, oral or written, to affect another person's behavior.
- **Sanctions:** Using organizationally based punishments to affect a person's behavior; coercive power, described earlier in the chapter. Used more with subordinates than with coworkers or superiors.
- **Exchange of benefits:** Using favors and benefits to influence another person, especially a coworker.
- **Upward appeal:** Getting support for a cause from higher levels in the organization.
- **Inspirational appeal:** Focusing on a person's values to arouse emotional support for a proposal. Similar to transformational and charismatic leadership.
- **Consultation:** Involving the person you want to influence in the decision process.

Recall that power flows in all directions: downward, laterally, and upward. Some research shows that managers often use consultation, rationality, inspirational appeal, and ingratiation in all three directions. Because power most easily flows downward in organizations, supervisors can use all political tactics in supervisor–subordinate relationships. For example, a supervisor could use sanctions to change the direction of someone's behavior in his work unit. Tactics that can work in lateral relationships include coalitions and upward appeals. A marketing manager who is trying to influence peer managers to accept a marketing campaign could appeal to a higher authority for support. The higher authority could then coerce the peer managers to accept the campaign. Upward influence efforts call for tactics that do not directly use formal authority. Impression management and rationality can help a junior team member affect the thinking of the team leader about the team's direction.

Political Skill

Political skill is a person's ability to interact effectively in various social situations to affect the behavior of another person or group. A politically skilled person gives the impression of sincerity. He leaves a social interaction with the other party or parties feeling a sense of trust and confidence. Politically skilled people can work successfully within an organization's political system, influence others in the desired direction, and gain positive results for himself and often the organization.

The social situations in which a person uses political skill can occur inside or outside an organization. Using political skill at a social event outside the organization can be as important as using the same skill inside the organization. Interactions also can occur over communication media such as voice-mail, e-mail, discussion boards, and chat rooms.

Political skill has the following four dimensions:

- **Social astuteness:** Has high self-awareness; accurately perceives varying social situa-

tions; insightfully observes other people's social behavior.
- **Interpersonal influence:** Flexibly adapts behavior in varying social situations to reach desired goals; convincing, but subtle, personal style.
- **Networking ability:** Deliberately gains positions in alliances and coalitions; creates opportunities that help in social interactions; uses those opportunities to own advantage; knows the powerful assets that exist in political networks.
- **Apparent sincerity:** Leaves an impression of openness and honesty (or the person is open and honest); perceived by others as genuine and honest in a social interaction. Apparent sincerity is a key factor in successful social interactions.

Current research suggests that political skill is a personality-level quality that almost anyone can learn. Various forms of management training and coaching can develop political skill. The recommended training goes beyond content-oriented training such as reading the previous paragraphs about political skill. It includes experientially based training, in which a person develops heightened self-awareness and practices the behaviors required for political skill. The latter includes drama-based theatrical training, in which a person learns emotional control, emotional expression, and the use of effective nonverbal behavior.

Political Diagnosis

A **political diagnosis** assesses where power is located in an organization and what type of political behavior is likely to happen. It identifies politically active individuals and coalitions in the organization, the amount of power they have, and the likely ways they will use their power. The diagnosis also examines political networks in the organization.

A political diagnosis helps an employee understand the political systems present in the organization. Some research shows that employees who understand the political systems have lower anxiety and greater job satisfaction. Members of minority groups in a diverse organization can use a political diagnosis to get political information that the majority group might try to withhold.

Individuals

A political diagnosis focused on individuals:

- Identifies the powerful and politically active people in the organization.
- Learns the power base of each person.
- Assesses each person's skill in using his power base.
- Decides how each person is likely to use power.
- Identifies the goals each person is trying to reach through power and political behavior.
- The political diagnosis collects information in each of those areas from organizational records and key informants inside and outside the organization.

Politically diagnosing individuals begins by identifying presumably powerful people in the organization from an organization chart and a description of titles and duties. This part of the diagnosis also includes identifying people external to the organization who play important roles in its political processes. External individuals might include union officials, regulatory agents, and key financial backers of the organization. Be careful when ascribing power to a person because of position and title. Some people with powerful-sounding titles might not have power.

You can interview a sample of people in the organization about the reputation of those initially identified as power holders. You can also identify major decisions and the people involved in those decisions. These steps test the conclusions from the first step.

After you identify the power holders, you need to assess their power base. The power base depends on both the resources available to the person and his political skill in using those resources. Resources include budget discretion, rewards, sanctions, and information. A power base is strong if the person has discretion in using resources that are important for major issues facing the organization. The power base becomes stronger when there is little substitute for the person's resources and when the resources apply to a wide range of situations.

A diagnosis assesses a person's ability to develop a general political strategy and use the political tactics described earlier. It also is necessary to assess the person's flexibility in using the resources available. This step in the diagnosis relies on both archival information, such as minutes of key decision-making groups and reports, and people in the organization familiar with the power holder's background. These sources can also give information about how the power holder is likely to use his power and the goals he wants to reach.

Coalitions

The political diagnosis then identifies and assesses coalitions in the organization. A **coalition** is an alliance of individuals who share a common goal. Coalitions are also interest groups that try to affect decisions in the organization. Coalitions can have members from widely scattered parts of the organization. The goals of a political diagnosis of coalitions are the same as those listed earlier for individuals.

Information from veteran informants inside and outside the organization can help identify coalitions. Reports of past major decisions are also a useful source of information. Any stable group of people who regularly affect major decisions is a coalition.

The power of a coalition depends on the power bases of its individual members. You can use the methods of assessing an individual's power base described earlier to do an initial assessment of a coalition's power. A coalition's power also depends on how stable its membership is and how effectively it manages group processes. An unstable, mismanaged coalition loses the advantages of its individual members' power. To assess the power of a coalition, you might need to observe the coalition in action. You can infer how a coalition is likely to use its power from the political styles of its high-status members. Often such members strongly affect the coalition's norms. The political goals of a coalition are most easily assessed from its public statements.

Political Networks

Diagnosing political networks gets at the heart of an organization's political processes. **Political networks** form from affiliations and alliances of individuals and coalitions. Political networks can control information and other resources throughout the organization. They also can give support to those in the network and provide a common ideological view.

The diagnosis of networks depends upon knowledge from informants and direct experience in the organization. The diagnosis should identify the people and coalitions that have major influence within the network. Information from the diagnosis helps identify those strategic positions

and should identify the individuals with informal access to the organization's decision-making processes. Such people play key political roles in affecting the results of major decisions.

The Dark Side of Organizational Politics: Deception, Lying, and Intimidation

Organizational politics also has a dark side: deception, lying, and intimidation. Machiavellian personalities (see Chapter 5) are especially well adapted to the dark side of organizational politics. Their resistance to social influence, lack of ethical concerns, and use of deception and manipulative tactics make the dark side an attractive part of organizational politics. These gloomy aspects of political behavior help explain why it has a negative image in the eyes of many people.

Deception

The following advice from Niccolò Machiavelli promotes the use of **deception** to build and hold power:

> A prince being thus obliged to know well how to act as a beast must imitate the fox and the lion, for the lion cannot protect himself from traps, and the fox cannot defend himself from wolves. One must therefore be a fox to recognize traps, and a lion to frighten wolves.
> …
> [A] prudent ruler ought not to keep faith when by so doing it would be against his interest, and when the reasons which made him bind himself

no longer exist. … [M]en are so simple and so ready to obey present necessities, that one who deceives will always find those who allow themselves to be deceived.

Today, hundreds of years after Machiavelli's observations, deceptive behavior is still a part of organizational life. Deception tricks another party into arriving at incorrect conclusions or picking the wrong alternative in a decision process. Deceptive behavior happens in organizations when an individual's personal goals become more important than the organization's goals. Here are some examples of deceptive behavior:

- A manager does not want change, but never actually says he does not want change. Instead, he authorizes an endless series of studies that result in everyone forgetting the proposed change.
- An executive appears to select successors based on ability, but really selects them based on loyalty to his ideas.
- An equal employment opportunity (EEO) manager proposes expanding his staff to develop a training program to improve job opportunities for underrepresented groups. Many judge the overt goal as the worthy pursuit of diversity. The EEO manager's covert goal is to increase his chances of a promotion to a higher level, something never discussed in the proposal.

The costs to organizations of the deceptive behavior in this list are clear: high economic costs of endless studies, selection of less-capable successors, and the higher cost of an otherwise worthy diversity-enhancement program.

Despite its costs, some argue that deceptive behavior is functional for organizations. Deceptive behavior brings political intrigue and a sense of uneasiness to an organization. It lends an air of excitement to otherwise routine daily activities. No one knows upon arriving at work which "hidden agenda" will play out on a given day.

Lying

Lying intentionally misstates the truth to mislead another party. Lying helps the liar build power by distorting information in favor of the liar. A person lies to gain a political advantage. Although lying can help a person reach his political goals, the long-term effects include a loss of power, especially if others discover the lie.

Intimidation

The third gloomy side to political behavior uses indirect and direct **intimidation** on someone who wants to reform organizational practices, but does not have the authority to cause such changes. Such people typically are in lower-level organizational positions. They may perceive middle management and upper management as incompetent or acting in illegal or immoral ways.

Managers perceive the reformer as threatening their authority. They first react by trying to intimidate the reformer indirectly. If indirect intimidation does not silence the reformer, the intimidation escalates to a more direct form. Here are some management actions that can intimidate a reform-minded subordinate:

- The manager assures the subordinate that he misperceives the situation, and his suggestions are not valid. If the reformer persists, the manager suggests an investigation to find the truth. The results of the investigation will show the reformer that the charges have no basis.

- The next level of intimidation isolates the reformer from others in the organization. The manager first reduces or ends communication with the reformer and restricts his interactions with others. If the reformer persists, the manager physically can isolate the person by transferring him to a position that has low visibility or is physically distant from the part of the organization to which the reformer objects.
- The third level of intimidation focuses on the character and motives of the reformer. The manager defames the reformer by suggesting to others that he is incompetent or even psychopathic.

These intimidation methods try to prevent the reformer from building support among others in the organization. The intimidation also tries to drive the reformer out of the organization. If none of these methods work, the manager can escalate to the last level—firing the reformer.

International Aspects of Power and Political Behavior in Organizations

This section presents some observations on the international aspects of political behavior in organizations. Some observations are speculative because little direct assessment of political behavior in organizations across cultures has been done. Several observations come from known cultural differences that can affect how power is attributed to a person and that person's political behavior.

People from different cultures hold different beliefs about the proper relationship between individuals who have power and those who do not. Some cultures see a directive and autocratic use of power as correct. Other cultures define a consultative or democratic approach as correct. Such cultural differences affect reactions to the use of power and related political behavior. Different individuals within those cultures, of course, can have different beliefs about power relationships.

People in the Philippines, Mexico, many South American countries, India, Singapore, and Hong Kong value a directive use of power. A manager who gives clear directions and instructions to subordinates receives more respect than a manager who consults subordinates. Workers in those countries ascribe power to a directive manager and weakness to a consultative one. Status symbols also play important roles in defining who has power and who does not. The political processes within the organizations of those countries should also mirror the power orientation of the underlying culture. Consultative-oriented managers have a distinct disadvantage when trying to maneuver through the political systems of power-directive cultures.

People in Israel, Switzerland, Austria, New Zealand, and the Scandinavian countries have an opposite orientation. Workers in those countries expect their managers to involve them in the decision-making process. A directive manager from India or Singapore, for example, would not be well accepted by workers in Scandinavian organizations. Although such a manager enjoys high power in his home culture, the same manager would have little power in Scandinavian cultures.

Cultures vary widely in their orientation to uncertainty. Some cultures value the reduction of uncertainty. Other cultures see uncertainty as a manageable part of organizational life. Workers in Greece and France expect managers to maintain low levels of uncertainty. A manager who cannot keep uncertainty low has little power and influence over his workers. Workers in Denmark and the United States, however, have a higher tolerance for uncertainty. Nonmanagers in those countries expect managers to make risky decisions. Such workers could ascribe high power to risk-taking managers and low power to those who avoid risk. The degree of power ascribed to various managers affects their ability to influence others with political tactics.

Workers in the United States, Australia, Great Britain, Canada, and the Netherlands are more individualistic than workers from many South American countries. The latter value family ties and conformity to social norms. South American workers expect managers to look after them. Managers who show genuine interest in their subordinates' private lives enjoy higher power in South American organizations than they do in North American organizations.

Ethical Issues about Power and Political Behavior in Organizations

Political behavior in organizations raises many questions about what is ethical and what is not. You may have sensed some ethical issues as you read this chapter. If any of the discussions of power or political behavior caused you to ponder the "rightness" of the observations, you were thinking of implicit ethical questions.

Using power and political behavior in an organization to serve self-interest is unethical, if you reject an egoistic view of ethics and accept a utilitarian view. Similarly, political behavior that uses excessive organizational resources to reach a personal goal is also unethical. These observations suggest that any political strategy and its associated tactics are unethical if they do not serve the organization's goals or the goals of a larger group of people than the single political actor. For example, an individual who ignores equipment maintenance to push products through a manufacturing process for personal gain is behaving unethically.

Using power or political behavior that violates another person's rights is also unethical. Political tactics such as blaming others, ingratiation, and co-optation violate others' rights. A co-opted individual, unless he understands the goal of the political actor, has not consented to be influenced. Making accusations against someone violates that individual's right to an impartial hearing of the charges.

A sense of justice strongly argues for fair treatment, fair pay, and the fair administration of rules and procedures. Treating someone preferentially to build a sense of obligation is unethical.

Does this discussion of ethics and political behavior mean political behavior is inherently unethical? No! If you accept the discussions of ethics, any political behaviors, uses of power, and efforts to affect others that have the following characteristics are ethical:

- The behavior should serve people outside the organization and beyond the single political actor.
- Individuals should clearly know the person's intent and give their implicit or explicit consent to be influenced.
- The right of due process should not be violated while the political behavior unfolds.
- Administering the organization's resources, procedures, and policies should allow fair treatment of all affected people.
- These guidelines should help you distinguish an organizational statesman from a person playing "dirty politics."

LEADERSHIP AND FOLLOWERSHIP

Debra L. Nelson & James Campbell Quick

eadership in organizations is the process of guiding and directing the behavior of people in the work environment. The first section of this chapter distinguishes leadership from management. *Formal leadership* occurs when an organization officially bestows on a leader the authority to guide and direct others in the organization. *Informal leadership* occurs when a person is unofficially accorded power by others in the organization and uses influence to guide and direct their behavior. Leadership is among the most researched but least understood social processes in organizations.

Leadership has a long, rich history in organizational behavior. In this chapter, we explore many of the theories and ideas that have emerged along the way in that history. To begin, we examine the differences between leaders and managers. Next, we explore the earliest theories of leadership, the trait theories, which tried to identify a set of traits that leaders have in common. Following the trait theories came behavioral theories, which proposed that leader behaviors, not traits, are what counts. Contingency theories followed soon after. These theories argue that appropriate leader behavior depends on the situation and the followers. Next, we present some exciting contemporary theories of leadership, followed by the exciting new issues that are arising in leadership. We end by discussing *followership* and offering some guidelines for using this leadership knowledge.

Leadership and Management

John Kotter suggests that leadership and management are two distinct yet complementary systems of action in organizations. Specifically, he believes that effective leadership produces useful change in organizations and that good management controls complexity in the organization and its environment. Sheryl Sandberg, COO of Facebook, knows about creating change while stabilizing. Since joining Facebook in 2007, she has helped to lead the company to great success, devising an advertising platform that's attracted the world's largest brands and creating a remarkably trusting partnership with Mark Zuckerberg, Facebook's 26-year-old founder. Healthy organizations need both effective leadership and good management.

For Kotter, the management process involves (1) planning and budgeting, (2) organizing and staffing, and (3) controlling and problem solving. The management process reduces uncertainty and stabilizes an organization. Alfred P. Sloan's integration and stabilization of General Motors after its early growth years are an example of good management.

By contrast, the leadership process involves (1) setting a direction for the organization, (2) aligning people with that direction through communication, and (3) motivating people to action, partly through empowerment and partly through basic need gratification. The leadership process creates uncertainty and change in an organization. Effective leaders not only control the future of the organization but also act as enablers of change. They disturb existing patterns of behaviors, promote novel ideas, and help organizational members make sense of the change process.

Abraham Zaleznik proposes that leaders have distinct personalities that stand in contrast to the personalities of a manager. Zaleznik suggests that both leaders and managers make a valuable contribution to an organization and that each one's contribution is different. Whereas *Leaders* agitate for change and new approaches, *managers* advocate stability and the status quo. There is a dynamic tension between leaders and managers that makes it difficult for each to understand the other. Leaders and managers differ along four separate dimensions of personality: attitudes toward goals, conceptions of work, relationships with other people, and sense of self. It has been proposed that some people are strategic leaders who embody both the stability of managers and the visionary abilities of leaders. Thus, strategic leaders combine the best of both worlds in a synergistic way. The unprecedented success of Coca-Cola and Microsoft suggests that their leaders, the late Roberto Goizueta (of Coca-Cola) and Bill Gates, were strategic leaders.

Early Trait Theories

The first studies of leadership attempted to identify what physical attributes, personality characteristics, and abilities distinguished leaders from other members of a group. The physical attributes considered have been height, weight, physique, energy, health, appearance, and even age. This line of research yielded some interesting findings. However, very few valid generalizations emerged from this line of inquiry. Therefore, there is insufficient evidence to conclude that leaders can be distinguished from followers on the basis of physical attributes.

Leader personality characteristics that have been examined include originality, adaptability, introversion–extraversion, dominance, self-confidence, integrity, conviction, mood optimism, and emotional control. There is some evidence that leaders may be more adaptable and self-confident than the average group member.

With regard to leader abilities, attention has been devoted to such constructs as social skills, intelligence, scholarship, speech fluency, cooperativeness, and insight. In this area, there is some evidence that leaders are more intelligent, verbal, and cooperative and have a higher level of scholarship than the average group member.

These conclusions suggest traits leaders possess, but the findings are neither strong nor uniform. For each attribute or trait claimed to distinguish leaders from followers, there were always at least one or two studies with contradictory findings. For some, the trait theories are invalid, though interesting and intuitively of some relevance. The trait theories have had limited success in being able to identify the universal, distinguishing attributes of leaders. Recent research investigated the effects of heritability among 178 fraternal and 214 identical female twins. Results indicated that genetic factors contribute to the motivation to occupy leadership positions among women leaders. Similarly, prior work experience also has a significant impact on the motivation to lead. Thus, it seems that both personal factors and experience affect a person's desire to become a leader.

Behavioral Theories

Behavioral theories emerged as a response to the deficiencies of the trait theories. Trait theories told us what leaders were like, but didn't address how they behaved. Three theories are the foundations of many modern leadership theories: the Lewin, Lippitt, and White studies, the Ohio State studies, and the Michigan studies.

Lewin Studies

The earliest research on leadership style, conducted by Lewin, Lippitt and White, identified three basic styles: autocratic, democratic, and laissez-faire. Each leader uses one of these three basic styles when approaching a group of followers in a leadership situation. The specific situation is not an important consideration because the leader's style does not vary with the situation. The *autocratic style* is directive, strong, and controlling in relationships. Leaders with an autocratic style use rules and regulations to run the work environment. Followers have little discretionary influence over the nature of the work, its accomplishment, or other aspects of the work environment. The leader with a *democratic style* is collaborative, responsive, and interactive in relationships and emphasizes rules and regulations less than the autocratic leader. Followers

have a high degree of discretionary influence although the leader has ultimate authority and responsibility. The leader with a *laissez-faire style* has a hands-off approach. A laissez-faire leader abdicates the authority and responsibility of the position, which often results in chaos. Laissez-faire leadership also causes role ambiguity for followers by the leader's failure to clearly define goals, responsibilities, and outcomes. It leads to higher interpersonal conflict at work.

Ohio State Studies

The leadership research program at The Ohio State University also measured specific leader behaviors. The initial Ohio State research studied aircrews and pilots. The aircrew members, as followers, were asked a wide range of questions about their lead pilots using the Leader Behavior Description Questionnaire (LBDQ). The results using the LBDQ suggested that there were two important underlying dimensions of leader behaviors. These were labeled initiating structure and consideration.

Initiating structure is leader behavior aimed at defining and organizing work relationships and roles, as well as establishing clear patterns of organization, communication, and ways of getting things done. *Consideration* is leader behavior aimed at nurturing friendly, warm working relationships, as well as encouraging mutual trust and interpersonal respect within the work unit. These two leader behaviors are independent of each other. That is, a leader may be high on both, low on both, or high on one while low on the other. The Ohio State studies were intended to describe leader behavior, not to evaluate or judge it.

Michigan Studies

Another approach to the study of leadership, developed at the University of Michigan, suggests that the leader's style has very important implications for the emotional atmosphere of the work environment and, therefore, for the followers who work under that leader. Two styles of leadership were identified: production oriented and employee oriented.

A production-oriented style leads to a work environment characterized by constant influence attempts on the part of the leader, either through direct, close supervision or through the use of many written and unwritten rules and regulations for behavior. The focus is clearly on getting work done.

In comparison, an employee-oriented leadership style leads to a work environment that focuses on relationships. The leader exhibits less direct or less close supervision and establishes fewer written or unwritten rules and regulations for behavior. Employee-oriented leaders display concern for people and their needs.

These three groups of studies—Lewin studies; Ohio State; and Michigan—taken together form the building blocks of many recent leadership theories. The studies identified two basic leadership styles; one focused on tasks (autocratic, production oriented, initiating structure), and the other focused on people (democratic, employee oriented, consideration). Use the "How Does Your Supervisor Lead?" box to assess your supervisor's task-oriented versus people-oriented styles.

The Leadership Grid: A Contemporary Extension

Robert Blake and Jane Mouton's *Leadership Grid*, originally called the *Managerial Grid*, was developed with a focus on attitudes. The two underlying dimensions of the grid are labeled Concern for Results and Concern for People. These two attitudinal dimensions are independent of each other and in different combinations form various leadership styles. Blake and Mouton originally identified five distinct managerial styles, and further development of the grid has led to the seven distinct leadership styles shown in Figure 15.1.

The *organization man manager (5,5)* is a middle-of-the-road leader who has a medium concern for people and production. This leader attempts to balance a concern for both people and production without a commitment to either.

The *authority-compliance manager (9,1)* has great concern for production and little concern for people. This leader desires tight control in order to get tasks done efficiently and considers creativity and human relations unnecessary. Authority-compliance managers may become so focused on running an efficient organization that they actually use tactics such as bullying. Some authority-compliance managers may intimidate, verbally and mentally attack, and otherwise mistreat subordinates. This form of abuse is quite common, with one in six U.S. workers reporting that they have been bullied by a manager. The *country club manager (1,9)* has great concern for people and little concern for production, attempts to avoid conflict, and seeks to be well liked. This leader's goal is to keep people happy through good interpersonal relations, which are more important to him or her than the task. (This style is not a sound human relations approach but rather a soft Theory X approach.)

The *team manager (9,9)* is considered ideal and has great concern for both people and production. This leader works to motivate employees to reach their highest levels of accomplishment, is flexible, responsive to change, and understands the need for change. The *impoverished manager (1,1)* is often referred to as a laissez-faire leader. This leader has little concern for people or production, avoids taking sides, and stays out of conflicts; he or she does just enough to get by. Two new leadership styles have been added to these five original leadership styles within the grid. The *paternalistic* "father knows best" manager (9+9) promises reward for compliance and threatens punishment for noncompliance. The *opportunistic "what's in it for me" manager (Opp)* uses the style that he or she feels will return the greatest self-benefits.

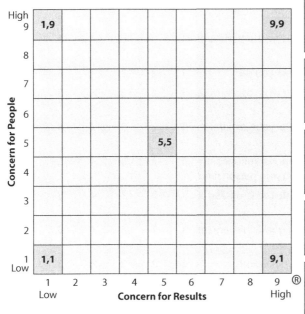

1,9 Country Club Management:
Thoughtful attention to the needs of the people for satisfying relationships leads to a comfortable, friendly organization atmosphere and work tempo.

9,9 Team Management:
Work accomplishment is from committed people; interdependence through a "common stake" in organization purpose leads to relationships of trust and respect.

5,5 Middle-of-the-Road Management:
Adequate organization performance is possible through balancing the necessity to get work out while maintaining morale of people at a satisfactory level.

1,1 Impoverished Management:
Exertion of minimum effort to get required work done is appropriate to sustain organization membership.

9,1 Authority-Compliance Management:
Efficiency in operations results from arranging conditions of work in such a way that human elements interfere to a minimum degree.

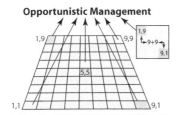

In Opportunisitic Management, people adapt and shift to any grid style needed to gain the maximum advantage. Performance occurs according to a system of selfish gain. Effort is given only for an advantage for personal gain.

9+9: Paternalism/Maternalism Management:
Reward and approval are bestowed to people in return for loyalty and obedience; failure to comply leads to punishment.

Figure 15.1 The Leadership Grid. *Source:* "The Leadership Grid®" figure, Paternalism figure, and Opportunism from *Leadership Dilemmas–Grid Solutions,* by Robert R. Blake and Anne Adams McCanse (formerly *The Managerial Grid* by Robert R. Blake and Jane S. Mouton). Houston: Gulf Publishing Company (Grid Figure: p. 29; Paternalism Figure: p. 30; Opportunism Figure: p. 31). Copyright 1991 by Blake and Mouton, and Scientific Methods, Inc.

How Does Your Supervisor Lead?

Answer the following sixteen questions concerning your supervisor's (or professor's) leadership behaviors using the seven-point Likert scale. Then complete the summary to examine your supervisor's behaviors.

	Not at All					Very Much	
1. Is your superior strict about observing regulations?	1	2	3	4	5	6	7
2. To what extent does your superior give you instructions and orders?	1	2	3	4	5	6	7
3. Is your superior strict about the amount of work you do?	1	2	3	4	5	6	7
4. Does your superior urge you to complete your work by the time he or she has specified?	1	2	3	4	5	6	7
5. Does your superior try to make you work to your maximum capacity?	1	2	3	4	5	6	7
6. When you do an inadequate job, does your superior focus on the inadequate way the job was done instead of on your personality?	1	2	3	4	5	6	7
7. Does your superior ask you for reports about the progress of your work?	1	2	3	4	5	6	7
8. Does your superior work out precise plans for goal achievement each month?	1	2	3	4	5	6	7
9. Can you talk freely with your superior about your work?	1	2	3	4	5	6	7
10. Generally, does your superior support you?	1	2	3	4	5	6	7
11. Is your superior concerned about your personal problems?	1	2	3	4	5	6	7
12. Do you think your superior trusts you?	1	2	3	4	5	6	7
13. Does your superior give you recognition when you do your job well?	1	2	3	4	5	6	7
14. When a problem arises in your workplace, does your superior ask your opinion about how to solve it?	1	2	3	4	5	6	7
15. Is your superior concerned about your future benefits like promotions and pay raises?	1	2	3	4	5	6	7
16. Does your superior treat you fairly?	1	2	3	4	5	6	7

The Leadership Grid is distinguished from the original Ohio State research in two important ways. First, it has attitudinal overtones that are not present in the original research. Whereas the LBDQ aims to describe behavior, the grid addresses the behavior and the attitude of the leader. Second, the Ohio State approach is fundamentally descriptive and nonevaluative, whereas the grid is normative

Add up your answers to Questions 1 through 8. This total indicates your supervisor's performance orientation:

Task orientation = _____

Add up your answers to Questions 9 through 16. This total indicates your supervisor's maintenance orientation:

People orientation = _____

A score above 40 is high, and a score below 20 is low.

Source: J. Misumi and M. F. Peterson, "The Performance-Maintenance Theory of Leadership: Review of a Japanese Research Program" *Administrative Science Quarterly* 30(2), p. 207, copyright 1985 by Sage Publications, Inc.

and prescriptive. Specifically, the grid evaluates the team manager (9,9) as the very best style of managerial behavior. This is the basis on which the grid has been used for team building and leadership training in an organization's development. As an organizational development method, the grid aims to transform the leader in the organization to lead in the "one best way," which according to the grid is the team approach. The team style is one that combines optimal concern for people with optimal concern for results.

Contingency Theories

Contingency theories involve the belief that leadership style must he appropriate for the particular situation. By their nature, contingency theories are "if–then" theories: If the situation is _____, then the appropriate leadership behavior is _____. We examine four such theories, including Fiedler's contingency theory, path–goal theory, normative decision theory, and situational leadership theory.

Fiedler's Contingency Theory

Fiedler's contingency theory of leadership proposes that the fit between the leader's need structure and the favorableness of the leader's situation determines the team's effectiveness in work accomplishment. This theory assumes that leaders are either task oriented or relationship oriented, depending on how the leaders obtain their primary need gratification. Task-oriented leaders are primarily gratified by accomplishing tasks and getting work done. Relationship-oriented leaders are primarily gratified by developing good, comfortable interpersonal relationships. Accordingly, the effectiveness of both types of leaders depends on the favorableness of their situation. The theory classifies the favorableness of the leader's situation according to the leader's position power, the structure of the team's task, and the quality of the leader–follower relationships.

The Least Preferred Coworker

Fiedler classifies leaders using the Least Preferred Coworker (LPC) Scale. The LPC Scale is a projective technique through which a leader is asked to think about the person with whom he or she can work least well (the *least preferred coworker,* or *LPC*).

The leader is asked to describe this coworker using sixteen eight-point bipolar adjective sets. Two of these sets follow (the leader marks the blank most descriptive of the LPC):

Efficient : : : : : : : : Inefficient
Cheerful : : : : : : : : Gloomy

Leaders who describe their LPC in positive terms (pleasant, efficient, cheerful, and so on) are classified as high LPC, or relationship-oriented, leaders. Those who describe their LPC in negative terms (unpleasant, inefficient, gloomy, and so on) are classified as low LPC, or task-oriented, leaders.

The LPC score is a controversial element in contingency theory. It has been critiqued conceptually and methodologically because it is a projective technique with low measurement reliability.

Situational Favorableness

The leader's situation has three dimensions: task structure, position power, and leader–member relations. Based on these three dimensions, the situation is either favorable or unfavorable for the leader. *Task structure* refers to the number and clarity of rules, regulations, and procedures for getting the work done. *Position power* refers to the leader's legitimate authority to evaluate and reward performance, punish errors, and demote group members.

The quality of *leader-member relations* is measured by the Group-Atmosphere Scale, composed of nine eight-point bipolar adjective sets. Two of these bipolar adjective sets follow:

Friendly   : : : : : : : : Unfriendly
Accepting : : : : : : : : Rejecting

A favorable leadership situation is one with a structured task for the work group, strong position power for the leader, and good leader–member relations. By contrast, an unfavorable leadership situation is one with an unstructured task, weak position power for the leader, and moderately poor leader–member relations. Between these two extremes, the leadership situation has varying degrees of moderate favorableness for the leader.

Leadership Effectiveness

The contingency theory suggests that low and high LPC leaders are each effective if placed in the right situation. Specifically, low LPC (task-oriented) leaders are most effective in either very favorable or very unfavorable leadership situations. By contrast, high LPC (relationship-oriented) leaders are most effective in situations of intermediate favorableness. Figure 15.2 shows the nature of these relationships and suggests that leadership effectiveness is determined by the degree of fit between the leader and the situation. Recent research has shown that relationship-oriented leaders encourage team learning and innovativeness, which helps products get to market faster. This means that most relationship-oriented leaders perform well in leading new product development teams. In short, the right team leader can help get creative new products out the door faster, while a mismatch between the leader and the situation can have the opposite effect.

What, then, is to be done if there is a misfit? That is, what happens when a low LPC leader is in a moderately favorable situation or when a high LPC leader is in a highly favorable or highly unfavorable situation? It is unlikely that the leader can be changed, according to the theory, because the leader's need structure is an enduring trait that is hard to change. Fiedler recommends that the leader's situation be changed to fit the leader's style.

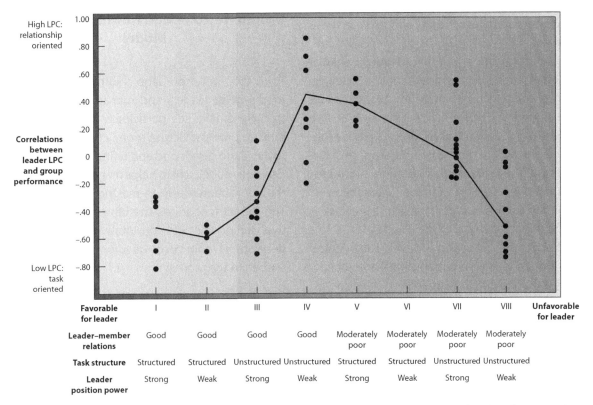

Figure 15.2 Leadership Effectiveness in the Contingency Theory. *Source*: F. E. Fiedler, *A Theory of Leader Effectiveness* (New York: McGraw-Hill 1964).

A moderately favorable situation would be reengineered to be more favorable and, therefore, more suitable for the low LPC leader. A highly favorable or highly unfavorable situation would be changed to one that is moderately favorable and more suitable for the high LPC leader. Fiedler's theory makes an important contribution in drawing our attention to the leader's situation.

Path–Goal Theory

Robert House developed a path–goal theory of leader effectiveness based on an expectancy theory of motivation. From the perspective of path–goal theory, the basic role of the leader is to clear the follower's path to the goal. The leader uses the most appropriate of four leader behavior styles to help followers clarify the paths that lead them to work and personal goals. The key concepts in the theory are shown in Figure 15.3.

A leader selects from the four leader behavior styles, shown in Figure 15.3, the one that is most helpful to followers at a given time. The *directive style* is used when the leader must give specific guidance about work tasks, schedule work, and let followers know what is expected. The *supportive style* is used when the leader needs to express concern for followers' well-being and social status. The *participative style* is used when the leader must engage in joint decision-making activities with followers. The *achievement-oriented style* is used when the leader must set challenging goals for followers and show strong confidence in those followers.

In selecting the appropriate leader behavior style, the leader must consider both the followers and the work environment. A few characteristics are included in Figure 15.3. Let us look at two examples. In Example 1, the followers are inexperienced and working on an ambiguous, unstructured task. The leader in this situation might best use a directive style. In Example 2, the followers are highly trained professionals, and the task is a difficult yet achievable one. The leader in this situation might best use an achievement-oriented style. The leader always chooses the leader behavior style that helps followers achieve their goals.

The path–goal theory assumes that leaders adapt their behavior and style to fit the characteristics of the followers and the environment in which they work. Actual tests of the path–goal theory and its propositions provide conflicting evidence. The path–goal theory does have intuitive appeal and reinforces the idea that the appropriate leadership style depends on both the work situation and the followers. Research is focusing on which style works best in specific situations. For example, in small organizations, leaders who used visionary, transactional, and empowering behaviors, while avoiding autocratic behaviors, were most successful.

Vroom–Yetton–Jago Normative Decision Model

The Vroom–Yetton–Jago normative decision model helps leaders and managers know when to have employees participate in the decision-making process. Victor Vroom, Phillip Yetton, and Arthur Jago developed and refined the normative decision model, which helps managers determine the appropriate decision-making strategy to use. The model recognizes the benefits of authoritative, democratic, and consultative styles of leader behavior. Five forms of decision making are described in the model:

- *Decide.* The manager makes the decision alone and either announces it or "sells" it to the group.
- *Consult individually.* The manager presents the problem to the group members individually, gets their input, and then makes the decision.
- *Consult group.* The manager presents the problem to the group members in a meeting, gets their inputs, and then makes the decision.
- *Facilitate.* The manager presents the problem to the group in a meeting and acts as a facilitator, defining the problem and the boundaries that surround the decision. The manager's ideas are not given more weight

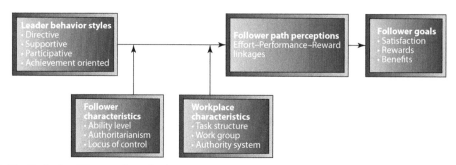

Figure 15.3 The Path–Goal Theory of Leadership

than any other group member's ideas. The objective is to get concurrence.

- *Delegate.* The manager permits the group to make the decision within the prescribed limits, providing needed resources and encouragement.

The key to the normative decision model is that a manager should use the decision method most appropriate for a given decision situation. The manager arrives at the proper method by working through matrices like the one in Figure 15.4. The factors across the top of the model (decision significance, commitment, leader expertise, etc.) are the situational factors in the normative decision model. This matrix is for decisions that must be made under time pressure, but other matrices are also available. For example, there is a different

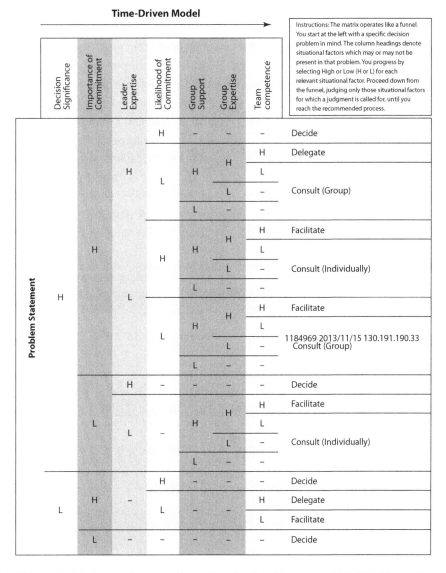

Figure 15.4 Time-Driven Model. *Source:* Reprinted from *Organizational Dynamics,* 28, by V. H. Vroom, "Leadership and the Decision-Making Process," pp. 82–94, Spring 2000.

matrix managers can use when their objective is to develop subordinates' decision-making skills. Vroom has also developed a Windows-based computer program called Expert System that can be used by managers to determine which style to use.

Although the model offers explicit predictions as well as prescriptions for leaders, its utility is limited to the leader decision-making tasks.

One unique study applied the normative decision model of leadership to the battlefield behavior of ten commanding generals in six major battles of the American Civil War. When the commanders acted consistently with the prescriptions of the Vroom–Yetton–Jago model, they were more successful in accomplishing their military goals. The findings also suggested that a lack of information sharing and consensus building resulted in serious disadvantages.

The Situational Leadership Model

The Situational Leadership model, developed by Paul Hersey and Kenneth Blanchard, suggests that the leader's behavior should be adjusted to the maturity level of the followers. The model employs the same two dimensions of leader behavior as used in the Ohio State studies: task-oriented and relationship–oriented. Follower maturity is categorized into four levels, as shown in Figure 15.5. Follower readiness is determined by the follower's ability and willingness to complete a specific task. Readiness can, therefore, be low or high depending on the particular task. In addition, readiness varies within a single person according to the task. One person may be willing and able to satisfy simple requests from customers (high readiness) but less able or willing to give highly technical advice to customers (low readiness). It is important that the leader be able to evaluate the readiness level of each follower for each task. The four styles of leader behavior

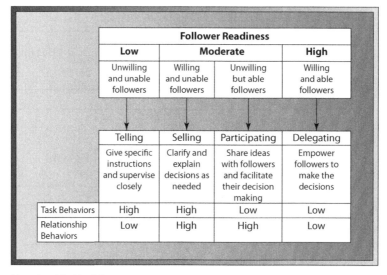

Figure 15.5 Situational Leadership Model

Source: From PHILLIPS/GULLY, *Organizational Behavior,* 1E. © 2012 Cengage Learning.

associated with the four readiness levels are depicted in the figure as well.

According to the Situational Leadership model, a leader should use a telling style when a follower is unable and unwilling to do a certain task. This style involves providing instructions and closely monitoring performance. As such, the telling style involves considerable task behavior and low relationship behavior. When a follower is unable but willing and confident to do a task, the leader can use the selling style in which there is high task behavior and high relationship behavior. In this case, the leader explains decisions and provides opportunities for the employee to seek clarification or help. Sometimes a follower will be able to complete a task but may seem unwilling or insecure about doing so. In these cases, a participating style is warranted, which involves high relationship but low task behavior. The leader in this case encourages the follower to participate in decision making. Finally, for tasks in which a follower is able and willing, the leader is able to use a delegating style, characterized by low task behavior and low relationship behavior. In this case, follower readiness is high, and low levels of leader involvement (task or relationship) are needed.

One key limitation of the Situational Leadership model is the absence of central hypotheses that could be tested, which would make it a more valid, reliable theory of leadership. However, the theory has intuitive appeal and is widely used for training and development in corporations. In addition, the theory focuses attention on follower maturity as an important determinant of the leadership process.

Leader–Member Exchange

Leader-member exchange theory, or LMX, recognizes that leaders may form different relationships with followers. The basic idea behind LMX is that leaders form two groups of followers: in-groups and out-groups. In-group members tend to be similar to the leader and are given greater responsibilities, more rewards, and more attention. They work within the leader's inner circle of communication. As a result, in-group members are more satisfied, have lower turnover, and have higher organizational commitment. By contrast, out-group members are outside the circle and receive less attention and fewer rewards. They are managed by formal rules and policies.

In-group members are more likely to engage in organizational citizenship behavior, while out-group members are more likely to retaliate against the organization. In-group members may also be more creative. When employees have a positive relationship with their supervisor, it increases their confidence or self-efficacy, which in turn increases creativity. The type of stress varies by the group to which a subordinate belongs. In-group members' stress comes from the additional responsibilities placed on them by the leader, whereas out-group members' stress comes from being left out of the communication network. One surprising finding is that more frequent communication with the boss may either help or hurt a worker's performance ratings, depending on whether the worker is in the in-group or the out-group. Among the in-group, more frequent communication generally leads to higher performance ratings, while members of the out-group who communicate more often with the superior tend to receive lower performance ratings. Perhaps the out-group members get to talk to the boss only when something has gone wrong!

Employees who enjoy more frequent contact with the boss also have a better understanding of what the boss's expectations are. Such agreement tends to lead to better performance by the employee and fewer misunderstandings between employer and employee.

In-group members are also more likely to support the values of the organization and to become models of appropriate behavior. If the leader, for example, wants to promote safety at work, in-group members model safe work practices, which lead to a climate of workplace safety.

Substitutes for Leadership

Sometimes situations can neutralize or even replace leader behavior. This is the central idea behind the substitutes for leadership theory. When a task is satisfying and employees get feedback about performance, leader behavior is irrelevant because the employee's satisfaction comes from the interesting work and the feedback. Other things that can substitute for leadership include high skill on the part of the employee, team cohesiveness, and formal controls on the part of the organization. Research on this idea is generally supportive, and other factors that act as substitutes are being identified. Even a firm's customers can be a substitute for leadership. In service settings, employees with lots of customer contact actually receive significant leadership and direction from customer demands, allowing the firm to provide less formal supervision to these employees than to workers with little customer contact. This finding adds new weight to the old adage about the customer being boss.

The Emergence of Inspirational Leadership Theories

Leadership is an exciting area of organizational behavior, one in which new research is constantly emerging. Three new developments are important to understand: transformational leadership, charismatic leadership, and authentic leadership. These three theories can be called inspirational leadership theories because, in each one followers are inspired by the leader to perform well.

Transformational Leadership

As we indicated earlier in the chapter, transactional leaders are those who use rewards and punishment to strike deals with followers and shape their behavior. By contrast, transformational leaders inspire and excite followers to high levels of performance. They rely on their personal attributes instead of their official position to manage followers. There is some evidence that transformational leadership can he learned. Transformational leadership consists of the following four sub dimensions: charisma, individualized consideration, inspirational motivation, and intellectual stimulation. We describe charisma in detail below. Individualized consideration refers to how much the leader displays concern for each follower's individual needs and acts as a coach or a mentor. Inspirational motivation is the extent to which the leader is able to articulate a vision that is appealing to followers. In the "Passion and People: Starbucks' Vision" box, read about how CEO Howard Shultz's vision and passion have led Starbucks through changes, including changing the iconic logo and experimenting with selling wine and beer in its stores.

Transformational leadership is very important for individuals as well as teams. Transformational leadership behavior focused on individuals increases task performance and personal initiative, whereas transformational behavior focused on a group increases team performance and helping behavior. Followers who work for a transformational leader are more satisfied, motivated, and perform better. Transformational leadership research conducted in China, Kenya, and Thailand also showed that it had positive effects on employee commitment and negative effects on employee work withdrawal.

Transformation leadership can increase firm performance. U.S. corporations increasingly operate in a global economy, so there is a greater demand for leaders who can practice transformational leadership by converting their visions into reality and by inspiring followers to perform "above and beyond the call of duty."

Leaders can be both transformational and transactional. Transformational leadership adds to the effects of transactional leadership, but exceptional transactional leadership cannot substitute for transformational leadership. One reason the latter is effective is that transformational leaders encourage followers to set goals congruent with the followers' own authentic interests and values. Because of this, followers see their work as important and their goals as aligned with who they are.

Men and women may differ on what aspects of transformational leadership are most important. Inspirational motivation has been found to be more important for men for promotion to CEO, but individualized consideration was more important for women with the same aspirations. For more information on transformational leadership

Passion and People: Starbucks' Vision

Howard Schultz, CEO of Starbucks, insists that Starbucks is not in the coffee business; instead, he says, it's in the people business, and it is all about human connection. When he came back from Italy in the 1980s to look for investors for the company, his vision was "to build a third place between work and home." That vision has served the company well even in tough times. After giving up the CEO role to serve as chairman, Schultz returned to the CEO role when Starbucks began losing its way. It had spread itself too thin, grown too fast, and needed refocusing. A lesson Schultz learned from the failure is that growth is not a strategy; it's a tactic.

Consistent with the vision, Starbucks' logo changed, removing the company name and the word "coffee" from the logo. This gives Starbucks the freedom to broaden its products to other beverages and foods. In several stores, wine and beer are now being sold in the afternoon. This experiment complements Schultz's vision of Starbucks as that "third place" between work and home. Another innovation is mobile phone payments for Starbucks store sales. Starbucks, in just three months, became the number one company in the United States for purchases by mobile phone.

Schultz's original vision to create a European espresso bar concept in the United States is not about selling coffee; instead, it's about human connection. Painting a picture of what a company's product stands for, not a picture of the product itself, is a hallmark of inspirational leadership.

Sources: A. Fisher, "How Starbucks Got Its Groove Back," *Fortune* (March 24, 2011), accessed at http://management.fortune.cnn.com/2011/03/24/how-starbucks-got-its-groove-back/; C. Gallo, "Starbucks CEO: Lesson in Communication," *Forbes* (March 25, 2011), accessed at http://blogs.forbes.com/canninegallo/2011/03/25/starbucks-ceo-lesson-in-communication-skills/.

Is It the Person or the Behavior?

Leadership research has long investigated the impact of both personality traits and leadership behaviors and their separate influences on leadership effectiveness. However, few studies have compared the impact of both traits and behaviors simultaneously. A recent study compared data from 59 studies to investigate the impact of traits and behaviors on four leadership effectiveness criteria: leader effectiveness, group performance, follower job satisfaction, and satisfaction with leader. The study found that, in general, leader behavior explained leadership effectiveness better than leader traits. Within this behavioral realm, leaders who were transformational were the most effective. Conscientiousness was the trait most common among effective leaders, while leaders' agreeableness improved group performance.

Passive leadership behavior or laissez-faire leadership was not effective. In fact, leaders are better off behaving in suboptimal ways than doing nothing at all. Leaders who engaged in task, relationship, and change behaviors were the most effective. This study provides clear guidance to leadership development programs to focus on all three types of leadership behaviors (task, relationship, and change) while also working to foster the dimensions of transformational leadership.

Source: D. S. DeRue, J. D. Nahrgang, N. Wellman, and S. E. Humphrey, "Trait and Behavioral Theories of Leadership: An Integration and Meta-analytic Test of Their Relative Validity," *Personnel Psychology*, 64 (2011): 7–52.

as well as the impact of traits and behaviors on leadership effectiveness, see the Science feature.

Charismatic Leadership

Steve Jobs, the pioneer behind the Macintosh computer and the growing music download market, had an uncanny ability to create a vision and convince others to become part of it. This was evidenced by Apple's continual overall success despite its major blunders in the desktop computer wars. Jobs's ability was so powerful that Apple employees coined a term in the 1980s for it, the *reality-distortion field*. This expression is used to describe the persuasive ability and peculiar charisma of managers like Steve Jobs. This reality-distortion field allowed Jobs to convince even skeptics that his plans are worth supporting, no matter how unworkable they may appear. Those close to these managers become passionately committed to seemingly impossible projects, without regard to the practicality of their implementation or competitive forces in the marketplace. Similarly, people who have worked with CEO Ken Chenault of American Express note that they admire him immensely and would do anything for him. He is known for chatting with executives and secretaries alike and is seen as someone who is free from the normal trappings of power.

Charismatic leadership results when a leader uses the force of personal abilities and talents to have profound and extraordinary effects on followers. Some scholars see transformational leadership and charismatic leadership as very similar, but others believe they are different. *Charisma* is a Greek word meaning "gift"; the charismatic leader's unique and powerful gifts are the source of his or her great influence with followers. In fact, followers often view the charismatic leader as one who possesses superhuman, or even mystical, qualities. Charismatic leaders rely heavily on referent power, and charismatic leadership is especially effective in times of uncertainty. Charismatic leadership falls to those who are "chosen" (born with the "gift" of charisma) or who cultivate that gift. Some say charismatic leaders are born, and others say they are taught.

Some charismatic leaders rely on humor as a tool for communication. Charismatic leadership carries with it not only great potential for high levels of achievement and performance on the part of followers but also shadowy risks of destructive courses of action that might harm followers or other people. Several researchers have attempted to demystify charismatic leadership and distinguish its two faces.

The ugly face of charisma is revealed in the personalized power motivations of Adolf Hitler and Osama Bin Laden. Both men led their followers into struggle, conflict, and death. The brighter face of charisma is revealed in the socialized power motivations of U.S. President Franklin D. Roosevelt. Former presidents Bill Clinton and Ronald Reagan, while worlds apart in terms of their political beliefs, were actually quite similar in their use of personal charisma to inspire followers and motivate them to pursue the leader's vision. In each case, followers perceived the leader as imbued with a unique vision for America and unique abilities to lead the country there. Charismatic leaders, both negative and positive, demonstrate that charisma is really in the eyes of the followers.

Authentic Leadership

A new form of leadership has started to garner attention thanks to the ethical scandals rocking the business world. In response to concerns about the potential negative side of inspirational forms of leadership, researchers have called for authentic leadership. *Authentic leadership* includes transformational, charismatic, or transactional leadership as the situation demands. However, it differs from the other kinds in that authentic leaders have a conscious and well-developed sense of values. They act in ways that are consistent with their value systems, so authentic leaders have a highly evolved sense of moral right and wrong. Their life experiences (often labeled "moments that matter") lead to authentic leadership development, and allow authentic leaders to be their true selves. Authentic leaders arouse and motivate followers to higher levels of performance by building a workforce characterized by high levels of hope, optimism, resiliency, and self-efficacy. Followers also experience more positive emotions and trust leadership as a result of transparency and a collective caring climate engendered by the leader. Researchers contend that this is the kind of leadership embodied by Gandhi, Nelson Mandela, and others like them throughout history. Only time and solid management research will tell if this approach can yield results for organizational leadership. One recent development in the identification of authentic leaders stems from the area of emotions. Emotions act as checks and balances that not only keep the ugly side of charisma in check but also provide certain cues to followers. For example, a leader who espouses benevolence (as a value) but does not display compassion (an emotion) might not be very authentic in followers' eyes. Similarly, a leader who displays compassion when announcing a layoff may be seen by followers as more morally worthy and held in higher regard.

Despite the warm emotions charismatic leaders can evoke, some of them are narcissists who listen only to those who agree with them. Whereas charismatic leaders with socialized power motivation are concerned about the collective well-being of their followers, charismatic leaders with a personalized power motivation are driven by the need for personal gain and glorification.

Charismatic leadership styles are associated with several positive outcomes. One study reported that firms headed by more charismatic leaders outperformed other firms, particularly in difficult economic times. Perhaps even more important, charismatic leaders were able to raise more outside financial support for their firms than noncharismatic leaders, meaning that charisma at the top may translate to greater funding at the bottom.

Emerging Issues in Leadership

Along with the recent developments in theory, some exciting issues have emerged of which leaders must be aware. These include emotional intelligence, trust, gender and leadership, and servant leadership.

Emotional Intelligence

It has been suggested that effective leaders possess emotional intelligence, which is the ability to recognize and manage emotion in oneself and in others. In fact, some researchers argue that emotional intelligence is more important for effective leadership than intelligence quotient (IQ) or technical skills. Emotional intelligence is made up of several types of abilities: the ability to perceive, understand, and facilitate emotion as well as emotion regulation.

Emotional intelligence affects the way leaders make decisions. Under high stress, leaders with higher emotional intelligence tend to keep their cool and make better decisions while leaders with low emotional intelligence make poor decisions and lose their effectiveness. Joe Torre, former manager of the New York Yankees, got the most out of his team, worked for a notoriously tough boss, and kept his cool. He was a model of emotional intelligence: compassionate, calm under stress, and a great motivator. He advocated "managing against the cycle," which means staying calm when situations are tough, but turning up the heat on players when things are going well. Now the manager of the Los Angeles Dodgers, Torre has written that his "triple play" in managing others includes fairness, trust, and respect.

Trust

Trust is an essential element in leadership. Trust is the willingness to be vulnerable to the actions of another. This means that followers believe that their leader will act with the followers' welfare in mind. Trustworthiness is also one of the competencies in emotional intelligence. Trust among top management team members facilitates strategy implementation; this means that if team members trust each other, they have a better chance of getting "buy-in" from employees on the direction of the company. And if employees trust their leaders, they will buy in more readily. Transformational leadership and servant leadership increase trust, which in turn increases team performance.

Trust in top business leaders may be at an all-time low given the highly publicized failures of many CEOs. Rick Wagoner, CEO of General Motors during 2000–2009, lost more money than any CEO in history, yet he continued to express confidence in his company and his strategy. He was fired by the government just before GM went bankrupt. In the midst of the biggest oil spill in history, Tony Hayward of British Petroleum suggested the environmental impact would be "very, very modest" and later mentioned he "would like his life back." As people scrambled to save their livelihoods, he took a day off to go yacht-racing with his son.

Effective leaders also understand both whom to trust and how to trust. At one extreme, leaders often trust a close circle of advisors, listening only to them and gradually cutting themselves off from dissenting opinions. At the opposite extreme, lone-wolf leaders may trust nobody, leading to preventable mistakes. Wise leaders carefully evaluate both the competence and the position of those they trust, seeking out a variety of opinions and input.

Gender and Leadership

An important, emergent leadership question is this: Do women and men lead differently? Historical stereotypes persist, and people characterize successful managers as having more male-oriented attributes than female-oriented attributes. Although legitimate gender differences may exist, the same leadership traits may be interpreted differently in a man and a woman because of stereotypes. The real issue should be leader behaviors that are not bound by gender stereotypes.

Early evidence shows that women tend to use a more people-oriented style that is inclusive and empowering. Women managers excel in positions that demand strong interpersonal skills. More and more women are assuming positions of leadership in organizations. Irene Rosenfeld is CEO of the

global food giant Kraft Foods. In the Real World 12.2, you can read her advice for future leaders. Interestingly, much of what we know about leadership is based on studies that were conducted on men. We need to know more about the ways women lead. Interestingly, recent research reports on the phenomenon of the *glass cliff* (as opposed to the *glass ceiling* effect). The *glass cliff* represents a trend in organizations of placing more women in difficult leadership situations. Women perceive these assignments as necessary due to difficulty in attaining leadership positions and lack of alternate opportunities combined with male in-group favoritism. On the other hand, men perceive that women are better suited to difficult leadership positions due to better decision making.

Servant Leadership

Robert Greenleaf was director of management research at AT&T for many years. He believed that leaders should serve employees, customers, and the community, and his essays are the basis for today's view called servant leadership. His personal and professional philosophy was that leaders lead by serving others. Other tenets of servant leadership are that work exists for the person as much as the person exists for work, and that servant leaders try to find out the will of the group and lead based on that. Servant leaders are also stewards who consider leadership a trust and desire to leave the organization in better shape for future generations. Servant leadership leads to higher team performance and increased organizational citizenship behaviors within teams. Although Greenleaf's writings were completed thirty years ago, many have now been published and are becoming more popular.

Abusive Supervision

Recently research has begun to investigate not only what make leaders effective but also the dark side of leader behavior. The most common negative leader behaviors include sexual harassment, physical violence, angry outbursts, public ridicule, taking credit for employees' successes, and scapegoating employees. Abusive supervision, as these behaviors are called, is estimated to effect about 13.6 percent of U.S. workers and leads to many negative consequences. Abused workers report diminished well-being, along with increased deviance behavior, problem drinking, psychological distress, and emotional exhaustion. In addition, abusive supervision increases absenteeism and reduces productivity. In fact, the cost of abusive supervision to U.S. corporations has been estimated at $23.8 billion. It is not clear why supervisors abuse others. Some research suggests that

---

Want to Be a CEO? Irene Rosenfeld, Kraft Foods

Ranked high on *Forbes'* Power Women list, the CEO of Kraft Foods, Irene Rosenfeld, knows a thing or two about leadership. She's head of the world's second largest food company, including brands like Maxwell House, Nabisco, Oreo, and Oscar Mayer, among others. She was asked for her advice for women aspiring to be CEOs, but what she said applies equally to men.

- *Make a difference.* A company should be better for your having worked there. Constantly push the envelope and challenge traditional business approaches.
- *Take risks.* Playing it safe won't help you get ahead. Take on challenging assignments and risky jobs.
- *Make sure you have mentors.* Mentors see that you avoid landmines and give you the inside scoop. They also help you be more visible to key decision-makers.
- *Ask for what you want.* Some of my best promotions were to jobs I campaigned strongly for. Be direct, and toot your own horn if you need to.

Rosenfeld practices what she preaches, having led Kraft through the $18.5 acquisition of Cadbury, a key player in the market for chocolates and sweets, including Green & Black's chocolates and Trident gum. With that acquisition, Kraft's revenue tops $49.2 billion. Snacks now make up half of its portfolio, and more than half of the company's business is outside North America. And Rosenfeld believes in giving back. Her leadership has produced major efforts in sustainability, and she has led efforts to fight world hunger—Kraft has donated nearly a billion dollars in food and money to that effort.

Sources: A. Zendrian, "Get Briefed: Irene Rosenfeld", *Forbes* (Nov. 1, 2010), accessed at http://www.forbes.com/2010/10/29/rosenfeld-buffett-cadbury-intelligent-investing-kraft.html; http://www.kraftfoodscompany.com/assets/pdf/kraft_foods_fact_sheet.pdf.

injustice experienced by supervisors increases the likelihood that they will abuse. Other studies suggest that abuse stems from self-regulatory failures in that abusive supervisors are experiencing large amounts of stress and lose their cool. Abusive supervisors are more likely to direct their aggression toward employees who are very negative, or toward those who appear weak or unwilling or unable to defend themselves.

THE MOST IMPORTANT LEADERSHIP QUALITY FOR CEOS? CREATIVITY

Austin Carr

For CEOs, creativity is now the most important leadership quality for success in business, outweighing even integrity and global thinking, according to a new study by IBM. The study is the largest known sample of one-on-one CEO interviews, with over 1,500 corporate heads and public sector leaders across 60 nations and 33 industries polled on what drives them in managing their companies in today's world.

Fast Company's annual list of the 100 Most Creative People in Business just took on a whole new depth. And this year's list will be revealed later this month.

Steven Tomasco, a manager at IBM Global Business Services, expressed surprise at this key finding, saying that it is "very interesting that coming off the worst economic conditions they'd ever seen, [CEOs] didn't fall back on management discipline, existing best practices, rigor, or operations. In fact, they [did] just the opposite."

About 60% of CEOs polled cited creativity as the most important leadership quality, compared with 52% for integrity and 35% for global thinking. Creative leaders are also more prepared to break with the *status quo* of industry, enterprise

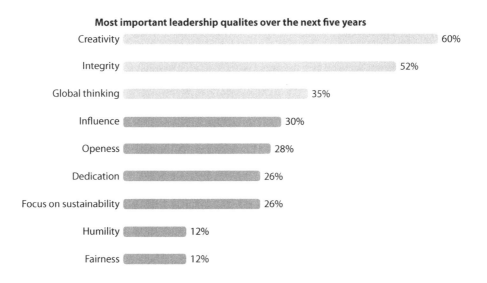

Most important leadership qualites over the next five years

Creativity	60%
Integrity	52%
Global thinking	35%
Influence	30%
Openess	28%
Dedication	26%
Focus on sustainability	26%
Humility	12%
Fairness	12%

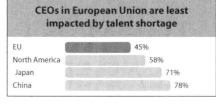

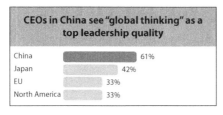

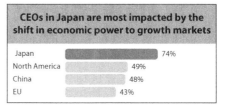

and revenue models, and they are 81% more likely to rate innovation as a "crucial capability."

Other key findings showed a large disparity between views of North American CEOs and those from other territories.

For example, in North America, 65% of CEOs think integrity is a top quality for tomorrow's leaders, whereas only 29-48% of CEOs in other territories view it as such.

Ironically, while company leaders in North America will bring more integrity to the job, they also expect far more regulation than foreign heads—both presumably reactions to negative public perception and heavy government

intervention following the recession. A full 87% anticipate greater government oversight and regulation over the next five years—only 70% of CEOs in Europe hold this opinion, and 50% and 53% in Japan and China, respectively. Meanwhile, nearly double the amount of CEOs in China view global thinking as a top leadership quality, compared with Europe and North America.

The area of focus the regions can all agree on is customer focus: 88% of all CEOs, and an astounding 95% of standout leaders, believe getting closer to the customer is the top business strategy over the next five years.

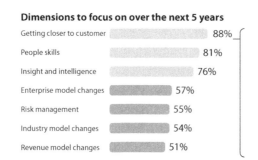

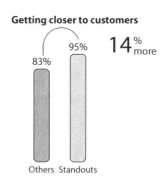

SEXUAL HARASSMENT

Annette M. Cremo & Richard C. Gaffney

What Trainers Need to Know

Sam, a supervisor, asks one of his employees, Debby, to go out with him on a date. Debby refuses, but Sam continues to ask her out.

George, the maintenance man, has pictures of scantily clad women pasted on his locker door. No one has complained to management—yet.

A high school principal gives a student after-school detention for leaving a sexually inappropriate note in a girl's locker and for "accidentally" bumping into her in the hallway.

An admittedly gay employee complains to his foreman that fellow employees are taunting him for being homosexual.

Sandi, a secretary who dates the region manager, has just received a promotion to office manager. She is delighted, but her co-workers are jealous.

Can you identify which, if any, of the above scenarios are actionable sexual harassment? Could you properly investigate a case of alleged sexual harassment? Could you mediate or arbitrate a dispute concerning sexual harassment in the workplace?

Does your organization have in place an effective policy on sexual harassment that includes a complaint procedure? Is management aware that the organization can be held strictly liable for the conduct of its supervisory personnel? Are managers and supervisors aware that they may be held personally liable for conduct that constitutes sexual harassment?

Could you develop and conduct a training course to raise management, supervisory, and employee awareness of sexual harassment? This issue, based on *Info-line* No. 9202, "Sexual Harassment: What Trainers Need to Know," provides the information you need to answer these questions and prepare you to educate and train your workforce on this rapidly evolving area of law. When it comes to sexual harassment, what you (and your organization) don't know can hurt you.

Trainers need to be familiar with all laws and policies that pertain to sexual harassment in the workplace. In the past few years, the public's awareness of workplace sexual harassment has grown greatly. Not surprisingly, the number of sexual harassment lawsuits also has exploded. This has often resulted in expensive and protracted litigation, which could otherwise have been avoided through effective training and development. The following pages contain detailed information regarding the laws and court decisions that affect the field of sexual harassment training, as well as an extensive discussion of the trainer's role and responsibility, plus guidelines for conducting training sessions.

Defining Sexual Harassment

What exactly is "sexual harassment"? What behavior crosses the line? And who exactly decides what conduct rises to the level of being actionable sexual harassment?

The U.S. Congress enacted Title VII of the Civil Rights Act of 1964 to make clear that discrimination on the basis of sex is unlawful. The federal judiciary has found that sexual harassment is a form of sex discrimination and therefore a violation of Sections 703–704 of Title VII of the Civil Rights Act of 1964 *as amended*. These court cases further define what behavior constitutes sexual harassment and what elements a plaintiff must prove for the harassment to be actionable.

EEOC Guidelines

The Equal Employment Opportunity Commission (EEOC) is the federal administrative agency charged with responsibility for investigating filed complaints of sexual harassment. The EEOC has defined the following behavior as constituting sexual harassment:

"Unwelcome sexual advances, requests for sexual favors, and other verbal or physical conduct of sexual nature constitutes sexual harassment when:

1. Submission to such conduct is made either explicitly or implicitly a term or condition of an individual's employment.
2. Submission to or rejection of such conduct by an individual is used as a basis for employment decisions affecting the individual.
3. Such conduct has the purpose or effect of unreasonably interfering with an individual's work performance or creating an intimidating, hostile, or offensive working environment."

In determining whether alleged conduct constitutes sexual harassment, the EEOC will look at the record as a whole and at the *totality of the circumstances,* such as the nature of the sexual advances and the context in which the alleged incidents occurred. The determination of the legality of a particular action will be made from the facts, on a case-by-case basis.

Applying Title VII principles, an employer, employment agency, joint apprenticeship committee, or labor organization (hereinafter "employer") is responsible for its acts, those of its agents, and supervisory employees with respect to sexual harassment, *regardless of whether the specific acts complained of were authorized or even forbidden by the employer and regardless of whether the employer knew or should have known of their occurrences*. The EEOC will examine the circumstances of the particular employment relationship, and the job functions performed, to determine whether a person acts in either a *supervisory or an agency capacity.*

Fellow Employees

With respect to conduct *between fellow employees,* an employer is responsible for acts of sexual harassment in the workplace where the employer, its agents, or supervisory employees, knows or should have known of the conduct—unless the employer can show that it took immediate and appropriate corrective (or remedial) action.

Nonemployees

An employer also may be responsible for the *acts of nonemployees,* with respect to sexual harassment of employees in the workplace, where the employer, its agents, or supervisory employees, knows or should have known of the conduct and fails to take immediate and appropriate corrective action. When examining these cases, the EEOC considers the extent of the employer's control and any other legal responsibility that the employer may have with respect to the conduct of nonemployees.

In other related practices, where employment opportunities or benefits are granted because of an individual's submission to the employer's sexual advances or requests for sexual favors, the employer may be held liable for unlawful sex discrimination against *other persons who were qualified but were denied that employment opportunity or benefit.*

In light of the extensive categories of employer liability for unlawful conduct, prevention is the best tool for elimination of sexual harassment. An employer should take all steps necessary to prevent sexual harassment from occurring by:

- raising the subject affirmatively
- expressing strong disapproval
- developing appropriate sanctions
- informing employees of the right to raise and how to raise the issue of harassment under Title VII
- developing methods to sensitize all employees through training

Workplace Rights and Responsibilities

The sexual harassment cases that have been decided in court have set out clear guidelines for the workplace. The following sections cover the terminology applicable to sexual harassment lawsuits, recent developments, implications for trainers, and the specific rights and responsibilities of employees, supervisors, and organizations.

Terminology

In 1986, the U.S. Supreme Court made clear that Title VII prohibits sexual harassment in the workplace. Since then, numerous cases have defined—and redefined—what constitutes sexual harassment, who may be held liable, and what damages are recoverable in a sexual harassment lawsuit. Traditionally, the law has focused on two main categories of actionable sexual harassment:

1. *Quid pro quo* harassment, in which sexual considerations are demanded in exchange for job benefits.
2. Hostile environment harassment that unreasonably interferes with an individual's job performance, or creates an intimidating, hostile, or offensive work environment, whether or not the harassment is linked to economic job consequences.

Quid pro quo harassment is unwelcome sexual conduct that causes or threatens to cause a tangible job detriment (for example, where an employer extracts or attempts to extract sexual favors either in exchange for favorable job action or under the threat of taking adverse job action).

Glossary

Hostile environment: one of two types of sexual harassment claims; requires showing of frequent, nontrivial acts of a sexual nature that create the effect of a hostile, offensive, or intimidating working environment.

Prima facie: legally sufficient to establish a fact or a case unless disproved.

Quid pro quo: unwelcome activity of a sexual nature in exchange for tangible job benefits or the loss of tangible job benefits because of the rejection of such activity.

Reasonable person/woman: a mythical judicial construct of an individual who thinks and responds the way an ordinary person would under such circumstances.

Sex discrimination: the favoring of one individual or group over another on the basis of gender or stereotypical assumptions associated with gender.

Sexual harassment: a cause of action grounded in sex discrimination; the imposition of unwelcome sexual conduct on an employee in the workplace.

Strict liability: the automatic imposition of liability, regardless of extenuating circumstances or intent.

Unwelcome conduct: behavior that is considered offensive to and undesirable by its recipient; behavior that is not encouraged or incited by its recipient.

Vicarious liability: indirect legal responsibility; for example, liability of an employer for the acts of an employee.

To establish a *prima facie* case of sexual harassment, a plaintiff must generally demonstrate the following circumstances:

- She or he is a member of the protected class.
- She or he was subjected to unwelcome sexual advances or requests for sexual favors.
- The harassment was based on sex.

- Submission to the unwelcome advances was an expressed or implied condition for receiving a job benefit or avoiding a job detriment.

Plaintiffs alleging **hostile environment** harassment do not need to establish deprivation of a job benefit (the fourth element described above). Instead, a claim is established by proof

Landmark Sexual Harassment Court Cases

Although Congress enacted Title VII of the Civil Rights Act of 1964, the federal and state courts have breathed life into the concept of sexual harassment. Through thousands of cases, the courts have placed their judicial gloss on the definition of sexual harassment. Here are some of the major cases that outline the courts' evolving definition of the concept.

- *Griggs v. Duke Power* (1971) was one of the first major rulings in the sexual harassment area, establishing that women have a right to compete for all jobs. *Griggs* mandated equal employment opportunity for both men and women.
- *General Electric Company v. Gilbert* (1976) established the illegality of sexual harassment. The court defined sexual harassment as submission to conduct [unwelcome sexual behavior] that is made explicitly or implicitly a term or condition of an individual's employment, a basis for employment decisions affecting the individual, or conduct that unreasonably interferes with an individual's work performance by creating an intimidating, hostile, or offensive environment.
- *Barns v. Costle* (1977) ruled that sexual harassment becomes unlawful only when it is unwelcome, thus clarifying when sexual harassment is illegal.
- *Henson v. City of Dundee* (1982) held that, for harassment to violate Title VII, it must be "sufficiently severe or pervasive" to create an abusive environment and alter the conditions of the victim's employment. *Henson* established that creating a hostile environment by sexual harassment violates Title VII of the Civil Rights Act.
- *Zabowicz v. West Bend Company* (1984) established the "reasonable person" standard. The standard states that the objective standpoint of a "reasonable person" determines whether challenged conduct is of a sexual nature. On the other hand, Title VII does not serve as a vehicle for "vindicating the petty slights suffered by the hypersensitive."
- *Meritor Savings Bank v. Vinson* (1986) determined that employers are liable for the creation of a hostile environment. The court also ruled that voluntary (not forced) submission to sexual activities does not necessarily indicate "welcomeness."
- *Yates v. Avco Corporation* (1987) also expanded the court's position on the liability of the organization. Yates stated that an employer is liable when it has "known, or upon reasonably diligent inquiry should have known," of the alleged harassment.
- *Fields v. Horizon* (1987) defined the "scope of employment." The court found that a supervisor's actions are generally viewed as being within the scope of his or her employment if the actions represent the exercise of authority actually vested in him or her.
- *Kyriazi v. Western Electric* (1981) established the precedent that individual employees or co-workers may be personally liable for acts of sexual harassment.
- *Swentek v. USAir, Inc.* (1987) expanded the definition of "unwelcomeness." The court found that any past conduct of the charging party that is offered to show "unwelcomeness" must relate to the alleged perpetrator of the harassment.

- *King v. Board of Regents of Univ. of Wis.* (7th Cir. 1990) instructed that "although a single act (of harassment) can be enough, … generally, repeated incidents create a stronger claim of hostile work environment with the strength of the claim depending on the number of incidents and the intensity of each incident."
- *Robinson v. Jacksonville Shipyards* (1991) added the "reasonable woman" clause to the "reasonable person" standard. The new standard was necessary because the courts found that women and men often have differing opinions about what sexual harassment is. An action may be considered sexual harassment if a reasonable woman considers it to be sexual harassment.
- *Faragher v. City of Boca Raton* (1998) and *Burlington Industries, Inc. v. Ellerth* (1998) changed the court's focus of inquiry concerning employer vicarious liability for actions of its supervisors and employees. The court's traditional analysis classifies complaints of sexual harassment as being either quid pro quo harassment or hostile environment harassment. In *Faragher* and *Ellerth,* however, the Supreme Court held that where a supervisor's sexual harassment of an employee results in a "tangible employment action," the employer is strictly liable for the harassment regardless of whether the employer knew or should have known about the harassment and regardless of whether the employer took remedial steps to end the harassment after learning of it. Going one step further, the Court said that even when a supervisor's sexual harassment does not result in a "tangible employment action," an employer may still be vicariously liable for the hostile environment created by its supervisor. The Court did allow for an employer defense. To avoid liability in the second class of cases, an employer must show by a preponderance of the evidence that (1) the employer exercised reasonable care to prevent and correct promptly any sexually harassing behavior, and (2) the employee "unreasonably failed to take advantage of any preventive or corrective opportunities provided by the employer to avoid harm."
- *Oncale v. Sundowner Offshore Services, Inc.* (1998) teaches that Title VII covers same-sex sexual harassment. Three federal district courts (in Maine, Minnesota, and New York), however, have been careful to note since then that discrimination based on sexual orientation is not discrimination "based on sex" under Title VII of the Civil Rights Act. Thus, at least in those districts, *Oncale* cannot be read to open the door to claims based on mistreatment of homosexuals in the workplace.
- In *Davis v. Monroe County Board of Education* (1999), the Court held in a 5–4 decision that students harassed by fellow students may sue schools for money damages under Title IX of the 1972 Education Amendments.

Adapted from Info-line No. 9202,
February 1992.

of unwelcome sexual conduct of such a severe or pervasive nature that it alters the victim's conditions of employment through the creation of an abusive work environment or hostile workplace. Although a single incident can be enough, it will generally be considered "trivial" and therefore not actionable. A key legal issue in establishing a prima facie case of sexual harassment under Title VII is whether the perpetrator's actions were unwelcome.

The Supreme Court made clear in *Meritor Savings Bank v. Vinson* that voluntary compliance

Handling Harassment

While it is not legally necessary to take any of the following actions, they may be valuable when dealing with harassment.

- Tell the person you do not like what he or she is doing and ask them to stop. Be specific and be firm.
- Document what is happening in the workplace. Get as much information as you can: who, what, where, when, witnesses, others who were harassed, if you asked the person to stop, what they said or did, and so forth. Always keep copies of your performance appraisals.
- Get support from a friend.
- Let your organization handle the problem through proper channels. Tell someone the harassment is happening—your supervisor or any other supervisor or manager in your organization, or go directly to the Human Resources Department.
- If you need to go outside the organization, other channels include the EEOC or your state agency.

Sexual Harassment Charge Process

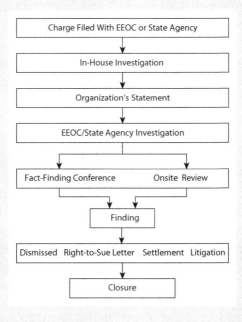

with a sexual overture does not prove that the overture itself was welcomed. The court recognized that a solicitation might be unwelcome even when an employee voluntarily participates in a sexual act, where the threat of adverse employment consequences exists. The correct inquiry, the court explained, "is whether (the plaintiff) by her conduct indicated that the alleged *sexual advances* were unwelcome, not whether her *actual participation* was voluntary." The unwelcome nature of a sexual advance is demonstrated by evidence "that the employee did not solicit or incite it, and the employee regarded the conduct as undesirable or offensive."

Recent Developments

When a plaintiff successfully establishes a prima facie case of sexual harassment, the case is treated as a sex discrimination case under Title VII, and the burden of proof shifts to the defendant.

Employers are held strictly liable for conduct of supervisory personnel that constitutes quid pro quo harassment. An employer's liability for hostile environment harassment depends on the answer to two questions:

1. Can the actions of the harassing supervisor(s) or co-worker(s) be imputed to the employer?
2. Did the employer take prompt and effective remedial action once it received notice of the harassment?

Two important Supreme Court decisions have clarified and redefined the way in which courts will treat vicarious liability of employers for employee claims of sexual harassment in the workplace (see *Faragher v. City of Boca Raton,* and *Burlington Industries, Inc. v. Ellerth,* in *Landmark Sexual Harassment Court Cases* at left).

Implications for Trainers

The *Faragher* and *Ellerth* cases imply that, to avoid liability, employers must not only implement sexual harassment policies but they must also inquire into the harassing behavior of their employees and provide a reasonable mechanism by which employees can report claims of workplace sexual harassment. This enables the employer to take action to prevent and correct promptly any sexually harassing behavior.

Courts will no longer mechanically focus on the existence of a formal sexual harassment policy, and such policies will no longer be an absolute defense to a hostile work environment claim. Indeed, the courts are now rejecting the traditional distinction of quid pro quo and hostile environment claims in favor of an inquiry into whether the alleged perpetrator of the harassment is in a supervisory or non-supervisory position.

These changes in the law imply that employers should reexamine their policies on sexual harassment, actively implement the policies, carefully train supervisory employees (because the employer's vicarious liability for actions of supervisory employees is nearly absolute), and provide a workable mechanism by which employees can report claims of workplace sexual harassment.

Employee Rights and Responsibilities

Employees have a right to work in an environment that is free from sexual harassment and sexual discrimination. So it follows that employees also have a responsibility to conduct their behavior so that they do not sexually harass or intimidate other employees, supervisors, managers, customers, or vendors—or contribute to a hostile, offensive, or intimidating work environment. All employees should understand the following things:

- the organization's policy concerning sexual harassment

- what behavior constitutes sexual harassment
- the procedures to follow if they feel that they have been sexually harassed
- the procedures to follow if they wish to file a complaint of sexual harassment with

the state or federal administrative agency (EEOC)

Supervisor Rights and Responsibilities

In addition to the rights and responsibilities they have as employees, supervisors need to

Conducting a Workplace Investigation

When an employee complains that he or she has been the victim of discrimination or harassment, it is imperative that the employer take prompt, effective remedial action. Many organizations outsource workplace investigations to ensure an impartial and unbiased investigation.

A critical part of any investigation is for the employer to generate and maintain solid documentation of the investigation, the employer's conclusions, and the employer's actions taken in response. Before creating any notes, it is important that investigators carefully consider that they are creating a record that may later be reviewed by an administrative agency (like the EEOC), a plaintiff, a plaintiff's attorney, judge, or a jury. Accordingly, a few simple guidelines must be followed:

- Place on paper only the facts received. Avoid editorial comments at all costs.
- Review all notes promptly after creation to check for factual errors, spelling, and grammar.
- Once created, never destroy documents except for working drafts.

Investigation Steps

To conduct an orderly investigation, follow these steps:

1. Begin by recording the facts that you already have.
2. Write down which facts you need to discover.
3. Review the organization's policy on sexual harassment and procedures for handling complaints.
4. Consult with inside or outside counsel to review and update yourself on developments in the law.
5. Engage the services of an independent, "objective" investigator.
6. Outline a plan of who will investigate; what steps will be taken; where you need to go to gather information; when the steps will be completed; and how you will proceed.
7. Ensure that senior management will support the investigation, its objectivity, and its confidentiality and that they are committed to following through on the disciplinary process.

Conducting Interviews

Interviewing techniques are critical to the success of any investigation. Follow these guidelines:

1. Always prepare a list of questions in advance of the interview.
2. Begin by explaining the purpose of the interview to the interviewee.
3. Use the "funnel" technique of questioning. Begin with open-ended and broad-based questions. First ask what the person knows. Then move to specific questions that focus on information you have already obtained.
4. Keep questions simple and direct.
5. Employ "active listening." Paraphrase answers. Reflect information back onto the speaker. Use silence to create subtle pressure to talk.
6. Always ask whether the person has anything to add to what they have already said.
7. Before concluding, review initial questions and notes. Summarize the witnesses' testimony and obtain the witnesses' declaration that the information they have given is true, complete, and accurate.

Writing a Sexual Harassment Policy

It is important for employers to communicate a clear policy on sexual harassment. This policy should include these elements:

- The organization's **values statement** (if one exists) affirming that employees are entitled to a workplace that is free from sexual harassment.
- A citation to currently applicable **federal and state laws** and regulations governing sexual harassment.
- A **working definition** of sexual harassment.
- Specific **complaint procedures,** including alternative channels through which employees can complain.
- Assurances of **confidentiality** throughout the complaint process.
- An **investigative process** that is prompt, impartial, and confidential.
- An **adjudication process,** including who will hear the complaint and how the hearing will proceed following the investigation.
- An **appeal process** for parties who feel aggrieved by the results of the adjudication process.
- A **disciplinary process** that clearly delineates the disciplinary measures that will be administered if there is a sufficient finding of sexual harassment. These measures should allow sufficient flexibility to address proceedings on a case-by-case basis.

- **Procedural rules,** including a timetable for progress through the process. It is important to complete this process thoroughly, but promptly, to preserve employee's legal rights and remedies.
- Clear, consistent **documentation procedures** for the following: the complaint, investigative, adjudication, appeal, and disciplinary processes; record retention; personnel file documentation or expungement; internal management communications; and communications with counsel.

understand that their behavior can result in personal liability and in liability for the organization. All supervisors should:

- thoroughly understand what behavior constitutes quid pro quo sexual harassment
- be sensitive to their own behavior and the behavior of the employees around them
- thoroughly understand what conditions might lead to a charge of hostile environment sexual harassment
- take affirmative steps to ensure that all employees understand the organization's policy on sexual harassment

Before harassment happens, supervisors should address their own behavior and awareness level. They should be role models, for their employees will look to their behavior for guidance. Moreover, they should know what is going on in their environment. There are no secrets in the workplace. Indicators that something is not right with a work group include the following:

- absenteeism
- fighting
- people not talking
- increased number of accidents
- poor morale
- low productivity
- increased number of mistakes

If harassment happens, supervisors should take action immediately. They should listen carefully, asking questions that will help put all the information together, but avoid criticism or judgments. Supervisors should inform the appropriate individuals and then conduct an investigation in accordance with the proper investigative and documentation procedures set up by the organization.

Organization Responsibility

A checklist of an organization's responsibility should include the following items:
- Adopt a no-harassment, zero-tolerance stance.
- Issue a policy and post it in many places in the organization.
- Distribute the policy to all employees.
- Train the entire workforce about the laws on sexual harassment as well as the policy.
- Be sure all new hires are trained.
- Provide managers and supervisors with additional training in communication skills, listening skills, negotiation skills, dealing with conflict, and the performance management systems. This ensures they are equipped with the tools they need to handle situations as they arise.
- Reinforce the information whenever possible. This could be done during organization meetings, during supervisory meetings, or as updates in memos.

- Reward appropriate behaviors.
- Practice what is taught. Be sure all management and supervisory personnel live the policy through their actions and words. A proactive supervisor or manager can put an end to inappropriate behavior and set the tone for the organization.
- Take action immediately should any complaints of sexual harassment arise.

Trainer Role and Responsibility

News coverage of sexual harassment and inappropriate behavior abounds. This coverage presents landmark decisions regarding what is appropriate and not appropriate in the workplace. It also tells of the huge awards victims receive due to certain workplace behavior that is prohibited by law.

What inappropriate behaviors occur in organizations that we know about, yet choose to ignore? How much goes on that we are unaware of? To restrict such inappropriate behavior, trainers must be the eyes and ears of the organization. They should work in tandem with management and human resources to help make the workforce aware of laws, policies, and the prevention of sexual harassment.

Many things that we do are subject to guidelines. Fishing rules and regulations, hunting rules, and guidelines for using equipment all exist so we know what we can do in that environment and what we should and should not do. Sometimes these rules are self-explanatory, and sometimes we need help in understanding them.

The guidelines for preventing sexual harassment in the workplace are no different. They tell us what we can and cannot do to maintain a harassment-free environment. Some rules are easy to understand, and some are a bit confusing. Yet, some organizations do nothing more than place a policy in the employee handbook—and hope the law will be followed.

Trainers help translate that law into appropriate behaviors in the workplace. They are integral to this process because their role requires them to do the following things:

- know what the laws are
- assist in the change process
- inform all employees (through a well-designed training process)

Content Trainers Need to Know

When teaching about sexual harassment, trainers need to be very familiar with all laws and policies that pertain to sexual harassment in the workplace. For example, there are federal laws, state laws, and organizational policies. State laws vary, and some states hold supervisors and managers personally liable for "aiding and abetting in an act of discrimination." In essence, if they themselves harass someone, or if they knew or had reason to know of such behavior in the workplace, they can be held personally liable.

Remember that every new court case shapes the law. It is imperative that trainers partner with the human resources department or have a legal contact to keep abreast of how laws are changing. Trainers also must be thoroughly aware of the organization's policy prohibiting sexual harassment. Some of these policies are more inclusive than federal and state law, incorporating legal rulings prohibiting age and disability discrimination (ADEA—Age Discrimination in Employment Act, and ADA—Americans with Disabilities Act).

Facilitating the Change

The face of the workplace has changed, laws have changed, and our workplace and employees must adapt if they are to survive and thrive. We all have a right to work in an environment that is free from unlawful harassment. To that end, the government has stepped in and given organizations guidelines for appropriate workplace behavior. Just as there is a code of conduct where we shop, where we socialize after work, and in our own homes, so is there a code of conduct in the workplace. Federal and state laws as well as organizational policies describe that code of conduct.

In some cases, we are asking our workforce to change the way they conduct themselves at work. Long-held patterns of behavior are no

Frequently Asked Questions

Training participants often ask similar questions to clarify acceptable behavior. Here are some of them—as well as the answers.

Where is the line? There is no line to cross that will make your behavior suddenly harassing. Harassment is something we do not like. What is harassment for one person may not be harassment for another.

Why can't people just leave if they don't like my jokes? People have jobs that require them to work at specific places. Leaving would adversely affect their job performance. They have a right to a job environment free from unlawful harassment.

Why are supervisors and managers liable for sexual harassment charges? According to some state statutes and some state common law, supervisors act as agents for the organization and can be liable for their own harassing behavior and for behavior they are aware of and choose to ignore.

What is my responsibility if I see one of my employees or another supervisor acting inappropriately? You must take action immediately. Remember your job as a supervisor is to maintain a harassment-free environment.

As an employee, if I see inappropriate behavior occurring, what is my responsibility? Legally you are not responsible for reporting such activity. But we all should help prevent harassment in the workplace. Tell your supervisor or any member of management immediately.

Can men be sexually harassed? Yes. While 91 percent of reported cases are filed by women, men can also be victims of sexual harassment. Men do not report incidents of sexual harassment for fear of ridicule or fear that some co-workers will make it more difficult on them if they tell.

We have 20 employees; are we covered by the law? Yes, you are covered under federal law. Organizations with fewer than 15 employees may be covered under another law applicable to their specific state, industry, or occupation. If you are unsure, consult legal counsel.

Must I tell the harasser I am offended by his or her behavior? It is not a legal requirement that you tell the harasser you are offended by the behavior for the behavior to be considered sexual harassment.

longer acceptable. Greater numbers of women and employees of diverse ethnicity have entered the workforce. Each of us has our own sensitivities, and we must respect one another's differences. Training teaches people what behavior is inappropriate, what behavior could be viewed as harassment, and which situations constitute sexual harassment.

Because change is uncomfortable for some people, they will be more amenable if they know why they are changing and what benefits they will achieve. Training must facilitate that change process in a nonthreatening way. Be firm about your stance on the laws and about what is appropriate and inappropriate in the workplace. Nevertheless, be cognizant of how the participants perceive and accept this information, understanding that there might be resistance at first. Overcome resistance by listening to participants' concerns and modeling behaviors that you expect of them. Assure participants that adhering to laws and organization policy will help the workplace become one that is healthy and harassment free.

Uncertainty about personal behavior is disconcerting to some. All training sessions include such questions as: "Where is the line?" or "How much can I do before I'm harassing someone?" That clear-cut line, in some instances, does not exist. Certainly, standards for appropriate and inappropriate behavior are clear. The line that tells a person when harassment starts is not as clear, however. What is harassment for one person, may not be harassment for another. Tell participants to stop and think before they engage in a questionable behavior, asking themselves, "What would my significant other (spouse, children, parents) think if they saw me behaving in this way?" To assist you in your training, see the sidebar opposite for a list of frequently asked questions and their answers.

Designing and Delivering the Training

Ideally, a male-female team should deliver the training. This helps break down any communication barriers between men and women in the audience. Of course this is not always possible. Therefore, it is important that you be sensitive and impartial. In many cases, training participants think sexual harassment is a male-versus-female issue. It is not. It is an individual issue, and it is about treating one another with respect.

Set up the training room to encourage participation and discussion. Be sure that you can interact with participants, and that participants can interact with one another. This training session might be the first opportunity members of the opposite sex have to talk honestly to one another.

In designing and conducting the training, break the content into digestible "chunks." Be sure to continually check for understanding after each chunk of information. For example, ask questions about the material, develop scenarios or case studies, or design short quizzes.

Introduction

Begin the training by giving an overview about harassment in the workplace—how prevalent it is, how it affects organizations, and how it can affect their lives or the lives of individuals they care about. Next, give participants an overview of what you will accomplish during the training session as well as the sequence of events. Review session goals and objectives for a clear understanding of what will be accomplished during the training.

If time permits, begin the training with an icebreaker—one that can be done in pairs. A good example is: "I'd like you and your partner to think of one question or piece of information you would like to know about sexual harassment. You can present this verbally or write it on an index card." At the conclusion of the icebreaker, ask each pair to share their response to your request. Post the answers where everyone can see them, and be sure to answer each concern by the end of the class. This activity gives you a gauge of their thoughts and concerns on the subject matter.

Give participants a pretest to open dialogue in the subject matter (see the job aid at the end of this issue). Encourage them to challenge anything they might find confusing or to seek clarification in areas where they need information. The pretest is designed to provide an overview of the material to be covered in the session, and the test results will give the trainer a flavor for the general knowledge of participants as well as their attitudes.

Core Content

The next part of the training focuses on a historical perspective of the law, both federal and state. Explain how it began, and take it to the point where it is today. During this time, explain the provisions of the law. For example, go over in detail both quid pro quo and hostile environment harassment and give detailed examples of both types. After explaining the law, read the organization's policy to explain and clarify its content—and to ensure that everyone has heard (not just read) it.

Examples provide a vivid picture of acceptable and unacceptable behavior. As you read or hear stories of actual occurrences in the workplace, make note of the general issues surrounding the examples and use them for future training. Nothing hits home harder than situations people can relate to.

Scenarios provide a check for understanding and give participants opportunities to apply analytical skills. They provide situations in which participants must decide if the described behavior is or is not sexual harassment. In addition, they must identify the rationale for their decision. A video

may be included at this point to help reinforce learning through a different medium. The following is a sample scenario:

Dru was the only woman in the crew. All of the men on the crew really did not want her there because she was awarded the job over one of their friends. Besides, the work they did they thought was a "man's" job. Dru did the job quite well— sometimes even better than her male counterparts. While there were no sexual jokes or pressuring for dates, the men would flatten the tires on her truck, put sugar in the gas tank, change the locks on the locker, or put petroleum jelly on the steering wheel. She did not like what was happening and complained to the supervisor. His response was, "They are just initiating you into the crew; you got to take it like one of the guys."

Was the supervisor right in what he said? What is your rationale?

Is this a case of harassment?

The next segment of the training session reviews the rights and responsibilities of employees and supervisors and the consequences organizations face when harassment occurs. A segment follows detailing steps to take if an employee is sexually harassed. When conducting supervisory training, be sure to detail specific supervisor responsibilities and liabilities. Supervisors and managers should then be given a chance to practice skills associated with handling claims of sexual harassment. Practicing in this nonthreatening environment allows participants to make and correct mistakes during the training session—not when they return to the work environment.

Summary

The session ends with an examination of case studies specific to the organization. Make the examples real to the participants by incorporating organizational terminology and situations that are potentially possible. During the debriefing of the scenarios, allow participants to explore "what if" situations. Although they will look to the trainer for the "correct" answers, encourage participants to explore options themselves and discover the appropriate determination.

In conclusion, explore what an organization free from unlawful harassment and discrimination looks like. How do people communicate? How do they interact? Allow participants to envision such a future for their own organization.

Putting It All Together

No two situations are alike. No two people are alike. What is right in one case does not apply to another. What trainers give participants is a guidebook or the rules of the road. In driving we know it is illegal to speed, yet how many of us go over the speed limit, watching at every turn for the flashing red lights. Some of us get caught; some of us do not. The same is true with the laws surrounding sexual harassment. Trainees will know the laws and the policy of the organization. They will know what is right and what is inappropriate. If they choose to break the laws, they know the consequence of their action.

Sample Curriculum

Session Objectives

At the conclusion of this workshop, participants will be able to do the following things:

- thoroughly understand and apply the organization's nonharassment policy
- discuss and apply federal laws, specifically Title VII, to workplace situations
- understand the applicable state laws
- define sexual harassment
- define discrimination
- identify sexual harassment in the workplace
- distinguish what is, what is not, and what could be sexual harassment
- understand implications of noncompliance
- describe supervisors' responsibilities in preventing sexual harassment
- deal effectively with and use proper procedures and organizational channels for complaints of sexual harassment
- identify appropriate and inappropriate behaviors in the workplace

Session Outline

I. Introduction
   A. Brief icebreaker and introductions.
   B. Reality check—what do we really know? Pretraining quiz (small group and discussion).
   C. Session objectives, outline, and logistics.
   D. The organization's policy.
II. Definitions and Provisions
   A. Definitions and terminology.
   B. Title VII.
   C. State law.
   D. Definition of sexual harassment as related to the law.
      • Quid pro quo.
      • Hostile environment.
      • What type of harassment it is (group exercise).
   E. Appropriate and inappropriate behavior.
   F. Scenarios (a small group activity to check for understanding).
VIDEO
BREAK
III. Roles and Responsibilities
   A. Employee responsibilities.
   B. Supervisor responsibilities.
   C. Procedures.
   D. Organizational responsibilities in maintaining a harassment-free environment.
   E. Case studies (to check for understanding of sexual harassment and of the methods for handling complaints).
   F. Debrief case studies "question-and-answer" session.
   G. Evaluation.

©Annette M. Cremo.

References & Resources

Articles

Baridon, Andrea P., and David R. Eyler. "Workplace Etiquette for Men and Women." *Training,* December 1994, pp. 31–37.

Barrier, Michael. "Sexual Harassment." *Nation's Business,* December 1998, pp. 14–19.

Bloch, Gerald D. "Avoiding Liability for Sexual Harassment." *HRMagazine,* April 1995, pp. 91–97.

Carmell, William. "Another Look at Sexual Harassment: Implications of the 1998 Supreme Court Decisions." *Diversity Facto,* Spring 1999, pp. 34–38.

Clark, Kathryn F. "Hands–Off Training." *Human Resource Executive,* January 1999, pp. 77–78.

Cole, Joanne. "Sexual Harassment: New Rules, New Behavior." *HRFocus,* March 1999, p. 1.

Crawford, Susan. "A Brief History of Sexual Harassment Law." *Training,* August 1994, pp. 46–49.

Fisher, Anne B. "After All This Time, Why Don't People Know What Sexual Harassment Means?" *Fortune,* January 12, 1998, p. 156.

Gallagher, Maureen M. "EEOC Speaks Plainly About Sexual Harassment." *HRFocus,* May 1994, p. 19.

Ganzel, Rebecca. "What Sexual Harassment Training Really Prevents." *Training,* October 1998, pp. 86–94.

Garland, Susan. "Finally, a Corporate Tip Sheet on Sexual Harassment." *Business Week,* July 13, 1998, p. 39.

Garvin, Stacey J. "Employer Liability for Sexual Harassment." *HRMagazine,* June 1991, p. 6.

Harris, Gloria G., and David A. Tansey. "Relearning Relationships."

HRMagazine, September 1997, pp. 116–120.

Kirshenberg, Seth. "Sexual Harassment: What You Need to Know." *Training & Development,* September 1997, pp. 54–55.

Laabs, Jennifer. "What You're Liable for Now." *Workforce,* October 1998, pp. 34–42.

Mallery, Michael P. "The Answers to Your Questions About Sexual Harassment." *Workforce Tools,* (Supplement), November 1997, pp. 7–9.

Moore, Herff L., Rebecca W. Gatlin–Watts, and Joe Cangelosi. "Eight Steps to a Sexual–Harassment–Free Workplace." *Training & Development,* April 1998, pp. 12–13.

Parliman, Gregory. "The Evolving Case Law of Sexual Harassment." *Employee Relations Law Journal,* Winter 1995/1996, pp. 77–87.

Payson, Martin F. "Avoiding the High Costs of Sexual Harassment: Beyond Sexual Harassment." *Supervisory Management,* January 1994, p. 10.

Pope, Barbara Spyridon. "Handling Sexual Harassment." *Across the Board,* March 1996, p. 57.

Raphan, Melissa, and Max Heerman. "Eight Steps to Harassment–Proof Your Office." *HRFocus,* August 1997, pp. 11–12.

Reynolds, Sana. "Confronting Sexual Harassment." *US Banker,* July 1996, pp. 79–81.

Risser, Rita. "Sexual Harassment Training: Truth and Consequences." *Training & Development,* August 1999, pp. 21–23.

Solomon, Charlene Marmer. "Don't Forget the Emotional Stakes." *Workforce,* October 1998, pp. 52–58.

Books

Baridon, Andrea P., and David R. Eyler. *Sexual Harassment Awareness Training: 60 Practical Activities for Trainers.* New York: McGraw–Hill, 1996.

Cornish, Tony, ed. *Zero Tolerance: An Employer's Guide to Preventing Sexual Harassment and Healing the Workplace.* Rockville, MD: BNA Communications, 1997.

Fitzwater, Terry. *The Manager's Pocket Guide to Preventing Sexual Harassment.* Amherst, MA: HRD Press, 1998.

Orlov, Darlene, and Michael T. Roumell. *What Every Manager Needs to Know About Sexual Harassment.* New York: AMACOM, 1999.

Info–line

Talley, B.D., and M.L. Waller. "Sexual Harassment: What Trainers Need to Know." No. 9202 (out of print).

Other

9 to 5, The National Organization for Working Women. 1430 W. Peachtree St., Ste. 610, Atlanta, GA 30309. Tel.: 800.522.0925.

Pretraining Assessment

Administer this questionnaire to participants prior to sexual harassment awareness training. Have them read each of the statements below and mark the appropriate box. The answer code follows on the next page.

	True	False
1. According to recent Supreme Court decisions, once an organization issues a policy prohibiting sexual harassment, distributes the policy, and conducts training, it can no longer be held liable for sexual harassment in the workplace.	o	o
2. If a supervisor asks an employee for sexual favors in return for job benefits, it is all right as long as both parties agree.	o	o
3. In the workplace, it is all right to tell a person they look nice.	o	o
4. Supervisors have no power in preventing sexual harassment.	o	o
5. Some states have laws preventing harassment in the workplace.	o	o
6. Sexual harassment is a form of discrimination.	o	o
7. We must treat alleged harassers fairly in the workplace. Therefore, we must tell them we don't like their behavior and give them a chance to stop before filing a complaint.	o	o
8. Criminal charges can be filed along with charges of sexual harassment.	o	o
9. Today's dress and behavior norms are causes of sexual harassment.	o	o
10. Organizations should allow supervisors to always conduct sexual harassment investigations because their employees feel most comfortable talking with them.	o	o
11. It is difficult for individuals to come forward with a complaint because they feel it is embarrassing, they fear retaliation, or the organization just will not do anything about the complaint.	o	o
12. Once there is proof of harassment, organizations must take a firm stance and apply appropriate disciplinary action, which may include termination.	o	o
13. There are very few cases of men filing sexual harassment charges because few things are harassing to men.	o	o
14. According to federal law, there are four types of sexual harassment: hostile environment, criminal acts, quid pro quo, and inappropriate dress.	o	o
15. Some organizations are using external investigators to investigate claims of sexual harassment because of their expertise in that specific area.	o	o

Answer Code

1. False. Organizations are ultimately liable for what happens in the workplace.
2. False. This could be considered quid pro quo type of harassment.
3. True. We don't want to take the humanness out of the workplace. Simply telling a person they look nice is all right.
4. False. Supervisors can prevent harassment in the workplace. They can tell employees about the policy, reinforce it at meetings, post the policy where employees can see it, and most important, model appropriate behavior.
5. True.
6. True. According to Title VII of the Civil Rights Act as amended.
7. False. You can file a complaint without telling someone you do not like what they are doing. You are not legally required to tell them, and telling them does not guarantee they will stop.
8. True.
9. False. Just because someone dresses inappropriately does not give us cause to harass him or her. We are in control of what we say and what we do at all times.
10. False. Sometimes it is supervisor who is doing the harassing.
11. True.
12. True.
13. False. While it is true men have a higher tolerance for certain behaviors, they do not file charges because they fear what others might say, or because if they do tell someone, it is brushed off.
14. False. Only hostile environment and quid pro quo.
15. True.

WHAT EXECS DON'T GET ABOUT OFFICE ROMANCE

John A. Pearce II

Should Coworkers have sex with each other? Should employers try to stop them?

The answer to the first question is that the question isn't worth answering—because office romance is inevitable anyway. The answer to the second is more interesting. And due to recent shifts in the legal climate, for companies, it's also more scary.

There is a misunderstanding at the epicenter of the office romance debate, even as it attracts increasing scrutiny due to famous examples such as the recent episode involving CBS Corp.'s "Late Show With David Letterman" host. Contrary to some commonly misread signals, managers are not interested in stamping out employee dating. Cohesive relationships among employees, including some that become romantic, can help build esprit de corps within the work team and affinity for the company. However, sexual relationships and romances change office dynamics in potentially problematic ways, presenting legal challenges such as allegations about sexual harassment and a hostile work environment, and those challenges need to be managed skillfully.

Before addressing the challenges, though, we should recognize just how common and unstoppable office romance is. Surveys provide convincing evidence:

- In a survey by CareerBuilder.com in 2009, 40% of respondents revealed that they have dated a coworker, with 18% indicating two or more such relationships.[1] An additional 12% are on the sidelines but eager to join the scrum.
- Office romances extend across the age spectrum. Employees between the ages of 35 and 44 are the most likely demographic to date a coworker, with 44% acknowledging that they had done so.[2] In the age group of 55 and older, 34% of employees admitted to having an office relationship.

To be clear, an office romance is a relationship between two individuals employed by the same company that advances beyond the socially acceptable employer-employee association and the work-related duties that require their interaction. The relationship can be of a sexual nature where employees engage in sexual activities in and outside work, or where one employee makes sexually suggestive remarks about the other. These relationships often involve a common grouping of situations, such as where the supervisor and subordinate engage in exclusive and frequent lunches, dinners and drinks together, or where the subordinate is extended invitations to private social events such as parties, birthdays or trips. Perhaps surprisingly, office romances can create problems for the company whether or not the couple's interpersonal relationship runs smoothly.

As an indication of the importance of office romances, the CareerBuilder.com survey found that three in 10 respondents say they married a person they dated at work. By permitting office romances, companies provide what many employees see as a prime benefit of employment with the company—an opportunity to enrich their social lives.

It's no wonder the frequency of office romances is high. In a Spherion Corp. survey, employees acknowledged the possibility that an office romance might jeopardize their job security or advancement opportunities, yet 42% of them said an open office romance is worth the risk compared with 35% who prefer to keep an office romance private in the office.[3]

Private or not, office romance will be with us as long as offices are.

About the Research

This research builds on my previous work to improve corporate strategy formulation by integrating legal insights into the processes of environmental and competitive analyses and strategic choice. Because there are legal implications of every strategic move, executives rely on in-house counsel or legal consultants to ensure that their plans comply with the law and judicial interpretations. However, using attorneys as post-decision advisers can preclude executives' consideration of options that derive from the rule of law. Laws both constrain action and help to delineate options that can produce optimal outcomes for the company. Thus, legal input can improve executive decision making on important topics such as how to deal with the issues that arise from office romance.

In the course of this research, I performed quantitative and case-based research. To ground the research in the experience of many managers and their employees, I reviewed a number of large database surveys, conducted by CareerBuilder.com, Chubb, *Glamour* magazine, Lawyers.com, Society for Human Resource Management, Spherion, Steelcase and Vault.com. These findings are complemented by published survey results from the U.S. Department of Labor.

I then reviewed U.S. federal and state legislation, including Title VII of the Civil Rights Act of 1964 and publications of the Equal Employment Opportunity Commission. Next, I investigated dozens of U.S. court case renderings on sexual harassment and hostile working environments.

Finally, I conducted a comprehensive review of corporate best practices pertaining to the development of a business policy designed to prevent inappropriate workplace behavior associated with the negative repercussions of office romance. I synthesized the key lessons of success and generalized them into a set of findings that can be used by executives to better design and implement a policy that optimizes a company's chances of avoiding legal entanglements while allowing its employees to enjoy social interaction.

The New Management Challenges of Office Romance

Difficulties stemming from office romances can arise for the company in three main ways.

The first one isn't new: Some employees object to being pursued romantically on the job, at some times and by some people. A survey by Vault.com reveals that 38% of employees report that they have received unwanted sexual advances from their coworkers.[4] A joint survey by *Glamour* magazine and Lawyers.com found that 47% of employees regard being asked on a date by their supervisor as uncomfortable attention, and 36% stated that being complimented on their body or physique by their supervisor of the opposite sex is inappropriate.[5]

And it's not just the boss-and-direct-subordinate pairing that causes problems. The CareerBuilder .com survey found that 22% of employees admitted dating a married coworker, and 27% said they had dated someone with a higher position in the organization than their own.

The second difficulty in office romance gets less attention: While office romances are stimulating, exciting and energizing for the couple involved, their noninvolved coworkers see these dalliances as destructive for everyone else. A 2008 workplace survey by Steelcase Inc. found that 85% of respondents believe that office romance is a workplace distraction.[6]

Of course, some romances are sweet and foster good feelings and well wishes. Some resemble live soap operas imbued with the likelihood of drama. However, everyone knows the key governing fact: Most office romances end, some with lingering awkwardness and animus.

When one member of the couple wishes that the romance could continue and the other does not, the "dangerous liaison" syndrome is likely to disrupt the workplace. Patterns of distrust emerge.

Sides are taken. Reputations are damaged. The possibilities of retaliation and retribution lurk in every assignment and evaluation. In fact, the survey published by Lawyers.com found that the fear of reprisal after a romance ends affects 67% of employees.

The third cause for managerial concern is the freshest, and is increasingly posing legal trouble for businesses. Difficulties for the company arise because many romances, certainly those involving a supervisor and a subordinate, can create resentment among other "third party" subordinates who second-guess the fairness of evaluations and rewards. If favoritism is detected or even suspected, motivation is undermined. The disruption in the workplace deteriorates toward a productivity death spiral—or, equally devastating, a hostile work environment lawsuit. According to U.S. Equal Employment Opportunity Commission regulations, an employer may be liable for a hostile work environment claim when there is unlawful sex discrimination against third-party employees who were qualified for but denied an employment opportunity or benefit, because it was given to an employee who was engaged in a romantic relationship with a supervisor.

Claims of sexual harassment and hostile work environment are traumatic for the individuals directly involved, their coworkers and for the company as a whole in terms of workplace disruption, threats to morale and company culture, and reputational damage. Performance losses result from absenteeism, low productivity and employee turnover.

Additionally, the legal ramifications are likely to bring unwanted attention on management prac tices and individuals' behavior and motivation. The legal proceedings that are likely to result are time-consuming, contentious and costly, regardless of the outcome. Although the vast majority of sexual harassment complaints are believed to be concluded through negotiated settlements that are acceptable to the victims, other charges are pursued by the plaintiff through litigation.

A Growing Problem

The evidence of the widespread nature of sexual harassment and hostile work environment problems in the workplace is compelling:

- The U. S. Department of Labor reports that 71% of working women cope with some form of sexual harassment during their careers.[7]
- A poll of the largest U.S. service and industrial companies finds that 66% of women vice presidents report that they personally have been sexually harassed.[8]
- According to a Chubb Corp. survey of the presidents of privately held companies, 22% report having employees file sexual harassment or hostile work environment complaints with the EEOC or a state agency.[9]
- The most recent available statistics show that in 2008, 13,867 cases alleging sexual harassment and hostile work environment were filed with the EEOC—the highest level in six years.[10]
- The direct monetary benefits paid by companies to settle sexual harassment and hostile work environment claims through the EEOC have averaged $47.8 million annually for the past 12 years. That doesn't sound like much, given the prevalence of the problem. Unfortunately, the bulk of financial costs don't show up in EEOC outcomes. The largest monetary payments—which are in addition to these amounts—are determined separately through litigation or through

arbitration that is commonly advocated by employers to reduce the corporate costs of litigation and to minimize public disclosures.

The recent high-profile revelations about David Letterman's office romances with subordinates in his production company highlight some of the dangers involved in an office romance. On October 1, 2009, Letterman mixed jokes and confessions during his nightly monologue in revealing on his TV program that he had had sexual relationships with multiple members of his 70-person staff.

Letterman's impetus for divulging his secret was that Robert J. Halderman had been arrested earlier in the day for trying to extort the late-night comedian. Halderman gave Letterman a package of materials about the affairs that "contained clear, explicit and actual threats that [were designed to] … destroy the reputation of Mr. Letterman and to submit him and his family to humiliation and ridicule." Unless Letter-man agreed to a payment of $2 million, Halderman threatened to make the information public. Letter-man informed authorities about the threats, and Halderman was arrested. Letterman admitted his actions to preempt the disclosures by the press.[11]

Questions surfaced immediately. Letterman appears to be an extortion target—but is he also guilty of victimizing his employees through criminal sexual harassment? Will any of his sexual partners decide to pursue legal action? Will they charge that they felt coerced into affairs with Letterman, even if the liaisons appeared to be consensual at the time?

Equally critical, there are questions concerning the impact that Letterman's behavior had on the workplace for all of his employees. Will other employees back their media interview claims with formal charges that their knowledge of Letterman's sexual relationships created a hostile work environment that was biased against them or in which it was difficult to work? Will coworkers bring formal charges that because of Letterman's office romances he showed favoritism toward his sexual partners, providing them with opportunities that nonromantically involved coworkers were unjustly denied?

The Special Dangers of a Hostile Work Environment

Media visibility, arbitrated decisions and courtroom judgments have alerted managers to the dangers of a "hostile work environment," which is the legal term that describes a pattern of offensive, hostile, abusive conduct or a favoritism atmosphere caused by management or coworkers.[12]

While sexual harassment complaints are most likely to center on two people, hostile work environment claims arise from the damage to the employment experiences of many more—486 employees in the case of Mitsubishi Corp., which agreed to pay $34 million to settle an EEOC suit on behalf of employees who were groped and subjected to lewd jokes while on the job.[13]

Managers and the legal system share a concern for hostile work environments that are sufficiently severe or pervasive that they interfere with employees' work performance. The situations of concern are serious. Sexual flirtation, innuendo or vulgar language that is trivial, or merely annoying, does not establish a hostile environment.

There is evidence that the emergence of a hostile work environment is directly related to a company's tolerance of office romances involving superiors and their subordinates. Although the law does not forbid a coworker's romantic involvement with a supervisor, managers need to

be concerned that the work environment will become fouled by a supervisor's actual or perceived sexual favoritism or preferential treatment of his or her paramour. Such behavior could lead other employees to believe that favorable treatment may be obtained from the supervisor in exchange for a romantic or sexual relationship. Unequal treatment of employees, combined with sexually explicit behaviors, creates an illegal hostile environment and raises legal and business problems.

Despite the jeopardy involved, the CareerBuilder.com survey found that among workers who have dated a coworker, a third admit that they have dated someone with a higher position in their company. Of those, 42% said that they have dated their boss.

An affair between the supervisor and subordinate, manifested by sexual horseplay in the office or preferential treatment of the subordinate that prevents coworkers from being evaluated on grounds other than their sexuality, makes an office romance likely to raise objections and provide circumstances that are legally actionable.

A hostile environment can come in uglier forms. An example is quid pro quo harassment in which a supervisor uses an employee's response to a sexually charged overture in the workplace as the basis for employment decisions affecting the employee, thereby attempting to force the subordinate to tolerate or participate in the sexual conduct.

Courts have determined the existence of a hostile work environment by evaluating such factors as the frequency of the offending conduct, its severity, whether it is physically threatening or humiliating or an utterance and whether it unreasonably interferes with an employee's work performance. The effect of the company's sexual culture on the employee's psychological well-being is also relevant in determining whether an employee found the environment abusive.

The courts and arbitrators consider whether the alleged harasser was a coworker or a supervisor, whether other employees joined in perpetrating the harassment and whether the harassment was directed at more than one individual. In this assessment, no single factor is required or determinative. Thus, the general work atmosphere for employees other than the plaintiff is relevant to determining if a hostile work environment exists.

What Managers Need to Know About Hostile Work Environment Law

The origin of hostile work environment law is found in Title VII of the Civil Rights Act of 1964, which makes it "an unlawful employment practice for an employer … to discriminate against any individual with respect to his compensation, terms, conditions, or privileges of employment, because of such individual's … sex." The Equal Employment Opportunity Commission regulations expand Title VII to protect against unwelcome sexual advances, requests for sexual favors and other verbal or physical conduct of a sexual nature when "such conduct has the purpose or effect of unreasonably interfering with an individual's work performance or creating an intimidating, hostile, or offensive working environment." (See "About the Research," p. 38.) Further, EEOC regulations provide that "where employment opportunities or benefits are granted because of an individual's submission to the employer's sexual advances or requests for sexual favors, the employer may be held liable for unlawful sex discrimination *against other persons* who were qualified for but denied that employment opportunity." (Emphasis mine.)

Within the framework of a hostile work environment, a third party, commonly a coworker of the subordinate involved in an office romance, sues the employer. Third parties may pursue litigation for hostile work environment by arguing that they were harmed by the favoritism of the supervisor toward the subordinate paramour.

When a supervisor or any organizational superior and a subordinate are engaged in a romantic relationship, coworkers may claim that the involved person-in-power favors that subordinate. The EEOC regulations define favoritism as a situation "where employment opportunities or benefits are granted because of an individual's submission to the employer's sexual advances or requests for sexual favors."

There are three categories of favoritism. The first involves isolated instances of favoritism toward a paramour. An isolated instance of preferential treatment based on consensual romantic relationships does not violate Title VII. Thus, for example, a female employee who is denied an employment benefit because it is awarded by her supervisor to her coworker who is his paramour would not have a viable Title VII claim based on this single, isolated instance of sexual favoritism. Such favoritism is not illegal, because an allegation claiming the existence of a hostile work environment should prove a pattern of repeated, routine or generalized level of harassing behavior by a supervisor, manager or employer.

The courts have judged a host of actions as being an insufficient basis for finding a company guilty of fostering a hostile work environment: a male supervisor looking down the low-cut blouse of a female employee, following her movements as she leaves the premises, blowing her kisses across the office, attending a private birthday lunch with her, having clandestine meetings in and out of the office with her, telling her during a company Christmas party that she is beautiful, giving her the largest year-end bonus and giving her a Christmas gift.[14] The principal shortcoming of these charges is that they were one-time events that did not prove a pattern of repeated, routine or generalized level of harassing behavior by the supervisor.

The second category of illegal favoritism that can result in a claim of hostile work environment is based on incidents of coerced sexual conduct. It occurs when an employee is coerced into submitting to unwelcome sexual advances in return for a job benefit. When this occurs, coworkers who were qualified for but denied the benefit could believe that sexual favors were generally a condition for receiving the benefit. Such an implied requirement would be evidence of favoritism in support of a legal claim that the coworkers, as well as the targeted employee, were victims of a hostile work environment.

In one case, for example, the court considered evidence of telephone calls made by a supervisor to proposition several female subordinates at their homes, descriptions of the supervisor's sexual encounters with subordinate female employees and the supervisor's engagements in suggestive behavior at work. The court found that the supervisor demonstrated a "total inability to separate his work life from 'personal' matters."[15]

This evidence, supplemented by confirmation of other harassing behaviors, led the court to side with the plaintiff, who was a coworker of a woman who was having an affair with their supervisor. The court found that when sexual favors play a role in determining individual rewards, including promotion and irrespective of qualifications, the supervisor is guilty of harassing the subordinate and creating a hostile environment for the subordinate and the subordinate's coworkers. The court ruled that the plaintiff's Title VII rights were violated because granting sexual favors was a condition for a promotion. The court also noted that even when an affair between supervisor and subordinate is consensual, the law has been broken if sexual favors play a role in the rewards process.

The third category of favoritism occurs when decisions based on sexual favors are widespread in a workplace. Offended employees can establish a hostile environment claim in violation of Title VII. The claim may be established regardless of whether any objectionable conduct is directed at them personally and regardless of whether those who were granted favorable treatment willingly provided the sexual favors.

An example of a hostile work environment caused by this form of favoritism involved a female employee who filed a claim against the Securities and Exchange Commission after five years of employment. The court concluded that evidence presented at trial established that "conduct of a sexual nature was so pervasive" at the department that it created "a hostile or offensive work environment," which affected employees who found the conduct offensive and repugnant.[16] The court found that the employee was forced to work in an environment in which managers harassed her and other female employees by "bestowing preferential treatment upon those who submitted to their sexual advances." This preferential treatment undermined the motivation and performance of the employees who did not submit to the sexual overtures and deprived them of promotions and other benefits.

Tactics to Prevent a Hostile Work Environment (and the Damages It Brings)

Managers can take proactive steps to protect their businesses from hostile environment claims and the associated consequences of lawsuits, large monetary jury awards, public embarrassment and damage to employee morale and productivity.

By developing a policy that declares the expectations of management, employers can help shield their company from legal liability by preventing or reducing unacceptable incidents of supervisor behavior that can create a hostile work environment. By enforcing the policy as necessary, employers can respond promptly and confidently to claims of sexual harassment or hostile work environment that stem from an office romance.

The elements of a policy to eliminate the downside consequences of office romance are similar to those needed to prevent sexual harassment in the workplace, since the problems have important commonalities. Both represent violations of Title VII of the Civil Rights Act and Equal Employment Opportunity Commission regulations. Both involve intense interpersonal dynamics. Both damage the involved employees' work performance or the productivity of their coworkers. Both can result in legal action by employees to hold the employer culpable unless executives of the company can prove that they took two steps:

- They took strong action to prevent office romance from degenerating into favoritism, sexual harassment or a hostile work environment, and
- If problems arose, the company activated a response plan to halt the suspected violation immediately, investigate the circumstances in a thorough and unbiased manner, penalize guilty perpetrators according to preestablished guidelines and take action to close the gap in the company's prevention plan.

Prevention is the best tool for minimizing the exposure of the company to lawsuits stemming from office romances and associated sexual harassment or hostile work environment claims. To prevent problems from occurring, an employer should educate employees on the company policy concerning office romance. That official notification can supplement the company's total and unqualified opposition to sexual harassment in the workplace, explaining its illegality, specifying appropriate sanctions for breaching of the policies and identifying the company's plan to sensitize all supervisory and nonsupervisory employees on the issues.

The cornerstone of an employer's efforts to prevent favoritism, sexual harassment and hostile work environments is a policy statement. That written and widely circulated document puts all employees on notice that the employer actively seeks to identify and eliminate all problems stemming from sexual dynamics. A carefully formulated and implemented policy to prevent favoritism, sexual harassment or a hostile work environment provides a useful defense against claims for liability and punitive damages if violations occur. Conversely, the absence of a policy makes it difficult for an employer to prove that it exercised reasonable care to prevent or correct the problem.

Yet, many companies do not have a formal written policy on office romance. A survey by the Society for Human Resource Management of 617 companies on workplace romance found that 72% of the respondents did not have a written policy, 13% had a policy and 14% said they had an unwritten, but well understood, norm in their workplace.[17] These figures may provide a clue as to why EEOC statistics on sexual harassment claims continue to increase.

To reduce the possibility of illegal employee behavior and associated company liability, employers should have a policy against favoritism, sexual harassment and hostile work environments. The policy should include an effective complaint procedure, a distribution plan, education for all employees and a system for timely investigations and corrective action. The policy statement should be clear, emphatic, easily understood, free of confusing legal terms and provide examples of conduct targeted for immediate dismissal.

A policy on office romance needs to specify prohibitions, enforcement and penalties. The main prohibition to be determined for managers pertains to dating between employees. A blanket prohibition against any employee dating any other employee is rare. Wal-Mart Stores Inc. has one, but they are difficult to enforce and unpopular among employees.

A policy that forbids dating between employees at different levels of the organization is more palatable among employees but often fails to address most troublesome relationships. However, a policy that explicitly forbids dating between a supervisor and a person under his or her direct chain of command directly addresses the most dangerous pairing of employees. Their power imbalance creates the opportunity for the supervisor to impose his or her will over the subordinate, to be vindictive or to show favoritism. A ban that proactively attempts to prevent these self-evident hazards is an intuitively appealing centerpiece of an office romance policy. Once set, a policy limiting office romance needs to be monitored vigilantly and the penalties consistently applied.

The importance of expressing concern for fairness is suggested by the findings of the survey by Lawyers .com, which reveals that 26% of workers claim that they have experienced sexual harassment at work. Only 52% of these workers had taken action, such as reporting the behavior, confronting the harasser or quitting their job. The respondents' most common reason for not acting was their sense that nothing would happen even if they complained (22%).

Incentive for Proactive Attention

When an employee complains to management about a negative consequence of an office romance—alleged favoritism, sexual harassment or a hostile work environment—the employer is obligated to investigate the allegation. If the claim has merit, an employer has established an affirmative defense by exercising reasonable care in advance of and in response to the claim. Different strategies exist to handle claims, and the employer has latitude in deciding how to respond. However, the courts look for evidence of the employer's zeal in investigating and resolving claims in judging the company's determination to address the current situation and to prevent any future violations.

The psychic, temporal and financial costs of romantically and sexually precipitated problems in the workplace can combine to cripple productivity and endanger employee relations. The dollar cost of defending against a claim of office favoritism, sexual harassment or hostile work environment can start at $250,000.[18] During resulting litigation, company records come into play. In addition, personal intrusions, including computer work files, e-mails and even personal e-mails from home accounts of all involved parties become relevant and discoverable. Unfortunately, data from the SHRM survey suggest that such events are likely, since an average of 4% of the employees involved in a failed office romance file a formal complaint.

Executives can construct safeguards by educating their employees about a policy of the company that is designed to prevent office romances from becoming a disruptive force. Then, if trouble strikes, executives can activate a formal response plan to deal quickly and fairly with any violation of the policy, to close the gap in the company's prevention plan and to restore a productive work environment that is respectful of all employees.

References

1. "Forty Percent of Workers Have Dated a Co-Worker, Finds Annual CareerBuilder.com Valentine's Day Survey," February 10, 2009, http://www.careerbuilder.com

2. R. Haefner, "Office Romances Rarely Kept Secret," February 13, 2008, www.cnn.com/2008/LIVING/worklife/02/13/office.romance/index.html

3. "Be My Valentine? Nearly 40 Percent of Workers Have Had a Workplace Romance, According to Latest Spherion Survey," January 29, 2007, http://www.spherion.com/press/releases/2007/workplace-romance.jsp

4. "Love Is Blooming by the Watercooler," Vault.com, April 1, 2009.

5. A. Kopit, "Research Reveals Rise in Interoffice Romance," 2004, http://research.lawyers.com/Research-Reveals-Rise-in-Interoffice-Romance.html

6. "Study Finds Office Culture, Not Corporate Policy, Deters Most Workers from Dating a Colleague," September 2, 2008, www.steelcase.com/na/office_culture_not_policy_de_News.aspx?f=36352

7. S.B. Kiser, T. Coley, M. Ford and E. Moore, "Coffee, Tea, or Me? Romance and Sexual Harassment in the Workplace," Southern Business Review 31 (spring 2006): 35–50.

8. M. Velasquez, "Sexual Harassment Today: An Update—Looking Back and Looking Forward,"2004, http://diversitydtg.com/articles/sex-harass-today.htm

9. "One in Four Private Companies Sued by Employees, Chubb Survey Finds," May 25, 2004, http://www.chubb.com/news/pr20040525.html

10. "Sexual Harassment Charges EEOC & FEPAs Combined: FY 1997–FY 2009," 2009, www.eeoc.gov/eeoc/statistics/enforcement/sexual_harassment.cfm

11. R. Adams and S. Schechner, "CBS Staffer Indicted in Letterman Plot," Wall Street Journal, October 3, 2009, sec. A, p.3; S. Adams, "How to Have a Successful Office Romance," August 23, 2009, http://www.forbes. com/2009/08/11/office-romance-affair-leadership-careers-sex.html; H. Kurtz, "Will Stupid Human Tricks Turn Off Letterman's Fans?" Washington Post, October 3, 2009, sec. C, p.1; and J. Schwartz, "The Letterman Situation: What Constitutes Harassment?" New York Times, October 2, 2009, http://mediadecoder.blogs.nytimes.com/2009/10/02/the-letterman-situation-what-constitutes-harassment/

12. Huston v. P&G Paper Products Corp., 2009 U.S. App. LEXIS 12437 (3rd Cir. Pennsylvania, June 8, 2009).

13. Equal Employment Opportunity Commission v. Mitsubishi Motor Manufacturing of America Inc., 990 F. Supp. 1059, 1073 (C.D. Illinois, 1998).

14. Proksel v. Gattis, 41 Cal. App. 4th 1626 (California App. 4th Dist., January 26, 1996).

15. Toscano v. Nimmo, 570 F. Supp. 1197, 1198 (D. Delaware, 1983).

16. Broderick v. Ruder, 685 F. Supp. 1269 (D.D.C., 1988).

17. S. Heathfield, "Tips About Dating, Sex and Romance at Work: What's Love Got to Do With Office Romance?" 2010, http://humanresources.about.com/cs/workrelationships/a/workromance_3.htm

18. A. Slavin, "Love, Labor, Losses: New Rulings Widen the Workplace Impact of Office Romance," Best's Review 110 (August 2009): 28–30, 32.

WHISTLE-BLOWERS: THREAT OR ASSET?

Dori Meinert

Cheryl Eckard repeatedly warned senior managers at GlaxoSmithKline that defective drugs were being produced at its Puerto Rico plant. Rather than address the problems, they fired her.

Eckard filed a whistle-blower suit. Last October, GlaxoSmithKline agreed to pay $750 million to settle criminal and civil complaints that the company knowingly sold contaminated drugs made at the now-closed plant. Eckard received $96 million.

The number of whistle-blower suits—and the related payouts—have been growing in recent years under federal and state laws aimed at uncovering fraud and protecting the public. Corporate lawyers fear another surge of whistle-blower complaints will result from passage of the Dodd-Frank Act. The law, which significantly increases rewards and protection to those blowing the whistle on securities violations, affects publicly held companies and their private subsidiaries and affiliates.

The U.S. Securities and Exchange Commission (SEC) is scheduled to release regulations implementing the law in April. Employers better get ready.

To reduce the risk of an expensive and embarrassing government investigation, company leaders must step up internal reporting procedures and management training to encourage employees to report their concerns to the company first, lawyers say. And HR managers must play a critical role in those processes.

The Tipsters

The share of workers who reported negative behavior rose to 63 percent in 2009, an increase from 58 percent in 2007, according to the Ethics Resource Center's *2009 National Business Ethics Survey* report. Women are more likely to report wrongdoing than men. Managers are more likely to report than line employees, and senior managers consistently report misconduct more than any other group, researchers found.

"There is a sense of urgency about ethics that didn't exist before," says Daniel F. Carey, director of human resources and employment counsel at O&G Industries Inc. in Torrington, Conn., and a member of the Society for Human Resource Management's (SHRM) Ethics Special Expertise Panel.

"The No. 1 defense that a company can muster against these new whistle-blower rules is positive employee relations," Carey says. "You need to have a relationship with your employees so they come to you, so they're not racing to the SEC to be the first ones to report this problem."

The Bounty

The GlaxoSmithKline case was prosecuted under the federal False Claims Act. The act has been the most successful avenue to date for whistle-blowers and government investigators who rely on them. The U.S. Justice Department collected $3 billion in civil settlements and judgments in cases involving fraud against the government last year—$2.3 billion with the help of whistle-blowers.

The so-called bounty system in False Claims Act cases was so useful that the SEC is now proposing to offer whistle-blowers up to 30 percent of any amount above $1 million that the government recovers. Corporate lawyers argue that the proposed regulations would entice disgruntled employees to circumvent internal reporting methods with the goal of getting hefty rewards.

"You're essentially creating a financial incentive for employees to breach their duty of loyalty to their employer by going to an agency before they go to the employer," argues Daniel P. Westman, a partner with Morrison & Foerster LLP in McLean, Va.

Steven J. Pearlman, a partner at Seyfarth Shaw LLP in Chicago, says he has been receiving calls from employers that want to know how to respond to the proposed regulations. Employers poured money and training into complying with the federal Sar-banes-Oxley Act, enacted in 2002 in response to the Enron scandal, Pearl-man says. Now, the SEC's proposed bounties pose a "risk of eviscerating, totally gutting, those compliance mechanisms," he says.

The Association of Corporate Counsel, in Washington, D.C., along with 270 in-house lawyers, urged the commission to require individuals to first report concerns through internal compliance systems.

However, whistle-blower advocates say that would allow corporate executives to sweep problems under the rug.

Stephen M. Kohn, executive director of the National Whistleblowers Center in Washington, D.C., says arguments raised by corporate officials imply that "a white-collar criminal has more rights than a blue-collar criminal. If you're a white-collar criminal and you're defrauding investors, why should you be told that you're going to be turned into the police? You've committed a crime. You should be reported."

When illegal behavior is condoned by senior managers, employees limited to internal reporting have no recourse, adds Kohn, whose organization supports whistle-blowers in court and before Congress.

Bounties offer safety nets for whistle-blowers who jeopardize their jobs and careers to provide government with information on lawbreakers.

For whistle-blowers with valid claims, bounties "reward them for the trouble and the risk," says Reuben A. Guttman, a director at the law firm of Grant & Eisenhofer and co-founder of Voices for Corporate Responsibility in Washington, D.C.

The Motives

In interviews with 26 whistle-blowers in the health care field, researchers found most were motivated by integrity, altruism or public safety, justice, and self-preservation, but integrity was cited most frequently, according to a 2010 study in the *New England Journal of Medicine*. The whistle-blowers frequently were exposed to questionable practices when they started new jobs or were promoted.

That was the case with John Schilling, hired in 1993 by Columbia Healthcare Corp., now HCA Inc., to oversee Medicare reimbursements for five hospitals. Within months, he discovered the company was claiming expenses not allowed by government. Senior managers ordered him to keep quiet and devised a plan to distract government auditors.

"I felt like it was stealing from the taxpayers, stealing from the Medicare beneficiaries we were supposed to be taking care of," Schilling recalls.

A lawyer told him he could be found personally liable if he didn't speak up. So Schilling worked undercover for federal investigators, recording phone calls and wearing wires to meetings. The government recovered more than $1.7 billion in 2003.

After Blowing the Whistle, Psychologist Faces Challenges

Janet Chandler, a Chicago psychologist, spent 12 years embroiled in lawsuits against her former employer, Cook County Hospital. In 1995, she reported to superiors her concerns about mismanagement of a $5 million federal research grant for a study of pregnant drug-dependent women. When she was fired several months later, she was shocked.

"I spent my career working with indigent minority women and children, those who didn't have a voice," Chandler says. "I was trained that if you have a concern, you bring it to higher-up officials. That's exactly what I did."

She developed stress-related health problems, including diabetes. Her husband left her. With no money coming in, her daughter had to drop out of college temporarily. Her sons, ages 7 and 12, watched as their car was repossessed. "It's burned in their memories—our lives before the suit and our lives after the suit," she says.

Chandler's case went to the U.S. Supreme Court in 2003, where judges sided with her in a landmark decision that found local governments could be held liable under the False Claims Act. In 2006, she collected less than $1 million; legal fees, taxes and debt left her with just $200,000. In 2008, at age 60, Chandler could afford to buy her first house, a bargain dwelling.

"I may have won in court, but I have to work for the rest of my life and I have no pension," says Chandler, who has a part-time private practice and does consulting. Yet, she doesn't regret her decision to report wrongdoing: "It was a concern for public safety and a matter of ethics and integrity," she says.

**Types of Retaliation
Experienced by Employees Who Report Misconduct**

Excluded from decision and work activity	62%
Given the cold shoulder	60%
Verbally abused by managers	55%
Almost lost job	48%
Not given promotion or raise	43%
Verbally abused by other co-workers	42%
Relocated or reassigned	27%
Other forms of retaliation	20%
Demoted	18%
Physical harm to person or property	4%

Figure 19.1 Multiple answers were permitted. *Source*: 2009 National Business Ethics Survey report, Ethics Resource Center.

The Consequences

Historically, companies have treated whistle-blowers "the same way that any animal views a threat," says Tom Devine, legal director with the Government Accountability Project, a whistle-blower advocacy group. "The more responsibility an employee has, the more significant the disclosure's potential and the more vicious the likely retaliation. That's because officials with more responsibility have the capacity to pose a greater threat to institutional wrongdoers so there's

---

Help Workers Speak Up

To encourage its 1,900 employees to report wrongdoing internally, AMN Healthcare in San Diego recently launched a program called "Speak Up."

"Statistically, it's the most important way you find out about wrongdoing—from your employees," says Senior Corporate Counsel Jennifer MacDougall. "A couple of principles that we try to make clear to everybody are that it's every employee's responsibility to report suspected misconduct; it's also every employee's right," she explains. "And, they don't have to know all the facts, just a good-faith suspicion. We want to make sure people know if there is something that doesn't seem right to them, they should come forward."

New employees get introduced to those principles at orientation, managers conduct face-to-face training, and longtime employees receive annual surveys asking about misconduct. Managers receive periodic training on how to encourage and handle reports.

Recently, MacDougall and Lisa Larson, the human resources director, took a lighter approach to capture employees' attention. They e-mailed employees interactive cartoons that imitate a game show—"To Call or Not Call?"—to teach the specific types of misconduct that should be disclosed.

As one of her final questions during exit interviews, Larson asks whether departing employees noticed any fraudulent acts or violations while at the company.

Similarly, Connie Eggleston, PHR, human resources manager for Farmers State Bank in Calhan, Colo., asks, "What did you think of how management handled complaints?"

Cheryl Sachse, employee relations manager for SkyWest Airlines in St. George, Utah, acknowledges that open-door policies can be abused by some employees who use reporting channels as gripe sessions. "There are some people who would never report anything, and when they do, you know it's serious; other people report every tiny thing."

more motive to engage in more intensified, uglier retaliation."

Jeffrey Wigand, a former tobacco executive whose testimony led to a historic $246 billion tobacco industry settlement with 40 states, says he received death threats that necessitated his being protected by two bodyguards for almost a year while helping government attorneys make their case. A bullet was left in his mailbox with a note threatening his children. He lost his job, his career and even his family after his wife divorced him.

In a 2007 study, the nonpartisan National Bureau of Economic Research found that in 82 percent of cases where whistle-blowers' identities were revealed, the employees were fired, quit under duress or lost significant job responsibilities.

The Ethics Resource Center's *2009 National Business Ethics Survey* report found that 15 percent of employees who reported misconduct said they experienced retaliation. Of those, nearly half said they almost lost their jobs, and 43 percent said they were denied raises or promotions.

In the *New England Journal of Medicine* study, six whistle-blowers reported divorces, severe marital strain or other family conflicts, and 13 reported health problems. "The prevailing sentiment was that the payoff had not been worth the cost," researchers reported.

Glenn DeMott of Columbus, Ohio, numbers among six whistle-blowers who aided federal officials in a case that led Pfizer to settle for $2.3 billion in 2009 for illegal marketing of drugs. DeMott, once a top salesman, prided himself on giving physicians accurate information. "I wasn't willing to make comments that were false and misleading," he says. Even before he was fired, he developed asthma and "was totally stressed-out." He still battles depression and has yet to find employment.

Is Anybody Listening?

A National Whistleblowers Center study last year found that 89.7 percent of employees who eventually filed False Claims Act lawsuits initially reported their concerns internally, either to supervisors or compliance officers.

Similarly, the Ethics Resource Center survey found that more than 90 percent of employees who blew the whistle went to someone inside the company; only 4 percent went outside the organization.

Employees typically go to an outside agency only when they are ignored or punished for speaking up within their organizations, Kohn says. "It's the retaliation that pushes them."

Instead of focusing on weeding out whistle-blowers, corporate leaders should consider "how they handle internal concerns and to what extent they are preventing retaliation of employees who come forward," says Donna C. Boehme, a principal with Compliance Strategists LLC in New Providence, N.J. She serves on the board of the RAND Center for Corporate Ethics and Governance and as program director for The Conference Board Council on Corporate Compliance and Ethics.

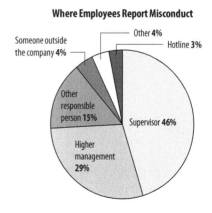

Figure 19.2 *Source: 2009 National Business Ethics Survey* report, Ethics Resource Center.

"Dodd-Frank shines a spotlight on how effective companies have been at creating real programs, rather than ones that just look good on paper," Boehme adds.

A SHRM poll conducted in January found that a minority of companies have hotlines. Of 361 respondents indicating they encouraged employees to use specific methods to report organizational wrongdoing, only 41 percent provided ethics hotlines.

The number of employers providing hotlines increased after the Sarbanes-Oxley Act required publicly traded companies to provide a confidential mechanism for employees to report misconduct. Confidentiality was supposed to help ease employees' fear of retaliation.

However, the Ethics Resource Center survey found that only 3 percent of all reports of wrongdoing come through hotlines—possibly indicating that employees don't trust them. They might be right: A study by the University of New Hamp-shire concluded that corporate officials take anonymous complaints less seriously and devote fewer resources to them.

There's a business reason for listening to employees' concerns: In a 2008 study examining 959 cases of fraud involving U.S. companies, the Association of Certified Fraud Examiners found that 46 percent were uncovered by whistle-blowers—more than the number of frauds discovered by audits or internal controls.

The Culture

The best way to keep out of legal trouble is to create a culture of integrity, starting with company leaders.

"A written policy is not enough," says Westman, the Virginia lawyer. "It's got to be talked about. It's got to be internalized. Employees have to be made to care about it. Of course, they won't if they think management doesn't."

HR managers, working with compliance and ethics officers if their companies have them, must persuade employees that it's safe to report wrongdoing through internal channels. That means creating and enforcing nonretaliation policies.

HR managers often are the first to hear complaints. They need to know how to react when people raise concerns. "One mistake you can make is to judge the veracity of the claim at the moment it's made," O&G Industries' Carey says. "In other words, don't jump to the conclusion that there's no basis."

HR professionals can train supervisors to be receptive to employees' complaints. Even a casual comment by the supervisor can send the wrong message. After an employee has complained internally or externally, managers shouldn't restrict access to documents or meetings, or do anything that could be perceived as retaliation and prompt a lawsuit, Carey says.

"Almost any action that an employer takes has the potential to be viewed as retaliation—even if it's 'No, you can't look at that file anymore,'" he explains. "It does get tricky. You can't diminish the person's position, even for access. They still should be able to go to the same meetings they went to before. In the eyes of the law, raising an issue to the SEC is not poor performance. It's not grounds for discipline. It's the opposite."

Boehme advises employers to develop clear guidelines for investigations and ensure that anyone conducting investigations is trained in those guidelines.

"I once reviewed a case where the security group, including a number of ex-law enforcement, decided to have seven questioners in a room interviewing a single employee, who was only a witness and not even the suspected wrongdoer," she says. "When managers are left to their own devices to conduct an investigation, even good people can make terrible judgments."

Names of employees should be kept confidential, and employees should be told not to discuss cases with anyone but investigators, Carey says.

However, in situations where employees work closely together and relationships might become tense, the HR manager should tell the accused and the accuser, in a clear and nonintimidating way, that they are still responsible for doing their jobs and may be subject to discipline if they don't, West-man advises.

"Angry managers who are accused may need special attention and counseling, including being advised that their visible reactions, or changed behaviors, in response to the situation may be used as evidence of retaliatory motive," he says. Company leaders should anticipate this kind of disruption to the workplace, discourage it at the outset, monitor how the work progresses and step in to reset relationships if necessary.

In extreme cases, Carey says, the HR team may create a temporary reporting structure to avoid friction between employees or may move workspaces, but it's better to make such changes at the employees' request to avoid any appearance of retaliation. Before making changes, the HR manager should consult with the company's attorney and document the reasons for the action.

The Reporting Channels

Company leaders should offer employees many ways to report wrongdoing, in case workers aren't comfortable going to managers. However, it's a mistake for employers to think they are in good shape because no reports come in. Employees may be too intimidated to report concerns, Westman notes.

Goodwin House Inc., an assisted-living facility in Alex-andria, Va., conducts surveys to gauge whether employees remain comfortable reporting wrongdoing, says Human Resources Manager Robin Wilson, SPHR.

Every report of wrongdoing should be investigated promptly. And, the employee who made

A Patchwork of Protection

There are 47 federal laws protecting the rights of corporate workers to report wrongdoing, including 12 passed by Congress in the past decade.

They are a patchwork of legal protection for employees in industries from airlines to food preparation. Most only offer fired whistle-blowers reinstatement and back pay. Only the Dodd-Frank Act, False Claims Act and an IRS statute offer whistle-blowers financial rewards for their help in uncovering wrongdoing.

In addition, every state except Alabama has some type of whistle-blower protection, according to the National Whistleblowers Center. Twenty-five states have false claims acts, and 46 states have statutory or common-law protections.

Recent Federal Whistle-Blower Protection Laws and Who They Cover

2000	Aviation Investment and Reform Act—airline workers
2002	Sarbanes-Oxley Act—employees at publicly traded companies
2005	Energy Reorganization Act amendments—nuclear power workers
2007	Surface Transportation Assistance Act amendments—truck drivers
2007	Federal Rail Safety Act—rail workers
2007	National Transit Systems Security Act—mass transit workers
2008	Consumer Product Safety Improvement Act—retail workers
2008	Department of Defense reauthorization—defense contractors
2009	American Recovery and Reinvestment Act—employees of any institution receiving stimulus funds
2010	Food Safety Modernization Act—food industry workers
2010	Patient Protection and Affordable Care Act—health care workers
2010	Dodd-Frank Act—employees at publicly traded companies and their private subsidiaries and affiliates

Source: The Government Accountability Project.

the report should be told afterward how the investigation was resolved so he or she knows it was taken seriously.

This type of follow-up "makes the employee much more trusting to go to the employer for future issues," says Connie Eggleston, PHR, human resources manager at Farmers State Bank in Calhan, Colo.

AMN Healthcare in San Diego periodically posts the results of investigations—with names deleted—on its intranet and in its electronic newsletter to employees. The HR department recently posted the comments of an employee whose report prompted changes in some procedures. Although this employee said she felt uncomfortable reporting her concerns at first, "I now am an advocate of speaking up when someone witnesses these types of experiences. HR kept me updated throughout the process. The right people were informed and asked to investigate, and my confidentiality was maintained."

Taking a page from government, some company officials are exploring offering rewards to encourage workers to report internally, Pearlman says. In the SHRM poll, 3 percent of respondents said their companies offer financial incentives to encourage employees to report wrongdoing. Boehme suggests creating incentives for ethical leadership as well, by incorporating ethics into managers' performance reviews.

Pearlman advises corporate leaders to require employees to certify several times a year whether they are aware of fraud or misconduct.

Executives often can minimize the fallout by discovering problems and reporting them to an outside agency before a whistle-blower does, so executives should establish procedures for self-reporting, lawyers say.

However, the best way for leaders to reduce the risk of whistle-blower lawsuits and expensive government investigations is to set high ethical standards and treat whistle-blowers as assets, Pearlman says. "If they know of fraud, they can detect it and bring it to your attention earlier so you can nip it in the bud."

ORGANIZATIONAL CULTURE

Debra L. Nelson & James Campbell Quick

The Key Role of Organizational Culture

The concept of organizational culture has its roots in cultural anthropology. As in larger human society, there are cultures within organizations. These cultures are similar to societal cultures. They are shared, communicated through symbols, and passed down from generation to generation of employees.

The concept of cultures in organizations was alluded to as early as the Hawthorne studies, which described work group culture. The topic came into its own during the early 1970s, when managers and researchers alike began to search for keys to survival for organizations in a competitive and turbulent environment. Since then, culture has been studied a great deal and most researchers as well as executives now accept that organizational cultures exist, are unique, and can be managed.

Culture and Its Levels

Many definitions of *organizational culture* have been proposed. Most of them agree that there are several levels of culture and that these levels differ in terms of their visibility and their ability to be changed. The definition adopted in this chapter is that *organizational (corporate) culture* is a pattern of basic assumptions that are considered valid and that are taught to new members as the way to perceive, think, and feel in the organization. Culture has been viewed both as what defines the values of the organization and as a toolkit as to how to behave in an organization. As such, culture influences desired organizational outcomes as well as the processes necessary to obtain those outcomes.

Edgar Schein, in his comprehensive book on organizational culture and leaderships, suggests that organizational culture has three levels. His view of culture is presented in Figure 20.1. The levels range from visible artifacts and creations to testable values to invisible and even preconscious basic assumptions. To achieve a complete understanding of an organization's culture, all three levels must be studied.

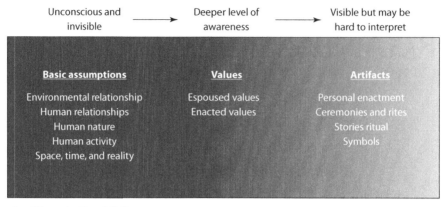

Figure 20.1 Levels of Organizational Culture

Artifacts

Symbols of culture in the physical and social work environment are called *artifacts*. They are the most visible and accessible level of culture. The key to understanding culture through artifacts lies in figuring out what they mean. Artifacts are also the most frequently studied manifestation of organizational culture, perhaps because of their accessibility. Among the artifacts of culture are personal enactment, ceremonies and rites, stories, rituals, and symbols.

The big "Blue Bag" that IKEA sells to customers for less than $1 rather than using plastic bags serves as an artifact for IKEA's cultural stance of protecting the planet. Similarly, the corporate culture of Google is apparent in the offices of its headquarters in Mountain View, California. The lobby is replete with lava lamps, pianos, and live searches on the Google search engine from around the world. The hallways house bikes and exercise machines, and office spaces are laid-back, featuring couches and occupied by dogs that go with their owners to work.

Personal Enactment

Culture can be understood, in part, through an examination of the behavior of organization members. Personal enactment is behavior that reflects the organization's values. In particular, personal enactment by the top managers provides insight into these values. Steve Irby is the founder and CEO of Still water Designs, the company that created Kicker audio speakers. He values good relationships and believes that people are the most important part of his company. Irby builds trust with his employees by sharing the financial results of the business each month. The employees know that if monthly sales are higher than the sales in the same month of the previous year, Irby will hold a cookout for the employees on the following Friday. Irby and the general manager always do the cooking. Eskimo Joe's, a Stillwater, Oklahoma, restaurant chain and one of the largest T-shirt sellers in the United States, could probably have become a national franchise years ago. But founder Stan Clark, who began as co-owner of the once-tiny bar, says his intent is to become better, not bigger. Clark still meets personally with new hires for the restaurant's serving staff, ensuring that they receive a firm grounding in his philosophy of food and fun.

Modeled behavior is a powerful learning tool for employees, as Bandura's social learning theory demonstrated. As we saw in Chapter 5, individuals learn vicariously by observing others' behavior and patterning their own behavior similarly. Culture can be an important leadership tool. Managerial behavior can clarify what is important and coordinate the work of employees, in effect negating the need for close supervision.

Ceremonies and Rites

Relatively elaborate sets of activities that are enacted time and again on important occasions are known as organizational ceremonies and rites. These occasions provide opportunities to reward and recognize employees whose behavior is congruent with the values of the company. Ceremonies and rites send a message that individuals who both espouse and exhibit corporate values are heroes to be admired.

The ceremonies also bond organization members together. Southwestern Bell (now AT&T) emphasized the importance of management training to the company. Training classes were kicked off by a high-ranking executive (a rite of renewal), and completion of the classes was signaled by a graduation ceremony (a rite of passage). Six kinds of rites in organizations have been identified:

1. *Rites of passage* show that an individual's status has changed. Retirement dinners are an example.
2. *Rites of enhancement* reinforce the achievement of individuals. An example is the awarding of certificates to sales contest winners.
3. *Rites of renewal* emphasize change in the organization and commitment to learning and growth. An example is the opening of a new corporate training center.
4. *Rites of integration* unite diverse groups or teams within the organization and renew commitment to the larger organization.

Company functions such as annual picnics fall into this category.
5. *Rites of conflict reduction* focus on dealing with conflicts or disagreements that arise naturally in organizations. Examples are grievance hearings and the negotiation of union contracts.
6. *Rites of degradation* are used by some organizations to visibly punish persons who fail to adhere to values and norms of behavior. Some CEOs, for example, are replaced quite publicly for unethical conduct or for failure to achieve organizational goals. In some Japanese organizations, employees who perform poorly are given ribbons of shame as punishment.

Berkshire Hathaway Inc. is an Omaha-based company that owns and operates a number of insurance firms and several other subsidiaries. Its chairman and CEO is Warren Buffett, known for his business acumen and for ensuring good returns on shareholder investments. Berkshire's annual shareholder meeting is a ceremony of celebration and appears more like a rock music festival than a corporate meeting. Each annual meeting starts with a short film poking fun at Berkshire's CEO and his cantankerous sidekick, Charlie Munger. The cast of the TV show "The Office" starred last year intimating that Buffet would take Michael Scott's job. Others who have made cameos in the past include Arnold Schwarzenegger, Donald Trump, and the women of Desperate Housewives. Over 20,000 shareholders, employees, and Warren Buffett attend the star-studded event annually.

Stories

Some researchers have argued that the most effective way to reinforce organizational values is through stories. As they are told and retold, stories give meaning and identity to organizations and are especially helpful in orienting new employees.

Part of the strength of organizational stories is that the listeners are left to draw their own conclusions, a powerful communication tool.

Some corporate stories even transcend cultural and political boundaries. Visit the Web site of Walmart China, and you will read the true story of Jeff, a pharmacist in Harrison, Arkansas, a small town deep in the Ozarks. When Jeff received an early morning weekend call telling him that a diabetic patient needed insulin, he quickly opened his pharmacy and filled the prescription. Although Arkansas and Beijing are worlds apart, stories such as this one help transfer Walmart's corporate personality to its new Asian associates. Research by Joanne Martin and her colleagues has indicated that certain themes recur in stories across different types of organizations:

1. *Stories about the boss.* These stories may reflect whether the boss is "human" or how the boss reacts to mistakes.
2. *Stories about getting fired.* Events leading to employee firings are recounted.
3. *Stories about how the company deals with employees who have to relocate.*

These stories relate to the company's actions toward employees who have to move, whether the company is helpful and takes family and other personal concerns into account.

4. *Stories about whether lower-level employees can rise to the top.* Often, these stories describe a person who started out at the bottom and eventually became the CEO. Nordstrom is well known for promoting from within and is one reason it has been voted to *Fortune's* "100 Best Companies to Work For" every year since 1998.
5. *Stories about how the company deals with crisis situations.* AIG's payout of $73 million in bonuses to seventy-three employees in the

unit that lost so much money that it forced a taxpayer bailout and made AIG the poster child for Wall Street greed, excess, and bad management.
6. *Stories about how status considerations work when rules are broken.* When Tom Watson, Sr., was CEO of IBM, he was once confronted by a security guard because he was not wearing an ID badge.

These are the themes that can emerge when stories are passed down. The information from these stories serves to guide the behavior of organization members.

To be effective cultural tools, stories must be credible. You can't tell a story about your flat corporate hierarchy and then have reserved parking spaces for managers. Stories that aren't backed by reality can lead to cynicism and mistrust. For example, Steve Jobs, the founder and CEO of Apple, made a commencement address at Stanford University and told stories relating his successful battle with cancer, his struggles with keeping Apple afloat, and his being fired and getting back on top. These stories were meant to reinforce his lesson that one should work toward whatever his or her passion might be.

Effective stories can also reinforce culture and create renewed energy. Lucasfilm is the home of director and producer George Lucas and the birthplace of such blockbusters as *Star Wars* and *Forrest Gump.* Stories of the company's legendary accomplishments are used to reinforce the creative culture and to rally the troops. When Gail Currey, former head of the company's digital division, found her 300 designers were grumbling, she reminded them of how they did *Gump* when everyone else said it was impossible and what a hit the film was. The designers would then head back to their computers to contribute to the company's success.

Rituals

Everyday organizational practices that are repeated over and over are rituals. They are usually unwritten, but they send a clear message about "the way we do things around here." Although some companies insist that people address each other by their titles (Mr., Mrs., Ms., Miss) and surnames to reinforce a professional image, others prefer that employees operate on a first-name basis from the top manager on down. Hewlett-Packard (HP) values open communication, so its employees address one another by first names only.

Founder of Facebook, Mark Zuckerberg, would end company meetings with a ritual that entailed his pumping his fist in the air and leading employees in a chant of "domination." Although he dropped this ritual eventually, he replaced it by quoting movie lines aimed at reminding employees that they are engaged in something greater and more meaningful than getting rich. As everyday practices, rituals reinforce the organizational culture by establishing role identities, and fixing values, beliefs, and norms. Insiders who commonly practice the rituals may be unaware of their subtle influence, but outsiders recognize it easily.

Symbols

Symbols communicate organizational culture by unspoken messages. Symbols are representative of organizational identity and membership to employees. Nike's trademark "swoosh" is proudly tattooed above the ankles of some Nike employees. Apple Computer employees readily identify themselves as "Apple People." Symbols are used to build solidarity in the organizational culture.

Personal enactment, rites and ceremonies, stories, rituals, and symbols serve to reinforce the values that are the next level of culture.

Values

Values are the second, and deeper, level of culture. They reflect a person's underlying beliefs of what should be or should not be. Values are often consciously articulated, both in conversation and in a company's mission statement or annual report. However, there may be a difference between a company's *espoused values* (what the members say they value) and its *enacted values* (values reflected in the way the members actually behave). Values also may be reflected in the behavior of individuals, which is an artifact of culture. One study investigating the gender gap in a Canadian sports organization found that coaches and athletes believed that inequities resulting from this gap were normal or natural, or they completely denied such inequities existed even though they were widespread. This was because even though the organization espoused gender equity as a value, its practices did not demonstrate and support gender equity.

A firm's values and how it promotes and publicizes them can also affect how workers feel about their jobs and themselves. A study of 180 managers looked at their employers' effectiveness in communicating concern for employees' welfare. Managers in organizations that consistently communicated concern for workers' well-being and that focused on treating employees fairly reported feeling better about themselves and their role in the organization. The lesson? Treat employees like valuable team members, and they are more likely to *feel* like valuable team members.

Values underlie the customer, environment, and high quality-focused culture at Whole Foods Market. As guides for behavior, they are reinforced in the aspirations statement and in the reward system of the organization. Whole Foods Market states that these values do not change from time to time, from person to person, or as the company grows but are the "soul" of the company's culture.

Some organizational cultures are characterized by values that support healthy lifestyle behaviors. When the workplace culture values worker health and psychological needs, there is enhanced potential for high performance and improved well-being. Clif Bar & Company, the energy bar maker, even has a forty-four-foot rock climbing wall in its corporate office.

When Harley-Davidson hires new customer service employees, they had better be ready to do more than just answer telephones. Working at Harley-Davidson is not only a job, it's about an entire subculture that revolves around Harleys. New employees are immersed in this culture, typically through working at a Harley owners' rally and taking demonstration rides. Over time, most employees

Zappos: A Happiness Culture

Zappos believes culture fit is so important that it offers to pay new employees for their time in training plus a $2,000 bonus if they quit and leave at the end of the first week. Who pays new employees to quit? The goal is to weed out employees who are just at Zappos for the paycheck. They look for people whose values fit the company's ten values:

1. Deliver WOW Through Service
2. Embrace and Drive Change
3. Create Fun and a Little Weirdness
4. Be Adventurous, Creative, and Open-Minded
5. Pursue Growth and Learning
6. Build Open and Honest Relationships with Communication
7. Build Positive Team and Family Spirit
8. Do More With Less
9. Be Passionate and Determined
10. Be Humble

Zappos is so passionate about culture fit that in the hiring phase, the manager and team do a standard interview about whether the person fits the job. A second round of interviews is conducted by HR solely for ensuring culture fit.

Happiness is a theme at Zappos too, which CEO Tony Hsieh says is composed of pleasure, passion, and purpose in life. His book Delivering Happiness focuses on work-life integration and being able to be yourself at work. He says that the best companies focus on combining profit, passion and purpose by thinking about how they can make customers, employees, and investors happier.

Sources: (http://about.zappoo.com/our unique culture/zappoo aoro values/deliver-wow-through-service; S. Rosenbaum, "The Happiness Culture: Zappos Isn't a Company, It's a Mission," *Fast Company* (June 6, 2010), accessed at http://www. fastcompany.com/1657090/the-happiness-culture-zappos-isn-t-a-company-it-s-a-mission).

become Harley riders or owners, which helps them provide better service to other Harley lovers.

At Zappos, the value system is focused on happiness for customers and employees alike. In the "Zappos" box, you can read about Zappos' values, and how they ensure that they hire people who share their values.

Assumptions

Assumptions are the deeply held beliefs that guide behavior and tell members of an organization how to perceive and think about things. As the deepest and most fundamental level of an organization's culture, according to Edgar Schein, they are the essence of culture. They are so strongly held that a member behaving in any fashion that would violate them would be unthinkable. Another characteristic of assumptions is that they are often unconscious. Organization members may not be aware of their assumptions and may be reluctant or unable to discuss them or change them.

Although unconscious assumptions often guide a firm's actions and decisions, some companies are quite explicit in their assumptions about employees. NetApp, a data storage solution provider, operates under the cultural assumption that treating its employees fairly reduces the need for too many rules or regulations. For example, its travel policy simply states, "We are a frugal company but don't show up dog-tired to save a few bucks." NetApp is one of Fortune's "Best Companies to Work For" in part due to its focus on trust and openness.

Now that you understand Schein's three levels of culture, you can use "Analyzing the Three Levels of Culture" to assess a culture you'd like to learn more about.

Analyzing the Three Levels of Culture

Select an organization you respect. Analyze its culture using the following dimensions. The artifacts of _____'s culture are as follows:

Personal enactment:
Rites and ceremonies:
Stories:
Rituals:
Symbols:
The values embedded in _____'s culture are as follows:
The assumptions of _____'s culture are as follows:

1. On what information did you base your analysis?
2. How complete is your view of this organization's culture?

Functions and Effects of Organizational Culture

In an organization, culture serves four basic functions. First, culture provides a sense of identity to members and increases their commitment to the organization. When employees internalize the values of the company, they find their work intrinsically rewarding and identify with their fellow workers. Motivation is enhanced, and employees are more committed.

Second, culture is a sense-making device for organization members. It provides a way for employees to interpret the meaning of organizational events. Leaders can use organizational symbols like corporate logos as sense-making devices to help employees understand the changing nature of their organizational identity. This is specifically so in an environment that is constantly changing. Sometimes symbols can remain the same to ensure that some things stay constant despite changing conditions; other times symbols may have to change to reflect the new culture in the organization. For example, McDonald's is known worldwide for its golden arches that have remained the same since its inception in 1955. By contrast, Southwest Airlines changed its logo in 2002 to mark its leadership in the airline industry as the "fun" airline and to capitalize on one of its most important trademarks, being "the love airline."

Third, culture reinforces the values in the organization. The culture at SSM Health Care emphasizes patient care and continuous improvement. The St. Louis-based company, which owns and manages twenty-one acute-care hospitals in four states, values compassionate, holistic, high-quality care. SSM was the first health care organization to win the Malcolm Baldrige National Quality Award.

Finally, culture serves as a control mechanism for shaping behavior. Norms that guide behavior are part of culture. If the norm the company wants to promote is teamwork, its culture must reinforce that norm. The company's culture must be characterized by open communication, cooperation between teams, and integration of teams. Culture can also be used as a powerful tool to discourage dysfunctional and deviant behaviors in organizations. Norms can send clear messages that certain behaviors are unacceptable. For example, the work group that an employee is involved with can have an impact on her or his absenteeism behavior. That is, if the work group does not have explicit norms in place discouraging absenteeism, members are more likely to be engaged in excessive absenteeism.

The effects of organizational culture are hotly debated by organizational behaviorists and researchers. Managers attest strongly to the positive effects of culture in organizations, but it is difficult to quantify these effects. John Kotter and James Heskett have reviewed three theories about the relationship between organizational culture and performance and the evidence that either supports or refutes these theories. The three are the strong culture perspective, the fit perspective, and the adaptation perspective.

The Strong Culture Perspective

The strong culture perspective states that organizations with "strong" cultures perform better than other organizations. A *strong culture* is an organizational culture with a consensus on the values that drive the company and with an intensity that is recognizable even to outsiders. Thus, a strong culture is deeply held and widely shared. It also is highly resistant to change. One example of a strong culture is IBM's. Its culture is one we are all familiar with: conservative, with a loyal workforce and an emphasis on customer service.

Strong cultures are thought to facilitate performance for three reasons. First, they are characterized by goal alignment; that is, all employees share common goals. Second, they create a high level of motivation because of the values shared by the members. Third, they provide control without the oppressive effects of a bureaucracy.

To test the strong culture hypothesis, Kotter and Heskett selected 207 firms from a wide variety of industries. They used a questionnaire to calculate a culture strength index for each firm, and they correlated that index with the firm's economic performance over a twelve-year period. They concluded that strong cultures were associated with positive long-term economic performance, but only modestly.

There are also two perplexing questions about the strong culture perspective. First, what can be said about evidence showing that strong economic performance can create strong cultures rather than the reverse? Second, what if the strong culture leads the firm down the wrong path? Sears, for example, is an organization with a strong culture, but in the 1980s, it focused inward, ignoring competition and consumer preferences and damaging its performance. Changing Sears' strong but stodgy culture has been a tough task, with financial performance only recently showing an upward trend.

The Fit Perspective

The fit perspective argues that a culture is good only if it "fits" the industry or the firm's strategy. For example, a culture that values a traditional hierarchical structure and stability would not work well in the computer manufacturing industry, which demands fast response and a lean, flat organization. Three particular characteristics of an industry may affect culture: the competitive environment, customer requirements, and societal expectations. In the computer industry, firms face a highly competitive environment, customers who require highly reliable products, and a society that expects state-of-the-art technology and high-quality service.

A study of twelve large U.S. firms indicated that cultures consistent with industry conditions help managers make better decisions. It also indicated that cultures need not change as long as the industry doesn't change. If the industry does change, however, many cultures change too slowly to avoid negative effects on firms' performance.

The fit perspective is useful in explaining short-term performance hut not long-term performance. It also indicates that it is difficult to change culture quickly, especially if the culture is widely shared and deeply held. But it doesn't explain how firms can adapt to environmental change.

The Adaptation Perspective

The third theory about culture and performance is the adaptation perspective. Its theme is that only cultures that help organizations adapt to environmental change are associated with excellent performance. An *adaptive culture* is one that encourages confidence and risk taking among employees, has leadership that produces change, and focuses on the changing needs of customers. 3M is a company with an adaptive culture in that it encourages new product ideas from all levels within the company.

To test the adaptation perspective, Kotter and Heskett interviewed industry analysts about the cultures of twenty-two firms. The contrast between adaptive cultures and nonadaptive cultures was striking. The results of the study are summarized in Table 20.1.

Adaptive cultures facilitate change to meet the needs of three groups of constituents: stockholders, customers, and employees. Nonadaptive cultures are characterized by cautious management that tries to protect its own interests. Adaptive firms showed significantly better long-term economic performance in Kotter and Heskett's study. One contrast that can he made is between HP, a high performer, and Xerox, a lower performer. The analysts viewed HP as valuing excellent leadership more than Xerox did and as valuing all three key constituencies more than Xerox did. Economic performance from 1977 through 1988 supported this difference: HP's index of annual net income growth was 40.2, as compared with Xerox's 13.1. Kotter and Heskett concluded that the cultures that promote long-term performance are those that are most adaptive.

Given that high-performing cultures are adaptive ones, it is important to know how managers can develop adaptive cultures. Although substantial research has supported the value of adaptive cultures, this framework is not the only one used to study culture. See the Science feature for another perspective. In the next section, we will examine the leader's role in managing organizational culture.

The Leader's Role in Shaping and Reinforcing Culture

According to Edgar Schein, leaders play crucial roles in shaping and reinforcing culture. The five most important elements in managing culture are (1) what leaders pay attention to, (2) how leaders react to crises, (3) how leaders behave, (4) how leaders allocate rewards, and (5) how leaders hire and fire individuals.

The Enron Corporation fiasco illustrates each of these roles. *Enron ethics* is the term applied to the gap between words and deeds, and it illustrates that leader behavior deeply affects organizational culture. Enron created deceptive partnerships and used questionable accounting practices to maintain its investment-grade rating. Employees recorded earnings before they were realized; they thought this was merely recording them early, not wrongly. Enron's culture was shaping the ethical boundaries of its employees, and Enron executives bent the rules for personal gain.

Table 20.1 Adaptive versus Nonadaptive Organizational Cultures

	Adaptive Organizational Cultures	**Nonadaptive Organizational Cultures**
Core values	Most managers care deeply about customers, stockholders, and employees. They also strongly value people and processes that can create useful change (e.g., leadership up and down the management hierarchy).	Most managers care mainly about themselves, their immediate work group, or some product (or technology) associated with that work group. They value the orderly and risk-reducing management process much more highly than leadership Initiatives.
Common behavior	Managers pay close attention to all their constituencies, especially customers, and initiate change when needed to serve their legitimate interests even if that entails taking some risks.	Managers lend to behave somewhat insularly, politically, and bureaucratically. As a result, they do not change their strategies quickly to adjust to or take advantage of changes in their business environments.

Source: John P. Kotter and James L. Heskett, *Corporate Culture and Performance* (FreePress, 1992).

What Type of Culture Would You Want to Work For?

The competing values framework investigates culture in terms of flexibility as well as whether the organization is more internally or externally focused. This framework suggests four types of organizations: the clan, the adhocracy, the market, and the hierarchy. The *clan* culture is focused on its human resources; this type of culture puts a lot of time and effort into selecting and retaining their employees and then gives these employees the power to make decisions. Clan cultures typically value communication, participation, and support. The *adhocracy* culture is based on the idea that change is fundamental to success. This culture encourages employees to take risks and be creative; it values growth, autonomy, and variety. The *market* culture is achievement focused and involves more organizational control. This type of culture is founded on the idea that clear goals and performance-related rewards motivate employees. Market cultures value competence and achievement. Finally, the *hierarchy* culture is characterized by control mechanisms; this type of culture values stability, formalization, and rules that foster efficiency.

A recent study investigated the effectiveness of each of these cultural strategies by comparing results from 84 different studies. Results indicated that clan cultures excel when it comes to relationships with employees as well as having quality products and services. Market cultures, however, lead the pack in financial success as well as innovation. When looking for a job, you should ask yourself what type of culture you want to work for.

Source: C.A. Hartnell, A.Y. Ou, & A. Kinicki, "Organizational Culture and Organizational Effectiveness: A Meta-analytic Investigation of the Competing Values Framework's Theoretical Suppositions," *Journal of Applied Psychology* (2011, January 17), advance online publication.

What Leaders Pay Attention To

Leaders in an organization communicate their priorities, values, and beliefs through the themes that consistently emerge from what they focus on. These themes are reflected in what they notice, comment on, measure, and control. If leaders are consistent in what they pay attention to, measure, and control, employees receive clear signals about what is important in the organization. If, however, leaders are inconsistent, employees spend a lot of time trying to decipher and find meaning in the inconsistent signals.

Enron leader Jeffrey Skilling paid attention to money and profit at all costs. Employees could take as much vacation as they wanted as long as they were delivering results; they could deliberately break company rules as long as they were making money. By contrast, leaders at Badger Mining Company pay attention to the environment. Their environmental stewardship, along with their cultural emphasis on trust, earned them recognition as the "Best Small Company to Work for in America."

How Leaders React to Crises

The way leaders deal with crises communicates a powerful message about culture. Emotions are heightened during a crisis, and learning is intense. With mergers and acquisitions, the way in which the leader reacts to change, transparency of the procedures used, and communication quality affect how followers perceive change and ultimately acceptance of any associated changes in the organizational culture.

Difficult economic times present crises for many companies and illustrate their different values. Some organizations do everything possible to prevent laying off workers. Others may claim that employees are important but quickly institute major layoffs at the first signal of an economic downturn. Employees may perceive that the company shows its true colors in a crisis and, thus, may pay careful attention to the reactions of their leaders.

When the Enron crisis became public, managers quickly shifted blame and pointed fingers. Before bankruptcy was declared, managers began systematically firing any employee they could lay blame on, while denying that there was a problem with accounting irregularities. During the crisis, managers responded with anonymous whistleblowing, hiding behind the Fifth Amendment, and shredding documents.

How Leaders Behave

Through role modeling, teaching, and coaching, leaders reinforce the values that support the organizational culture. Employees often emulate leaders' behavior and look to the leaders for cues to appropriate behavior. Many companies are encouraging employees to be more entrepreneurial—to take more initiative and be more innovative in their jobs. A study showed that if managers want employees to be more entrepreneurial, they must demonstrate such behaviors themselves. This is the case with any cultural value. Employees observe the behavior of leaders to find out what the organization values.

The behavior of Enron's managers spoke volumes; they broke the law as they created fake partnerships. They ignored and then denied that problems existed. Although employees were unable to dump their Enron stocks, managers were hastily getting rid of their shares, all the while telling employees that the company would be fine.

How Leaders Allocate Rewards

To ensure that values are accepted, leaders should reward behavior that is consistent with the values. Some companies, for example, may claim that they use a pay-for-performance system that distributes rewards on the basis of performance. When the time comes for raises, however, the increases are awarded according to length of service with the company. Imagine the feelings of a high-performing newcomer who has heard leaders espouse the value of rewarding individual performance and then receives only a tiny raise.

Some companies may value teamwork. They form cross-functional teams and empower them to make important decisions. However, when performance is appraised, the criteria for rating employees focus on individual performance. This sends a confusing signal to employees about the company's culture: Is individual performance valued, or is teamwork the key?

At Enron, employees were rewarded only if they produced consistent results, with little regard for ethics. Managers were given extremely large bonuses to keep the stock price up at any cost. Performance reviews were done in public, and poor performers were ridiculed.

How Leaders Hire and Fire Individuals

A powerful way that leaders reinforce culture is through the selection of newcomers to the organization. With the advent of electronic recruitment practices, applicant perceptions of organizational culture are shaped by what the organization advertises on its recruitment Web site. Typical perception-shaping mechanisms are organizational values, policies, awards, and goals. Leaders often unconsciously look for individuals who are similar to current organizational members in terms of values and assumptions. Some companies hire individuals on the recommendation of a current employee; this tends to perpetuate the culture because the new employees typically hold similar values. Jeffrey Swartz, CEO of The Timberland Company, has a unique way of hiring people. He has his recruiter call the applicants in advance and have them wear anything they feel passionately about other than Timberland shoes. Senior applicants go through a day of community service with Timberland executives because Swartz claims that anyone can be smarter than he is in an interview, but the service work helps them decide who to hire by bringing out the real person.

The way a company fires an employee and the rationale behind the firing also communicate the culture. Some companies deal with poor performers by trying to find a place within the organization where they can perform better and make a contribution. Other companies seem to operate under the philosophy that those who cannot perform are out quickly.

The reasons for terminations may not be directly communicated to other employees, but curiosity leads to speculation. An employee who displays unethical behavior and is caught may simply be reprimanded even though such behavior is clearly against the organization's values. Other employees may view this as a failure to reinforce the values within the organization.

Enron hired employees who had aggressiveness, greed, a desire to win at all costs, and a willingness to break rules. It fired nonproductive employees, using a "rank and yank" system whereby the bottom 15–20 percent of employees were let go each year. Peers were required to rank each other, which led to cutthroat competition and extreme distrust among employees.

In summary, leaders play a critical role in shaping and reinforcing organizational culture. The Enron case illustrates how powerful, and potentially damaging, that influence can be. The lesson for future managers is to create a positive culture through what they pay attention to, how they react to crises, how they behave, the way they allocate rewards, and how they hire and fire employees. Research results from a study of finance professionals in Greece support this view. Transformational leaders create a more adaptive culture, which in turn increases business unit performance.

Socialization

We have seen that leaders play key roles in shaping an organization's culture. Another process that perpetuates culture is the way it is handed down from generation to generation of employees. Newcomers learn the culture through *organizational socialization,* the process by which newcomers are transformed from outsiders to participating, effective members of the organization. The process is also a vehicle for bringing newcomers into the organizational culture. As we saw earlier, cultural socialization begins with the careful selection of newcomers who are likely to reinforce the organizational culture. Once selected, newcomers pass through the socialization process.

The Stages of the Socialization Process

The organizational socialization process is generally described as having three stages: anticipatory socialization, encounter, and change and acquisition. Figure 20.2 presents a model of the process and the key concerns at each stage of it.

It also describes the outcomes of the process, which will be discussed in this chapter's next section.

Anticipatory Socialization

Anticipatory socialization, the first stage, encompasses all of the learning that takes place prior to the newcomer's first day on the job. It includes the newcomer's expectations. The two key concerns at this stage are realism and congruence.

Realism is the degree to which a newcomer holds realistic expectations about the job and about the organization. One thing newcomers should receive information about during entry into the organization is the culture. Information about values at this stage can help newcomers begin to construct a scheme for interpreting their

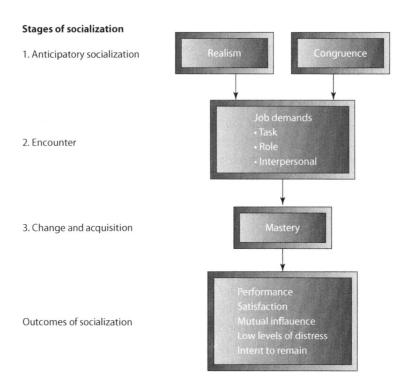

Figure 20.2 The Organizational Socialization Process: Stages and Outcomes. *Source:* D. Nelson, *Organizational Socialization: A Demands Perspective*, doctoral dissertation, The University of Texas at Arlington, 1985.

organizational experiences. A deeper understanding of the organization's culture will be possible through time and experience in the organization. Furthermore, a recent study found that when organizations not only give realistic job previews that highlight major stressors but also teach various coping strategies to deal with these stressors, newcomers feel less stressed and report higher levels of adjustment six and nine months post entry.

There are two types of congruence between an individual and an organization: congruence between the individual's abilities and the demands of the job, and the fit between the organizations values and the individual's values. Organizations disseminate information about their values through their Web pages, annual reports, and recruitment brochures. Value congruence is particularly important for organizational culture. It is also important in terms of newcomer adjustment. Newcomers whose values match the company's values are more satisfied with their new jobs, adjust more quickly, and say they intend to remain with the firm longer.

Encounter

The second stage of socialization, *encounter*, is when newcomers learn the tasks associated with the job, clarify their roles, and establish new relationships at work. This stage commences on the first day at work and is thought to encompass the first six to nine months on the new job. Newcomers face task demands, role demands, and interpersonal demands during this period,

Task demands involve the actual work performed. Learning to perform tasks is related to the organization's culture. In some organizations, newcomers are given considerable latitude to experiment with new ways to do the job, and creativity is valued. In others, newcomers are expected to learn the established procedures

for their tasks. Early experiences with trying to master task demands can affect employees' entire careers. Auditors, for example, are often forced to choose between being thorough, on the one hand, and being fast in completing their work on the other. By pressuring auditors in this way, firms often set themselves up for problems later, when these pressures may lead auditors to make less-than-ethical decisions.

Role demands involve the expectations placed on newcomers. Newcomers may not know exactly what is expected of them (role ambiguity) or may receive conflicting expectations from other individuals (role conflict). The way newcomers approach these demands depends in part on the culture of the organization. Are newcomers expected to operate with considerable uncertainty, or is the manager expected to clarify the newcomers' roles? Some cultures even put newcomers through considerable stress in the socialization process, including humility-inducing experiences, so newcomers will be more open to accepting the firm's values and norms. Long hours, tiring travel schedules, and an overload of work are part of some socialization practices.

Interpersonal demands arise from relationships at work. Politics, leadership style, and group pressure are interpersonal demands. All of them reflect the values and assumptions that operate within the organization. Most organizations have basic assumptions about the nature of human relationships. The Korean *chaebol* (business conglomerate) LG Group strongly values harmony in relationships and in society, and its decision-making policy emphasizes unanimity.

In the encounter stage, the expectations formed in anticipatory socialization may clash with the realities of the job. It is a time of facing the task, role, and interpersonal demands of the new job.

Change and Acquisition

In the third and final stage of socialization, *change and acquisition*, newcomers begin to master the demands of the job. They become proficient at managing their tasks, clarifying and negotiating their roles, and engaging in relationships at work. The time when the socialization process is completed varies widely, depending on the individual, the job, and the organization. The end of the process is signaled by newcomers being considered by themselves and others as organizational insiders.

Outcomes of Socialization

Newcomers who are successfully socialized should exhibit good performance, high job satisfaction, and the intention to stay with the organization. In addition, they should exhibit low levels of distress symptoms. High levels of organizational commitment are also marks of successful socialization. This commitment is facilitated throughout the socialization process by the communication of values that newcomers can buy into. Successful socialization is also signaled by mutual influence; that is, the newcomers have made adjustments in the job and organization to accommodate their knowledge and personalities. Newcomers are expected to leave their mark on the organization and not to be completely conforming.

When socialization is effective, newcomers understand and adopt the organization's values and norms. This ensures that the company's culture, including its central values, survives. It also provides employees a context for interpreting and responding to things that happen at work, and it ensures a shared framework of understanding among employees.

Newcomers adopt the company's norms and values more quickly when they receive positive support from organizational insiders. Sometimes this is accomplished through informal social gatherings. Socialization also impacts the social connections or networks that newcomers form at work. Social networks serve as resources for employees and can be very important to newcomer success.

Although socialization occurs when an employee enters the organization, studies indicate that for best results, a supervisor should show high levels of support for newcomers for at least two years. Successful socialization is not all the organization's responsibility; newcomers who are more curious and adaptable adjust to their new jobs in more effective ways, leading to better performance. Additionally, newcomers with proactive personalities (discussed in Chapter 3) adjust more effectively in organizations because they are more likely to seek out the information they need to become socialized.

Socialization as Cultural Communication

Socialization is a powerful cultural communication tool. Even though the transmission of information about cultural artifacts is relatively easy, the transmission of values is more difficult. The communication of organizational assumptions is almost impossible since organization members themselves may not be consciously aware of them.

The primary purpose of socialization is the transmission of core values to new organization members. Newcomers are exposed to these values through the role models they interact with, the training they receive, and the behavior they observe being rewarded and punished. Newcomers are vigilant observers, seeking clues to the organization's culture and consistency in the cultural messages they receive. If they are expected to adopt these values, it is essential that the message reflect the underlying values of the organization.

One company known for its culture is The Walt Disney Company. Disney transmits its culture to employees though careful selection, socialization, and training. The Disney culture is built around customer service, and its image serves as a filtering process for applicants. Peer interviews are used to learn how applicants interact with each other. Disney tries to secure a good fit between employee values and the organization's culture. To remind employees of the image they are trying to project, employees are referred to as "cast members" and they occupy a "role." They work either "on stage" or "backstage" and wear "costumes" rather than uniforms. Disney operates its own "universities," which are attended by all new employees. Once trained at a Disney university, cast members are paired with role models to continue their learning on-site.

Companies such as Disney use the socialization process to communicate messages about organizational culture. Both individuals and organizations can take certain actions to ensure the success of the socialization process.

MANAGING CHANGE

Debra L. Nelson & James Campbell Quick

Lewin's Change Model

Kurt Lewin developed a model of the change process that has stood the test of time and continues to influence the way organizations manage planned change. Lewin's model is based on the idea of force field analysis. This model contends that a person's behavior is the product of two opposing forces; one force pushes toward preserving the status quo, and the other force pushes for change. When the two opposing forces are approximately equal, current behavior is maintained. For behavioral change to occur, the forces maintaining the status quo must be overcome. This can be accomplished by increasing the forces for change, by weakening the forces for the status quo, or by a combination of these actions.

"Applying Force Field Analysis" asks you to apply force field analysis to a problem in your life.

Lewin's change model is a three-step process, as shown in Figure 21.1. The process begins with *unfreezing*, which is a crucial first hurdle in the change process. Unfreezing involves encouraging individuals to discard old behaviors by shaking up the equilibrium state that maintains the status quo. Change management literature has long advocated that certain individuals have personalities that make them more resistant to change. However, recent research indicates that only a small portion of a study's respondents (23 percent) displayed consistency in their reactions to three different kinds of change: structural, technological, and office relocation. The majority of respondents (77 percent) reacted differently to these various kinds of change, suggesting that reactions to change might be more situationally

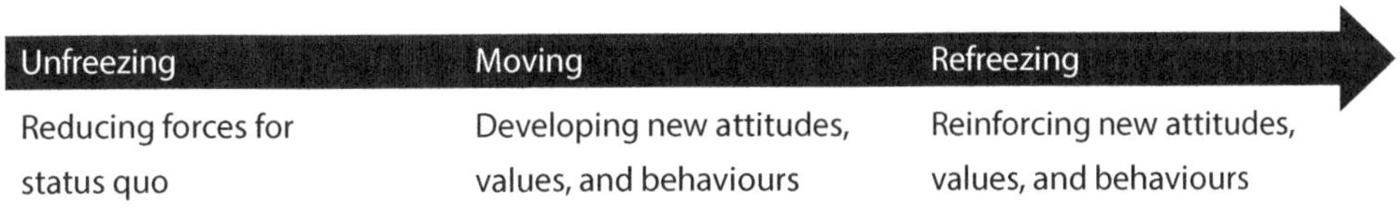

Unfreezing	Moving	Refreezing
Reducing forces for status quo	Developing new attitudes, values, and behaviours	Reinforcing new attitudes, values, and behaviours

Figure 21.1 Lewin's Change Model

Applying Force Field Analysis

Think of a problem you are currently facing. An example would be trying to increase the amount of study time you devote to a particular class.

1. Describe the problem as specifically as possible.
2. List the forces driving change on the arrows at the left side of the diagram.
3. List the forces restraining change on the arrows at the right side of the diagram.
4. What can you do, specifically, to remove the obstacles to change?

5. What can you do to increase the forces driving change?
6. What benefits can be derived from breaking a problem down into forces driving change and forces restraining change?

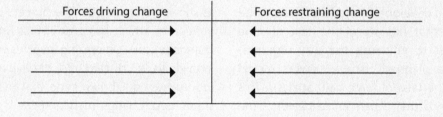

driven than was previously thought. Organizations often accomplish unfreezing by eliminating the rewards for current behavior and showing that current behavior is not valued. By unfreezing, individuals accept that change needs to occur. In essence, individuals surrender by allowing the boundaries of their status quo to be opened in preparation for change.

The second step in the change process is *moving*. In the moving stage, new attitudes, values, and behaviors are substituted for old ones. Organizations accomplish moving by initiating new options and explaining the rationale for the change, as well as by providing training to help employees develop the new skills they need. Employees should be given the overarching vision for the change so that they can establish their roles within the new organizational structure and processes.

Refreezing is the final step in the change process. In this step, new attitudes, values, and behaviors are established as the new status quo. The new ways of operating are cemented in and reinforced. Managers should ensure that the organizational culture and formal reward systems encourage the new behaviors and avoid rewarding the old ways of operating. Changes in the reward structure may be needed to ensure that the organization is not rewarding the old behaviors and merely hoping for the new behaviors. A study by Exxon Research and Engineering showed that framing and displaying a mission statement in managers' offices may eventually change the behavior of two percent of the managers. By contrast, changing managers' evaluation and reward systems will change the behavior of 55 percent of the managers almost overnight.

The approach used by Monsanto Company to increase opportunities for women within the company is an illustration of how to use Lewin's model effectively. First, Monsanto emphasized unfreezing by helping employees debunk negative stereotypes about women in business. This also helped overcome resistance to change. Second, Monsanto moved employees' attitudes and behaviors by diversity training in which differences were emphasized as positive, and supervisors learned ways of training and developing female employees. Third, Monsanto changed its reward system so that managers were evaluated and paid according to how they coached and promoted women, which helped refreeze the new attitudes and behaviors.

One frequently overlooked issue is whether the change is consistent with the company's deeply held core values. Value consistency is critical to making a change "stick." Organizations whose members perceive the changes to be consistent with the firm's values adopt the changes much more easily and fully. Conversely, organizations whose members' values conflict with the changes may display "superficial conformity," in which members pay lip service to the changes but ultimately revert to their old behaviors.

Although Lewin presents these steps as a progressive process, some research indicates that the steps can occur simultaneously. Leaders may hedge their bets and unfreeze and refreeze simultaneously. This research also indicates that leaders should also take care in how they unfreeze and refreeze their followers because employees will often embellish and retell a leader's stories in ways counterproductive to the change effort. For example, consider a manager who wants to implement change in a sales process. She may attempt to "unfreeze" the process by stating it is cumbersome and causes missed sales. Instead of interpreting this explanation to mean that the process needs to be improved upon (as the manager intended), an employee may retell the story stating that the sales department is in jeopardy because of excessive missed sales. Organizations that wish to change can select from a variety of methods to make a change become reality. Organization development is a method that consists of various programs for making organizations more effective.

Organization Development Interventions

Organization development (OD) is a systematic approach to organizational improvement that applies behavioral science theory and research in order to increase individual and organizational well-being and effectiveness. This definition implies certain characteristics. First, OD is a systematic approach to planned change. It is a structured cycle of diagnosing organizational problems and opportunities and then applying expertise to them. Second, OD is grounded in solid research and theory. It involves the application of our knowledge of behavioral science to the challenges that organizations face. Third, OD recognizes the reciprocal relationship between individuals and organizations. It acknowledges that for organizations to change, individuals must change. Finally, OD is goal oriented. It is a process that seeks to improve both individual and organizational well-being and effectiveness.

OD has a rich history. Some of the early work in OD was conducted by Kurt Lewin and his associates during the 1940s. This work was continued by Rensis Likert, who pioneered the use of attitude surveys in OD. During the 1950s, Eric Trist and his colleagues at the Tavistock Institute in London focused on the technical and social aspects of organizations and how they affect the quality of work life. These programs on the quality of work life migrated to the United States during the 1960s. During this time, a 200-member OD network was established, and it has grown to more than 4,100 members worldwide. As the number of practitioners has increased, so has the number of different OD methods. One compendium of organizational change methods estimates that more than 300 different methods have been used.

ORGANIZATIONAL CHANGE AND DEVELOPMENT

Joseph E. Champoux

Reasons for Resistance to Change

Organizational change resistance occurs for several reasons. Some people might perceive the change as causing them to lose something valued. For example, a change could reduce an individual's or a group's social status. If the individual or group valued their status, they are likely to resist the change. The change could also create a feeling of future unfairness in rewards and sanctions distribution.

Misunderstandings about the intended change goal or lack of trust between the change target and the change agent can create resistance reactions. Misunderstandings can arise because the change agent did not fully explain the goal of the change. Lack of trust might develop because the change agent is an outsider or comes from a part of the organization that the target has long distrusted.

Resistance to change can also occur when all parties involved in the change do not share a common perception about the value of the change. The change agent and the change target often have different expectations about the effects of the change. Later, this section discusses how such

differences make resistance to change a valuable tool for managing change.

The people who are the change target may have low tolerance for change and the uncertainty associated with it. People vary in their ability to change their behavior quickly. Those who resist change because of low tolerance may believe the change is good for them and the organization, but they simply cannot alter their behavior as fast as the change requires.

Managers' Orientation to Resistance to Change

Managers can react to resistance to change in two ways. They can treat the resistance as a problem to overcome or view it as a signal to get more information about the reasons for the resistance. Managers who view resistance as a problem to overcome might try to forcefully reduce it. Such coercive approaches often increase the resistance.

Alternatively, managers may see resistance as a signal that the change agent needs more information about the intended change. The targets that will be affected by the change may have valuable insights about its effects. An alert change agent will involve the targets in diagnosing the reasons for the resistance. In this way, managers can use resistance to change as a tool to get needed information.

Should managers and change agents see the absence of resistance to change as a stroke of good fortune? Many reasons suggest that they should not. The absence of resistance is also a signal to managers and change agents to get more information. A change that is automatically accepted can be less effective than one that has been resisted and actively debated. The resisters play an important role by focusing the change agent's attention on potentially dysfunctional aspects of the proposed change.

Managing the Change Process to Reduce Resistance

Resistance reactions might focus on the change, the method of change, or the change agent. The method or methods used to reduce resistance partly depend on the target of the resistance to change.

Resistance often develops when the change agent and the target of change differ strongly in such characteristics as education level, physical appearance, values, and language. Using change agents with characteristics congruent with those of the target reduces resistance reactions. For example, if the target of the change effort were a group of people who dress informally at work, a change agent would be ill advised to wear formal business clothes.

Using dramatic ceremonies and symbols to signal disengagement from the past can quickly move a system forward with little resistance. The ceremony can include recognition of a job well done on some program that is ending. This approach to managing a change effort can be especially effective in industries such as aerospace, where shifts in technology make old programs obsolete. Ceremoniously burying the old program and launching the new one can go a long way to reducing resistance to change.

Communicating information about the change is another way to head off resistance. The communications can be written or oral, presented to groups or to single individuals. Extensive conversations between a manager and each person reporting to her will help the change process. The communication should explain the reasons for the change, how it will happen, and the effects it will have on various groups in the organization. Especially with highly technical change, an explanation in simple and understandable terms helps reduce resistance reactions.

Involving the key people who will be affected by the proposed change also helps reduce resistance. They should be involved early in the change effort, especially in diagnosing the system to assess whether change is needed. This suggestion does not mean inviting members of the target system to participate simply to give them a superficial sense of contributing to the change. Their involvement is necessary to get crucial information from those most intimately involved in the target system. Such information lets managers and change agents design an effective change effort.

Managers can support a major change effort by committing enough resources to make the change easier on those affected. Ample resources are particularly important if the change involves moving to a new and complex technology. Managers can expect resistance reactions when people must learn new, more complex ways of doing their work. Management can head off such resistance by committing enough resources to train people to use the new technology.

When a powerful person or group is a potential source of resistance, negotiation may be necessary. These people may not be powerful enough to prevent the change, but they can create a significant source of resistance. Negotiations are common in situations asking for change in work behavior from unionized employees. Changes in a union contract might be needed to get major changes in the way work is done.

A more indirect and politically based approach than the methods described involves manipulating (in various ways) those who are the target of change. Co-optation is a political tactic that aims to gain endorsement of the change from important individuals or groups by inviting such people to play a role in designing the change effort. Co-optation is different from involvement, described earlier. Here, the change agent is not seeking information to build an effective change program. The change agent or manager wants the important person or group to accept the change program. Of course, co-optation can backfire on the manager or change agent. The co-opted individual or group could affect the design of the change effort to benefit the individual or the group at the expense of the organization's goals.

Managers and change agents sometimes have no other choice than to force change onto the target system. Such a coercive reaction often happens when the change must come quickly or when the change is undesirable to the target system. Pressing or forcing a system to change also can increase resistance to change, making the manager or change agent's job even more difficult.

Leadership and Organizational Change

Leaders can change organizations; managers operate with what they now have. Leaders play a major role in organizational change.

A leader's vision of an organization's future can play a compelling role in successful organizational change. A vision offers powerful imagery of the future. An effective vision is "future oriented, compelling, bold, aspiring, and inspiring, yet believable and achievable."

Several types of leaders can create strong changes in organizations. A leader with the leadership mystique has a sense of mission (vision), can build a power base for change, and has a will to survive and persevere during stormy periods. Transformational leaders use their charismatic qualities to inspire followers in pursuit of desired changes. Charismatic leaders combine an inspirational vision with the leader's charisma to move organizations out of a turbulent period to a new equilibrium period. All three types of leaders usually know what is in the organization's roots that they want to keep for the future. Without leaders at many levels in an organization, successful change is unlikely.

CAREER MANAGEMENT

Debra L. Nelson & James Campbell Quick

Preparing for the World of Work

When viewed from one perspective, you might say that we spend our youth preparing for the world of work. Educational experiences and personal life experiences help an individual develop the skills and maturity needed to enter a career. Preparation for work is a developmental process that gradually unfolds over time. As the time approaches for beginning a career, individuals face two difficult decisions: the choice of occupation and the choice of organization.

Occupational Choice

In choosing an occupation, individuals assess their needs, values, abilities, and preferences and attempt to match them with an occupation that provides a fit. Personality plays a role in the selection of occupation. John Holland's theory of occupational choice contends that there are six types of personalities and that each is characterized by a set of interests and values. Holland's six types are as follows:

1. *Realistic:* stable, persistent, and materialistic.
2. *Artistic:* imaginative, emotional, and impulsive.
3. *Investigative:* curious, analytical, and independent.
4. *Enterprising:* ambitious, energetic, and adventurous.
5. *Social:* generous, cooperative, and sociable.
6. *Conventional:* efficient, practical, and obedient.

Holland also states that occupations can be classified using this typology. For example, realistic occupations include mechanic, restaurant server, and mechanical engineer. Artistic occupations include architect, voice coach, and interior designer. Investigative occupations include physicist, surgeon, and economist. Real estate agent, human resource manager, and lawyer are enterprising occupations. The social occupations include counselor, social worker, and member of the clergy. Conventional occupations include word processor, accountant, and data entry operator.

Holland's typology has been used to predict career choices with a variety of international participants, including Mexicans, Australians, Indians, New Zealanders, Taiwanese, Pakistanis, South Africans, and Germans.

An assumption that drives Holland's theory is that people choose occupations that match their own personalities. People who fit Holland's social types are those who prefer jobs that are highly interpersonal in nature. They may see careers in physical and math sciences, for example, as not affording the opportunity for interpersonal relationships. To fulfill the desire for interpersonal work, they may instead gravitate toward jobs in customer service or counseling in order to better match their personalities.

Although personality is a major influence on occupational choice, it is not the only influence. There is a host of other ones, including social class, parents' occupations, economic conditions,

Teach for America: On a Mission

Teach for America (TFA) is a nonprofit organization founded by Wendy Kopp, who developed the idea in her senior project at Princeton University. She wanted to eliminate education inequity in the United States by enlisting the best and brightest college student leaders in a corps that would teach in low-income communities. The goal of TFA is to involve promising leaders in a two-year teaching stint and to encourage them to become lifelong leaders in promoting quality, equitable education. TFA corps members work for their local school districts, not TFA, and serve faculty members at their schools, earning the same salary and benefits as their peers. Corps members also receive an education voucher that can be used to cover student loans or fund further education. TFA has reached its 20-year anniversary with an annual budget of $212 million and a staff of 1,400.

TFA does not emphasize making a career out of teaching; its goal is to recruit future leaders to teach two years; however 52 percent of alumni remain in teaching after their two-year commitment and include 548 district and state "Teacher of the Year" winners. The TFA philosophy is that education requires leaders in a variety of roles; 67 percent of TFA alumni are in fields related to education, including principals, school district leaders, politicians, and foundations.

Each corps member brings a unique set of talents and experiences to the classroom, and TFA provides initial training, networking, and ongoing support. Research indicates that TFA corp members have equal or greater impact than experienced teachers in the same school.

If your mission is to improve education, teaching with TFA might be for you. Even if you are not inclined to teach, joining the nonprofit's staff could make you a happy camper. TFA was recently named a Fortune "Best Company to Work For," fueled by zeal to make education better.

Sources: http://www.teachforamerica.org; A. J. Rotherham, "Teach For America: 5 Myths that Persist 20 Years On, Time," February 10, 2011, accessed at http://www.time.com/time/nation/article/0,8599,2047211,00.html; Best Companies to Work For: Teach for America, accessed at http://money.cnn.com/magazines/fortune/bestcompanies/2011/snapshots/82.html

and geography. Individuals are often attracted to organizations whose mission matches their passions and values. One such organization, Teach for America, is on a mission to fix public education in the United States, as you can see in the "Teach for America: On a Mission" box. Once a choice of occupation has been made, another major decision individuals face is the choice of organizations.

Organizational Choice and Entry

Several theories of how individuals choose organizations exist, ranging from those that postulate logical and rational choice processes to those that offer seemingly irrational processes. Expectancy theory can be applied to organizational choice. According to the expectancy theory view, individuals choose organizations that maximize positive outcomes and avoid negative outcomes. Job candidates calculate the probability that an organization will provide a certain outcome and then compare the probabilities across organizations.

Other theories propose that people select organizations in a much less rational fashion. Job candidates may satisfice—that is, select the first organization that meets one or two important criteria—and then justify their choice by distorting their perceptions.

The method of selecting an organization varies greatly among individuals and may reflect a combination of the expectancy theory and theories that postulate less rational approaches. Entry into an organization is further complicated by the conflicts that occur between individuals and organizations during the process. Figure 23.1 illustrates these potential conflicts. The arrows in the figure illustrate four types of conflicts that can occur as individuals choose organizations and organizations choose individuals. The first two conflicts (1 and 2) occur between individuals and organizations. The first is a conflict between the organization's effort to attract candidates and the individual's choice of an organization. The individual needs complete and accurate information to make a good choice, but the organization may not provide it. The organization is trying to attract a large number of qualified candidates, so it presents itself in an overly attractive way.

The second conflict is between the individual's attempt to attract several organizations and the organization's need to select the best candidate. Individuals want good offers, so they do not disclose their faults. They describe their preferred job

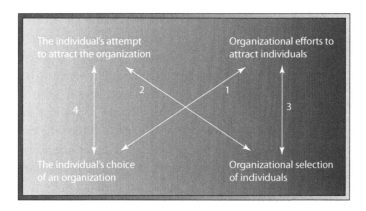

Figure 23.1 Conflicts during Organizational Entry. *Source:* Figure in L. W. Porter, E. E. Lawler III, and J. R. Hackman, *Behavior in Organizations,* New York: McGraw-Hill, Inc., 1975, p. 134.

in terms of the organization's opening instead of describing a job they would really prefer.

Conflicts 3 and 4 are internal to the two parties. The third is a conflict between the organization's desire to recruit a large pool of qualified applicants and the organization's need to select and retain the best candidate. In recruiting, organizations tend to give only positive information, which results in mismatches between the individual and the organization. The fourth conflict is internal to the individual; it is between the individual's desire for several job offers and the need to make a good choice. When individuals present themselves as overly attractive, they risk being offered positions that are poor fits in terms of their skills and career goals.

The organizational choice and entry process is very complex due to the nature of these conflicts. Partial responsibility for preventing these conflicts rests with the individual. Individuals should conduct thorough research of the organization through published reports and industry analyses. They also should conduct a careful self-analysis and be as honest as possible with organizations to ensure a good match. The job interview process can be stressful, but also fun.

Partial responsibility for good matches also rests with the organization. One way of avoiding the conflicts and mismatches is to utilize a realistic job preview.

Realistic Job Previews

The conflicts just discussed may result in unrealistic expectations on the part of the candidate. People entering the world of work may expect, for example, that they will receive explicit directions from their boss, only to find that they are left with ambiguity about how to do the job. They may expect that promotions will be based on performance and find that in fact they are based mainly on political considerations. Some new hires expect to be given managerial responsibilities right away; however, this is not often the case.

Giving potential employees a realistic picture of the job they are applying for is known as a *realistic job preview (RJP)*. When candidates are given both positive and negative information, they can make more effective job choices. Traditional recruiting practices produce unrealistically high expectations, which produce low job satisfaction when these unrealistic expectations hit the reality of the job situation. RJPs tend to create expectations that are much closer to reality, and they increase the numbers of candidates who withdraw from further consideration. This occurs because candidates with unrealistic expectations tend to look for employment elsewhere. Time Warner Cable posts videos with realistic job previews on their Web site. These videos show current employees discussing the skills necessary for dealing with the challenges and frustrations associated with the various job within the company.

RJPs can also be thought of as inoculation against disappointment. If new recruits know what to expect in the new job, they can prepare for the experience. Newcomers who are not given RJPs may find that their jobs don't measure up to their expectations. They may then believe that their employer was deceitful in the hiring process, become unhappy and mishandle job demands, and ultimately leave the organization.

Job candidates who receive RJPs view the organization as honest and also have a greater ability to cope with the demands of the job. RJPs perform another important function: uncertainty reduction. Knowing what to expect, both good and bad, gives a newcomer a sense of control that is important to job satisfaction and performance.

With today's emphasis on ethics, organizations need to do all they can to be seen as operating consistently and honestly. RJPs are one way companies can provide ethically required information to newcomers. Ultimately, RJPs result in more effective matches, lower turnover, and higher organizational commitment and job satisfaction. There is much to gain, and little to risk, in providing realistic job information.

In summary, the needs and goals of individuals and organizations can clash during entry into the organization. To avoid potential mismatches, individuals should conduct a careful self-analysis and provide accurate information about themselves to potential employers. Individuals should also ask all the appropriate questions. Newcomers tend to focus on seeking information about organizational rewards rather than on employee contributions. Seeking out information on both is important in obtaining a RJP. Organizations should present RJPs to show candidates both the positive and negative aspects of the job, along with the potential career paths available to the employee.

After entry into the organization, individuals embark on their careers. A person's work life can be traced through successive stages, as we see in the career stage model.

The Career Stage Model

A common way of understanding careers is viewing them as a series of stages through which individuals pass during their working lives. Figure 23.2 presents the career stage model, which will form the basis for our discussion in the remainder of this chapter. The career stage model shows that individuals pass through four stages in their careers: establishment, advancement, maintenance, and withdrawal. It is important to note that the age ranges shown are approximations; that is, the timing of the career transitions varies greatly among individuals.

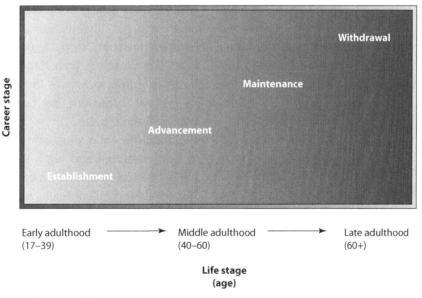

Figure 23.2 The Career Stage Model

Establishment is the first stage of a person's career. The activities that occur in this stage center on learning the job and fitting into the organization and occupation. *Advancement* is a high-achievement-oriented stage in which people focus on increasing their competence. The *maintenance* stage finds the individual trying to maintain productivity while evaluating progress toward career goals. The *withdrawal* stage involves contemplation of retirement or possible career change.

Along the horizontal axis in Figure 23.2 are the corresponding life stages for each career stage. These life stages are based on the pioneering research on adult development conducted by Levinson and his colleagues. Levinson conducted extensive biographical interviews to trace the life stages of men and women. He interpreted his research in two books, *The Seasons of a Man's Life* and *The Seasons of a Woman's Life*. Levinson's life stages are characterized by an alternating pattern of stability and transition. Throughout the discussion of career stages that follows, we weave in the transitions of Levinson's life stages. Work and personal life are inseparable, and to understand a person's career experiences, we must also examine the unfolding of her or his personal experiences.

You can see that adult development provides unique challenges for the individual and that there may be considerable overlap between the stages. Now let us examine each career stage in detail.

The Establishment Stage

During the establishment stage, the individual begins a career as a newcomer to the organization. This is a period of great dependence on others, as the individual is learning about the job and the organization. The establishment stage usually occurs during the beginning of the early adulthood years (ages eighteen to twenty-five). During this time, Levinson notes, an important personal life transition into adulthood occurs: the individual begins to separate from his or her parents and becomes less emotionally and financially dependent. Following this period is a fairly stable time of exploring the adult role and settling down.

The transition from school to work is a part of the establishment stage. Many graduates find the transition a memorable experience. The following description was provided by a newly graduated individual who went to work at a large public utility: We all tried to one-up each other about jobs we had just accepted … bragging that we had the highest salary, the best management training program, the most desirable coworkers, the most upward mobility … and believed we were destined to become future corporate leaders. … Every Friday after work, we met for happy hour to visit and relate the events of the week. It is interesting to look at how the mood of those happy hours changed over the first few months … at first, we jockeyed for position in terms of telling stories about how great these new jobs were or how weird our bosses were. … Gradually, things quieted down at happy hour. The mood went from "Wow, isn't this great?" to "What in the world have we gotten ourselves into?" There began to be general agreement that business wasn't all it was cracked up to be.

Establishment is, thus, a time of big transitions in both personal and work life. At work, three major tasks face the newcomer: negotiating effective psychological contracts, managing the stress of socialization, and making a transition from organizational outsider to organizational insider.

Psychological Contracts

A *psychological contract* is an implicit agreement between the individual and the organization that specifies what each is expected to give and receive in the relationship. Individuals expect to receive salary, status, advancement opportunities, and challenging work to meet their needs. Organizations expect to receive time, energy, talents, and loyalty in order to meet their goals. Working out the psychological contract with the organization begins with entry, but the contract is modified as the individual proceeds through the career.

Psychological contracts form and exist between individuals. During the establishment stage, newcomers form attachment relationships with many people in the organization. Working out effective psychological contracts within each relationship is important. Newcomers need social support in many forms and from many sources. Table 23.2 shows the type of psychological contracts, in the form of social support, that newcomers may work out with key insiders in the organization.

One common newcomer concern, for example, is whose behavior to watch for cues to appropriate behavior. Senior colleagues can provide modeling support by displaying behavior that the newcomer can emulate. This is only one of many types of support that newcomers need. Newcomers should contract with others to receive each of the needed types of support so that they can adjust to the new job. Organizations should help newcomers form relationships early and should encourage the psychological contracting process between newcomers and insiders.

Broken or breached psychological contracts can have very negative outcomes. When a breach occurs, employees can have very negative emotional reactions which can lead to loss of trust, reduced job satisfaction, and lower commitment to the organization and higher turnover intentions. The influence of a broken psychological contract is often felt even after an employee leaves a job. Laid-off employees who

Table 23.2 Newcomer-Insider Psychological Contracts for Social Support

Type of Support	Function of Supportive Attachments	Newcomer Concern	Examples of Insider Response/Action
Protection from stressors	Direct assistance in terms of resources, time, labor, or environmental modification	What are the major risks/ threats in this environment?	*Supervisor* cues newcomer to risks/ threats.
Informational	Provision of information necessary for managing demands	What do I need to know to get things done?	*Mentor* provides advice on informal political climate in organization.
Evaluative	Feedback on both personal and professional role performances	How am I doing?	*Supervisor* provides day-to-day performance feedback during first week on new job.
Modeling	Evidence of behavioral standards provided through modeled behavior	Whom do I follow?	Newcomer is apprenticed to *senior colleague*.
Emotional	Empathy, esteem, caring, or love	Do I matter? Who cares if I'm here or not?	*Other newcomers* empathize with and encourage individual when reality shock sets in.

Source: Table from D. L. Nelson, J. C Quick, and J. R. Joplin, "Psychological Contracting and Newcomer Socialization: An Attachment Theory Foundation," from *Journal of Social Behavior and Personality* 6 (1991): 65.

feel that a psychological contract breach has occurred are not only unhappy with their former firms but may also be both more cynical and less trusting of their new employers.

The Stress of Socialization

In Chapter 16, we discussed three phases that newcomers go through in adjusting to a new organization: anticipatory socialization, encounter, and change and acquisition. (You may want to review Figure 23.2.) Another way to look at these three phases is to examine the kinds of stress newcomers experience during each stage.

In anticipatory socialization, the newcomer is gathering information from various sources about the job and organization. The likely stressor in this stage is ambiguity, so the provision of accurate information is important. During this stage, the psychological contract is formed. It is essential that both parties go into it with good intentions of keeping up their end of the agreement.

In the encounter phase, the demands of the job in terms of the role, task, interpersonal relationships, and physical setting become apparent to the newcomer. The expectations formed in anticipatory socialization may clash with the realities of organizational life, and reality shock can occur. This very predictable surprise reaction may find the new employee thinking, "What have I gotten myself into?" The degree of reality shock depends on the expectations formed in the anticipatory socialization stage. If these expectations are unrealistic or unmet, reality shock may be a problem.

Although most organizations allow some time for newcomers to adapt, as little as two to three months may be allotted for new hires to reach some level of independence. This unwritten rule will mean that new hires who cannot quickly get up to speed on the organization's and their work

group's norms and procedures will quickly find themselves experiencing negative feedback from coworkers. Adaptability is the key during the early stages of the socialization process. New hires who adapt themselves to fit the environment rather than trying to change the environment are more effective at achieving fit in a new organization.

In the change and acquisition phase, the newcomer begins to master the demands of the job. Newcomers need to feel that they have some means of control over job demands.

Easing the Transition from Outsider to Insider

Being a newcomer in an organization is stressful. The process of becoming a functioning member of the organization takes time, and the newcomer needs support in making the transition. A successful transition from outsider to insider can be ensured if both the newcomer and the organization work together to smooth the way.

Individual Actions

Newcomers should ask about the negative side of the job if they were not given an RJP. In particular, newcomers should ask about the stressful aspects of the job. Other employees are good sources of this information. Research has shown that newcomers who underestimate the stressfulness of job demands do not adjust well. In addition, newcomers should present honest and accurate information about their own weaknesses. Both actions can promote good matches.

During the encounter phase, newcomers must prepare for reality shock. Realizing that slight depression is natural when adjusting to a new job can help alleviate the distress. Newcomers can also plan ways to cope with job stress ahead of time. If, for example, long assignments away from home are typical, newcomers can plan for these trips in advance. Part of the plan for dealing with reality shock should include ways to seek support from others. Networking with other newcomers who empathize can help individuals cope with the stress of the new job.

In the change and acquisition stage of adjusting to a new organization, newcomers should set realistic goals and take credit for the successes that occur as they master the job. Newcomers must seek feedback on job performance from their supervisors and coworkers. Newcomers should be proactive because proactive personality in newcomers has been shown to relate to creativity on the job and increased career satisfaction. Organizations also can assist newcomers in their transition from outsiders to insiders.

Organizational Actions

RJPs start the relationship between the newcomer and the organization with integrity and honesty. Careful recruitment and selection of new employees can help ensure good matches.

During the encounter phase, organizations should provide early job assignments that present opportunities for the new recruit to succeed. Newcomers who experience success in training gain increased self-efficacy and adjust to the new job more effectively. Newcomers who face early job challenges successfully tend to be higher performers later in their careers. Providing encouragement and feedback to the newcomer during this stage is crucial. The immediate supervisor, peers, other newcomers, and support staff are important sources of support during encounter. Starbucks takes onboarding and socialization a step further, and promotes open communication and feedback from newcomers. New hires are encouraged to express concerns and request new programs or changes to the socialization process. Any newcomer can write the CEO and is guaranteed a response. The idea is that if new hires can express their needs and ideas, they will be more likely to stay with Starbucks, for example.

By contrast, some firms do little to help newcomers adjust. A recent survey of information technology firms found that only 38 percent have formal company policies regarding training for new employees. The remaining 62 percent answered that when it comes to new-hire training, they simply "wing it."

During the change and acquisition phase, rewards are important. Organizations should tie the newcomers' rewards as explicitly as possible to performance.

Feedback is also crucial. Newcomers should receive daily, consistent feedback. This communicates that the organization is concerned about their progress and wants to help them learn the ropes along the way. Supervisory support is important during and even beyond the first few months. A recent study found that on average newcomers perceived less supervisory support during the six to twenty-one months after starting the job, and this resulted in role confusion and lower job satisfaction, and even delayed the receipt of salary increases over time.

The establishment stage marks the beginning of an individual's career. Its note-worthy transitions include the transition from school to work, from dependence on parents to dependence on self, from organizational outsider to organizational insider. Individuals who successfully complete the establishment stage go through many positive changes, including increased self-confidence, interpersonal skills, and self-knowledge. Once they have met their need to fit in, individuals move on to the advancement stage of their careers.

The Advancement Stage

The advancement stage is a period when individuals strive for achievement. They seek greater responsibility and authority and strive for upward mobility. Usually around age thirty, an important life transition occurs. Individuals reassess their goals and feel the need to make changes in their career dreams. The transition at age thirty is followed by a period of stability during which the individual tries to find a role in adult society and wants to succeed in the career. During this stage, several issues are important: exploring career paths, finding a mentor, working out dual-career partnerships, and managing conflicts between work and personal life.

Career Paths and Career Ladders

Career paths are sequences of job experiences along which employees move during their careers. At the advancement stage, individuals examine their career dreams and the paths they must follow to achieve them. For example, suppose a person dreams of becoming a top executive in the pharmaceutical industry. She majors in chemistry in undergraduate school and takes a job with a nationally recognized firm. After she has adjusted to her job as a quality control chemist, she reevaluates her plan and decides that further education is necessary. She plans to pursue an MBA degree part-time, hoping to gain expertise in management. From there, she hopes to be promoted to a supervisory position within her current firm. If this does not occur within five years, she will consider moving to a different pharmaceutical company. An alternate route would be to try to transfer to a sales position, from which she might advance into management.

The career paths of many women have moved from working in large organizations to starting their own businesses. Currently, there are 10.6 million women-owned firms in the United States, comprising almost half of all privately held firms in the country. What is the motivation for this exodus to entrepreneurship? The main reasons are to seek additional challenge and self-fulfillment and to have more self-determination and freedom.

A *earner ladder* is a structured series of job positions through which an individual progresses in an organization. For example, at Southwestern Bell, it is customary to move through a series of alternating line and staff supervisory assignments to advance toward upper management. Supervisors in customer service might be assigned next to the training staff and then rotate back as line supervisors in network services to gain experience in different departments.

Some companies use the traditional concept of career ladders to help employees advance in their careers. Other organizations take a more contemporary approach to career advancement. Sony encourages creativity in its engineers by using nontraditional career paths. At Sony, individuals have the freedom to move on to interesting and challenging job assignments without notifying their supervisors. If they join a new project team, their current boss is expected to let them move on. This self-promotion philosophy at Sony is seen as a key to high levels of innovation and creative new product designs. There has been heightened interest in international assignments by multinational corporations in response to globalization and global staffing issues. One challenge in this regard has been that most expatriate assignments are not successful, and organizations have been facing the challenge of properly training and preparing individuals for such assignments. Alternative international work assignments (e.g., commuter work assignments, virtual assignments, short-term assignments) can be used to help in-dividuals gain international work experience in preparation for higher levels in the organization.

Another approach used by some companies to develop skills is the idea of a "career lattice"—an approach to building competencies by moving laterally through different departments in the organization or by moving through different projects. Top management support for the career lattice is essential because in traditional terms an employee who has made several lateral moves might not be viewed with favor. However, the ca-reer lattice approach is an effective way to develop an array of skills to ensure one's employability.

Exploring career paths is one important activ-ity in advancement. Another crucial activity dur-ing advancement is finding a mentor.

Finding a Mentor

A *mentor* is an individual who provides guidance, coaching, counseling, and friendship to a protégé. Mentors are important to career success because they perform both career and psychosocial func-tions. Sir Richard Branson, head of Virgin Group, has a passion for mentoring and attributes his own success to having good mentors. In The Real World you can see that Branson's mentoring pro-grams are global in nature.

The career functions provided by a mentor include sponsorship, facilitating exposure and visibility, coaching, and protection. Sponsorship means actively helping the individual get job ex-periences and promotions. Facilitating exposure and visibility means providing opportunities for the protégé to develop relationships with key figures in the organization to advance. Coaching involves providing advice in both career and job performance. Protection is provided by shield-ing the protégé from potentially damaging

experiences. Career functions are particularly important to the protégé's future success. One study found that the amount of career coaching received by protégés was related to more promo-tions and higher salaries four years later.

The mentor also performs psychosocial func-tions. Role modeling occurs when the mentor displays behavior for the protégé to emulate. This facilitates social learning. Acceptance and confirmation is important to both the mentor and protégé. When the protégé feels accepted by the mentor, it fosters a sense of pride. Likewise, positive regard and appreciation from the junior colleague provide a sense of satisfaction for the mentor. Counseling by a mentor helps the pro-tégé explore personal issues that arise and require assistance. Friendship is another psychosocial function that benefits both mentor and protégé alike.

There are characteristics that define good mentoring relationships. In effective mentoring relationships, there is regular contact between mentor and protégé that has clearly specified purposes. There should be mutual trust between the protégé and mentor. Mentoring should be consistent with the corporate culture and the organization's goals. Both mentors and protégés alike should be trained in ways to manage the relationship. Mentors should be held account-able and rewarded for their role. Mentors should be perceived (accurately) by protégés as having considerable influence within the organization. Though it may be tempting to go after the "top dog" as your mentor, personality compatibility is also an important factor in the success or failure of a mentoring relationship. Mentors who are similar to their protégés in terms of personality traits like extra version, and whose expectations are largely met by the relationship, are more likely to show interest in continuing the arrange-ment. Cigna Financial Advisors takes a proactive approach to integrating new employees. As part of the company's Partnership Program, all new hires work for up to twenty-seven months under the oversight of an experienced, successful mentor. This relationship provides the new hires with hands-on instruction in how to sell more effectively, as well as increasing sales levels for the mentors themselves. Cigna demonstrates its commitment to this approach by hiring no more new producers than it can assign to individual mentors.

Mentoring programs are also effective ways of addressing the challenge of workforce diversity. The mentoring process, however, presents unique problems, including the availability of mentors, issues of language and acculturation, and cultural sensitivity, for minority groups such as Hispanic Americans. Negative stereotypes can limit minority members' access to mentoring relationships and the benefits associated with mentoring. To address this problem, companies can facilitate access to mentors in organizations. Informal mentoring programs identify pools of mentors and protégés, give training in the development of effective mentoring and diversity issues, and then provide informal opportunities for the development of mentoring relationships. Network groups are another avenue for mentoring. Network groups help members identify with those few others who are like them within an organization, build relationships with them, and build social support. Network groups enhance the chance that minorities will find mentors. Dell, for example, has several

Richard Branson: Mentoring on a Global Scale

Sir Richard Branson, head of Virgin Group, believes mentorship has the power to change the world. He cites his parents as his most important mentors, along with Sir Freddie Laker, the British airline entrepreneur. Laker was the mentor who taught him that only a fool never changes his mind. Branson claims that piece of advice is the best he ever received.

Branson has implemented mentorship programs of several kinds, some of them on a global scale. The Branson Centre of Entrepreneurship supports and mentors aspiring young entrepreneurs in South Africa and the Caribbean. The centre provides access to mentors, advisors, coaches, and financing assistance. The Young Upstarts report, produced by the centre, found that a full 65 percent of young South Africans want to start their own businesses, and that they recognize the need for role models and mentors in helping them get started.

In addition, Branson joined forces with Peter Gabriel to found and fund The Elders, a group of ten visionary leaders without vested personal interests who work together to promote peace-building and solve global conflicts. Using their collective skills to promote peaceful resolutions to conflicts, the Elders include Nelson Mandela, Jimmy Carter, Desmond Tutu, and Gro Brundtland among others. Branson sees The Elders as a group of experienced, trusted advisors to the world.

Branson's gratitude toward his parents, as his most cherished mentors, is what drives him to implement mentoring initiatives that are his passion.

Sources: http://www.theelders.org/, http://www.bransoncentre.org/, http://motivatedonline.com/ sir-richard-branson-on-a-mission-to-mentor/.

CAREER MANAGEMENT 317

Employee Resource Groups that serve networking functions. Some of these groups are aDellante, for Hispanic Americans; Asians in Motion, for Asian Americans; Building Relationships in Diverse Group Environments, for African Americans; and PRIDE, for gay, lesbian, and bisexual individuals. These groups serve as links to their respective communities within Dell. Networks also increase the likelihood that individuals have more than one mentor. Employees with multiple mentors, such as those gained from mentoring networks, have even greater career success than those with

only one mentor. Recently, scholars have identified the specific advantages of having a network of mentors. See the Science feature for more on developmental networks.

Some companies have formal mentoring programs. PricewaterhouseCoopers (PWC) also uses the mentoring model to help its interns. Each intern is assigned both a peer mentor to help with day-to-day questions and an experienced mentor to help with larger issues, such as career path development. As an international firm, PWC also employs similar methods overseas. In PWC's

How to Be Extraordinary

Individuals who are extraordinary at their job often have a team of mentors or "developers" from both inside and outside their employing organizations. These developmental networks provide career and/or psychosocial support throughout the individuals' careers. Until recently, little was known about who these developers are, what they do, or what type of developmental network is most effective. A recent study investigated 62 National Baseball Hall of Famers and addressed these questions.

Who are developers? Developers are mentors from five primary categories: family, support (friends and fans), company, professional developers such as former coaches, and heroes/idols. *What do developers do?* Developers provide a range of support including coaching, job-related feedback, the opportunity for skill development and exposure. Developers also fulfill psychosocial functions, such as emotional support, counseling, inspiration and motivation.

What type of developmental network is most effective? To answer this question, the researchers divided the players into two groups (the best of the best and a great but lower tier) to see whether the developmental networks of the two groups differed. The best of the best group had more developers and these mentors were both within and across more career categories (an average of 22 developers across 4.3 career categories versus 11 developers across 2.9 career categories). The higher tier also had more developers specifically from the family, company and support categories. They also had a greater depth and breadth of psychosocial and career support.

So what's the take home lesson for those who want to be extraordinary? Develop a large and diverse network of individuals willing and able to provide you with plenty of career and psychosocial mentoring.

Source: R.D. Cotton, Y. Shen, R. Livne-Tarandach. "On Becoming Extraordinary: The Content and Structure of the Developmental Networks of Major League Baseball Hall of Famers" *Academy of Management Journal* (2011) 54:15–46.

Czech Republic operations, a team of two mentors, one of whom is called a counselor, fills the same guidance role as the two mentors generally fill for U.S. employees.

Mentoring has had a strong impact in shaping the identities of the Big Four accounting firms. In one study, every partner who was interviewed reported having at least one mentor who played a critical role in his or her attainment of the partnership and beyond. Protégés' identities are shaped through mentoring, and their work goals, language, and even lifestyles reflect the imperatives of the Big Four firm. Protégés are schooled on partners'"hot buttons" (what not to talk about), what to wear, to "tuck in the tie," and not to cut the grass without wearing a shirt.

Although some companies have formal mentoring programs, junior employees more often are left to negotiate their own mentoring relationships. The barriers to finding a mentor include lack of access to mentors, fear of initiating a mentoring relationship, and fear that supervisors or coworkers might not approve of the mentoring relationship. Individuals may also be afraid to initiate a mentoring relationship because it might be misconstrued as a sexual advance by the potential mentor or others. This is a fear of potential mentors as well. Some are unwilling to develop a relationship because of their own or the protégé's gender. Women report more of these barriers than men, and individuals who lack previous experience report more barriers to finding a mentor. There are other gender differences found in mentoring relationships. Male protégés report receiving less psychological support than female protégés. Additionally, male mentors report giving more career development support, whereas female mentors report giving more psychological support. Mentoring can be particularly important for women in male-dominated professions. In these environments, women who have male mentors also have the highest compensation and career progress satisfaction.

Organizations can encourage junior workers to approach mentors by providing opportunities for them to interact with senior colleagues. The immediate supervisor is not always the best mentor for an individual, so exposure to other senior workers is important. Seminars, multilevel teams, and social events can serve as vehicles for bringing together potential mentors and protégés.

Mentoring relationships go through a series of phases: initiation, cultivation, separation, and redefinition. There is no fixed time length for each phase, because each relationship is unique. In the *initiation* phase, the mentoring relationship begins to take on significance for both the mentor and the protégé. In the *cultivation* phase, the relationship becomes more meaningful, and the protégé shows rapid progress because of the career and psychosocial support provided by the mentor. Protégés influence mentors as well.

In the *separation* phase, the protégé feels the need to assert independence and work more autonomously. Separation can be voluntary, or it can result from an involuntary change (the protégé or mentor may be promoted or transferred). The separation phase can be difficult if it is resisted, either by the mentor (who is reluctant to let go of the relationship) or by the protégé (who resents the mentor's withdrawal of support). Separation can proceed smoothly and naturally or can result from a conflict that disrupts the mentoring relationship.

The *redefinition* phase occurs if separation has been successful. In this phase, the relationship takes on a new identity as both parties consider themselves colleagues or friends. The mentor feels pride in the protégé, and the protégé develops a deeper appreciation for the support from the mentor.

Why are good mentors so important? Aside from the support they provide, the research shows that mentors are vital to the protégé's future success. For example, studies have demonstrated that individuals with mentors have higher promotion rates and higher incomes than individuals without them. In fact, mentorship has been shown to add increase career success above and beyond an individual's education, training, work experience, pro-activity in their careers, and networking. Professionals who have mentors earn between $5,600 and $22,000 more per year than those who do not. Individuals with mentors also are better decision makers. And it is not just the presence of the mentor that yields these benefits. The quality of the relationship is most important. Be aware that bad mentoring experiences can do extensive damage. These experiences increase withdrawal and depression at work, even more so than good experiences reduce these outcomes. So it's not a good idea to remain in negative mentoring relationships.

During the advancement stage, many individuals face another transition: They settle into a relationship with a life partner. This lifestyle transition requires adjustment in many respects: learning to live with another person, being concerned with someone besides yourself, dealing with an extended family, and many other demands. The partnership can be particularly stressful if both members are career oriented.

Dual-Career Partnerships

The two-career lifestyle has increased in recent years due in part to the need for two incomes to maintain a preferred standard of living. *Dual-career partnerships* are relationships in which both people have important career roles; unfortunately, both organizations and organizational research often ignore the prevalence of dual-careers and, therefore, we don't know a lot about what organizations and individuals can do to successfully manage dual careers. This type of partnership can be mutually beneficial, but it can also be stressful. Often these stresses center around stereotypes that providing income is a man's responsibility and taking care of the home is the woman's domain. Among married couples, working women's satisfaction with the marriage is affected by how much the husband helps with childcare. Men who adhere to traditional gender beliefs may be threatened when the wife's income exceeds their own. Beliefs about who should do what in the partnership complicate the dual-career issue.

One stressor in a dual-career partnership is time pressure. When both partners work outside the home, there may be a time crunch in fitting in work, family, and leisure time. Another potential problem is jealousy. When one partner's career blooms before the other's, the less successful partner may feel threatened.

Another issue to work out is whose career takes precedence. For example, what happens if one partner is transferred to another city? Must the other partner make a move that might threaten his or her own career in order to be with the individual who was transferred? Who, if anyone, will stay home and take care of a new baby?

Working out a dual-career partnership takes careful planning and consistent communication between the partners. Each partner must serve as a source of social support for the other. Couples can also turn to other family members, friends, and professionals for support if the need arises.

Work-Home Conflicts

An issue related to dual-career partnerships that is faced throughout the career cycle, but often first encountered in the advancement phase, is the conflicts that occur between work and personal life. Experiencing a great deal of work-home conflict negatively affects an individual's overall quality of life. Such conflicts can lead to emotional exhaustion. Dealing with customer complaints all day, failed sales calls, and missed deadlines can magnify negative events at home, and vice versa. Responsibilities at home can clash with responsibilities at work, and these conflicts must be planned for. For example, suppose a child gets sick at school. Who will pick up the child and stay home with him or her? Couples must work together to resolve these conflicts. Even at Eli Lilly and Company, only 36 percent of workers said it is possible to get ahead in their careers and still devote sufficient time to family. This is surprising, because Lilly has a reputation as one of the world's most family-friendly workplaces. When one partner has a lot of work-home conflict, it negatively affects the other partner. A recent study found that one partner's work-home conflict impacts how couples interact with one another and increases behaviors aimed at expressing negative feelings, criticizing or actually negatively impacting the other's goal attainment which eventually leads to exhaustion in that other partner.

Work-home conflicts are particular problems for working women. Women have been quicker to share the provider role than men have been to share responsibilities at home. When working women experience work-home conflict, their performance declines, and they suffer more strain. Work-home conflict is a broad topic. It can be narrowed further into work-family conflict, in which work interferes with family, versus family-work conflict in which family or home life interferes with work. Additionally, egalitarian individuals who believe men and women should identify equally with their contributions at home and work experience more guilt associated with work-home conflict than individuals who are more traditional.

In fact, traditional individuals tend to feel more guilt associated with home interfering, with work.

Cultural differences arise in these types of conflicts. One study showed that while Americans experience more family-work conflict, Chinese experience more work-family conflict. For example, women in management positions in China were very positive about future advancements and carried a strong belief in their ability to succeed. This, in turn, caused them to reevaluate their personal and professional identities. Such an identity transformation is marked by happiness associated with career advancement even though many women foresaw emotional costs with such career advancement. This study indicated that female Chinese managers experience work-family conflict in part because the Chinese culture emphasizes close social ties and *guanxi*, or personalized networks of influence.

To help individuals deal with work-home conflict, companies like Ernst & Young offer *flexible work schedules*. These programs give employees freedom to take care of personal concerns while still getting their work done. Telecommuting enables people to work no matter where they are located, and breaks down barriers of time and space. At Cisco Systems, employees who telecommute experienced higher productivity, work-life flexibility, and job satisfaction. Employees reported fuel cost savings of $10.3 million per year from telecommuting. Cisco saves $277 million per year in time and productivity costs. At Cisco, telecommuting is a green practice as well. In a single year, Cisco telecommuters stopped 47,320 metric tons of greenhouse gases from being released.

Company-sponsored childcare is another way to help. Companies with on-site day-care centers include Johnson & Johnson, Perdue Farms, and Campbell Soup, Mitchell Gold, an award-winning furniture maker, believes that treating people right must come first. Aflac insurance company offers not only on-site daycare but also on-site medical care from licensed physicians and nurses so that employees don't have to miss work to care for a sick child. Whereas large companies may offer corporate daycare, small companies can also assist their workers by providing referral services for locating the type of childcare the workers need. For smaller organizations, this is a cost-effective alternative. At the very least, companies can be sensitive to work-home conflicts and handle them on a case-by-case basis with flexibility and concern.

A program of increasing interest that organizations can provide is *eldercare.* Often workers find themselves part of the sandwich generation: They are expected to care for both their children and their elderly parents. This extremely stressful role is reported more often by women than men. The impact of caring for an aging loved one is often underestimated. But 17 percent of those who provide care eventually quit their jobs due to time constraints, and another 15 percent reduce their work hours for the same reason. Caring for an elderly dependent at home can create severe work-home conflicts for employees and also takes a toll on the employee's own well-being and performance at work. This is especially true if the organization does not provide a supportive climate for discussion of eldercare issues. Harvard University has taken steps to help its faculty and staff deal with eldercare issues by contracting with Parents in a Pinch, a firm that specializes in nanny services and now also offers eldercare. KPMG offers an award-winning eldercare program with services including care referrals, backup care, and a shared leave program in which employees can donate leave to coworkers who need it.

Alternative work arrangements such as flextime, compressed workweeks, telecommuting, part-time hours, job sharing, and leave options can help employees manage work-home conflicts. Managers must not let their biases get in the way of these benefits. Top managers may be less willing to grant alternative work arrangements to men than to women, to supervisors than to subordinates, and to employees caring for elderly parents rather than for children. It is important that family-friendly policies be applied fairly.

The advancement stage is filled with the challenges of finding a mentor, balancing dual-career partnerships, and dealing with work-home conflicts. Developmental changes that occur in either the late advancement stage or the early maintenance stage can prove stressful, too. The midlife transition, which takes place approximately between ages forty and forty-five, is often a time of crisis. Levinson points out three major changes that contribute to the midlife transition. First, people realize that their lives are half over and that they are mortal. Second, age forty is considered by people in their twenties and thirties to be "over the hill" and not part of the youth culture. Finally, people reassess their dreams and evaluate how close they have come to achieving those dreams. All of these factors make up the midlife transition.

Stage

Maintenance may be a misnomer for this career stage because some people continue to grow in their careers although the growth is usually not at the rate it was earlier. A career crisis at midlife may accompany the midlife transition. A senior product manager at Borden found himself in such a crisis and described it this way: "When I was in college, I had thought in terms of being president of a company. … But at Borden I felt used and cornered. Most of the guys in the next two rungs above me had either an MBA or fifteen to twenty years of experience in the food business. My long-term plans stalled."

Some individuals who reach a career crisis are burned out, and a month's vacation will help, according to Carolyn Smith Paschal, who owns an executive search firm. She recommends that companies give employees in this stage sabbaticals instead of bonuses. This would help rejuvenate them.

Some individuals reach the maintenance stage with a sense of achievement and contentment, feeling no need to strive for further upward mobility. Whether the maintenance stage is a time of crisis or contentment, however, there are two issues to grapple with: sustaining performance and becoming a mentor.

Sustaining Performance

Remaining productive is a key concern for individuals in the maintenance stage. This becomes challenging when one reaches a *career plateau*, a point where the probability of moving further up the hierarchy is low. Some people handle career plateauing fairly well, but others may become frustrated, bored, and dissatisfied with their jobs.

To keep employees productive, organizations can provide challenges and opportunities for learning. Lateral moves are one option. Another option is to involve the employee in project teams that provide new tasks and skill development. The key is keeping the work stimulating and involving. Individuals at this stage also need continued affirmation of their value to the organization. They need to know that their contributions are significant and appreciated.

Becoming a Mentor

During maintenance, individuals can make a contribution by sharing their wealth of knowledge and experience with others. Opportunities to be mentors to new employees can keep senior workers motivated and involved in the organization and lead to positive job attitudes. It is important for organizations to reward mentors for the time and energy they expend. Some employees adapt naturally to the mentor role, hut others may need training on how to coach and counsel junior workers.

Kathy Kram notes that there are four keys to the success of a formal mentoring program. First, participation should be voluntary. No one should be forced to enter a mentoring relationships and careful matching of mentors and protégés is important. Second, support from top executives is needed to convey the intent of the program and its role in career development. Third, training should be provided to mentors so they understand the functions of the relationship. Finally, a graceful exit should be provided for mismatches or for people in mentoring relationships that have fulfilled their purpose.

Maintenance is a time of transition, like all career stages. It can be managed by individuals who know what to expect and plan to remain productive, as well as by organizations that focus on maximizing employee involvement in work. According to Levinson, during the latter part of the maintenance stage, another life transition occurs. The age fifty transition is another time of reevaluating the dream and working further on the issues raised in the midlife transition. Following the age fifty transition is a fairly stable period. During this time, individuals begin to plan seriously for withdrawing from, their careers.

The Withdrawal Stage

The withdrawal stage usually occurs later in life and signals that a long period of continuous employment will soon come to a close. Older workers may face discrimination and stereotyping. They may be viewed by others as less productive, more resistant to change, and less motivated. However, older workers are one of the most undervalued groups in the workforce. They can provide continuity in the midst of change and can serve as mentors and role models to younger generations of employees.

Discrimination against older workers is prohibited under the Age Discrimination in Employment Act. Organizations must create a culture that values older workers' contributions. With their level of experience, strong work ethic, and loyalty, these workers have much to contribute. In fact, older workers have lower rates of tardiness and absenteeism, are more safety conscious, and are more satisfied with their jobs than are younger workers.

Planning for Change

The decision to retire is an individual one, but the need for planning is universal. A retired sales executive from Boise Cascade said that the best advice is to "plan no unplanned retirement." This means carefully planning not only the transition but also the activities you will be involved in once the transition is made. All options should be open for consideration. One recent trend is the need for temporary top-level executives. Some companies are hiring senior managers from the outside on a temporary basis. The qualities of a good temporary executive include substantial high-level management experience, financial security that allows the executive to choose only assignments that really interest him or her, and a willingness to relocate. Some individuals at the withdrawal stage find this an attractive option.

Planning for retirement should include not only financial planning but also a plan for psychologically withdrawing from work. The pursuit of hobbies and travel, volunteer work, or more time with extended family can all be part of the plan. The key is to plan early and carefully, as well as to anticipate the transition with a positive attitude and a full slate of desirable activities.

Retirement

There are several retirement trends right now, ranging from early retirement to phased retirement to never retiring. Some adults are choosing a combination of these options, leaving their first career for some time off before reentering the workforce either part-time or full-time doing something they enjoy. For more and more Americans, the idea of a retirement spent sitting beside the swimming pool lacks appeal. Factors that influence the decision of when to retire include company policy, financial considerations, family support or pressure, health, and opportunities for other productive activities.

During the withdrawal stage, the individual faces a major life transition that Levinson refers to as the late adulthood transition (ages sixty to sixty-five). One's own mortality becomes a major concern, and the loss of one's family members and friends becomes more frequent. The person works to achieve a sense of integrity—that is, the encompassing meaning and value—in life.

Some retirement-aged individuals may go through a second midlife crisis. People are living longer and staying more active. Vickie Ianucelli, for example, bought a condo on a Mexican beach, celebrated a birthday in Paris, bought herself a

9.5-karat ring, and got plastic surgery. And it's her second midlife crisis. She's a psychologist who is also a sixty-plus grandmother of two.

Retirement need not be a complete cessation of work. Many alternative work arrangements can be considered, and many companies offer flexibility in these options. *Phased retirement* is a popular option for retirement-age workers who want to gradually reduce their hours and/or responsibilities. There are many forms of phased retirement, including reduced workdays or workweeks, job sharing, and consulting and mentoring arrangements. Many organizations cannot afford the loss of large numbers of experienced employees at once. In fact, although 50 percent of all U.S. workers are officially retired by age sixty, only 11 percent fully withdraw from work. This means there is an increase in *bridge employment,* which takes place after a retirement from a full-time position but before permanent withdrawal from the workforce. Bridge employment is related to retirement satisfaction and overall life satisfaction.

Some companies are helping employees transition to retirement in innovative ways. Retired individuals can continue their affiliation with the organization by serving as mentors to employees who are embarking on retirement planning or other career transitions. This helps diminish the tear of loss some people have about retirement because the retiree has an option to serve as a mentor or consultant to the organization.

Lawrence Livermore National Labs (LLNL) employs some of the best research minds in the world. And when these great minds retire from full-time work, they have numerous opportunities to continue contributing. LLNL's retiree program Web site lists a wide variety of requests, ranging from leading tours and making phone calls to providing guidance on current research and helping researchers make contact with other researchers. Programs like these help LLNL avoid the typical knowledge drain that takes place when seasoned veteran employees retire.

Now that you understand the career stage model, you can begin to conduct your own career planning. It is never too early to start.

Career Anchors

Much of an individual's self-concept rests on a career. Over the course of a person's work life, career anchors are developed. *Career anchors* are self-perceived talents, motives, and values that guide an individual's career decisions. Edgar Schein developed the concept of career anchors based on a twelve-year study of MBA graduates from the Massachusetts institute of Technology (MIT). Schein found great diversity in the graduates' career histories but great similarities in the way they explained the career decisions they had made. From extensive interviews with the graduates, Schein developed five career anchors:

1. *Technical/functional competence.* Individuals who hold this career anchor want to specialize in a given functional area (e.g., finance or marketing) and become competent. The idea of general management does not interest them.

2. *Managerial competence.* Adapting this career anchor means individuals want general management responsibility. They want to see their efforts have an impact on organizational effectiveness.

3. *Autonomy and independence.* Freedom is the key to this career anchor, and often these individuals are uncomfortable working in large organizations. Autonomous careers such as writer, professor; or consultant attract these individuals.

4. *Creativity.* Individuals holding this career anchor feel a strong need to create something. They are often entrepreneurs.
5. *Security/stability.* Long-term career stability, whether in a single organization or in a single geographic area, fits people with this career anchor. Some government jobs provide this type of security.

Career anchors emerge over time and may be modified by work or life experiences. The importance of knowing your career anchor is that it can help you find a match between you and an organization. For example, individuals with creativity as an anchor may find themselves stifled in bureaucratic organizations. Textbook sales may not be the place for an individual with a security anchor because of the frequent travel and seasonal nature of the business.

Managerial Implications: Managing Your Career

The challenges of globalization, diversity, technology, and ethics have provided unique opportunities and threats for career management. The tough economic downturn has created high rates of unemployment and, although the private sector is beginning to add jobs, state and local governments will likely continue to downsize. The flattening of the organizational hierarchy has resulted in fewer opportunities for promotion. Forty-year careers with one organization, a phenomenon Baby Boomers saw their parents experience, are becoming less and less the norm. Negotiating the turbulent waters of the U.S.

employment market will be a challenge in the foreseeable future.

Many industries are experiencing sinking employment, but there are some bright spots. According to Labor Department projections, the U.S. economy will add approximately 15.3 million jobs by the year 2018, most of them in service industries. Of all the occupations expected to have faster than average employment growth, above-average earnings, and below-average unemployment, the ones shown in this chart have the largest number of projected openings. Many of these jobs require at least a bachelor's degree. Business students could consider becoming a manager of some of these occupations.

Andy Grove, chairman of Intel, suggests that as a general rule, you must accept that no matter where you work, you are not an employee. Instead, you are in a business with one employee: yourself. You face tremendous competition with millions of other businesses. You own your career as a sole proprietor. Grove poses three key questions that are central to managing your career. Continually ask the following questions:

1. *Am I adding real value?* You add real value by continually looking for ways to make things truly better in your organization. In principle, every hour of your workday should be spent increasing the value of the output of the people for whom you're responsible.
2. *Am I plugged into what's happening around me?* Inside the company? The industry? Are you a node in a network of plugged-in people, or are you floating around by yourself?
3. *Am I trying new ideas, new techniques, and new technologies?* Try them personally—don't just read about them.

The key to survival is to add more value every day and to be flexible.

CREDITS

John Wagner and John Hollenbeck, "Chapter 1: Introduction to OB," *Organizational Behavior: Securing Competitive Advantage*, pp. 5–7. Copyright © 2010 by Taylor & Francis Group LLC. Reprinted with permission. • John Wagner and John Hollenbeck, "Chapter 2: Management and Managers," *Organizational Behavior: Securing Competitive Advantage*, pp. 13–34. Copyright © 2010 by Taylor & Francis Group LLC. Reprinted with permission. • Ricky W. Griffin and Gregory Moorhead, "The Changing Environment of Organizations," *Organizational Behavior: Managing People and Organizations*, pp. 32–46. Copyright © 2014 by Cengage Learning, Inc. Reprinted with permission. • Ricky W. Griffin and Gregory Moorhead, "Foundations of Individual Behavior," *Organizational Behavior: Managing People and Organizations*, pp. 66–81. Copyright © 2014 by Cengage Learning, Inc. Reprinted with permission. • John Schermerhorn, Richard Osborne and Mary Uhl-Bien,Excerpts from: "Ch. 2: Values" and "Ch. 3: Emotions," *Organizational Behavior*, pp. 38–40, 56–60. Copyright © 2013 by John Wiley & Sons, Inc. Reprinted with permission. • J. Owen Cherrington and David J. Cherrington, "A Menu of Moral Issues: One Week in the Life of *The Wall Street Journal*," *Journal of Business Ethics*, pp. 255–265. Copyright © 1992 by Kluwer Academic Publishers. Reprinted with permission. • Joseph E. Champoux, "Communication Processes," *Organizational Behavior: Integrating Individuals, Groups and Organizations*, pp. 320–337. Copyright © 2011 by Taylor & Francis Group LLC. Reprinted with permission. • Joseph E. Champoux, "Conflict in Organizations," *Organizational Behavior: Integrating Individuals, Groups and Organizations*, pp. 264–279. Copyright © 2011 by Taylor & Francis Group LLC. Reprinted with permission. • Joseph E. Champoux, "Groups and Intergroup Processes," *Organizational Behavior: Integrating Individuals, Groups and Organizations*, pp. 232–251. Copyright © 2011 by Taylor & Francis Group LLC. Reprinted with permission. • Joseph E. Champoux, "Decision-Making and Problem-Solving Processes," *Organizational Behavior: Integrating Individuals, Groups and Organizations*, pp. 345–362. Copyright © 2011 by Taylor & Francis Group LLC. Reprinted with permission. • Debra Nelson and James Quick, "Motivation and Work Behavior," *Organizational Behavior: Science, the Real World and You*, pp. 162–181. Copyright © 2013 by Cengage Learning, Inc.. Reprinted with permission. • John Wagner and John Hollenbeck, "Work Motivation and Performance," *Organizational Behavior: Securing Competitive Advantage*, pp. 88–98. Copyright © 2010 by Taylor & Francis Group LLC. Reprinted with permission. • Ricky W. Griffin and Gregory Moorhead, "Managing Stress and the Work-Life Balance," *Organizational Behavior: Managing People and Organizations*, pp. 181–197. Copyright © 2014 by Cengage Learning, Inc. Reprinted with permission. • Joseph E. Champoux, "Power and Political Behavior," *Organizational Behavior: Integrating Individuals, Groups and Organizations*, pp. 371–387. Copyright © 2011 by Taylor & Francis Group LLC. Reprinted with permission. • Debra Nelson and James Quick, "Leadership and Followership," *Organizational Behavior: Science, the Real World and You*, pp. 432–450. Copyright © 2013 by Cengage Learning, Inc. Reprinted with permission. • Austin Carr, "The Most Important Leadership Quality for CEOs? Creativity," *Fast Company Magazine*. Copyright © 2010 by Mansueto Ventures LLC. • Annette Cremo Richard Gaffney, "Sexual Harassment." Copyright © 2001 by American Society for Training and Development (ASTD). Reprinted with permission. • John Pearce, "What Execs Don't Get About Office Romance," *MIT Sloan Management Review*, vol. 51, no. 3, pp. 37–44. Copyright © 2010 by MIT Sloan Management Review. Reprinted with permission. • Dori Meinert, "Whistle-Blowers: Threat or Asset," *HR Magazine*, vol. 56, no. 4, pp. 26–32. Copyright © 2011 by Society for Human Resource Management (SHRM). Reprinted with permission. • Debra Nelson and James Quick, "Organizational Culture," *Organizational Behavior: Science, the Real World and You*, pp. 592–607. Copyright © 2013 by Cengage Learning, Inc. Reprinted with permission. • Debra Nelson and James Quick, "Managing Change," *Organizational Behavior: Science, the Real World and You*, pp. 681–683. Copyright © 2013 by Cengage Learning, Inc. Reprinted with permission. • Joseph E. Champoux, "Organizational Change and Development," *Organizational Behavior: Integrating Individuals, Groups and Organizations*, pp. 460–462. Copyright © 2011 by Taylor & Francis Group LLC. Reprinted with permission. • Debra Nelson and James Quick, "Career Management," *Organizational Behavior: Science, the Real World and You*, pp. 631–650. Copyright © 2013 by Cengage Learning, Inc. Reprinted with permission. • Uchora Udoji, "Team Productivity through Management of Agreement—the Abilene Paradox." Copyright © 2006 by The Case Centre. Reprinted with permission.

CPSIA information can be obtained at www.ICGtesting.com
Printed in the USA
LVOW01s0905210814

400126LV00003B/19/P